Iran's Economy
under
The Islamic Republic

JAHANGIR AMUZEGAR

I.B.Tauris & Co Ltd
Publishers
London • New York

Published in 1993 by
I.B.Tauris & Co. Ltd
45 Bloomsbury Square
London WC1A 2HY

175 Fifth Avenue
New York
NY 10010

In the United States of America
and Canada distributed by
St Martin's Press
175 Fifth Avenue
New York
NY 10010

A CIP record for this book is available from the British Library

Library of Congress cataloging-in-publication card number:
A full CIP record is available from the Library of Congress

ISBN 1–85043–603–7

Printed and bound in Great Britain by
WBC Ltd, Bridgend, Mid-Glamorgan

Table of Contents

Preface

Since the establishment of the Islamic Republic in Iran in February 1979, not a year has passed without some voice in the opposition predicting the new regime's approaching, if not imminent, collapse. Soon after the revolution, it was believed that the triumphant *clergy* would be ousted by the well-organized Left (for example, the Mojahedin-e Khalq [Islamic Marxists] and the [communist] Tudeh party), or by the traditional Right (the army). After the Iraqi attack in September 1980, the theocracy's days were thought to be numbered on account of Iran's decimated and leaderless armed forces.[1] In the mid-1980s, the *bazaar*'s irritation and discontent with economic controls and state encroachment seemed to foretell a second revolution.[2] Later in the decade, Ayatollah Khomeini's impending death was expected to create a void in leadership and open a rift among clerical factions, thereby paving the way for unavoidable political disintegration – or civil war.

As this book goes to press, the Islamic Republic is in its fifteenth year of effective rule, having defied all threats to its survival. During this period, however, there have been notable changes in the regime's socio-economic agenda, management strategy and political outlook. The significance and implications of these changes and developments should be of more than passing interest to students of Iranian politics, Islamic economics, or theocratic statecraft.

A good deal has been written about the Islamic Republic's relations with the outside world, the Iran-Iraq war, and the regime's design for the Persian Gulf region and the Moslem republics of the former Soviet Union. But information on the

Iranian *economy* has been limited to press reports, monthly or quarterly news bulletins, occasional research papers of special interest, and a few partisan works in Persian. At the same time, interest in the direction and performance of the Iranian economy has continued to be felt, not only among scholars and researchers in the field, but also within the world's business and diplomatic communities. Earlier efforts made by Islamic authorities to expand state domination in the economy and recent attempts toward deregulation and marketization also seem to be of special interest to both economic analysts and practising businessmen, traders and investors. Accurate, reliable, and up-to-date information on various aspects of the Islamic economy is needed, not only for comparison with the past, but also for charting the proper course of action for the future. This study is an attempt to fill the current void in a modest way.

The book is divided into five parts, following a short introduction on the state of the Iranian economy prior to the revolution: the Islamic Republic's politico-economic agenda; an overview of the developments during the 1980s; the role of the state in the economy; sectoral structure and developments; and performance and prospects. Individual chapters discuss the regime's search for an Islamic order; the constitutional framework of the economy; major developments in output, employment, and the price level; government policies regarding the national budget, banking, development planning, and foreign trade; the operation and achievements of major economic sectors; and, finally, the economy's balance sheet, and its task ahead.

The focus of this study is on major economic *developments* since the revolution, and not on a detailed *structure* of the economy. Thus, major changes in output, employment, internal and external balances, and national economic policies will be examined, and basic trends in agriculture, hydrocarbons, and industry will be discussed. But descriptions of Iran's economic geography, resources, production facilities, distribution system, service outlets, health, education, and other socio-economic subsectors will either be left out, or kept to a minimum.

An examination of major macro-economic trends and main sectoral developments is to provide a reasonable basis for an objective assessment of the economy's performance. In the process, answers will be sought to two cardinal questions: firstly, how has the economy's performance in terms of commonly accepted criteria measured up to the regime's main objectives? And secondly, taking into account both the endogenous and the exogenous constraints which the authorities had to confront, were the objectives of the Islamic Republic realistic and achievable?

The preparation of this book has been hampered by a lack of adequate information. Data on many aspects of the Iranian economy have been relatively scarce, fragmentary, and often conjectural in nature. Although the government has recently taken a somewhat more relaxed attitude towards the publication and dissemination of economic data, sufficient transparency has not yet been achieved.[3] An accurate portrayal of the economy is further made difficult by the inconsistency of available official data. Scattered information made available by state agencies is often unverifiable from other sources, and replete with discrepancies. Figures on many aspects of the economy, such as employment and unemployment, national debt, foreign exchange reserves, and the financial status of some parastatal organizations, are not regularly published. Within published data, sizeable incongruities in certain items make it impossible to detect real trends in the economy, or to analyze the nature of the government's involvement and objectives. Furthermore, there are significant differences in published data on the same subjects by different government agencies (for example, Bank Markazi [the central bank] and the Plan Organization), as well as incompatibilities in figures supplied by a given agency on different accounts (such as Bank Markazi's data on national accounts and its balance-of-payments tables). Discrepancies also abound in the repeated revisions of the same data in subsequent years.

In addition to the shortcomings of official data – some of which Iran shares with other countries – there is the matter of divergence between official and private estimates. In the case of certain sensitive data such as unemployment, inflation, reserves, and debt, private figures differ – sometimes considerably – from official data. In the delicate issue of comparing the Islamic Republic's economic performance with achievements during the Shah's reign, even the reliability of published materials is questionable. Finally, there is ambiguity in the treatment of public and private sectors: some nationalized industrial enterprises, for example, are counted as part of the private sector; and some foundations, which carry out a number of public functions, are treated as private, or independent.

For these and other reasons, almost all available data ought to be considered subject to correction and revision. Certain figures should be regarded as approximations or estimates. No hard and fast lines should be drawn between expenditures and investments by the public and private sectors, since the large and unexplained items in the national and fiscal accounts tend to mask both the size of the public and private sectors, as well as the sectoral shares in the national product.

Discussions and analysis in this book are based on a variety of materials drawn from official publications of the Islamic Republic, private research papers, documents available in Iran and elsewhere, and the data-base of international financial and economic organizations. In the absence of more reliable alternatives, occasional use has been made of reports in the popular press, both domestic and foreign, without necessarily vouching for their accuracy or authenticity. In all such cases, the referenced accounts have been the only available source of information. Care has been taken to separate editorials from reported statistics. Tables are based on data published, or otherwise made available, by national and international organizations.

Internal sources used in this study are, for the most part, Bank Markazi-e Jomhuri-ye Eslami-ye Iran (the central bank), Sazman-e Barnameh va Budgeh (Plan and Budget Organization), and Markaz-e Amar-e Iran (Iranian Statistical Center). International organizations referenced here are mainly the International Monetary Fund and The World Bank group, supplemented by publications of the United Nations, the Organization for Economic Cooperation and Development, the Food and Agricultural Organization, and the Organization of Petroleum Exporting Countries. For brevity's sake, references to specific documents from each agency are omitted. All errors of omission or commission are the author's sole responsibility, and not those of organizations cited.

In a limited number of cases where official data themselves showed discrepancies in different publications, certain minor adjustments have been allowed. In all such cases, proper notations have been made. In chapters dealing with specific sectors, extensive use has been made of many internal reports and documents with certain restrictions over their direct quotations or attribution. Since the intention here is to examine the Iranian economy – and not to rewrite Iran's post-revolution economic history – no attempt has been made to change or revise official data even when their accuracy has been doubted by critics.

Despite conscious efforts made to provide an inclusive and reasonably accurate profile of Iran's post-revolution economy, the study should still be treated as a record of past performance, and not a blueprint for the future. The unsettled contours of Islamic economics, the volatility of revolutionary politics, and unanswered questions regarding both the letter and the spirit of the 1979 Constitution, disallow any meaningful prognosis beyond the obvious, and rather elementary, trends. Not only are data on various aspects of the economy in need of continuous updating and revision as time passes, but also the essential thrust of economic policy must be constantly reviewed and re-examined in the light of internal political developments and shifts of direction.

Regulations regarding imports and exports, exchange rates and availability, domestic credit ceilings and allocations, rates of return on deposits and investments, taxes on income and expenditure, and other variables have undergone repeated changes in the past dozen years, and promise to follow a similar pattern in the future. The rapid pace of change in both the structure and direction of the Iranian economy may therefore make even the very latest facts and figures out of date.

NOTES

1. See, for example, *The Economist*, (London), February 21 and September 5, 1981.
2. See Terrence Smith, 'Iran: Five Years of Fanaticism', *The New York Times Magazine*, February 12, 1984.
3. Foreign analysts believe that official statistical data should be treated with caution as they tend to be used for 'political ends'. See The Economist Intelligence Unit, 'Iran', Country Report No. 4, 1991. One of the regime's own newspapers complains that statistics and information needed for making a comprehensive analysis of the economy have been locked up under the seal of confidentiality, and made available to only a few experts to prepare internal memoranda to still fewer higher-ups. (*Ettela'at-e Siasi-Eqtesad-i,* 21 Tir 1367.)

Acknowledgements

I wish to express my sincere thanks to a number of individuals who have assisted me in the preparation of this study. Without their help, insight and input, this book would have been incomplete.

I owe an enormous debt of gratitude to Mohammed Yeganeh who generously placed his extensive collection of materials on the Iranian economy at my disposal, read part of an early draft, and as usual offered many cogent and helpful suggestions. I am equally grateful to Farrokh Najmabadi and Bahram Nowzad who took time to review the entire manuscript and made valued and indispensable comments for its improvement in both style and substance. Special words of appreciation should also go to Shaul Bakhash, Hashem Pesaran, Homayoun Jaber Ansari, Abbas Ordoobadi and Shahram Chubin who provided me in different ways with valuable information and support.

A large number of Iranian and foreign friends and former colleagues who, for reasons of their own, prefer to remain anonymous, have supplied me with additional source materials and research aids for which I cannot be thankful enough. They all deserve much of the credit for this study's contents and contributions while the responsibility for its deficiencies are solely mine.

I
INTRODUCTION

1

The Iranian economy on the eve of the revolution

Much has been written about the Iranian economy under the Pahlavis. Its basic features, principal socio-political priorities, and progressive development (particularly during the 1960s and 1970s) have been detailed in several studies by Iranian and foreign analysts.[1] What follows here is a brief summation of the underlying economic conditions preceding the 1979 revolution. The aim is to provide a backdrop against which the problems and prospects in the period after the change in political regime can be understood.

A PRE-REVOLUTION PANORAMA

On the eve of the 1979 revolution, Iran had just completed nearly two decades of rapid economic growth and impressive social development. Between 1960 and 1978, the Iranian economy was for the most part thriving, vibrant, and expansive, albeit somewhat unbalanced and in some ways fragile. During this period, the country was systematically transformed from a largely agrarian and stagnant economy into a modern, progressive society by way of structural changes in the tradition-bound socio-economic order. Through public planning, guidance and assistance, the economy was led on a path of urbanization, industrialization, and diversification. Basic priorities set by the government emphasized rapid growth, sectoral modernization, improved social welfare, and integration into the global economy. This agenda was a matter of consensus among the regime's supporters. Dissent within government circles was centered mostly on specific strategies and policies, and not on the basic orientation and direction. Thanks to the growing revenues from oil – a state monopoly – the government undertook a comprehensive program of multi-billion-dollar public investment in infrastructure, industry, agriculture, and hydrocarbons. Through appropriate legislation, management guidance, labor training, and other incentives, the government helped create a vigorous and exuberant private sector.

While annual domestic private investment accounted for a substantial portion of gross fixed capital formation – larger than public investment during 1960–1967 – the public sector exercised an increasingly active role in the economy. The growing dominance of the government, however, was not due to an ideological bias, but was the result of rising public expenditure financed by oil revenues. And, despite the state's expanding involvement in certain basic economic activities (oil and gas, metals, petrochemicals, and defense industries), the private sector was predominant in others (for example, automobiles, textiles, pharmaceuticals, and food processing). In other activities, the two sectors were in competition. In agriculture, the government owned a number of agribusinesses and farm corporations – some in joint ventures with foreign interests. Small and mid-size farming, however, was largely in private hands. In industry, apart from certain consumer-goods factories inherited from the Reza Shah period, the government's involvement was limited to the very large industries and public utilities, high-tech and heavy machinery projects which were not attractive to, and could not be afforded by, the private sector. The state's entry into other, smaller projects was also prompted by the need to serve as a catalyst for establishing new industries, helping to renovate others, and offering management know-how to ailing private sector firms.

Furthermore, the third principle of the Shah's 'White Revolution' promised that state enterprises would be sold to the public, and more than 30 factories (or nearly 40 per cent) of those destined for sale were subsequently sold either wholly or in part. In addition, the 1975 Law for the Expansion of Ownership of Productive Enterprises (based on the 13th principle of the 'White Revolution') called for 49 per cent of the shares of large, private industrial firms, and 99 per cent of the shares of state industrial units (except in strategic industries) to be sold to the workers of each company, and then to other workers, farmers, and the general public.

As acknowledged even by critics of the Pahlavi regime, the expansion of public sector ownership and management did not crowd out the private sector: the domestic economic boom generated by soaring public expenditure served as a great stimulus to private entrepreneurs. The mining and manufacturing sector that was given the pivotal role in the development process was expected to serve as a powerful locomotive for growth through its backward and forward linkages in the economy. The rapidly rising oil revenues, surrogating as enormous and painless national savings, fuelled the expansion without the historical necessity of belt-tightening, or heavy foreign borrowing. As a result, national output rose from slightly more than $4 billion in 1960/61 to over $77 billion in 1977/78 at current prices and official rial/dollar exchange rates.

Throughout these years, the government was successful in attaining most of its economic, social, and defense objectives. Data published by the World Bank show that, compared with other Third World countries, Iran's annual real growth rate of nearly 9.6 per cent during 1960–1977 was roughly double the average of the countries in the middle-income category, and higher than the average for any other group of countries in the world. Impressive rates of growth were also achieved in other main economic variables – investment, saving, consumption, employment, and per capita income. Gross domestic investment grew at an average annual rate of more than 16 per cent, reaching 33 per cent of gross domestic product (GDP) in 1977/78. Public consumption rose nearly 18 per cent a year; private consumption rose 10 per cent. Per capita income went up by about 8 per cent a year on average. All sectors of the economy also showed significant expansion, albeit at different rates. Between 1960 and 1978, agriculture grew by 4.8 per cent a year, industry by 8.7 per cent, and services by 13 per cent on average. The annual growth rate of agriculture, although lower than the other sectors, was respectable by world standards. Diversification was achieved as industry, oil, and service sectors gradually claimed larger shares of the gross domestic product. The share of agriculture was reduced from 29 per cent of GDP in 1960 to less than 10 per cent in 1977; by contrast, the share of industry (including energy) went up from 33 per cent to about 50 per cent; while the service sector's share remained roughly the same.[2]

In oil and gas, the average annual growth rate was 14.5 per cent a year during 1960–74, but declined to less than 1 per cent per annum in 1974–78. Nevertheless, the sector's progress in the two decades before the revolution was remarkable. Crude oil exports rose from approximately 1 million barrels per day (mb/d) in 1963 to around 4 mb/d in 1971, reaching a peak of 5.4 mb/d in 1974. By the time of the revolution, oil exports were about 4.5 mb/d. At the same time, oil production capacity had reached 6.5 mb/d.

Domestic oil consumption, almost totally supplied by domestic refineries, rose from 80,000 b/d in 1963 to nearly 543,000 b/d by 1979. Refined product exports averaged about 192,000 b/d for the 1960–1977 period. The government's revenues from crude oil exports rose from $723 million in 1960 to about $22 billion by the time of the revolution.[3] In the meantime, the country's dependence on oil income as a source of foreign exchange rose from 88 per cent in 1960 to 97 per cent in 1977. Production of natural gas during the same period rose seven-fold. The share of the oil sector in GDP, which was about 15 per cent in the early 1960s reached nearly 35 per cent in 1973 before declining to 32.5 per cent in 1977/78.

The manufacturing sector registered an average annual real growth of nearly 14 per cent during 1963–1978, the second highest in the world after South Korea, and more than twice the growth rate of other developing countries in the same group as Iran. Production per worker grew to 10.5 per cent a year in manufacturing (compared to 5 per cent in agriculture and 8 per cent in the economy as a whole). The share of employment in manufacturing went up from 16.5 per cent to 19 per cent, partially absorbing the labor released from agriculture.

In foreign trade, the share of consumer goods in the value of total imports declined from 24 per cent in 1963 to 18 per cent in 1977, while the share of capital goods rose from 20 per cent to 28 per cent. Although the share of non-oil exports in the country's foreign sales remained low (between $120 million in 1963 and about $800 million in 1977), the contribution of industrial goods to total non-oil exports rose from 6 per cent in 1963 to 22 per cent in 1977.

Inflation was kept at an uncommonly low rate of 2.5 per cent a year during 1960–67, and 3.7 per cent a year between 1968 and 1973. Even during the oil boom of the mid-1970s, the 1974–77 annual rise in the consumer price index averaged 15.5 per cent – still below the average of Third World countries (22 per cent). The overall external payments balance for much of the 1970s was positive. The exchange and trading system was liberal even by Western standards, and, by the second half of the 1970s, the Iranian rial had effectively become a convertible currency. Government finances, while in deficit, were in manageable order, and internal debt was easily serviceable. Iran's foreign exchange assets were estimated at $15 billion (with reserves of nearly $11 billion) against an estimated long-term external debt of some $7.5 billion.[4]

Thanks to considerable outlay allocated to education and health, great strides were made in improving social welfare. Infant mortality, malnutrition, endemic diseases, and illiteracy were reduced considerably, while caloric intake, student population, and life expectancy all increased appreciably. The ratio of value added by farm workers to that of workers in non-oil sectors slightly improved. While the gap between rural and urban income, and income inequalities within each sector, did not demonstrably change, indications are that absolute poverty was measurably reduced.

THE OIL BOUNTY: A CURSE IN DISGUISE?

As indicated in a separate study,[5] the beginning of the civil unrest and economic turmoil that culminated in the overthrow of the Pahlavi regime coincided with the end of the Fifth Development Plan (1973/74–1977/78). This, final five-year plan, implemented during the Shah's reign, turned out to be the most ambitious, and least successful, of all post-1954 planning endeavors.[6] The preamble of the revised Fifth Plan declared it to be 'the spearhead of one of the country's most brilliant and significant transformations', designed to guide Iran more rapidly to the period of the 'Great Civilization'.[7] While this ultimate goal was not precisely defined, it meant a militarily strong, modern, industrial nation, faithful to Iran's cultural heritage, and concerned about social welfare for all. The plan – which was hastily revised after the 1973 oil price rise, from a total investment target of $36 billion over the five-year period to nearly $70 billion – turned out to be highly unrealistic in its revenue projections, and unduly confident over the feasibility of its goals. While planned public and private investment outlays were nearly seven times the size of the just-completed Fourth Plan (1968–73), the planners still believed them to be within the country's absorptive capacity.

The Tehran Oil Agreement of December 1973 boosted the Iranian government's oil export revenues for the year 1973/74 to $4.6 billion, an increase of about 65 per cent over the 1972/73 figure of $2.8 billion. The figure for 1974/75, $17.8 billion, represented a three-fold increase within the space of two years.[8] Based on this substantial increase in oil receipts, both current and development expenditures went up sharply. Credit to the private sector and domestic liquidity rose precipitously. The result was a two-year superboom which generated a broadening gap between aggregate supply and demand, and double-digit inflation.

Domestic production, although increasing, did not meet unexpectedly rising demand. A number of physical and managerial bottlenecks (such as in port capacity, transport facilities, warehousing and customs clearance) hampered imports. Accelerated private and public investments in a wide range of economic activities accentuated the shortages of skilled manpower, building materials, and electric power. The raw materials boom in world markets, and the ensuing virulent worldwide inflation, added cost-push pressures on top of rising aggregate demand. By the end of 1975/76 the economy was out of balance.

The government's earnest efforts, and its emergency high-cost rescue programs, proved unable to break supply shortages, and stemmed inflation only temporarily. An effective means of combating inflation required fundamental (albeit politically difficult) policies to increase domestic competition, reduce the oligopolistic power of a few leading industrialists, encourage agricultural production, and restrict public expenditure. The urgency of the situation, however, combined with political expediency, led the authorities to resort to seemingly easier measures, such as price controls and penalties against hoarding. The immediate impact of these measures was to shake business confidence.

The year 1976/77 proved to be the undoing of the boom. The earlier euphoria was dampened by a fall in world demand for oil, a drop in real oil prices, and a decline in anticipated oil revenues. With the increase in expenditure rapidly outpacing increases in receipts, the national budget, which had been in the black for two years, showed gross deficits in the last two years of the plan. Iran returned to the international market for borrowing to meet development project needs.

By the close of its five-year period in March 1978, the Fifth Plan registered a mixed record. Unlike the two previous five-year plans that showed steady upward growth during 1963–73, the Fifth Plan exhibited an erratic boom-and-bust pattern. For the entire Plan period, the yearly economic growth averaged 8.5 per cent (Table 1.1). (For detailed economic indicators before the revolution, including a comparison of different five-year plans, see Tables 1.1, 1.2 and 1.3.)

In retrospect, the Fifth Plan's shortfalls – apart from its overly ambitious and virtually unattainable goals, and an unexpected decline in oil revenues – were caused by: a lack of careful calculation of emerging demand for housing, electricity, water, transportation, and other infrastructural facilities; too much confidence in the technocrats' ability to manipulate essential market forces; and undue haste in revising the plan in 1974/75. An overall picture of the economy during the Fifth Plan is shown in Table 1.2. A careful review of this picture shows that, once allowance is made for the arbitrary and unrealistic targets that the Fifth Plan had set for itself, its record was highly satisfactory. Although overall growth lagged behind the two previous plans because of a nearly stagnant oil sector, the rest of the economy performed well. Indeed, the non-oil GDP's growth at over 15 per cent a year on average compared remarkably well with the 11 per cent average annual expansion in the Fourth Plan.

The need for a mid-course correction brought about a change in government in the summer of 1977. A 12-point program, proposed by the new government, promised more attention to social welfare, increased productive capacity, an effective campaign against infla-tion, relaxation of price controls, decreased dependence on oil, reversal of rural migration, greater global competitiveness for domestic industry, development of alternative sources of energy, expansion of infrastructure, support of the private sector, improved distribution of income, and better consumer protection.[9]

The new government adopted an anti-inflationary program through budget cuts, credit restrictions, and land-price regulation. The growth of money supply was reduced; total public expenditure was slashed; prices of 'non-strategic' items were freed from con-trols; oil and gas prices were raised to encourage energy conserva-tion; certain farm price supports were boosted as incentives to increase production; import bans on a number of items were lifted to raise local competitiveness; and, in a major policy shift, emphasis was diverted from large agribusiness projects to small and medium-size farms.

These measures had some good short-term effects. Electricity generation increased, and power blackouts were reduced. Cargo discharge was improved. The cost-of-living index was temporarily brought down. But these deflationary measures came too late and too fast. A slackening of construction activities caused pockets of unemployment, especially among unskilled and semi-skilled work-ers. Putting the economy back on course, and reducing growth to a sustainable level, required a slow cooling-off period. But the earlier decision to catapult the economy to the position of a major industrial power within one generation had created a momentum which defied quick retrenchment.

It was hoped to bring many of these run-away developments under control in the Sixth Plan, starting in March 1978. But the preparation of the Sixth Plan (1978/79–1982/83) turned out to be virtually impossible. While the projected public revenues during the coming five-year period (based on a 30 per cent increase in oil receipts) was no more than $128.6 billion, the budgetary demands of public institutions surpassed $500 billion! In this financial quagmire, the first tentative draft of the Sixth Plan showed that the total anticipated revenues would be fully absorbed by only seven 'high-priority' programs (military bases and housing; nuclear power generation; the second gas pipeline to the Soviet Union and Europe; capacity expansion in oil, gas, and petrochemicals; electrification of the railroad; a 15 million-ton a year steel production; and a satellite telecommunications complex). All other programs and projects had to be left out.

Faced with the Sixth Plan's limited prospects and a number of other painful alternatives, it was decided to do away with five-year planning altogether, and to proceed with annual development budgeting for each economic or social program (for example, steel, nuclear energy, petrochemicals, transport, literacy and health) within 10- and 25-year 'guidelines'. Before the new planning procedure could be put into effect, however, there was a change in the government in August 1978. A further series of politically-inspired disturbances brought in three further governments in quick succession, and ultimately led to the triumph of the revolution. In the process, the Sixth Plan became a moot exercise, and was later overtaken by events.

TOO MUCH, TOO SOON

Iran's development during the two decades before the revolution – if not exactly the 'economic miracle' that the Shah's supporters liked to call it – was undoubtedly one of the world's clearest success stories in the second half of the twentieth century. Despite harsh and unrelenting criticism of the Pahlavi regime's economic strategies and policies – some of them justified at the time, and others mostly in hindsight – the Iranian experience was beyond even the most optimistic expectations of knowledgeable observers, both domestic and foreign.

Numerous factors were responsible for the incontrovertible economic achievements. During most of the 1963–78 period, Iran enjoyed a good measure of political stability and national self-confidence. The relationship between the public and private sectors, while not ideal, was mutually supportive, and the private investment climate was attractive to both domestic and foreign investors. Rising demand for investment was spurred by Iran's substantial natural resources, a rich supply of human capital, extensive new physical and institutional infrastructure, a solid banking system, and – above all – a large and expanding domestic market protected from foreign competition. The government's helping hand in the form of heavy trade protection, generous tax incentives, easy bank credit, bilateral trade agreements, exclusive licensing, and liberal exchange facilities served as an unparalleled promoter of private enterprise and initiative.

From all indications, Iran's pre-revolution economy, despite its imbalances and fragility, was a *workable* system, capable of self-correction and survival in the face of many *economic* challenges. But, as it turned out, the elaborate economic superstructure could not withstand hostile political forces and a revolutionary onslaught. It was gradually weakened by unreasonable demands on its fragile capabilities, and finally immobilized by the ferocity of the opposition's attacks on its nerve centers (for example, oil exports, customs clearance, banking transactions, treasury disbursements, and transport facilities).

In retrospect, the regime's quest for military superiority in the Persian Gulf region, its drive to join the ranks of the world's major industrial powers within a generation, plus its desire to create a Western European welfare state – all simultaneously, with the aid of oil money – proved to be too ambitious a target and too heavy a burden. Significant socio-economic achievements and considerable military capacity thus failed to establish a solid base of support for the leadership, which meant that the regime could not withstand the onslaught of adverse forces and inopportune circumstances. The country's sizeable investment in infrastructure, human resources, and defense equipment, however, enabled the new regime to cope with many formidable problems more easily than expected or imagined. The proven ability of the Islamic republic to defend Iran's territorial integrity against the Iraqi aggression, to sustain its fast-growing population (albeit at reduced standards), and to pay its external debt (albeit with reseves inherited from the past) was to a very large extent due to the enormous investment and capital accumulation which occurred during the previous regime.

NOTES

1. For a partial list of these studies see J. Amuzegar and M. A. Fekrat, *Iran: Economic Development under Dualistic Conditions* (Chicago: University of Chicago Press, 1971); Jahangir Amuzegar, *Iran: An Economic Profile* (Washington: The Middle East Institute, 1977); Hossein Bashiriyeh, *The State and Revolution in Iran, 1962–1982* (London: Croom Helm, 1984); Robert Graham, *Iran: The Illusion of Power* (New York: St Martin's Press, 1979); Fred Halliday, *Iran:*

Dictatorship and Development (New York: Penguin Books, 1979); Eric Hooglund, *Land and Revolution in Iran, 1960–1980* (Austin: University of Texas Press, 1982); J. W. Jacqz (ed.), *Iran: Past, Present, and Future* (New York: Aspen Institute, 1975); Massoud Karshenas, *Oil, State and Industrialization in Iran* (Cambridge: Cambridge University Press, 1990); George Lenczowski, *Iran Under the Pahlavis* (Stanford: Hoover Institution, 1975); M. M. H. Malek, *The Political Economy of Iran under the Shah* (London: Croom Helm, 1986); H. Razavi and F. Vakil, *The Political Environment of Economic Planning in Iran 1971–1983* (Boulder: Westview Press, 1984); Ebrahim Razzaqi, *Eqtesad-e Iran* (Tehran: Nashr-e Ney, 1367 [1988]); Bahram Tehrani, *Pajuheshi dar Eqtesad-e Iran 1354–1364* [1975–1985] (Paris: Khavaran, 1986).

2. All figures are based on data in *World Development Report, 1980* (Washington: The World Bank, 1980).

3. Figures of Iran's annual revenues from oil exports published by Bank Markazi, OPEC, and the International Monetary Fund do not always correspond, due to differences in the accounting year, statistical discrepancies, and other (unexplained) reasons.

4. The figures for foreign assets and external debts are mere estimates since accurate data are not available, and published figures differ considerably.

5. Jahangir Amuzegar, *The Dynamics of the Iranian Revolution* (Albany: SUNY Press, 1991), Chapter XII.

6. Jahangir Amuzegar, *Iran: An Economic Profile* (Washington: The Middle East Institute, 1977), Chapter 4.

7. *Iran's Fifth Development Plan, Revised 1973–78: A Summary* (Tehran: Plan and Budget Organization, January, 1975), p. 1.

8. For details about oil price changes during 1973–74 see *The Middle East and North Africa 1979/80* (London: Europa Publications Ltd., 1981).

9. For details, see Jahangir Amuzegar, 'Growth Without Pain: The New Iranian Development Strategy', *Middle East Problem Paper No. 18* (Washington: The Middle East Institute, September, 1978).

II
THE
ISLAMIC REPUBLIC'S
POLITICO-ECONOMIC
AGENDA

2

The search for an Islamic economic order

The uneasy coalition of opposition groups that supported Ayatollah Khomeini's challenge to the Pahlavi regime had no specific economic agenda acceptable to all factions. Each group had its own notion of an ideal future for the Iranian economy. Sharp rifts existed between these groups on nearly every major aspect of this future, including national socio-economic objectives, the nature of policy reforms, the role of the state and the private sector in the economy, economic ties with the outside world, and the overall structural transformation of the socio-economic order.

The glue that kept the disparate groups together was their opposition to the Pahlavis' vision and plans for Iran. The revolutionaries blamed Mohammad Reza Shah's regime for what each faction regarded as a mistaken economic strategy or policy. The Pahlavi regime was called to task by some for adopting a Western development model that neglected national interests, and made Iran dependent for its survival on Western technology, management know-how, industrial inputs, and capital. It was criticized by others for rapidly exhausting the country's oil reserves to serve foreign interests and to pay for 'worthless' arms, for neglecting agriculture and upsetting traditional rural systems, and for following a modernization and industrialization strategy responsible for subjecting Iran to foreign dictate. Insufficient attention to non-oil exports was said to have caused Iran's dangerous reliance on the volatile petroleum market, and placed the domestic economy at the mercy of oil cartels and multinationals. Encouragement given to consumerism and material welfare was castigated for having detracted the populace from the path of contentment and virtue.

The regime's overall economic stance was blamed for encouraging non-productive speculations, and widening the gap between the rich and the poor, the urbanites and the rural folk.

As forcefully put by one of its academic supporters in the West, the Islamic Republic inherited 'a semi-peripheral country following almost three decades of a dependent capitalist growth path'. The country, accordingly, experienced technological dependency, uneven development, and speedy destruction of its traditional culture through rapid industrialization, modernization, and integration into the world economy. The 1979 revolution, in the opposition's view, reflected the failure of the economic model to benefit the majority; it was a cultural and nationalistic reaction to Western imperialism; and it represented a strong will to rebuild the society after an ideal homegrown model. In short, the Shah's economic legacy was depicted as an economy heavily dependent on oil and the capitalist world for industrial inputs, technology, and food; unevenly developed across social classes, regions and economic sectors; and largely directed toward production and imports for consumption by a tiny minority of the rich and the upper-middle classes. The economy's 'growth first, redistribution later' strategy caused industries and urban centers to gain at the expense of agriculture and rural areas.[1]

GROPING FOR A NEW WAY

A new and indigenous way had thus to be found to rescue the economy from its 'unhealthy' dependence on the 'capitalist world'. But no one in the anti-Shah opposition possessed a home-grown model which appealed to the rest. At issue were the questions of the nation's economic *orientation*, the shape of its basic economic *institutions*, and the *direction* of economic policies. Marxists and the radical Left (represented by the Tudeh [Communist] party, the Mojahedin-e Khalq, and other splinter factions) followed the standard Marxist-Leninist line with a sprinkling of Islamic rhetoric. Even during the short tenure of the Bazargan government, and before the ultimate triumph of theocracy, the ideological slogans of leftist revolutionaries included such far-out visionary promises as liberating man from the dominance of nature and class and giving him more time for truly human activities. There was talk about sending the population into the countryside to do more productive work. An 'ideal' society (where food, clothing, housing, health, and education were to be free) was contemplated by the followers of *divine harmony* economists; to be established through rejecting consumerism, decentralizing all decisions into Soviet-type units, and distributing oil revenues in inverse proportion to population density in regions.[2] Democratic secularists of the National Front, and Islamic progressives (led by Mehdi Bazargan), advocated a kind of Euro-socialist system suffused with nationalistic or Islamic undertones. Moslem fundamentalists (most closely linked with Ayatollah Khomeini himself) talked about a return to an Islamic economy reminiscent of the Prophet's time. Center-right groups of liberal-democratic secularists, the *bazaar*, the industrial and agricultural bourgeoisie, and the conservative clergy wished to preserve the free-enterprise foundation of the Pahlavi regime and introduce only supplemental changes in the direction of a more democratic, or a more Islamic, identity. The orthodox Shi'ite hierarchy in this camp took their cue from certain passages in the Qor'an in support of private property, freedom of enterprise, and individual initiative.

In Ayatollah Khomeini's own thinking, perhaps, a truly Islamic society had to place greater emphasis on the theological at the expense of the material. Economics had to play a secondary role to spiritual considerations. According to some Western observers, Iran's Islamic revolutionary faction rejected the idea of material improvement in favor of 'generalized austerity' or shared poverty. The Ayatollah is repeatedly quoted as having once declared that the revolution was about Islam, not about the price of melons.[3] The supreme leadership's preference was said to be a return to the idyllic times of prophet Mohammad in simplicity, appearance, and outlook. His Islamic economic order, according to his followers, was one in which the poor and the deprived stood at the center. The objective of this order was to abolish poverty and establish justice by renouncing the accumulation of wealth. Economic growth was secondary to man's intellectual, cultural and spiritual development. An austere and puritanical lifestyle was the key to such development.[4]

Eventually, with the victory of the clerical faction over other anti-Shah groups in the design of the 1979 Constitution, all secular socio-economic agendas were laid to rest, or given an Islamic hue. The Islamic Republic had to have an Islamic society and an Islamic economy. The political revolution had to be followed by a cultural revolution. The new leadership's main task was thus to delineate the contours of an Islamic social system, and to formulate the essential characteristics of an Islamic economic model. Yet, since no such integral Islamic system existed anywhere in the globe (even in Saudi Arabia, which the Iranian Shi'ite fundamentalists did not, in any case, wish to emulate) a new order had to be designed and constructed by the Islamic Republic.

The basic *principles* of an Islamic economy had already been talked about by close Khomeini aides as a 'third path' between laissez-faire capitalism and outright Marxism. The emphasis was on the uniqueness of the Islamic approach compared to the East-West alternatives. Islamic economics, invoking some of the liberal and populist teachings of the holy book, promised to create a healthier and more desirable society through an equitable distribution of wealth, and greater social welfare for the so-called disenfranchised, dispossessed and deprived masses (*mostazafan*). Some basic theoretical aspects of 'Islamic economics' had also been advanced by a number of (mostly non-Iranian) clerical and lay scholars familiar with modern economic thought.[5]

Iran's own Islamic scholars (including Ali Shariati, Morteza Motahhari, and Mahmud Taleqani) dealt with an Islamic economic culture in such generalities as the denunciation of exploitation poverty, inequality, and injustice. The pliant domestic press also advanced the thesis that the test of true economic independence (which the Shah had allegedly sacrificed at the altar of *comprador* capitalism) was the nation's ability to take care of its basic needs through its own domestic means, and to be able to withstand 'imperialist' pressures by relying on internal resources.

Beyond these simplified (if not simplistic) notions, there was no concrete, mutually agreed Islamic economic model to follow. A series of expedient but haphazard (and untried) policies with a distinct leftist slant were rushed through the Revolutionary Council by the Provisional Government. But subsequent escalation of conflict between secularist-progressive elements and clerical-fundamentalist groups resulted in the forced resignation of Prime Minister Bazargan on November 6, 1979. The road was thus cleared for the theocratic design of a new constitution, and the eventual takeover of the government by the clerics and their fundamentalist allies. The in-fighting for the imposition of an Islamic model on the rest of the coalition partners was nowhere more evident than in the drafting of the new Constitution where two vastly different texts, and scores of amendments, were proposed and voted on. And nowhere were the uneasy compromises in the final draft of the Consitution as striking as in the obvious incongruity of many constitutional clauses, each reflecting the views of a distinct constituency with different politico-religious backgrounds and oreintation.[6]

As detailed in the next chapter, the 1979 Constitution devoted a good part of its text to economic matters and the fundamental principles of an Islamic economy. Within this constitutional framework, certain specific objectives and policies of an Islamic society, and certain basic tenets of Islamic economics, were provided by the leaders of the Islamic Republic in their Friday prayer meetings. The most detailed and influential description of these principles were offered by Hojat ol-Islam Hashemi Rafsanjani in his capacity as Tehran's interim Friday *imam*, in addition to his position, first, as speaker of the *Majles* (the Islamic parliament) and, later, as president of the Islamic Republic.

AN ISLAMIC ECONOMY

Abstracting from its minute and specific prescriptions regarding interest, taxes, alimony, inheritance, and business contracts, Islamic economics – as defined by the regime's leadership – refers to a set of socio-economic principles concerning production, consumption, and distribution that are designed to create a 'just society', and certain invididual attitudes and behavior that are likely to ensure a society of 'divine unity'. Islamic economics, in other words, functions within, and is an integral part of, what may be called an Islamic economic *culture*.

In an Islamic economy, private ownership originates from human labor, and the fruits of ownership may be transferred to others through bequest, inheritance, confiscation, and other legitimate social contracts and covenants. Except for natural resources (such as minerals, forests and rivers), that belong to the nation, there is no prohibition against accumulation of wealth as long as it is legitimately acquired, used in 'God's way', and for the benefit of other people (that is, *enfaq*). Islamic ownership, however, is never absolute in the capitalist bourgeois sense. Private ownership is circumscribed by several caveats. In general, Moslems are endowed with freedom to conduct their lives and manage their property. Yet, the exercise of such freedoms cannot transgress the lives or properties of others. Nor is the power to exercise ownership *total*: it is constrained by necessity and moderation. That is, the use of property is limited to productive, non-extravagant, and rational activity. Owners, for example, are *not* free to destroy, dissipate, misuse or abuse their possessions; but they are free from other people's transgressions and usurpations. Thus, while private property is recognized and sanctioned in Islam, it is subjected to a number of stringent limitations and social obligations.[7]

Ownership is also divided between public and private sectors, with most natural resources belonging to the state. Private ownership and operation of productive means are considered perfectly legitimate activities. But the Islamic private sector is deemed to be different from its non-Islamic counterparts. In the Islamic culture, private enterprises based on private ownership cannot engage in a free-wheeling, *caveat emptor*, type of operation. Private business activity has to be healthy, humane, self-sacrificing, and in conformity with the Islamic criterion of social justice.[8] In a word, it has to be *responsible*.

Self-interest, ambition, and material incentives are recognized as necessary and constructive. But the government has the duty to direct these instincts and desires into 'proper paths'. The individual is not a mere cog in the state machinery (as in communism); he is free to improve his lot. But he is not allowed to pursue selfish interests in an unbridled, greedy fashion (as in capitalism); the state has the responsibility to control individual excesses.[9] Islamic economics allows individual freedom in choice of employment and activity, trade, production, and other legitimate endeavors. State control and guidance, however, are used to make sure that no one is deprived of an opportunity to earn a living. Yet, since even with state control and guidance some people will still get ahead and others will be left behind, while life's accidents will disadvantage others, Islam calls for the creation of an integral society where brotherly love and friendship among people are so strong that they thwart any feeling of resentment and envy emanating from differences in wealth and status. To mitigate such differences, a truly Islamic society encourages people of different means to become 'contractual brothers', whereby each is allowed to share the other's wealth and possessions.[10]

On personal consumption, Islamic economics counsels moderation (*e'etedal*) and abhors economic waste (*esraf*) in daily habits. Islam, it is emphasized, has nothing against beauty, pleasure, attractiveness, ornamentation, or a good healthy life; it is only opposed to waste, profligacy, extravagance, lavishness, and ostentation. The ideal is 'moderation', which, while not precisely defined, refers to a state or condition that is different from anything which is clearly considered to be 'showing off' by local community standards, anything that creates envy or a sense of deprivation among one's friends, neighbors and associates. This emphasis on homogeneity in lifestyle is part of the Islamic economic culture where individuals are not guaranteed equal income, status, or wealth, but are simultaneously enjoined from being conspicuously different.

Income distribution in an ideal Islamic economy is expected to be 'equitable' in such a way that there are neither prodigal consumers nor needy people. Equity in the distribution of income is to be attained through obligatory individual contributions (for example, *khoms* and *zakat*)[11] to the state and society, and voluntary sharing of wealth and income by the well-to-do (i.e. *enfaq*). An individual's moral duty toward his fellow men thus goes beyond the payment of his dues; it also requires further humanitarian behavior. A lavish and dissipated life, hoarding, the idle holding of wealth, and similar 'anti-social' behavior are considered contrary to the creation of a healthy, brotherly, and non-discriminatory environment. In an ideal Islamic society, there is no greed, no hiding of supply, no price gouging, no abuse of economic power. Opposed to such a society of virtuous, committed, and generous faithfuls are the greedy, the oppressor, the tyrant (*taghut*). Wealth should not be an end in itself, but only a means of contributing to the welfare of others. A true Moslem elevates himself toward God by going through three stages of personal development: charity (*movasat*); equality of wealth-sharing (*mosavat*); and the highest stage, self-sacrifice (*ithar*).[12]

The Qor'anic verses and religious statements attributed to Shi'ite *imams* that are cited by the leadership in defining such a homogeneous society of contractual brotherhood sometimes come perilously close to certain Marxian distributional prescriptions. Each true Moslem, according to Hojat ol-Islam Rafsanjani, is morally obligated to share the fruits of his ability or possessions with those in need. Certain anecdotes (*ravayat*) from the Prophet and Imam Ja'afar Sadeq, almost seem to hint at communist ownership and wealth-sharing. For example, it is reported that when the hat was once passed around among the faithful gathered in a mosque, some of the wealthy present put money in according to their ability and status, while some poorer brethren were allowed to take money from it according to their need.[13]

In three other specific areas, the Islamic Republic's version of Islamic economics and Islamic culture in the early years of the revolution took a radical position fundamentally at odds with that of the *ancien regime*. A major clergy-dominated Tehran newspaper proposed eliminating all political and cultural dependence on the West (particularly the United States); resorting to import substitution instead of export promotion; and assuming greater economic self-reliance approaching virtual autarky. The economy's major sectors had to become self-contained and strategically self-sufficient. Manufacturing industries had to become inward-oriented and reliant on domestic demand. A 20-year economic perspective prepared by the government's Plan and Budget Organization in 1982/83, projecting an annual rise in consumer imports, was sharply criticized as being against the goal of ultimate agricultural self-sufficiency, and contrary to the nation's long-term interests. Reliance on exports to raise living standards was rejected as futile in the face of an internationally hostile environment and the industrial powers' enmity toward the Islamic revolution. The proper direction for the economy was thought to be the expansion of industries that were independent of imported inputs, and supported by mineral-based exports.[14]

Iran's industrial independence was also seen as attainable only through the pursuit of an 'Islamic consumption model'. Taking the old regime to task for advocating 'a Peykan automobile in every garage' and encouraging consumerism as a means of reaching the 'Great Civilization', the government was urged by the press to take a firm stand against lavish spending, luxury consumption, and consumer imports. The corollary of this posture was to reduce imports to items not producible at home, and to limit the latter to only capital and intermediate goods. An Islamic consumption model was to be proposed by the government on the basis of 'society's real needs' as seen by the state. By limiting national consumption to real needs, the government was to eliminate economic dependence, restructure internal consumption patterns, eliminate unnecessary imports, and guide domestic industries toward the production of essential goods.[15]

The Islamization of the economy also involved educational curricula, technical training, and criteria for admission to the institutions of higher learning. The pre-1979 university system was suspended for more than three years in order to effectuate cultural adjustment (that is, the purging of foreign influences among students and in the faculty). Admission to university later become contingent upon commitment to Islamic tenets and the applicant's 'potential value' to the new Islamic society. Higher education was also used as a means to enhancing social justice. Thus, a certain percentage of total annual enrolment was earmarked for the rural poor, the children of 'martyrs' and their families, and other deserving groups.

The revolution's cultural criteria also affected other aspects of formal education. A 'fundamental' restructuring of the system, demanded by Ayatollah Khomeini in March 1980, called for the Islamization not only of ideas, but also of textbooks and teaching methods.[16] On the whole, all universities and institutions of higher learning were placed under the Islamic watch of a seven-man Cultural Revolution Committee. Islamic students' committees in each university (like similar committees in the ministries and government agencies), while still a minority representing no more than 25 per cent of the student body, had considerable power over the conduct of university affairs.

Finally, the Islamic culture placed greater emphasis on religious commitment (*ta'ahod*) than on technical competence (*takhassos*) as a criterion for public sector employment. A similar priority was given to public enterprise managers over private sector entrepreneurs in the social and professional hierarchy. While Western economic culture often regarded *public* ownership and direction of the economy as detrimental to maximum efficiency, the reverse was said to be true of Islamic management. Islamic managers were claimed to be the most virtuous, the most faithful and most sincere individuals; they were thus the most qualified to guide and direct the economy.[17] An Islamic manager was believed to spend more time, show more initiative, and be more diligent and decisive when in charge of the people's trust than when he tended to his own private business, because public trusteeship was part of his religious duties.[18]

THE ISLAMIC ECONOMY IN ACTION

The economic order that gradually evolved in Iran during the 1980s was undoubtedly influenced by these ideas and ideals. As shown in later chapters, the Provisional Government that was installed by Ayatollah Khomeini under the Revolutionary Council, the new constitution that was ratified by a national referendum, and the new *Majles* (Islamic parliament) that was elected in the general elections all attempted to introduce basic Islamic tenets into the hitherto secular society and largely free economy. The official policy was to re-orient Iranian society toward Islamic social justice, and to restructure the Iranian economy to attain self-reliance and self-sufficiency.

Forthcoming chapters will examine the extent to which the Islamic Republic has been able to establish a truly new Islamic economic order on promised patterns.[19] Iran's experience is, in turn, expected to show how difficult it is for a contemporary nation to adopt a type of economy vastly different from that of its trading partners in the current interdependent world.

NOTES

1. Hooshang Amirahmadi, *Revolution and Economic Transition: The Iranian Experience* (Albany: SUNY Press, 1990), pp. 1, 16. For

further criticism of the Shah's economic strategy from two other points of view, see Ezat Mossallanejad, *The Political Economy of Oil* (New Delhi: Criterion, 1986); and Kamran Mofid, *The Economic Consequences of the Gulf War* (London: Routledge, 1990).

2. See *Financial Times*, November 28, 1979.
3. Fred Halliday, 'The Iranian Revolution: Uneven Development and Religious Populism', *Journal of International Affairs*, Winter, 1983, p. 187; and Fouad Ajami, 'The Impossible Revolution', *Foreign Affairs*, January 1989, p. 155.
4. See *Kayhan Havai*, June 10, 1992 and May 27, 1992.
5. For some theoretical discussions of Islamic economics see M. A. Choudhuri and U. A. Malik, *The Foundation of Islamic Political Economy* (London: Macmillan, 1992); M. H. Besheshti, *Eqtesad-e Eslami* (Islamic Economics) (Tehran: 1370 [1990]); M. B. Sadr, *Eqtesadona* (Our Economics) (Beirut: 1961); Mahmud Teleqani, *Eslam va Malekiyat* (Islam and Property Ownership) (Tehran: 1344 [1965]); M. A. Mannan, *Islamic Economics* (Dehli: Adabiat-i Dehli, 1970); Imam Musa Sadr, *Eqtesad dar Maktab-e Eslam* (Economics of Islamic School) (Tehran: 1350 [1971]); S. M. Yusuf, *Economic Justice in Islam* (Lahore: Ashraf, 1971); Ali Tehrani, *Eqtesad-e Eslami* (Islamic Economics) (Mashad: Khorasan Press, 1353 [1974]); A. H. Bani Sadr, *Eqtesad-e Towhidi* (Economics of Divine Unity) (n.p., 1978); Kurshid Ahmed, ed., *Studies in Islamic Economics* (Leicester: Islamic Foundation, 1980); and M. N. Siddigi, *Muslim Economic Thinking* (Leicester: Islamic Foundation, 1981). For further references see Shaul Bakhash, *The Reign of the Ayatollahs* (London: I. B. Tauris, 1985), Ch. 7.
6. There were basically two main drafts – one by the clerical faction and the other by the radical Left – as working papers. The strong influence of Ayatollah Mohammad Hossein Beheshti in pushing the final version of the Constitution closer to the clerical draft has been widely acknowledged.
7. See Ali Akbar Hashemi Rafsanjani, 'Private and Public Ownership in Islam', *Ettela'at*, 3 Bahman 1361; and 16 Bahman 1362.
8. Press interview with the Minister of Agriculture, *Ettela'at*, 23 Aban, 1361.
9. See *Ettela'at*, 23 Aban 1361.
10. *Ettela'at*, 31 Bahman 1362.
11. *Khoms* is a tax of one-fifth on monetary profit and other gains. *Zakat* (or alms) is another religious tax equal to 2.5 per cent of income.
12. A. A. H. Rafsanjani, 'Charity, Empathy and Cooperation in an Islamic Society', *Ettela'at*, 16 Bahman 1362.
13. Friday prayer sermons of Hojat ol-Islam Hashemi Rafsanjani in *Ettela'at*, 11 Dey 1362; 25 Dey 1362; and 9 Bahman 1362.
14. See *Ettela'at*, 23 Bahman 1361.
15. Press interview with the Deputy Minister of Industry, *Ettela'at*, 20 Azar 1362, p. 4.
16. The use of dice in teaching the theory of probability was reportedly

shunned as a 'satanic gambling device', and replaced with a sack of balls of various colors. See *The New York Times*, July 19, 1980.

17. Press interview with the Minister of Agriculture, *Ettela'at*, 23 Aban 1361, p. 2.

18. For a broader discussion of the issue, see Cyrus Bina and Hamid Zanganeh, *Modern Capitalism and Islamic Ideology in Iran* (New York: St Martin's, 1992).

19. Thanks to the delicately nuanced contingency of Islamic thought, and the possibility of widely varied but equally valid interpretations of scripture, the regime is still claiming Islamic legitimacy for all its policies and strategies. On Islam's ideological resilience, see Shahrough Akhavi, *Religion and Politics in Contemporary Iran* (Albany: SUNY Press, 1980); and Maxime Rodinson, *Islam and Capitalism* (Austin: University of Texas Press, 1978).

3

The ideological framework of the economy

The referendum of March 1979 that officially changed the monarchy to an Islamic republic was the first step toward the Islamization of Iranian society and economy. Of the 73 members of the Assembly of Experts, elected nationwide in the summer of 1979 to debate and ratify a draft constitution (already approved by Ayatollah Khomeini and the Revolutionary Council), 55 were clerics. As expected, under the Ayatollah's strict order to make the constitution 'one hundred per cent Islamic', a large majority of the constitutional assembly – between 70 and 80 per cent – consistently voted in favor of the various 'Islamic' clauses of the document.

The final draft, ratified by a popular referendum on December 2–3, 1979, requires 'all civil, penal, financial, economic, administrative, cultural, military, political, and other laws and regulations in the country to be based on "Islamic criteria"' (Article 4).[1] To make sure that laws passed by the *Majles* adhere to the Islamic *sharia*, the Constitution provides for a Council of Guardians, composed of 12 members – six Islamic scholars and six jurists specializing in different areas of the law – to review all legislation and declare their compatibility with both the *sharia* and the Constitution (Article 96).[2]

THE 1979 CONSTITUTION AND THE ECONOMY

The economic framework of the Islamic Republic is described in several chapters and clauses of the 1979 Constitution, which is itself ideologically based on the concept of *velayat-e faqih* (mandate of the Islamic jurist). The preamble to the Constitution states the fundamental goal of the economy to be the 'satisfaction of the material needs of man in the course of his overall growth and development'. This principle is explicitly declared to be in contrast with non-Islamic economic systems where the aim is 'the concentration and accumulation of wealth and the maximization of profit'. In the Islamic culture, the economy is not an *end* in itself, but only a *means* 'to contribute to the attainment of the ultimate goal': i.e. a 'movement toward God'.

Article 3 of Chapter I sets out the economic objectives of the Islamic government as: firstly, the planning of a correct and just economic system in order to create prosperity, remove poverty, and abolish all forms of deprivation with respect to food, housing, work, and health care, and the provision of universal insurance; and, secondly, the attainment of self-sufficiency in industrial, agricultural and military science, technology, and all related matters.

Chapter IV (Articles 43 to 55) deals exclusively with the 'Economy and Financial Affairs'. As a means of creating a just society, the economy has to be independent of 'foreign domination' and must strive to eliminate 'poverty and deprivation'. Article 43 declares the underlying criteria of the Islamic economy to be the provision of such basic necessities as housing, food, clothing, health, and education for all citizens; possibilities of employment for everyone; national economic planning towards individual self-development, political participation and initiative; prohibition of monopoly, hoarding, usury, labor exploitation, and wasteful consumption; prevention of foreign economic domination; and a drive towards self-sufficiency. Other provisions of Article 43 reaffirm the right of every Iranian citizen to choose his own line of work, and define basic necessities to include 'housing, food, clothing, health care, medicine, education, and the necessary facilities for the establishment of a family for all'. The right to work is upheld for everyone, and the government is charged with the responsibility of providing 'every citizen with the opportunity to work'. The state has, furthermore, the duty of creating 'equal conditions' for finding employment. At the same time, Article 43 states that, in carrying out its constitutional duties, the government must not itself become 'a major or dominant employer'.

Article 44 divides the economy into three sectors: 'public, cooperative, and private'. The public sector includes 'all large-scale and basic industries; foreign trade; major mineral resources; banking; insurance; energy; dams and large-scale irrigation networks; radio, television, post, telegraph and telephone; aviation; shipping, roads, railroads and the like'. The cooperative sector is to include cooperative companies and institutions engaged in production and distribution 'in accordance with Islamic criteria'. The private sector consists of activities concerned with 'agriculture, animal husbandry, industry, trade and services that supplement the economic activities of the state and cooperative sectors'. The precise scope of each sector, as well as the regulation and conditions governing their operation, are to be specified by the *Majles*.

Articles 22, 44, 45, 46 and 47 deal with public and private ownership of property. Public property includes unclaimed lands, minerals, bodies of water, forests, unenclosed pastures, heirless estates, and confiscated private property. Article 22 holds private property to be 'inviolate, except in cases sanctioned by law'. Article 46 declares that everyone is 'the owner of the fruits of his legitimate business and labor', and Article 47 affirms that private property 'legitimately obtained is to be respected'. In order for it to be protected, however, Article 44 requires property to meet three conditions: that ownership must 'not go beyond the bounds of Islamic law', that the property itself should 'contribute to the economic growth and progress of the country', and that the property must not 'harm society'.

Article 49 defines the general criteria for 'legitimate' ownership by citing what is 'illegitimate', and setting forth violations of property obligations. Illegitimate assets to be confiscated by the government include all holdings resulting from usury, usurpation, bribes, embezzlement, theft, gambling, misuse of endowments, mishandling of public contracts and transactions, appropriation of public lands, operations of unlawful business, and other illicit sources. Article 50 expands the list of prohibited economic activities to include those that 'tend consistently to pollute the environment or inflict irreparable damage on it'.

Articles 47 and 49 impose stringent limitations on private property. Since the relevant criteria for legitimate acquisition of property are to be determined by the *Majles*, there is evidently no constitutional protection against arbitrary confiscation of property by a *Majles* law, except perhaps the vague provision that all legislation must conform to Islamic principles. These principles, however, are themselves subject to different interpretations. A liberal interpretation of Article 49, for example, may make virtually all wealth of substantial size in the hands of certain categories of individuals 'illegitimate'. And due to the absence of objective critiera and retroactivity of the law to past acquisitions, there may be no recourse to constitutional protection.

Chapter III of the Constitution, entitled the 'Right of the People', devotes its Articles 28 to 31 to *economic* rights. Thus, every citizen has the right to employment; social security with respect to retirement, unemployment, old age, disability, and destitution benefits; and entitlement to emergency assistance, health services, medicine, and medical care. Article 30 calls on the government to provide all citizens with free education to the end of high school, and to expand higher education facilities to the level required for national self-sufficiency. Article 31 obligates the government to make land available to every individual and family in Iran to own 'a dwelling commensurate with one's needs'. Articles 51 to 55 deal with taxes, annual budgets, disbursement of public funds, and fiscal audits.

Finally, Chapter VI of the Constitution deals in part with foreign economic relations. Thus, Article 77 requires that all 'international treaties, conventions, contracts and agreements' be ratified by the *Majles*.[3] Article 80 makes any government borrowing from abroad contingent upon parliamentary approval (as in the 1906 Constitution). The *Majles* can, however, authorize certain governmental agencies to borrow from abroad for specific purposes and within a specified amount. Also, Article 81 states that 'granting of concession to foreigners for the establishment of companies or organizations in the commercial, industrial and agricultural fields or for the extraction of minerals is strictly forbidden'.[4]

A careful scrutiny of these rights and obligations shows how the 1979 Constitution reflects the views and political pressures of various factions in the 73-member Assembly of Experts, both religious and secular. The so-called radical clergy's input can be detected in the first part of Chapter IV on economics and finance which calls for: national economic planning; the provision by the government of basic necessities; national independence from foreign domination; and state monopoly of all natural resources, transport, communications, public utilities, large-scale industries, banking, insurance and, most significantly, foreign trade.

The influence of secular nationalists (as well as advocates of 'neither East nor West' foreign policy) is evident in the passage on foreign relations. Stung by the exploitative character of concessions granted to foreign interests in the Qajar dynasty, and mindful of Dr Mossadeq's injunction against the granting of oil exploration rights to either Britain or Russia in the early 1950s, the framers of the new constitution wished to make sure that history would not repeat itself.

The conservative clergy's influence is shown in Article 46 which entitles everyone to the fruits of his legitimate business and labor, and Article 47 which specifically recognizes private ownership if legitimately acquired according to Islamic law. But, by far the most solid triumph of the conservatives was in the passage of Article 4 which requires that all laws (including, by implication, even constitutional clauses) to be in conformity with Islam. Since all legislation by the *Majles* must be reviewed by the Council of Guardians, the Council is in a position to nullify all radical provisions of the Constitution by finding them 'un-Islamic'.[5]

Interestingly, the numerous economic clauses of the Constitution, with their populist appeal and egalitarian terminology, were approved without much debate despite their sharp contrast with previously held notions that Islam was a conservative religion in favor of private property and free enterprise. This apparent contradiction reflected the strong influence of the radical Left in the Constitutional Assembly at the time, and the political environment created by Ayatollah Khomeini's own populist stance with which the conservative clergy did not dare to quarrel.

THE POLITICAL ENVIRONMENT

The 1979 Constitution's inherent contradictions and inconsistencies opened a Pandora's box of endless legal and ecclesiastic disputes. Soon after its official ratification, serious divisions of opinion emerged among politico-religious leaders on almost every major policy issue affecting the structure and direction of the national economy. Despite their overwhelming majority in the Assembly of Experts, and their success in redrafting the 1979 Constitution in favor of a theocracy headed by a religious leader called *vali-ye faqih*, the clerical establishment could not present a unified stance on matters of either principle or policy. While the supreme spiritual and political leadership of Ayatollah Khomeini was never openly challenged by his followers, several Islamic factions tried tirelessly to solicit the Imam's support in setting the republic's politico-economic agenda. Each faction, invoking the Ayatollah's name and authority, and drawing on both the Qor'an and the 1979 Constitution, volunteered to define and create an *Islamic* economy, and to formulate a consensual Islamic economic model.

Friction among these groups was unavoidable. One reason for the conflicts was that the Qor'an and other sources of Islamic jurisprudence can be interpreted to sanction both capitalism and collectivism. 'For every verse in the scripture calling for redistribution and sanctioning a command economy', writes a Moslem commentator, 'there is another, sanctioning the right of property, decreeing inequality to be the natural order of things'.[6] Another reason for the divergence of views was the imprecise and ambiguous provisions of the 1979 Constitution itself, which tried to strike a balance between Islamic ideals of justice and the efficiency requirements of a modern economy. But by far the most significant reason has been differences in the theological schooling and family roots of the major clerical leaders.

One major tendency – dogmatic in essence and populist-statist in action – has favored 'the good of society' over individual rights. It has advocated nationalization of all vital economic resources and institutions, drastic limits on property ownership, extensive reforms in the direction of income redistribution and wealth-sharing, state control over foreign trade, central planning, wage-price controls through regular or parastatal agencies, and maximum national economic self-reliance. Pitched against this group has been the conservative tendency, favoring sanctity of private property, freedom of enterprise and commerce, reduced government interference in the economy, international economic cooperation, and an open-door policy. The third tendency – the pragmatist faction – has gradually evolved from the ranks of disillusioned early interventionists. This group initially advocated a militant Islamic position, and an isolationist closed-door policy designed to safeguard Iran's economic independence from the superpowers. Having risen to positions of power and responsibility, and witnessed the deteriorating state of the economy over time, this faction has subsequently downplayed early slogans, and become a reluctant convert to the value of an eclectic path between the other two tendencies. Pragmatic in outlook and mildly libertarian in orientation, this group now favors a limited role for the state in the economy, maximum respect for 'legitimate' private property rights, nationalization only in areas where national interest is clearly concerned and a minimum of tampering with the former *status quo*.

These three tendencies do not use terms like hardliners, radical, moderate, pragmatist, and similar Western terminology to describe their ideological or political essence.[7] All consider themselves and their views to be purely Islamic, and invoke various principles of Islamic jurisprudence (such as the Qor'an, precedence, attribution, consensus, and reason) in support of a set of general objectives and specific means. Depending on whether an issue is of special interest to them, they come together or go their separate ways. The stance taken on different politico-economic issues is therefore not always consistent, exclusive, or unaltered over time. This has made it difficult to identify many major individual politicians, religious leaders, or even special groups as *irrevocably* radical, conservative, or moderate. Some conservatives on domestic economic policy are fiercely radical on the question of foreign cooperation and *rapprochement* with the West. And some radicals, favoring drastic internal economic restructuring, have shown no objection to opening up the economy to the rest of the world.

Broadly speaking, the ideological divisions seem to have followed economic class lines. For example, Ayatollah Khomeini's students and disciples – mostly poor, provincial, and steeped in the Faizieh Seminary's puritanical tradition – have as a rule supported radical social reforms in favor of the oppressed, the downtrodden, the dispossessed and the disenfranchised. This group's standard bearers and intellectual gurus have been economically dependent radical *mollahs*, the group of militant clergy calling themselves 'followers of the Imam line', left-wing elements infiltrating the high ranks of the *Majles* and the bureaucracy, and a few secular anti-West politicians. Conservatives, on the other hand, with their strong financial and blood ties to the *bazaar* have tended to represent the interests of landlords and the urban bourgeoisie. Among them have been some religious notables in the cities of Najaf, Mashad and even Qom, as well as other influential clerics reflecting the views of major monied interests. This faction has sometimes been identified with the right-wing and militantly Islamic *hojjatieh* society with its close links with the well-to-do. Pragmatists or moderates have also had close affiliations with the wealthy, but they have, as a rule, mainly *managed* and handled national wealth rather than *owned* it. They have emerged, after Khomeini's death, as closet free-marketeers and economic internationalists.[8]

While Ayatollah Khomeini was alive, these factions invoked his authority, and his occasional intervention, to gain ascendancy over their rivals. But no faction's position was ever secure or clearly dominant. Throughout his supreme leadership of the Islamic Republic, the Ayatollah remained ambiguous and non-committal on most economic issues debated by his subordinates. His position seemed to have only one constant: to save the Islamic hegemony at all costs. He played his cards close to his chest at all times and revealed little about his inner thoughts on any subject. He also frequently changed sides on controversial issues. It was not difficult to see that on numerous occasions he sided with whichever party was on the defensive, just to restore balance and to prevent any faction from inadvertently jeopardizing the revolution, the perpetuation of which was always his overriding concern. His ultimate acceptance of peace with Saddam Hussein – after eight years of vowing to pursue the war to the bitter end at any price – was in his own words, as painful as 'drinking poison'. But he did just that in order to preserve the revolution which was apparently in serious jeopardy at the time.

Born to a clerical village family, with mannerisms and accent that revealed his humble provincial background, Ayatollah Khomeini was bound to be a populist reformer in favor of income redistribution, public subsidies, and social welfare for the poor. Yet, whenever he faced strong resistance to his own economic agenda by the conservative clergy and wealthy *bazaar* merchants, he backed down or remained non-partisan. The same proclivity for preserving a balance between controversial economic policies was shown by the Ayatollah in the choice of state officials. For example, no serious efforts were ever made by him in the mid-1980s to resolve fundamental policy differences between his conservative heir-apparent at the time (Ayatollah Hossein Montazeri), his radical prime minister (Mir Hossein Musavi), the moderate speaker of the *Majles* (Hojat ol-Islam Rafsanjani) and the enigmatic president of the republic (Hojat ol-Islam Ali Khamenei). Nor did he apparently mind a theological rift between the majority of *Majles* deputies and the Council of the Guardians; the Guardians and the cabinet; individual ministers and the head of the state; or the head of the state and the head of government. In a dispute between his own protégé in favor of free enterprise, Ayatollah Montazeri, and the interventionist Prime Minister, Musavi, he did little for a long time to resolve the impasse. When asked by one of his aides whether state intervention or free trade should prevail, he reportedly replied that he 'approves both and neither'. On another occasion, after the ceasefire in the Iran-Iraq war, he urged national economic self-reliance while at the same time approving foreign participation in rebuilding war-torn Iran.[9] In still another case involving the private sector's role in foreign trade, he is reported to have said that the public should be allowed to import whatever they wanted, but only under government supervision so as not to flood the market with a clutter of merchandise such as was the case during the Shah's time.[10]

The hallmark of this astute and calculated ambivalence was the theocracy's survival. Notwithstanding profound and often publicized rifts among high-ranking officials, no antagonist holding a leadership position after 1982/83 ever abandoned his unwavering commitment to the objectives of the Islamic state. No one questioned the legitimacy of the clerical rule, or the supremacy of religion in social life. Also, theocratic differences among the religious divines who manned the republic's ruling elite were always contained within clerical bounds, known as *ejtehad* (or judicial view), and seldom allowed to be exploited by secular outsiders.[11]

As a result of this clannish solidarity, the pragmatist tendency under the leadership of the Islamic Republican Party (IRP) managed to ward off all open challenges to its political primacy from the Marxist left, the secular and lay center, and the fundamentalist right. Between 1984/85 and 1988/89, the IRP-dominated faction consolidated its position in both the political and economic arenas – nearly always with Ayatollah Khomeini's tacit or explicit support. It was the IRP leadership that convinced the Ayatollah to accept the United Nations resolution 598 for a cease-fire in the Iran-Iraq war after nearly a year of hesitation and procrastination. The party was later dissolved when it had accomplished its mission.

STRUGGLE FOR POWER

The revolutionaries' triumph in February 1979 was greeted with an economy in total disarray. More than a year of political turmoil, public disturbances, strikes, sabotage, and physical destruction had left the economy in chaos. Economic activity was in deep recession. Oil production and exports were down to half their annual levels, as were government revenues. The banking system faced an imminent collapse due to massive withdrawals, and increasing non-functioning loans. Unemployment, inflation and capital flight were on the rise. Foreign trade, domestic investment, and public confidence were on the decline. A large number of half-finished projects from the Shah's time faced an uncertain fate. Agriculture was the only sector that was less affected by the disruptions.

The appointment of Mehdi Bazargan as the first post-revolution prime minister was heralded by most oppositionists as a move towards political freedom and free enterprise. As a seasoned human-rights activist and the head of Iran's Liberation Movement, he was expected to continue the country's previous economic thrust in a more authentic and less autocratic manner. But caught between pressures from the Left and the Right, and paralyzed by interference from the free-wheeling revolutionary *komitehs*, self-appointed ecclesiastic judges, and Khomeini's own close aides, he became, as he himself said, like 'a knife without a blade'. Thus, in the early months after the revolution, the political economy was rudderless, confused and chaotic. The Provisional Government wanted to maintain the decision-making apparatus of the old regime, discipline militant workers, continue selling oil to the old customers, resume industrial production, and stop the flight of people and capital from the country. But certain members of the Revolutionary Council, as well as most of the radical elements in the anti-Shah coalition, demanded fundamental revisions of the *status quo*, and a wholesale restructuring of the economy. When selecting the economy's major new players and decision-makers, the government also had difficulty in deciding which would be the overriding criteria: Islamic virtue and revolutionary commitment, or professional expertise and technical skills.

Nevertheless, for a few early months, Bazargan had the public support of Ayatollah Khomeini and most of the secular factions. For a short period after its formation, the Provisional Government also enjoyed active cooperation from the West, including the United States. Despite Washington's earlier criticism of the Shah's human rights record, and despite repeated declarations of non-interference in Iran's internal affairs, the Carter administration seemed ready to help Tehran with military spare parts and equipment (including Cobra helicopter gunships) even though Islamic revolutionary justice had publicly denounced Western concepts of human rights, and the weapons were clearly destined to be used in the central government's fight against Kurdish rebellion. Both Europe and the United States were seemingly anxious to show their willingness to resume old relationships with Iran, to demonstrate that they had recognized the 'Islamic revolution', and that they had no intention of helping the anti-Khomeini opposition at home or abroad to regain power.[12] The prevailing opinion among many Western diplomats and analysts was that if the Islamic government should fail, people might be ready to follow the Marxist minority. The Left – the Tudeh, the Mojahedin and the Fedai'yan, among some fifty assorted leftist groups in Iran – was, indeed, waiting for such an eventuality and biding its time. With middle-class parties in Iran virtually out of the picture, the only way people could express opposition to the government's failings was thought to be a turn to the left.[13]

As could be expected, the Provisional Government was soon mired in the realities of economic life. The promises for free housing, water, electricity and public transport, plus a direct share of the oil revenues, which had been made to the people as a reward for their anti-Shah uprising, proved impossible to honor, particularly in the midst of an emerging economic recession. Under the crushing forces of Islamic hegemonists from the right, and Marxist pretenders from the left, Prime Minister Bazargan and his hapless colleagues not only failed to unleash the creative energies of a politically suppressed society, but also found themselves deprived of the talent and skills of thousands of secular social reformers who rejected both communism and theocracy, and fled the country in droves. The central government's inability to cope with arbitrary, unauthorized and capricious interference in the economy by the Revolutionary Council, the local *komitehs*, burgeoning revolutionary courts, and self-appointed religious judges made the country's economic management an impossible task.

The prevailing expectations were for an imminent change. In fact, the general opinion among Western observers was that an Islamic republic under Ayatollah Khomeini could hardly be the answer to Iran's myriad economic problems. The victorious clerics were believed to have neither the knowledge nor the experience to run a semi-industrial economy such as Iran's. It was argued that the theocratic government's inability to tackle Iran's collapsing economy (with a reported 30 per cent inflation, 2–3 million unemployed, widespread demand for wage increases, and strikes) would gradually sap the Ayatollah's spiritual authority and the real basis of his power. Economic discontent was thought to unite the army and non-clerical revolutionaries to push Khomeini out and establish a secular government. In short, once the accumulated economic fat on which Iran was living ran out, and unrepaired machines fell quiet, it was believed that the civil service's passive resistance would make itself felt.[14]

The threatening insurgencies of Iran's ethnic minorities (in Gorgan and Gonbad, Kurdestan, Azarbaijan, and Baluchestan) and demands for greater local autonomy were also believed to threaten Iran's territorial integrity, and to result in the country's break-up. Prolonged resistance by the Kurds, under the Kurdestan Democratic Party's leadership, was believed likely to create similar movements for a distinctive minority status among Southwest Arabs and Southeast Baluchis – perhaps with outside help. *The Economist* bluntly asked: 'How can a country the size, intelligence and importance of Iran survive government by a turmoil of theologians chasing one another into ever more rigid obscurantism?'[15]

As it turned out, the clergy-dominated Islamic faction gradually succeeded in methodically eliminating almost all of its secular rivals and former co-revolutionaries. The establishment in January 1979 of the Revolutionary Council with a clerical majority, and its reshuffle in February in favor of more religious/radical elements at the expense of moderate/secular members tended to weaken the lay contingents of the anti-Shah opposition. The Council, acting as the supreme decision-making and legislative organ of the Khomeini regime, issued a number of decrees dealing with economic matters. With the formation of the Islamic Republic Party (IRP) by Ayatollah Mohammad Beheshti and his clerical colleagues on the Revolutionary Council, the religious group began to take on the Provisional Government. In July, three clerical members of the Council joined the government and took formal executive responsibilities. As detailed in a previous section, the Assembly of Experts, elected by popular ballots to draft the Constitution, had 55 clerics among its 73 members due to the victory of a coalition of Islamic organizations led by the IRP. The new document reflected the Islamic faction's dominance in the assembly.

The Islamic Republic's first presidential elections under the new Constitution took place in January 1981, and resulted in the victory of Abol Hassan Bani-Sadr – thought to be Khomeini's undeclared, but real, choice. Bani-Sadr had both the pretension and the reputation for being the architect of the new Iranian economic regime. It was partly at his instigation that, during the summer of 1979, the Revolutionary Council began its statist, radical, nationalization programs (see Chapter 4).

Although the reasons for the public takeover of major financial and industrial organizations were many, and perhaps only partially ideological, Bani-Sadr took most of the credit. To believe the Western press, the transformation of the Iranian economy into Islamic radicalism started shortly after the revolution under Bani-Sadr's intellectual as well as political stewardship, in his capacity as Khomeini's economic theoretician, principal adviser, minister of finance, and finally the Islamic Republic's first elected president (although he was later ousted by the Ayatollah).[16]

Bani-Sadr's economics of *divine unity* was fundamentally based on certain warmed-over, left-of-center presumptions regarding the anti-social role of Western-type private enterprise and the remedial responsibilities of the government. There was a marked antagonism toward bigness in business, interdependence with multi-national corporations, accumulated wealth by individuals, and unbridled private ownership. Similarly, there was a manifest bias in favor of self-sufficiency in basic products, redistribution of wealth and income, and the extension of state control over credit and resource allocation, the means of production, and foreign trade.

The impeachment and removal of Bani-Sadr from the presidency in June 1981 followed the political demise of other secular revolutionary groups in the anti-Shah coalition: namely, the Marxist elements (both the Fedai'yan and the Mojahedin); moderate secular oppositionists (the National Front); and the Islamic reformers (Mehdi Bazargan and his Liberation Movement). The IRP now had to contend only with other religious factions in the *Majles* and elsewhere in the government until late in the 1980s when it was no longer needed.

UNRESOLVED ISSUES

The Iranian economy's operational framework is still unsettled and in a state of flux. This fluidity in the economy's evolving character can be seen in the stop-go economic policies of the regime, reflecting the ideological skirmishes between the major clerical factions.[17] These decade-long philosophical clashes are centered on what may be called the 'Islamicly-correct' direction and management of the economy. As already noted, starting with the 2nd *Majles* in 1984/85, an open rift developed between the two factions within the legislature on the question of the management of the national economy. One group favored maximum state intervention in the economy for the sake of preserving Islamic values and promoting social justice. The other advocated a large role for the private sector – ironically, to reach the same objectives. Debates on how to run the economy on a purely Islamic platform have continued to this day without producing a consensus agenda. In the process, not only have certain provisions of the Constitution never been implemented, but the exclusivity of state functions in certain other areas has been gradually eroded by the growth of hybrid institutions and the emergence of extra-constitutional arrangements.

At the macro-economic level, although the Constitution specifically divides the economy into public, private, and cooperative sectors, the scope, jurisdiction, responsibilities, and scale of operation of none have so far been clearly delineated. For example, after years of debates and delays, the legislation on the nature and objectives of the cooperative sector was finally approved in 1992, leaving the role and status of the other two sectors still officially in limbo. The all-embracing objectives and functions of cooperatives as described in the new legislation – for example, the creation of national full-employment, the prevention of monopolies, hoarding, and inflation, and the attainment of Islamic social justice – present a good measure of confusion and overlap with the other sectors. Ironically also, the *Majles*'s new emphasis on cooperatives clashes with the post-1988 government's intention to privatize the economy. For this reason, the new *démarche* is interpreted by some foreign analysts as a bold step by the radical faction to thwart the Rafsanjani administration's efforts to reduce the public sector's domain in favor of private enterprise. The cooperative sector could serve as a bulwark against wholesale marketization and the rise of industrial and commercial corporate structures.[18]

At the micro level, the two most controversial issues between interventionists and free enterprisers have been the nature of land ownership and the management of external commerce. These will be discussed below in the chapters dealing with agriculture and foreign trade. At this level, several other major policy issues have also remained controversial or at a stalemate. Notable among these have been such questions as the primacy of agriculture versus industrial development; financial integration in the global economy (particularly long-term borrowing); the status of private properties owned by officials of the old regime or sequestered from their former owners; use and allocation of unoccupied urban land and control of land prices; the magnitude and nature of taxation; and the overall issue of the state's role in the economy. Differences have also persisted on such secondary issues as the desired volume of oil exports, the sale of oil for cash or via barter; the duties and responsibilities of semi-public 'foundations' in performing public functions; and the nature of the foreign exchange system.

Symptomatic of lingering ideological rifts and political confusion over the management of the Iranian economy has been the debate on the implementation of the country's current five-year development plan. Thus, while President Rafsanjani and his technocratic team have been painting a rather rosy picture of the plan's first three years of operation, Islamic hardliners have lost no opportunity to attack the government for having violated the Constitution and the national interest, for having ignored the plan law, and for lacking a clear national economic policy with respect to private profiteering, and equitable taxation.[19]

NOTES

1. This, and all subsequent quotations are taken from Constitution of the Islamic Republic of Iran (Berkeley: Mizan Press, 1980).
2. The name of the *Majles-e Shora-ye Melli* (the national consultative assembly) was changed to the *Majles-e Shora-ye Eslami* (the Islamic consultative assembly) under the 1989 amendment of the Constitution.
3. The Council of Guardians has subsequently ruled that contracts made for commercial purposes between Iranian and foreign companies, both public and private, are not subject to Article 77 except in individual cases when mandated by special legislation.
4. This article has subsequently been clarified by the Council of Guardi-

ans to mean the granting of monopolistic rights of exploitation rather than commercial joint ventures.

5. Since half of the council members are supposed to be full-fledged divines, and few clerics are able to reach that position in their youth, most appointees are of necessity aging clerics who do not share their younger brethrens' radical interpretation of Islam.

6. Fouad Ajami, 'Where God Sets Prices', *US News and World Report* February 20, 1989.

7. The leadership emphatically asserts that the categorization of religious groups into hardliners, radicals, moderates, conservatives, and pragmatists is an invention of the Western press: These factions may quarrel over certain means concerning the economy and foreign policy, but they all share one common objective, and that is Islam, Khomeini, and the *velayat-e faqih*.

8. See *The New York Times*, May 11, 1991.

9. *The New York Times*, January 2, 1989. The Ayatollah's intellectual supporters attribute this ambivalence to his pragmatism rather than to any ideological skepticism. His younger devotees argue that he was personally farsighted, radical, and idealist. However, as the supreme leader of a nation faced with mundane challenges, he was forced to accept policies and decisions with which he was personally uncomfortable. It was in this context that he appeared inconsistent to outside observers.

10. *Kayhan Havai*, July 29, 1992, p. 8.

11. For a brief account of the early years see Eric Hooglund, 'Iran 1980–85: Political and Economic Trends', in N. R. Keddie (ed.), *The Iranian Revolution and the Islamic Republic* (Syracuse: Syracuse University Press, 1986).

12. See 'The US and Khomeini', *The Washington Post*, September 26, 1980.

13. The *Wall Street Journal*, January 18, 1980.

14. See *The Economist*, September 8, 1979, and *Financial Times*, September 5, 1979.

15. *The Economist*, November 10, 1979, p. 15.

16. *The Economist*, February 23, 1980.

17. For a detailed presentation of the clashes and skirmishes among the various revolutionary groups in the first two years of the revolution, and the ideological rifts among the clergy afterwards see A. Rahnema and F. Nomani, *The Secular Miracle: Religion, Politics & Economic Policy in Iran* (London: Zed Books, 1990).

18. For the text of the new law on cooperatives see *Kayhan Havai*, January 8, 1992.

19. *Kayhan Havai* editorial, January 22, 1992.

III
MACRO-ECONOMIC
TRENDS

4

National output and income

In the years following the establishment of the Islamic Republic in February 1979, the Iranian economy has experienced periods of relatively sharp decline in real output, matched by years of respectable growth. There was a four-year recession in 1978/79–1981/82; a four-year recovery between 1982/83 and 1985/86; another economic slowdown between 1986/87 and 1988/89; and a new cycle of renewed growth after 1989/90 (see Table 4.6).

The chequered record of the real gross domestic product (GDP) – the annual value of all goods and services produced – can be attributed to a number of internal developments as well as external forces of varying origins and nature. Internal factors include: post-revolutionary turmoil, ethnic insurgencies, and labor agitation; the exodus of hundreds of thousands of entrepreneurs, business managers, professionals, and skilled technicians, as well as billions of dollars of capital from the country; the multiplicity of parallel decision-making centers; ambiguities regarding labor laws, property rights, and legitimate economic activity; the emphasis on commitment to Islam and loyalty to the clerical government as the overriding criterion for employment; the takeover of large business enterprises, combined with the inexperience of new managers, which resulted not only in reduced productivity but also in increased corruption; and rapid population increase unmatched by domestic raw materials, and other inputs.

External factors include: a long and costly war with Iraq; major turbulence in the world oil market resulting in reduced oil incomes and oil-financed imports; freezing of Iranian foreign exchange assets abroad following the American hostage crisis; sanctions on credit, trade, and technology imposed on Iran by Western industrial powers in the aftermath of Iran's refusal to abide by UN resolutions; the influx of an estimated three million Afghani and Iraqi refugees into the country; and Iran's virtual politico-economic isolation from the community of nations for much of the period.

ECONOMIC POLICY DEVELOPMENTS

In the first period of struggle over economic restructuring, the crisis caused by the revolution was particularly aggravated by the sudden exodus of seasoned administrators, business managers, skilled workers, foreign technicians, bankers, and other professionals who rejected the theocratic rule, or were not themselves acceptable to the Islamic republic. The loss of this vital human element was exacerbated by an acute shortage of raw materials, spare parts and semi-processed goods due to reduced imports. Industrial plants run by new and inexperienced managers, and plagued with material shortages, were further strangled by widespread strikes, slow-downs, and rebellions among left-leaning workers demanding managerial privileges and participatory rights in decision-making. Construction activities, which served as the mainstay of Iran's 1974–77 economic boom, had come to a virtual standstill due to the consequences of the revolutionary turmoil. These difficulties were, in turn, topped by a liquidity shortage caused by private currency hoardings outside the banks from fear of confiscation, or loss of confidence in the banking system; by virtual cessation of private sector imports; and by earlier wage and salary increases given to workers to appease industrial unrest.

In this period, when leftist elements, secular centrists, and religious groups were jockeying for power, the country's economic strategy was subjected to three ideological slogans: public denunciation of oppression, inequality and poverty as inimical to an Islamic economy; advocacy of social justice and fair reward for productive labor along with opposition to profiteering and the exploitation of man by man; and the need for shifting the structure of the economy from reliance on the oil sector toward domestic resources and home activities (particularly agriculture). As indicated earlier, the Provisional Government headed by Mehdi Bazargan was not keen on any radical changes in the economy's institutions and structures beyond a minimum of democratization and Islamization. Liberal-bourgeois in economic tradition and outlook, and supported by the secular intelligentsia, middle and upper bureaucracy, professional cadres, and modern private business establishments, the Provisional Government was squarely behind assistance to distressed industries, cooperation with exiled investors and managers, and even for attraction of foreign private investment, albeit under more equitable terms.[1] It opposed wildcat strikes, abolished the 1963 workers' profit-sharing scheme, and privately fought against the nationalization of financial enterprises. The Revolutionary Council and some of Khomeini's radical and fundamentalist aides and supporters, however, were anxious to implement their statist agenda as soon as they could. Backed by leftist and 'progressive' forces, the Council and the newly-established Islamic Republic Party (IRP) pushed for the nationalization of major economic sectors. Accordingly, in the summer of 1979, all banks, insurance companies, and some 50 industrial corporations were nationalized by a Council decree. Although this was essentially a political decision, there were also several economic reasons for the state takeover. Eight of the nationalized (and subsequently merged) banks were insolvent at the time; others had excessive domestic and foreign exposure; some were still engaged in facilitating a sizeable flight of capital owned by wealthy Iranians who had left the country or were about to leave. Most major private insurance companies were also in bad financial shape due partly to huge accumulated claims and poor investments. Large industrial firms also were heavily indebted to the banking system, but unable to service their debts due to strikes, workers' takeovers, or the absence of owners and managers who had abandoned them by leaving the country.

Foremost among the immediate revolutionary changes introduced by the Provisional Government in this period were: the nationalization of foreign trade; extension of full public ownership and control over the oil sector; a move towards the establishment of Islamic, interest-free banking; transfer of ownership and management of certain non-financial enterprises to a number of parastatal 'foundations' outside the regular government's structure, regulations, and accountability; and an overall extension of the state's allocative, distributional, and regulatory role in the economy.

The regime's ideological leaning during this brief and uncertain period was decidedly *expropriative* rather than *productive*. The forced takeover of private property by revolutionary forces was not only allowed, but also condoned. The Provisional Government and revolutionary courts sanctioned the sequestration of commercial farms, manufacturing industries, construction firms, and other financial assets of individuals and groups associated with the previous regime – without compensation. National output during this period plummeted for many reasons, none of which was unrelated to this expropriative climate. The 'one-shot' transfer of wealth from a relatively small group of well-to-do individuals to a much larger active, aggressive (and not necessarily the poorest) group within the nation involved some obvious revolutionary gratification and personal gain. But the long-term social and economic costs of this redistribution were the loss of business confidence and a decline in private investment.

The second period – the beginning of which may be identified with either the ratification of the 1979 Constitution, the triumph of the Islamic fundamentalists over their various rivals, or the outbreak of war with Iraq – was a period of wartime austerity, restrictions, regulations, and controls. As the economic turmoil and internal power struggle were overcome in 1981, and the national economy resumed its 'normal' operation under wartime conditions, the government chose to deal with ensuing shortages, bottlenecks, and declining oil revenues through intervention: quantitative import restrictions (to save foreign exchange); rationing of basic necessities (to ensure fair distribution); foreign exchange allocation (to prevent capital flight); and wage-price controls (to maintain internal balance). Constraints imposed by the war, the assets freeze, Western economic sanctions, and oil market volatility, however, prevented the leadership from managing the economy on a sustainable, systemic basis. A five-year plan that was worked out in great detail in 1982–1983 never got off the ground.

The necessity of pursuing a 'muddle-through' strategy from year to year – dependent on the oil fortune – resulted in a public course of action and policy formulation based on what may be called 'expedient discrimination'. This strategy manifested itself in: establishing a dozen different exchange rates for different categories of imports; granting various types and amounts of subsidies to domestic producers; setting up different foreign exchange quotas for various industries, activities and institutions; designating different rates and volumes of foreign exchange surrender obligations for non-oil exporters; offering different price subsidies to essential consumer goods; allowing different entitlements to certain privileged business operators; and guaranteeing discretionary protection of property rights belonging to different groups and individuals. These discriminatory practices were also frequently accompanied by arbitrary (unlawful, or extra legal) decisions on the part of government officials in charge of policy implementation. The most outstanding feature of this period was the regime's extraordinary resilience in seeking, sorting, interpreting, and justifying pragmatic, *ad hoc* solutions.

The third period, which began after the ceasefire in 1988 and Ayatollah Khomeini's death, continues to this day. In this third phase, when the reconstruction of the war-ravaged economy has become the overriding national issue, a series of heated debates has re-emerged among major political factions within the Islamic hierarchy. Considerable controversy has again surfaced over the new moral and spiritual underpinnings of the postwar economy, as well as the direction of the reconstruction strategy. Radical hardliners − known as Islamic fundamentalists − have once again emphasized the primacy of (Islamic) spirituality over (Western) materialism. They have argued that success in achieving economic welfare and national prosperity should not result in religious and doctrinal defeats; nor should economic adjustment be sought at the expense of political and moral principles embodied in the 1979 Constitution. The Islamic revolution's ideological and ethical imperatives are said to require that Iran remain the bastion of Islamic fundamentalism and the champion of the world's oppressed nations against the forces of imperialist hegemony led by the United States. The solution to the country's economic crisis, the radicals have argued, should not result in a moral and cultural setback.[2] Any *rapprochement* with the West has been termed by the hardliners a deviation from Ayatollah Khomeini's Islam and a return to a 'decadent' Western way of life. This faction has placed long-term Islamic and nationalistic considerations ahead of short-term reconstruction needs and faster economic growth through free-market institutions and devices. Labelling the moderate and pragmatist factions derisively as 'neo-internationalists', and their faith as 'American-style Islam' (*Eslam-e Amrika'î*), these doctrinaire politician/clerics have remained opposed to almost any *rapprochement* with the 'first world'.

The pragmatist faction, by contrast, has argued that the Islamic revolution and the Islamic Republic cannot succeed and survive *politically* unless they also succeed *economically*. Acutely aware of the rising discontent among the urban masses over inflation, unemployment, and shortages, this faction has concluded that the government can no longer ask people for further sacrifices in the name of the revolution or the 'imposed' war. Meaningful relief needs to be provided in order to keep faith.

Parallel debates have also raged within the group that recognizes the urgent need for economic revival and improvements in the people's welfare. The debate among these 'economics-first' advocates revolves around the nature and direction of the reconstruction strategy. While speedy economic growth, reconstruction of war-damaged cities and facilities, caring for the families of war casualties ('the martyrs'), and a new defense build-up have been on nearly everyone's agenda, the preferred means to achieve these ends has been in dispute. On one side have stood the advocates of an 'open-door' policy, emphasizing domestic private enterprise, price de-control, trade liberalization, business deregulation, export promotion, attraction of foreign private investment, and repatriation of Iranian capital, management and entrepreneurship. Led by conservative *bazaaris*, Islamic middle-class industrialists, the main-line clergy (e.g. Ayatollah Azari Qomi, the editor of the newspaper *Resalat*), and business-rooted politicians (including the president himself), this faction has opted for a revived market economy. Guided by a large cadre of Western-trained technocrats in the cabinet and the bureaucracy, this group has also been in favor of more business incentives for private risk-taking, early termination of rationing and subsidies, speedy exchange rate adjustment, and wholesale privatization of non-defense industries.

The other faction – variously labelled by the press as hardliners, radicals, or statists – has taken a decidedly opposite view on both the basic strategy and attendant policies. Championed by former interior minister Ali Akbar Mohtashami, former prosecutor Musavi Khoeiniha, and former prime minister Mir Hossein Musavi, and backed by a large faction of current and former *Majles* deputies, members of this group have continued to cling energetically to the early revolutionary platform and slogans. They have insisted, through the newspaper *Salam*, on continued self-reliance; import substitution; extensive protection of home industries; public control of prices and wages; state ownership and management of major industries; avoidance of foreign joint ventures, external borrowing, and association with multinational corporations; and, finally, keeping up the value of the Iranian rial.

QUANTITATIVE TRENDS IN NATIONAL OUTPUT

Data on Iran's national accounts are collected and computed by Bank Markazi, and published annually in the central bank's economic report and balance sheet. Two separate reports entitled *Hesabhaye Melli-ye Iran* (Iran's national accounts for the years 1974–87 and 1988–91) have been separately published by the bank. While no basis for the updating of the old figures is identified, significant discrepancies between earlier and revised data make a meaningful analysis of yearly fluctuations in sectoral developments nearly impossible.[3] For this reason, detailed data appearing in Tables IV.1 to IV.6 should be regarded as indications of an order of magnitude rather than precise accounting values. The very large and frequently contradictory and inexplicable upward and downward movement in various sectors detailed in Bank Markazi's annual reports, and its very latest volume on national accounts, should thus be treated with caution and subject to further change.[4] The significance of these tables can thus be found not so much in their year-to-year accuracy, but in the trends over the years.

Given these warnings, the officially-sanctioned data show the economy's real performance since the revolution to have passed through four phases of slowdown and recovery. After a four-year period of recession, the economy partially recovered in the first half of the 1980s with a relatively fast growth of output, and somewhat restrained inflation. The recovery was followed by a period of decline in the rate of annual production, and an acceleration of inflation in the second half of the 1980s. A broad-based economic revival got under way in the last year of the decade, and continued into the 1990s only to be marred by a devastating earthquake in the summer of 1990, and a massive inflow of refugees from the Persian Gulf conflict (i.e. Kurds and Iraqi Shi'ites). But the level of overall economic growth has remained strong.

The first period of downward trend actually began in 1978/79 with nationwide strikes, street demonstrations, physical damage to property, and other revolutionary events that cut down productive economic activity. The negative trend continued in the first year of the revolution, and was accelerated in the second year due to a significant fall in oil revenue, flight of capital and skilled labor, political in-fighting within the leadership, the consequences of the American hostage crisis, the war with Iraq, and a sharp overall drop in investment. Economic activity in the second half of 1978/79 showed a precipitous decline, followed by an equally drastic fall in oil exports, industrial activity, construction, and government revenues. Only agriculture showed a notable growth. Real gross domestic product (GDP) at factor cost experienced a decline of 10.9 per cent during 1978/79, followed by another 5.2 per cent fall in 1979/80. Again, agriculture was the only area to show growth, along with the services sector. The oil sector, on the other hand, experienced a 19.4 per cent decline (on top of a 28.7 per cent fall in the previous year), and industry showed a 15.7 per cent drop. The slump in industrial output (combined with the smaller than expected rise in farm output and reduced imports due to trade sanctions) caused both unemployment and inflation to rise. Industry's dependence on imports of raw materials and spare parts in the face of a foreign exchange shortage caused industrial output to decline below the already depressed level of 1979/80. In 1980/81, oil exports showed a drastic 65.8 per cent drop in value from the year before, causing real GDP to undergo another 14.9 per cent decline.

The substantial economic deterioration in 1980/81 was intensified by the Iraqi invasion, and continued Western economic sanctions. The war almost totally destroyed Khorramshahr (Iran's largest port), caused enormous damage to the Abadan oil refinery, made the country dependent on imports of refined oil products, and reduced industrial and agricultural output in the Iraqi occupied territories in the west and south. The dependence of domestic industries on scarce foreign parts and materials resulted in a drastic drop in capacity utilization. While causing government revenues to decline, the war helped to increase government expenditures and the budget deficit.

During the four-year recession 1978–81, the decline in the growth of real output amounted to about 33 per cent, bringing the real 1981/82 GDP to the same levels as those of the early 1970s. Additional causes for this precipitous decline were growing uncertainties regarding private ownership and enterprise, and the government's own partial paralysis (due to the lack of a clear, consistent and comprehensive economic policy). As could be expected, the most negatively affected sector after oil (see Chapter 13) was manufacturing, where the mass exodus of top owner/managers, tension between remaining bosses and the revolutionary workers' councils, shortage of foreign exchange, and severe difficulties in obtaining raw materials from either domestic or foreign suppliers played havoc with the normal production process. Nearly 1.4 million workers – 12 per cent of the labor force – were officially out of work in 1981/82. Private estimates put the figure at twice the official number.

In his 'state of the economy' message to the nation in April 1981, President Abol Hassan Bani-Sadr blamed the country's last three years of severe recession on such factors as the absence of security, bureaucratic chaos, anarchic exercise of power by unauthorized groups, and inconsistencies in national plans and policies.[5] The (state controlled) local press added other reasons for the early economic setbacks: the lack of proper national planning; sabotage by domestic 'economic terrorists' (hoarders, smugglers and speculators); infiltration of hostile or incompetent individuals into certain key government positions; and the lingering attachment to a 'consumerist culture' among affluent groups.[6]

With the partial restoration of political stability and a gradual return of public confidence, real output resumed its pre-revolution growth trend in 1982/83. As the Islamic faction eliminated both its radical-left and secular-centrist rivals, resolved the American hostage crisis, and achieved a modicum of political calm, real GDP began to recover. The ensuing four-year recovery period was largely underwritten by the resumption of oil exports, and particularly by the relatively firm prices of crude oil. Rising oil revenues enabled the government to finance larger imports of industrial inputs and other raw materials needed for industrial growth. For the four-year period, the average annual real growth was a respectable 6.9 per cent, albeit from a low base, with real GDP in 1985/86 still below that of 1977/78.

The favourable growth cycle was reversed in 1986/87, and continued through 1988/89, as a result of a drastic fall in the price of oil, and the loss of oil export volumes caused by attacks on oil facilities and oil tankers in the Persian Gulf. Soaring war expenditures, the fall in oil income, and exhausted foreign exchange resources, brought almost all foreign-dependent domestic economic activities to a standstill. Real GDP dropped by 8.8 per cent in 1986/87 when capacity utilization in industry fell as low as 30 per cent in certain activities, and other sectors also experienced large declines. A drop in farm output in 1988/89, combined with the lingering recession in the industry and services sectors contributed to another negative growth rate of 3.6 per cent in that year.

Buoyed by the more pragmatic and less ideological stand adopted by the Rafsanjani government, the economy began to recover from the recession and high inflation. Substantial resources released from the war efforts, and a noteworthy improvement in oil production and exports, helped the industrial sector to recover, the budget deficit to decline, and inflation to recede. With the launching of a new five-year plan in 1989/90, and a distinct shift in the government's priorities and policies, a broad-based expansion in all productive sectors helped the 1989/90 GDP realize a 4.2 per cent rise in real terms. The momentum picked up speed in 1990/91 when the oil and industry sectors took the lead and pushed GDP up by an 11.5 per cent. Enhanced public confidence in the new economic liberalization measures promised by the government, and new expectations of a better private investment climate, helped the growth trend to continue into 1991/92. Detailed preliminary figures in Table 4.2 indicate a GDP growth rate of 8.6 per cent for that year. The double-digit growth for the second year in a row was led by increased output in the water and power sub-sector, mining and manufacturing, petroleum, construction, services, and agriculture, in that order. The unprecedented sharp increase in imports of machinery, spare parts, and raw materials helped the industrial sector grow by over 18 per cent, and spearhead the aggregate GDP growth. As could be expected, the high growth rate subsequently slowed down when idle industrial capacity was used up, oil revenues projections did not materialize, and imports fell. Preliminary official estimates indicate that oil export revenues in 1992/93 amounted to about $14.5 billion, or $2 billion below budget calculations, as the average daily export of crude at 2.39 mb/d was 15 per cent less than the budget level. Imports at $17 billion for the year were about $4 billion below target, and only two-thirds of the previous year's. As government revenues also fell by 17 per cent (and the budget deficit doubled), the GDP growth rate for the year ending March 1993 was put at about 6–7 per cent, and a similar growth rate is forecast for 1993/94. For the entire post-revolutionary period, however, the economy's overall performance has been distinctly disappointing. GDP in constant 1982/83 prices, as well as real per capita income, had still not reached the levels of 1977/78. Even at the end of 1991/92 – some 14 years after the revolution, and 3½ years after the Iran-Iraq war – real GDP had still only reached a level less than 2 per cent above that of 1977/78, putting the overall annual growth rate for the 14-year period at little more than two-tenths of 1 per cent. Per capita real GDP was only about 62 per cent of the level obtained before the revolution.

More discouraging still, the fall in output and standard of living was accompanied by a steady depletion and deterioration of the country's extensive infrastructure and large industrial capacity inherited from the Shah's regime. In a candid assessment of the economy's plight, President Rafsanjani acknowledged in a press conference in May 1991 that the country had lagged in the rehabilitation and maintenance of *all* its infrastructural facilities (e.g. water, power, oil exploration and refining, transport, and others).[7] Without such sizeable accumulation of capital (including the defense equipment), the nation's impoverishment would probably have been even worse. Tables 4.1 and 4.2 show the development of the gross domestic product at current and constant prices, respectively, during 1977/78–1991/92.

CONSUMPTION AND INVESTMENT

The actual magnitude of consumption and gross fixed capital formation (GFCF) during the period under discussion is somewhat obscured by several deficiencies in published data. Despite these and other shortcomings, however, certain basic trends in the composition and growth of domestic output can be identified. First, aggregate demand during the entire period under review was affected by the level of economic activity which itself reflected the effects of the war, the crucial behavior of the oil sector, and the somewhat marginal impact of economic sanctions. Aggregate real consumption expenditure increased for much of the first half of the 1980s but steadily declined in the second half before the trend was reversed after 1990/91. Table 4.5 shows the composition of domestic consumption and investment at current prices. In real terms, the ratio of aggregate consumption to GDP rose from 57.5 per cent before the revolution to over 71 per cent in 1991/92, reflecting a rapid rise in population. Furthermore, while public consumption in 1977/78 was more than 30 per cent of total real consumption, the figure for 1991/92 was less than 15 per cent, indicating a sharp decline in the supply of basic public services. Still further, the average annual increase in real consumption, lagging far behind the yearly increase in population, showed the economy's eroding productive capacity. Part of the decline in consumption was due to shortages of basic products. At one time or another throughout the 1980s, there was rationing of nearly all staples (sugar, meat, chicken, eggs, rice and cooking oil) and other essential items (gasoline, soap, cigarettes, and kerosene). Only bread was available without ration coupons at all times. A recent survey of urban family expenditure shows that between 1977/78 and 1990/91, the average annual consumption of red meat, rice and pulses declined by 35 per cent; that of sugar, shortening and butter by 50 per cent or more. Consumption was also down in all other food categories except for powder milk, seafood and, particularly, bread whose per capita consumption reached twice that of the figure in the developed countries, and 45 per cent higher than the amount in the developing nations.[8]

The composition of aggregate investment was also affected by the revolutionary upheaval, trade sanctions, Iraq's invasion, and, particularly, the volatile oil revenues. The ratio of total real investment to real GDP fell from more than 24 per cent in 1977/78 to less than 12 per cent in 1991/92. Furthermore, total gross domestic capital formation in the latter year was less than 50 per cent of the real outlays in the year before the revolution – reflecting the falling fortunes of the oil sector and exigencies of the war. Still further, while the relative share of public investment in the total GFCF declined steadily between 1980/81 and 1989/90, there was a shift of investment outlays away from machinery (which depended on foreign exchange) in favor of residential construction (which used mostly local materials). During 1979–1989 there was a slight increase in the share of agricultural investment in the total GFCF, and a drastic fall in the share of oil and gas. While industry's total share of long-term investment remained essentially the same, the share of services improved a little thanks to the possibility of making a quick profit and the easier availability of bank credit.

There were several impediments to larger *private* investment, among which reduced public confidence, and the crowding-out effect of public sector borrowing were the most significant, with the disruption caused by the war and uncertainties regarding private ownership and enterprise also playing supplementary roles. As a result, a large number of projects that had started prior to the revolution and had absorbed substantial investment were left unfinished, to be completed after 1990.

The casualty of economic events during the last two years of the 1970s and the second half of the 1980s was clearly the level of investment in productive capacity. As indicated earlier, a larger share of resources shifted in favor of public and private consumption and away from capital formation. The growth of output during part of the period was financed by drawing on accumulated net foreign exchange reserves and other foreign assets left from the Pahlavi regime. The use of these assets to meet the country's defense and consumption needs is witnessed by the chronic trade deficits, implying a steady negative aggregate resource balance in the post-revolution economy. At the same time, almost all the major projects completed by the Islamic Republic have been those that had been already started by the previous regime.

SECTORAL DEVELOPMENTS

Agriculture (consisting of crops, livestock, forestry, and fisheries) has been a star performer among all sectors of the Iranian economy during the entire period. A number of reasons help to explain this, including the high public priority attached to food security and agricultural self-sufficiency. Demand for farm products, particularly foodstuffs, steadily grew during the period in response to rapid population growth, food subsidies, and shortages of other items in the market basket. Agricultural output increased by about 4.7 per cent a year on average during the 14 years after the revolution, with highest rates in the first half of the decade. Average yield per acre and the area under cultivation both rose modestly for food grains, and somewhat better for a few other farm products (such as onions and potatoes). The relatively better performance of agriculture compared to other sectors reflected the expansion of acreage under food grains, generous use of fertilizers and pesticides, subsidized utilization of farm machinery, guaranteed prices, crop insurance, and other incentives.

The 4.7 per cent average real growth in farm output, however, concealed an uneven pattern, caused mainly by weather conditions and the impact of the war. As Table 4.6 shows, annual growth rates in real terms ranged from 8 per cent in 1990/91 to 1.9 per cent in 1981/82. The year 1988/89, however, proved disastrous for this sector when, for the first time since the revolution, the value-added in agriculture showed a decline in almost all of its sub-sectors except forestry.[9] Despite agriculture's relatively favorable performance over the period as a whole, however, imports of foodstuffs continued to increase, and exports of farm products continued to decline.

In the energy sector as a whole, by virtue of a deliberate public policy adopted shortly after the revolution, the Islamic Republic reduced Iran's oil production and exports; cut back on the oil majors' involvement in marketing Iranian oil abroad; showed little interest in foreign joint ventures or downstream operations; put a virtual end to the old regime's nuclear energy program; abandoned plans for the construction of a second gas pipeline (IGAT II); and stopped the sale of gas to the Soviet Union. Crude oil was sold directly to a number of foreign customers for cash or kind – sometimes at discounts from OPEC's target prices – with traditional markets being gradually lost.

The oil industry's performance and growth were severely hampered by the heavy damage to oil installations (e.g. refineries, transport facilities, and offshore rigs) at the height of the war. As detailed in Chapter 13, crude oil output fell to a low of 1.47 mb/d on average in 1981/82 from nearly 6 mb/d in 1977/78. Even with considerable recovery later in the decade, average daily production was less than half the peak rates of the mid-1970s. As a result, the share of the oil sector in GDP declined sharply from more than 30 per cent in 1977/78 to about 8 per cent in 1991/92. Responsible for this volatile swing were such diverse factors as an early decision by the Islamic Republic to 'save' oil by cutting down output, foreign economic sanctions, damage inflicted by war, reluctance to deal with international oil majors, wild fluctuations in world prices for crude oil, and poor maintenance of oil wells.

Industrial output declined by an average of nearly 12.5 per cent a year in the first two years of the revolution due mostly to the disarray in industrial enterprises abandoned by their former owner/managers, a collapse in private sector confidence caused by the arbitrary actions of the revolutionary committees, and Tudehinspired workers' agitation in most factories. An injection of bank credit, renewed public and private investments, and efforts by new public managers helped output to edge up somewhat in 1980/81. In 1983/84, a temporary boom in the oil sector, and the availability of foreign exchange to finance imported inputs, put new life into the sector, and output increased by nearly 20 per cent. Yet, even in relatively prosperous years, basic metals and machine-building industries lagged measurably behind 1977/78. Large industrial enterprises had an average growth rate of about 5 per cent a year in the 1980–1984 period (compared to nearly 16 per cent in the mid 1970s). The downturn in oil prices, and the damage to productive capacity, made the industrial sector contract by over 4.2 per cent a year on average during the next four-year period ending 1988/89. The decline in the manufacturing sub-sector was even greater, mostly because of shortages of imported inputs and raw materials, but also partly due to curtailed investments on the part of hesitant private entrepreneurs. Chemicals, basic metals, machine tools and paper were among the industries most negatively affected by wartime shortages of funds. By the end of the war, output in enterprises under government supervision reportedly operated at the record low of only 30 per cent of capacity.

With the ceasefire in place, a more pragmatic government in power, and the new Five-Year Plan favoring private enterprise and operation, industrial activity revived and industrial output showed an estimated average growth rate of 12.8 per cent a year in the subsequent three years, mainly due to increased imports and capacity utilization. The recovery was also in large part due to increased availability of badly needed imported parts and raw materials, and new access to foreign technical and managerial sources. The removal of credit restrictions and the elimination of quantitative limitations on food exports also helped.

After the recovery from the 1978/79 slump, manufacturing grew rather erratically for six years, but subsequently declined steadily for three years through 1988/89, with the steepest fall in food and beverages, followed by machinery and equipment. Only some mining products and basic metals bucked the trend. The post-ceasefire liberalization policies, particularly deregulation of prices and production, higher wages, and profit-sharing schemes for managers, led to increased mineral output.

Construction activity experienced a decline in every year of the period bar five. Only residential housing and defense-related buildings and facilities escaped the fall. In 1978–80, private and public investments in this sub-sector dropped considerably, despite a number of financial incentives offered by state banks. The virtual nationalization of vacant urban lots in various cities in 1982/83, and the sale of some 4.5 million square meters of these lands to individuals and corporations at regulated prices, temporarily revived some construction activities. In the second half of the 1980s, however, construction's annual decline was much larger than the average for the industrial sector as a whole. In 1990/91, the government helped the recovery by starting the rebuilding of cities destroyed or damaged during the war. The greater availability of construction materials and reduced fear of war damage also helped in the sector's rehabilitation. The water and power sub-sector was the only one where there was increased activity almost steadily throughout the decade, due largely to increased investment in power generating capactiy.

The services sector had an equally chequered growth record. The slowdown of economic activity in manufacturing, construction and other directly productive sub-sectors in the mid-1980s did not affect many of the services. Most service activities were not only somewhat immune to exogenous factors, but did in fact pick up some of the slack in the other sectors. Generally speaking, services were most negatively impacted in the nationalized areas (e.g. banking and insurance) and in domestic trade, reflecting primarily government controls. However, the relative ease of entry into small trade and business, comparative immunity from government supervision and regulation, and the prospect of making quick profits undetectable to the taxman were some of the reasons for this sector's visibly better performance in most years.

According to the 1986/87 census, the number of units engaged in trade and business almost doubled compared with ten years earlier. The increased fragmentation of activities in this sector seems to have resulted in a considerable fall in productivity. The sector's overall small average annual growth has been chiefly due to a precipitous drop in the profit of the banking system, and a rise in transport costs. The performance was also affected by a decline in such sub-sectors as transport and communications (due to the wear-and-tear on unreplaced capital stock), and public services (due to the fiscal crunch).

CHANGES IN SHARE OF SECTORS

Shifts in the relative share of different sectors in aggregate output and employment have been sizeable and noteworthy. As shown in Table 4.6, the output share of agriculture reached 24 per cent of GDP in 1991/92 compared to 9.7 per cent in 1977/78, essentially because of a sharp decline in oil output, but also partly due to the special priority accorded to this sector, and its immunity from foreign exchange constraints. The share of agriculture in non-oil GDP rose from 19.1 per cent in 1977/78 to 21.5 per cent in 1991/92. In terms of employment, agriculture's share declined from nearly 33.5 per cent of the employed workforce in 1977/78 to 27.5 per cent in 1990/91. There was also a shift of occupation toward larger numbers of owner/operator families in lieu of wage-earning farm workers, as the latter took over the farms left by their former owners or were given new land by the state.

In the oil sector, the sectoral value-added fell from more than 30 per cent of GDP in 1977/78 to about 8 per cent in 1991/92. The shift was mostly due to a sharp drop in the volume of oil exports from nearly 5 mb/d before the revolution to 2.7 mb/d at the end of 1991/92. The calculation of oil export revenues at the official exchange rate in the national accounts also played a part in the downward shift. The petroleum sector's employment share – historically small in comparison with other sectors – remained rather unaffected at about 100,000 on average.

The share of industrial production edged up from 19.4 per cent of the GDP in 1977/78 to more than 21 per cent in 1991/92. Measured against non-oil GDP, the share of industry declined from 27 per cent before the revolution to about 21 per cent. Rescuing the sector from even larger contraction was the significant and increasing contribution of the water and power sub-sector which nearly tripled its value-added over the same period. The share of employment in the industrial sector also suffered a decline under the revolution. Employing some 32 per cent of the employed workforce in 1977/78, industry's share fell to 24.9 per cent by 1990/91, indicating a smaller labor contingent even in absolute terms. The loss of jobs was most pronounced among small rural industries and in the construction sub-sector. The absolute loss of employment in this sector was due to the general fall in industrial activity, and particularly to drastic under-utilization of capacity in some industries for much of the period. Since the reduction in industrial employment did not match the fall in capacity utilization, labor productivity was measurably reduced.

The services sector shows a different pattern from manufacturing and petroleum in terms of both output and employment shares. The output share of services in GDP rose from 40.5 per cent in 1977/78 to 54.5 per cent in 1988/89 before falling back to about 47 per cent in 1991/92. The rise in the contribution of this sector to total GDP during the period was due largely to the relative decline in the shares of oil and industry. In terms of employment, some 46.5 per cent of the employed labor force in 1990/91 were engaged in services as compared to about 33 per cent in 1977/78. Nearly nine out of ten jobs created each year after the revolution were service-related. To be sure, a sizeable portion of this employment was concentrated in petty trades, fast-food restaurants, taxis, street peddling, foreign currency dealings, and a whole list of illicit or extra-legal activities from selling smuggled foreign cigarettes to buying and selling government-issued ration coupons. The rise of this 'middlemanism' has frequently been deplored by the leadership, but it is an unavoidable phenomenon given the lack of opportunities in other sectors, inadequate investments by the private sector, and, most significantly, the high profitability of these activities. The disproportionate rise of employment in these trades can best be understood by the fact that in 1976/77 there were reportedly fewer than 1 million people in Iran engaged in 'middleman' jobs, while the number in 1986/87 had surged to 3.5 million. The broader ratio of non-productive to productive employment, which in 1976/77 had stood at 1.5 times, reportedly reached 7.5 times in 1986/87.[10] The main reason for the shift was that the mass exodus of the rural population could not be absorbed in urban industries or in more productive service jobs. Nevertheless, to the extent that the services sector was able to absorb most of the rural migrants, and to accommodate most of the new entrants into the job market, it helped reduce higher open unemployment in the economy.

THE OVERALL TREND

In the 14 years after the 1979 revolution, the Iranian economy was beset by a host of political, social and economic problems which directly or indirectly shaped the size and composition of the gross domestic and national product. Disregarding non-economic considerations (e.g. human suffering, personal hardship, individual sacrifice, etc.) the record in purely economic terms has been less than flattering. Since the revolution, economic growth has been almost nil, with GDP registering a decline in 6 out of the 14 years. Unemployment has hovered around 12–14 per cent of the labor force. Dependence on food imports has increased. With population up by nearly 62 per cent, and real GDP about the same as the pre-revolution level, per capita income has fallen 38 per cent There has also been a decline in per capita public and private consumption. But the most distressing aspect has been reduced total investment.Consequently, the contribution to real GDP of both the *hydrocarbons* and public service sectors in 1991/92 was smaller than the corresponding values in 1977/78. Equally disturbing has been a notable shift of resources (including labor) from more productive endeavors to low-value-added activities in the over-crowded and highly inefficient services. Since the revolution, there has been a decline in employment in agriculture and manufacturing, and a small rise in gainful occupation in construction and water and power. The services sector has provided nearly all the new jobs for the rising labor force in the private sector.

NOTES

1. *The New York Times,* July 31, 1979.
2. See statement of Ahmad Khomeini, and *Majles* debates in *Kayhan Havai,* September 11, 1991, p. 3 and August 14, 1991, pp. 3, 24.
3. In some years, for example, Bank Markazi's annual report shows a distinct decline of value-added in a given sector while the compendium indicates a spectacular rise (e.g. a minus 2.5 per cent vs. a plus 25.6 per cent for the services sector in 1985/86, or a minus 1.6 per cent vs. a plus 4.8 per cent in agriculture in 1983/84).
4. In cases where the difference between the two publications has been uncommonly wide, a reconciliation is sought through a recourse to supplementary sources.
5. 'Report of the President to the Nation on the State of the Economy', *Ettela'at,* 9 Farvardin 1360.
6. Press interview by *Ettela'at*'s economic service with government authorities, *Ettela'at,* 10 Mehr 1362, p. 5.
7. See press conference with Tehran University students, *Kayhan Havai,* May 15, 1991, p. 26.
8. See *Tahlili bar Natayej-e Barrasi-e budgeh-e Khanevar 1369* (An Analysis of the Family Budget Survey 1990/91) (Tehran: Bank Markazi, n.d.).
9. The year-to-year behavior of agriculture shown in Bank Markazi's annual reports often differs from the picture portrayed by the figures in the *National Accounts 1974/75–1987/88.* Attempts at reconciliation have proved futile.
10. See *Iran Focus,* May 1991, p. 13.

5

Population, labor force and employment

Iran's total population was estimated at 33.5 million inhabitants in the 1976/77 census with a male/female ratio of 51 to 49. The rate of growth of population between 1966/67 and 1976/77 was estimated at nearly 2.9 per cent per year. Tehran, with a population of 3.4 million, housed about 10 per cent of the nation. In the two decades before the revolution, the annual growth rate had been on the decline from a peak of 3.1 per cent to about 2.7 per cent by the time of the revolution, thanks in part to a number of population control measures and planned parenthood.

DEMOGRAPHIC TRENDS

The 1986/87 census put the population at 49.4 million, indicating nearly 14 million more people since the revolution, and a net annual increase of 3.9 per cent since the 1976/77 census.[1] Responsible for the upward trend is said to have been such factors as the regime's encouragement of large families in the early years of the revolution; a reduced legal age of marriage; initial opprobrium of the use of contraceptives; growing poverty and rising unemployment; re-emergence of polygamy; lack of entertainment outlets outside the home; distribution of ration coupons according to the size of family; and the influx of refugees from neighboring countries. The number of marriages reportedly doubled from 4.6 per thousand of population in 1975/76 to 9.8 per cent in 1983/84. The ratio of employed people to total population declined from 38 per cent to 36 per cent for the decade, and unemployment rose from 10 per cent of the labor force to 14 per cent.

Other salient features of the demographic changes in the ten-year period indicate a continued increase in urban population; a rise in the size of the 'non-productive' group (below 14 years of age and over 64); growing unemployment in the 'productive' sectors category and in rural occupations; a fall in gainful employment among women; a drastic 42 per cent decline in industrial employment accompanied by a spectacular 73 per cent rise in service jobs (mostly public); and a large 43 per cent concentration of urban employment in the so-called 'non-classified' category.[2]

Preliminary results of a new census conducted in 1991/92, show the country's population to have reached 58.2 million, with Tehran's population at 7.2 million. Nearly 46 per cent of the total population was reported to be less than 15 years of age. The average rate of increase of population between 1986/87 and 1991/92 ran at 3.28 per cent a year. The illiteracy rate was put at 25 per cent.[3] Of the total population, some 25.2 per cent formed the active labor force.

According to a study carried out by UNICEF in 1991, Iran, with 45.9 per cent of its total population in the 0–14-year age group, ranked as the third highest in the world in this category (behind Kenya and Nigeria). At the prevailing growth rate in the 1980s, Iran's population was expected to double every 22 years (compared with 1,000 years for Germany and 630 years for Austria). Infant mortality (death before 5 years of age) in Iran was found to be 56 per thousand (as compared with 8 per thousand in Japan and Canada, and 174 per thousand in Nigeria). The number of physicians in Iran was 3.4 per 10,000 of population (compared to 27 in Germany, and 0.6 in Kenya). For each 10,000 people in Iran, there were 4–5 nurses (compared with 79 in Canada).[4] The UN Human Development Report 1992 puts Iran at measurably below average in adult literacy and life expectancy among 21 states in the Middle East and North Africa region.

EMPLOYMENT AND UNEMPLOYMENT

Published employment data are available only for the general government in the public sector, and for large manufacturing enterprises in the private sector. Due to the growing size of the public sector after the revolution, the share of private enterprise in the total employed work force has shrunk. Between 1976/77 and 1990/91 perhaps no more than a million new jobs were created in the private sector – less than 30 per cent of the total of 3.41 million. A large proportion of these jobs were in small trade and businesses dealing in self-employed services that required little investment and promised a quick return.

According to the latest data published by the Iranian Statistical Center, in 1986/87 nearly 560,000 people were employed in large industrial workshops with ten or more employees. The total was up by only about 4 per cent since 1982/83, having reached a peak of 593,000 wage and salary earners in 1984/85. Nearly 26 per cent of total employment in these workshops were in textile and leather, 21 per cent in machine tools and fabricated metals, 16 per cent in food and tobacco, 15 per cent in non-energy mineral products, and the rest in chemicals, basic metals, paper, and wood products.[5]

In 1990/91, 4.7 million people – or nearly one-third of the total labor force – were employed in the broadly-defined public sector. Of this total an estimated 2.2 million constituted the regular government's wage and salary employees – an increase of over 1 million since 1976/77. Moreover, according to certain estimates, in the late 1980s, more than 80 per cent of the nearly half-a-million college graduates in the country, 85 per cent of the nation's 1.1 million scientific, technical and specialist cadres, and a majority of 45,000 top management and administration personnel worked for the state.[6] More than two-thirds of the new jobs created each year on average since the revolution seem to have been absorbed in the public sector, mostly in service-related occupations, and in urban centers. The rise in public sector employment since the revolution is attributed to the wholesale nationalization of large industrial and financial enterprises. The government's willingness (and obligation) to be the employer of first resort was an additional reason.

Data available on the distribution of the labor force by economic sectors and activities is weak. Information supplied by Bank Markazi and the Plan and Budget Organization puts total employment in 1977/78 at about 9 million of whom 33.5 per cent were employed in agriculture, 33.3 per cent in industry and oil, and 33.2 per cent in services. By contrast, figures for 1990/91 suggest a total employed force of 12.2 million of whom about 28 per cent were engaged in agriculture, 25 per cent in industry and oil, and nearly 47 per cent in services. As indicated in Table 5.1, the largest portion of jobs created after the revolution was absorbed by the services sector while agriculture and industry showed marginal gains. Within services, structural employment shifts were most pronounced in the public sector, in low-paying private-sector jobs, and among the least productive occupations. Table 5.1 also shows that while the labor force increased by about 43 per cent between

1977/78 and 1990/91, gainful employment expanded by no more than 35.5 per cent, and the jobless rate more than doubled. And since GDP in constant prices was actually smaller, per capita labor productivity showed a decline of 30 per cent during the period. The loss in productivity was particularly conspicuous in the services sector where an increase in employment amounting to nearly 89 per cent resulted in no more than an 18 per cent rise in added value (Table 4.2). In industry the outcome was equally disappointing as real output declined by about 7 per cent despite a larger labor contingent of roughly 5 per cent. Only in agriculture did an increase of some 12 per cent in the workforce result in a 38 per cent rise in output over the 13-year period. Improved productivity in agriculture was also due to larger and higher quality non-labor inputs rather than better skills or training on the part of small farmers.

Published official unemployment statistics are generally inadequate and often inaccurate because the majority of the gainfully employed work for themselves in the services sector, or are employed in a large number of very small industrial enterprises (with less than 10 workers). Also, a high proportion of employed workers are in agriculture where underemployment is rampant. The 1986/87 census showed a total population of 49.4 million, of which about 34 million were ten years old or older. The total labor force was estimated at 12.8 million and the employed population at 11 million – indicating an official, open, jobless rate of 14 per cent (or about 1.8 million).[7] The relatively small percentage of the active labor force in Iran (26 per cent compared to the world average of 44 per cent) is indicative of the very large under-age composition of the population and the inadequate use of women in productive employment during the post-revolution period. Table 5.1 shows employment and unemployment in Iran since the revolution. Table 5.2 provides certain estimates on the basic manpower categories.

Between 1977/78 and 1990/91, Iran's population grew about 62 per cent, and the economically active labor force increased by nearly 43 per cent (or 4.3 million workers). In the same period, only about 3.2 million paying jobs were created in the economy, thus adding about 1 million people to the ranks of the unemployed. In 1990/91, out of an officially estimated population of 56.1 million, and a workforce of 14.3 million, only about 12 million were gainfully employed. And perhaps as many as 3.5–4 million among the latter consisted of part-time workers, street vendors, hustlers, panhandlers, or underemployed service personnel.[8] If the large group of people in the disguised unemployment category is added to the officially jobless group, the total number of unemployed and underemployed civilians might be considerably higher than official figures, and perhaps as high as 30 per cent.[9]

The estimates of nationwide open unemployment during the 1980s shown in Table 5.1, are largely conjectural due to lack of reliable data on population, labor force, and the employed contingent. Except for the year 1986/87, when a nationwide census was conducted and various categories officially identified, the annual data supplied by the Iranian Statistical Center for other years are only rough estimates that are revised repeatedly. For this reason, labor information published by Bank Markazi, the Plan and Budget Organization, and international agencies frequently differ from one another and from year to year. Consequently, the ratio of the economically active labor force to total population, which should generally remain stable over a ten-year period, shows notable variations from year to year in Bank Markazi's annual reports, ranging from 25.3 per cent to 29.3 per cent. In the absence of detailed data on employment, the number of unemployed workers is also subject to a great deal of guesswork. Unofficial estimates of unemployment have always been measurably higher than government figures. Some private publications, for example, put the number of unemployed at 3.8 million in 1986/87 – indicating an unemployment rate of 28.6 per cent.[10] Official and private estimates, however, are both subject to large margins of error due to differences in definition, deficiencies of estimation, and other reasons. The estimates of national unemployment shown in Table 5.1, for the years 1982/83–1985/86, for example, are considerably lower than some other published estimates.[11] Foreign publications, referring to the Plan and Budget Organization estimates, put unemployment in early 1991 at 3.5–3.8 million,[12] while PBO itself gives a figure of 2.1 million persons, or 15.2 per cent of the labor force. Population estimates in Table 5.1 are also at variance with figures cited by different government agencies (which are not themselves uniform).

Information on the breakdown of total unemployment among various age or occupation groups is even more scarce. Indications are, however, that with nearly two-thirds of the workforce between 15 and 39 years of age, unemployment has been highest (twice the national average) among youth (15–24 year olds). The jobless rate has also been highest in urban areas, and, quite naturally, during the recessionary periods, 1978/79–1980/81 and 1986/87–1988/89. Unemployment has also been highest in the less developed regions of the country, among the ranks of the uneducated, and in the construction sub-sector. Most disturbing of all has been the increasing number of women out of work, and seeking employment out of necessity. Despite Islam's emphasis on the equality between sexes with respect to work, women have not enjoyed either the same opportunity for employment, or the same status in managerial jobs. According to a private estimate, while urban unemployment among women was 12 per cent in 1974/75, it stood at 60 per cent in 1991/92. Fourteen women held prominent political positions in the country for a female labor force of about 7 million.[13]

Detailed characteristics of employment, unemployment and the labor force are so far available only for the city of Tehran. According to data released in late 1992, of Tehran's total population of 6 million in 1986/87, some 1.7 million were in the active workforce, of which 88 per cent were men and 12 per cent women. Nearly 1.46 million of the labor force were employed, and about 240,000 (or 14.2 per cent) were jobless. Unemployment among men was 12.7 per cent, and among women, 26.4 per cent. Among unemployed men, a total of 11,530 (or 38 per cent) were university graduates; the number for women was nearly 4,000 (or 6 per cent).[14]

RURAL–URBAN MIX

Information on the composition of population and labor relocation is more readily available, and generally more reliable. Data published by the Iranian Statistical Center show a continuous and uninterrupted migration of rural people to the cities in every year since the revolution. As a result, the rural population, which stood at 52.2 per cent of the total inhabitants in 1977/78, declined to merely 42.2 per cent in 1990/91, while the urban population increased from 47.8 per cent to 57.8 per cent. The number of cities – defined as urban centers with 5,000 population and a municipality – increased from 373 in 1976/77 to 496 in 1986/87 and 512 in 1990/91.[15] Rapid urbanization of the population – largely due to larger public subsidies to city people, and lower costs of certain amenities – not only aggravated the housing shortage, but also increased urban unemployment. As the number of city jobs lagged considerably behind new job seekers, urban unemployment rose faster than rural joblessness. In 1977/78 an estimated 30 per cent of the unemployed lived in the cities; in 1990/91, by contrast, 72.7 per cent of the people out of work were city dwellers.

In the first post-revolution *Majles*, a radical, pro-labor law was passed to regulate employment and guarantee high levels of worker security by giving workers' councils broad management authority and responsibility. However, the law was vetoed by the Council of

Guardians. Another bill, this time somewhat 'anti-labor,' with no provisions for legal strikes and giving the employer right of dismissal without severance compensation, (bitterly fought against by leftist elements) was passed in 1987, but the Council rejected some of its provisions once again. A subsequent labor act was passed by the *Majles* in 1990 and, after a new veto by the Council of Guardians, was referred to the Council on Expediency and Discernment for final determination. The last, 203-article, version of the law which finally passed all the legislative processes in 1991 is believed by some observers to be fairly liberal toward labor. It recognizes workers' rights to collective bargaining, to strike (called work stoppage), and to generous benefit provisions (e.g. maternity leave for women workers).[16]

WORK FORCE AND JOB MARKET

According to experts, the alarming growth of the child-bearing segment of the female population, with girls reaching 15 years of age in 1991/92 outnumbering women of age 49 by 3.5 to 1, makes it difficult to reduce the annual population growth from the prevailing rate unless drastic measures are adopted. Even if new-born babies were to be limited to no more than two per couple from now on, Iran's population is likely to rise by at least 20 million by the year 2010. Under a more realistic scenario, based on the number of women of child-bearing age, population may be expected to exceed 100 million in the next 20 years.

Preliminary reports by Iranian health officials on the government's population control measures sound encouraging. According to the Health Minister, family planning programs involving 15,500 rural and urban centers have resulted in a reduction in the rate of population growth to 2.7 per cent in 1991/92 and 2.5 per cent in 1992/93 – the lowest since the revolution.[16] Neutral observers tend to question the accuracy of these figures, and doubt if the decade-long demographic trend could be turned around so quickly. This skepticism is reinforced by the diversity of the population growth rates estimated by other official agencies (e.g. the Ministry of Interior, the Iranian Statistical Center, the Bureau of Vital Statistics) ranging from as low as 2 per cent a year to as high as 3.17 per cent.

In any event, assuming a plausible rate of 2.9 per cent per annum, the Iranian economy has to create some 600,000 new jobs, 40,000 classrooms, 10,000 college-educated teachers, and 500,000 houses to accommodate the additions.

The current five-year plan projects the creation of 394,000 additional positions each year. However, the first year into the plan period has reportedly produced no more than 260,000 jobs. Another effect of a too-rapid population growth is expected to be the falling ratio of educational facilities to children of school age. In 1991/92, some 1.8 million school-age youth (out of 12 million) were reportedly unable to enter schools. According to press reports, out of the 900,000 applicants for admission to the Iranian universities each year, no more than 150,000 can be absorbed, due to lack of funds, facilities, and faculty. According to the Education Minister, no more than 60 per cent of the nation's educational needs is currently met.[18] This shortfall is larger, both absolutely and relatively, than in the Shah's time. Thus, a large segment of a potential managerial class, which Iran so desperately needs, is mostly wasted. What is often lost in the current debate on economic issues within the Islamic regime is the fact that now, more than ever before, the key to Iran's future viability and progress lies not so much in the country's oil, gas, and other natural resources as it does in the quality of its classrooms, libraries, and laboratories.

Iran's annual government expenditure on education of about 4 per cent of GNP is, according to UNESCO estimates, lower than similar rates in many Third World (and several Moslem) countries. Furthermore, shortages of classrooms, teachers and educational materials are aggravated by sub-optimal teaching efficiency. Thus drop-outs of 30 to 50 per cent in senior high schools imply a significant waste of manpower and resources. Iran's development is further hampered by the inadequacies of education in rural areas and for women, and by the system's inability to match academic curricula with national socio-economic priorities. Thus in a country which wishes to be self-sufficient in agriculture, less than 1 per cent of all senior high school students enroll in agricultural courses. In a country desperately short of mid-level technicians and skilled workers, less than 15 per cent of high school enrolment is in technical/vocational/agricultural schools. In a country that aspires to be independent of Western technology, less than 7 per cent of college-age men and women are able to receive a higher education. And in an overstretched public university system that can hardly accommodate 15 per cent of its best and brightest, nearly half of the admission capacity is reserved for politically endorsed candidates who are not required to take the standard entrance examination.[19] At the same time, the lack of gainful employment for all high-school graduates leads them to seek still sub-standard higher education, postponing the day of reckoning and aggravating the unemployment problem.

NOTES

1. See *Iran in the Mirror of Statistics* (Tehran: Iranian Statistical Center 1990).
2. Doubts have been expressed on the accuracy of these data for many reasons, including the lack of published figures on the exact size of Afghani and Iraqi refugees, the true number of war casualties, and the reliable fertility pattern.
3. Iran News Agency (IRNA) broadcast in English, June 20, 1991; and *Kayhan Havai* September 25, 1991, p. 5, and June 3, 1992, p. 4.
4. *Kayhan Havai*, July 24, 1991, p. 4. Comparison in each case is with the opposite extreme.
5. Iranian Statistical Center, *Statistical Yearbook 1369* (1990/91), p. 294.
6. Mohammad Alizadeh, *Specific Trends of Labor Market in Iran 1976/77–1986/87* (Tehran: Plan and Budget Organization, 1988).
7. Concealed unemployment and under-employment was estimated to be 33 per cent. *Kayhan*, 28 Shahrivar, 1370.
8. According to a government official, one-fifth of the total employed population is not engaged in useful production. *Iran Focus*, January 1989, p. 16.
9. In the boom years prior to the revolution, open unemployment in Iran was nationally insignificant and limited to scattered pockets among different sectors and localities.
10. See, for example, *Echo of Iran*, 'Political Bulletin' 6, No. 10 (March 10, 1987); and *The Economist Intelligence Unit*, 'Iran: Country Profile', 1988–1989.
11. See, for example, Amirahmadi (1990), p. 187.
12. *The Economist Intelligence Unit*, 'Iran', Report No. 1, 1991, p. 12; and 'Country Profile 1991–92', p. 20.
13. *The New York Times*, March 14, 1992, p. 2.
14. *Kayhan Havai*, November 25, 1992, p. 10.
15. Report of the Minister of Housing to the *Majles*, reported in *Kayhan Havai*, November 11, 1992.
16. See The Middle East Economic Digest (*MEED*), February 21, 1992.
17. See *MEED*, July 31, 1992, p. 12.
18. *Kayhan* (Tehran), 28 Shahrivar 1370, p. 5; and *Financial Times* (London), February 8, 1993 p. iv.
19. Of more than 1 million high-school graduates taking the college entrance examination in 1993, only about 130,000 were expected to gain admission to the country's institutions of higher learning.

6

Wages, prices and inflation

Information on wage and price movements under the revolution is not only rather sketchy and incomplete; there are sharp differences between official figures and private estimates. Statutory price controls, ceilings on profit margins, rationing of basic necessities, subsidies to essential commodities, and the parallel existence of a 'free' market for many goods and services, tend to mask the accuracy of both the magnitude and direction of specific variables. The consensus among foreign analysts is that Bank Markazi's wage and price indices understate the true level of wage and price inflation in Iran for both technical and political reasons. Statistical methodology and data collecting procedures are admittedly in need of technical refinement and updating.[1] However, critics believe that the lack of technical sophistication is only partly to blame.

WAGES

Data on overall or sectoral wage developments are not available. Published figures refer to wages or workers in large manufacturing enterprises, as well as construction workers in the private sector. Information obtained by international organizations on wage and salary income are derived from the published data on disposable income figures of urban and rural families, industrial wages in certain large establishments, and the 1986/87 population survey offering some data on government salaries. Private estimates are equally inadequate, and often partial.

By all accounts, during the few months before and the few

months after the change of the regime, while national output experienced a continuous decline, factory wages rose rapidly under strong political pressure from the burgeoning workers' councils. In some factories, wages were adjusted upward four or five times in a short period. The result was double-digit increases in both wages and consumer prices. The economy, in turn, faced both recession and inflation. After the revolutionary turmoil and the leftist influence in industrial enterprises subsided considerably, wage increases became more moderate. Interestingly, urban wage earners were normally able to negotiate higher incomes in the early part of the decade, while rural family income tended to rise after 1986/87.

According to published data, wages, salaries and bonuses in large industrial enterprises registered an upward trend through the post-revolution years. In 1978/79 these rose more than 25 per cent on average, with as much as a 60 per cent increase in some industries. With a rise in across-the-board minimum wages in 1979/80, payments to workers in large establishments increased by more than 60 per cent on average, with 100 per cent or more pay raises in textiles, shoes, cement, rubber, and farm machinery. In 1979, the Provisional Government raised the minimum wage rate for workers in large manufacturing enterprises from Rls 210 to Rls 567 a day. The minimum was raised again by 12 per cent in 1980. The rate of increase slackened in the following year to 18.5 per cent, and was limited to about 9 per cent in 1981/82. The moderation in wage increases continued in 1982/83 with a rise of less than 12 per cent, but 1983/84 again showed a rise of 15.7 per cent, followed by 13.3 per cent in 1984/85. A slackening of industrial output due to the shortage of foreign exchange in 1985/86 caused a clamp down on industrial wage increases, and the index rose by only 11.9 per cent. A sharp decline in industrial production in 1986/87, however, resulted – for the first time in the post-revolution period – in a *fall* of 3.4 per cent in industrial wage rates. In 1987/88, however, despite another decline in manufactures, wages increased by more than 8 per cent. The continued recession in industrial output in 1988/89 was also accompanied by a 14.6 per cent increase in industrial wages. The industrial sector's robust recovery in 1989/90 and 1990/91 resulted in wage and salary increases of 11.8 per cent and 22.6 per cent respectively. Notwithstanding the steady increase in wages and salaries in large manufacturing enterprises over the years, the overall wage and salary indices in these establishments still often lagged behind the consumer price index.

According to Bank Markazi data, the index of real wages, salaries and benefits in the construction industry rose 34.4 per cent in 1977/78 and 17.7 per cent in 1978/79. The inflow of rural families into Tehran and other large cities in the hope of acquiring cheap dwellings created a new boom in construction activities, and wages went up by 15 per cent in 1979/80, followed by 19.4 per cent in 1980/81, 16.2 per cent in 1981/82, and 20.5 per cent in 1982/83. The recovery of the housing sector in 1983/84 from a long recession revived the pressure on wages, and the index rose by nearly 25 per cent. The aborted boom in 1984/85, however, brought the index down to a rise of about 14 per cent. The slump in construction activities during 1985/86 kept construction wages down to a rise of only 7.2 per cent. But despite the continued recession, construction wages rose by 18 per cent in 1986/87, and again by 20.5 per cent in 1987/88. With the partial recovery in this sector, the rise in wages continued in 1988/89 at 21.4 per cent. In the following two years, the annual increase in wages was cut down to 18.1 per cent and 9.3 per cent respectively. In 1991/92, there was again a surge to 15 per cent. For this group of workers, too, wage increases did not keep up with inflation.

For other groups in society, available data are limited to information on family income in the urban and rural sectors. Scattered and indirectly obtained data show private sector wages during the 1980s rose by 10 per cent a year for urban families, and 16 per cent in rural areas. During the same period, public sector salaries increased by 8 per cent and 14 per cent a year for urban and rural regions respectively. More than 80 per cent of government employees on average reportedly received 30 per cent below comparable wages for industrial workers. One estimate indicates that the real take-home pay of government employees fell by at least half between 1980 and 1986. In the second half of 1990, an *ad hoc* wage increase of Rls 20,000 a month was granted to all public sector employees under a new 'salary-adjustment' policy to compensate for income erosion; the rise was made tax-exempt. Further increases were approved in 1991 and 1992.[2]

The government's wage and salary policy had a direct effect on employment and output. The policy of periodically adjusting nominal wages and salaries to increases in the cost of living, combined with the decision to increase overall employment (by making the public sector an employer of first resort) led to the expansion of aggregate demand, and private consumption. Due to the reasons already indicated, real output did not keep pace with the growing aggregate demand. The result was a steep rise in prices and sharp decline in real wages and income. At the same time, the policy of maintaining real wages at higher levels than warranted by labor productivity discouraged the private sector from increasing labor employment, particularly because price controls and foreign exchange overvaluation tended to increase labor costs relative to other costs. These policies resulted in creating an excess supply of workers. Thus, despite the government's efforts to maintain full employment, the rate of joblessness increased throughout the decade.

In the post-ceasefire environment of deregulation and reforms, wages and salaries in both private and public sectors began to rise at an accelerated tempo. Civil service pay across the board was raised more than once. There were also 'unofficial' benefits granted to special groups within the civil service. In the private sector, skilled labor wages soared to new highs. Frequent strikes under a new liberal labor law resulted in quick settlements in favor of strikers' demands for higher wages. The minimum wage as of March 1993 was raised 32 per cent to Rls 2994 a day (or about $1.87 at the floating exchange rate). All other wages of workers covered by the labor law were to increase by 22.5 per cent to an average of Rls 4856. Corresponding provisions were established for salaried employees.

PRICES AND INFLATION

Data on price developments are more detailed in content and coverage and more readily available than information on wages and employment. Bank Markazi regularly publishes price indices on consumer goods, wholesale products, imports, and exports. As can be expected, however, official statistics on wholesale, retail, and export prices generally reflect administered prices, and price movements in the controlled or regulated markets. For this reason, published figures do not always give a complete or true picture of the real situation. Controlled prices for certain basic necessities sold through government outlets against ration coupons, for example, differ significantly from prices of the same items sold in the parallel 'free market'. These differences, as reported in Tehran newspapers during the 1980s, often ranged from a minimum of twice (for gasoline and local cigarettes) to as much as 12–18 times (for cheese, rice, cooking oil and detergents). To be sure, the relative weight, volume of transaction, and number of customers for the high-priced items was not large enough to raise the true rate of inflation by the same multiples. Yet there is no dispute that the government figures measurably underestimated the real rise in prices.[3]

Despite the downward bias in official data, price developments over the years can still show reasonably clear trends. Figures supplied by Bank Markazi for all years since the revolution point to a persistently upward inflationary movement, albeit at different and erratic annual rates. A Central Bank survey of the early period shows that a series of measures adopted before the revolution to combat inflation in the housing sector resulted in a decline in the housing price index from a rise of 37.8 per cent in 1977/78 to zero in 1978/79 and minus 0.5 per cent in 1979/80. Due to the heavy weight of the dwelling index in the consumer price index, the rise in the overall consumer price for the latter two years was held down to less than 11 per cent on average, despite a 20 per cent average price rise in the index for food.[4] Other factors, such as a decline in private sector liquidity, a reduction in public expenditure, the outflow of considerable volumes of bank notes from the country, and a decline in the velocity of money, also helped to keep inflation in check.[5]

In 1980/81, inflation once again became one of the government's major economic headaches. With the outbreak of the war with Iraq in September 1980, a devastating decline in oil production and revenues, and significantly reduced imports of consumer goods and industrial inputs, domestic costs began to rise. Despite a modest rise in the housing index, a substantial (29 per cent) rise in the food index and a similar rise (24 per cent) in clothing pushed the CPI for the year to 23.5 per cent. Of greater concern, however, was a rise in the wholesale price index (WPI) from 19.8 per cent in the previous year to 30.5 per cent. Bank Markazi cited such factors as a 35 per cent rise in money supply, trade sanctions, a decline in private sector confidence resulting in reduced private investment, growing monopolies in production and distribution, and rising public expenditures, as some of the major reasons. The only offsetting factor was a reduction in the velocity of money in circulation.

The government's main response was to establish the Economic Mobilization Center to control prices and distribution channels. Despite these efforts, the CPI and WPI in 1981/82 still rose by 22.8 per cent and 19.4 per cent respectively, while indicating some response to new controls as well as the sale of war-induced rationed products (e.g. sugar, soap, and cooking oil) at controlled prices. By Bank Markazi's own estimation, the three-year post-revolution increases in the CPI reduced fixed-income earners' real purchasing power by 50 per cent.

In 1982/83, consumer prices rose by 19.2 per cent and wholesale prices by 13.7 per cent, according to official estimates, bringing the post-revolution total to more than 100 per cent in both indices.

Due to the recovery in the industrial sector, greater availability of foreign exchange, and increased imports of basic goods and raw materials, the rise in the CPI and WPI indices was reduced from the previous year. In 1983/84, rice was added to the list of rationed goods and sold at controlled prices. A total of Rls 106 billion in subsidies was also granted to the basic staples in order to keep down production costs. As a result, price rises were contained at below 15 per cent for CPI, and below 8 per cent for WPI.

Stringent government policies, such as price controls, rationing, and subsidization, that were adopted after the Iraq war gradually worked themselves through the economy and cut down the price spiral. In 1984/85 consumer prices rose by only 10.4 per cent, and wholesale prices by 7.6 per cent. A reduction in the current and public investment expenditures (with the resulting fall in budget deficit), accompanied by a slower rate of increase in private sector liquidity, resulted in a fall in aggregate demand. On the supply side, increased output in both agriculture and industry helped the balance. Some Rls 121 billion of new subsidies paid to essential goods also moderated their rise in price. Inflation on both the wholesale and consumer price levels was brought down further. A recession in agriculture and industry that developed in 1985/86 helped bring down the rise in the official CPI index (calculated on a new base period) to a record low of 6.9 per cent, and the official WPI to 7.3 per cent. The price rise on the old series was even lower. A sharp reduction in public sector investment was the major cause. Continued government subsidization of basic necessities and a fall in the circulation of money supply were additional factors.

The intensification of hostilities in the mid-1980s, combined with an enormous decline in oil revenues, the more effective impact of economic sanctions on both exports and imports, and the delayed but inevitable effects of sharply expanded domestic liquidity, fuelled the inflationary fires once again. Price deceleration was suddenly reversed in 1986/87, and the CPI and WPI both soared to 23.7 per cent and 25.1 per cent respectively. The most direct cause of the upsurge was the unprecedented one-year rise in the government budget deficit due to a sharp decline in oil revenues. Rising costs of imports, low domestic output, increased excise taxes, and higher priced public services also added to the price hike – despite continued rationing, price controls and subsidies. The post 1985/86 inflationary spiral continued in 1987/88 with CPI and WPI rising by 27.7 per cent and 29.7 per cent respectively. The main causes, again, were a large budget deficit (equal to 36 per cent of total expenditures), an 18.1 per cent rise in money supply, the administered rises in the price of some public goods and services, and a hike in certain excise taxes. The 1987/88 inflation was particularly disturbing because it occurred despite the state's considerable price subsidies and despite a rise of food imports to $2.5 billion from $1.2 billion in the previous year.

The fall in the global price of crude oil in 1988/89 negatively affected public revenues and foreign exchange earnings. With more than 50 per cent of the year's public expenditures being financed by borrowing from the central bank, and a 24 per cent rise in liquidity, inflationary pressures were further fuelled. The CPI and WPI rose by 28.9 and 22 per cent respectively. The ceasefire in August 1988 eased military expenditure and the subsequent fall in the free-market rate of exchange helped lower the rial cost of certain import items. The expanded aggregate supply resulting from the redirection of resources to peacetime activities, combined with a lower budget deficit and smaller monetary growth, contributed to a fall in the inflation rate. Consumer prices rose by 17.4 per cent and wholesale prices by 18.4 per cent in 1989/90. Considerable deregulation of economic activity in 1990/91, along with a sharply lower budget deficit and a smaller rise in money supply, brought the CPI index down to 9 per cent in that year, although wholesale prices were still up by 23.9 per cent. Growing demands for construction materials, basic commodities, industrial parts, and skilled labor in 1991/92 put new pressure on prices and the CPI rose by an estimated 19.6 per cent, and the WPI by 28.1 per cent. Private estimates go as high as 50 per cent. Table 6.1 traces price developments in the post-revolution period as officially reported.

Despite regular publication of detailed price indices by Bank Markazi, the true magnitude of inflation during the period of Islamic rule is hard to determine with any degree of reasonable accuracy. Critics claim total open and repressed inflation of some 20 times between 1977/78 and 1991/92.[6] Whatever the real size of the price rise, there is no doubt that the economy suffered from virulent inflation. Responsibility for the perennial rise in the consumer and wholesale price indices can be blamed on many internal and external factors. Reference has already been made to such exogenous elements as the trade embargo and Western sanctions; the high cost of obtaining needed foreign supplies through third parties; a relatively depressed global oil market in much of the 1980s compared to the 1979/82 period; and a long and costly war with Iraq. Among internal causes, the emphasis has been placed on the combination of rapid increases in population and demand pressures; a demographic shift from productive to non-productive categories (i.e. larger groups below 10 and above

64 years of age); supply bottle-necks; the growth of multi-tiered middlemen and widespread insufficiencies in the distribution process; intensification of private and public monopolies; ineffective monetary policies; and permeative corruption.

In addition to these elemental factors, the root cause of Iran's high inflation – although still relatively moderate by Third World standards – ought to be sought in two other related phenomena: the government's budget deficits and a rise in private sector liquidity. The officially estimated increase in the consumer price index during the 14-year period bears an uncanny relationship to the public sector deficit, the rise in nominal aggregate demand (and liquidity), and the so-called foreign exchange gap. The inflation rate can easily be seen to have soared in the early 1980s when the general government's deficit as a percentage of GDP was in the double-digit range. As the ratio of the government's budget gap to GDP was reduced from 6 per cent in 1982/83 to 4 per cent in 1985/86, the CPI also declined from 19.2 per cent a year to 6.9 per cent in the same period. Later in the second half of the decade, when the budget deficit climbed again, inflationary pressures intensified. After 1989, the regular government's budget deficit was reduced through the sale of foreign exchange in the free market and reduced subsidies to money-losing public enterprises. But the latter borrowed from the banking system to cover their losses, and the public sector's deficit remained large: giving rise to a renewed burst of inflation. The CPI in 1992/93 is unofficially estimated at 23 per cent, with higher figures of 30–40 per cent projected for 1993/94.

The correlation with the money supply and private sector liquidity is equally striking, although again not unexpected. During 1981/82 and 1982/83, when liquidity (i.e. broad money) increased by an annual average of nearly 20 per cent, the CPI rose by 21 per cent a year. When the expansion of liquidity was reduced to 12 per cent per annum between 1983/84 and 1985/86, the CPI also fell to about 10 per cent a year. After 1986/87, both indices rose almost in tandem until 1989/90. (See Tables 8.4 and 6.1.)

The link between price rises and foreign exchange shortages has also been plainly evident. The clearest linkage between the fall in exchange revenues and the rise in prices was apparent in the increases in liquidity resulting from budget shortfalls and the consequent resort to the printing press. Since oil revenues normally consitututed a substantial part (as much as 67 per cent) of total government revenues, any drastic decline in the budgeted petroleum income was bound to result in a correspondingly larger budget deficit. And, since the budget deficit was ordinarily financed by borrowing from Bank Markazi (that is, by an increase in the money supply), prices tended to rise as more rials began to chase limited supplies of goods and services. The second reason why the foreign currency shortage contributed to inflationary pressures was the central bank's reduced opportunity to curtail the excess money supply through the sale of oil dollars for rials in the highly devalued free foreign currency market. Foreign currencies sold by the central bank at open-market rates of exchange to Iranian importers, travellers, and other customers routinely provided the most successful means of mopping up the rial overhang in the economy. Foreign exchange shortages precluded this clean-up operation.

The third linkage between foreign exchange reserves and inflation was more circuitous, but no less effective. While the other two links worked through changes in aggregate demand, the third worked through a reduction of aggregate supply. The heavy dependence of Iran's industrial sector on foreign inputs of raw materials and semi-processed items directly linked the level of industrial production to the availability of foreign exchange. The shortage of foreign currencies, in turn, led to reduced industrial output, and, thus, more inflation. This inherent weakness was further intensified by the government's policy of maintaining a highly over-valued official exchange rate, and controlling the prices of domestically produced goods, without being able to keep domestic production costs down. As the limited and rationed foreign exchange funds reduced imports, while the shortage of raw materials (along with the lack of profit incentives and price controls) depressed domestic output, aggregate supply was unable to meet increasing demand.

ANTI-INFLATIONARY POLICIES

The government's anti-inflationary measures since the revolution consisted of rationing, price controls, subsidies to essential inputs and basic products, and the distribution of essential goods via official channels. Price controls were established immediately after the war with Iraq. Wages and salaries were frozen in 1980. Price ceilings were designated for wheat, sugar, vegetable oil, milk and fertilizers. Several public organizations became involved in the implementation of the government's fight against inflation. The Organization for the Protection of Consumers and Producers was placed in charge of pricing policy. The OPCP determined and adjusted domestic output prices in accordance with the overall price index and the costs of production. Prices of imported goods were also controlled on the basis of a complex politico-economic formula that presumably took output costs and social needs into consideration. The organization had its enforcing agents at the city and county levels.

The Center for Economic Mobilization (*Setad-e Basij-e Eqtesadi*), established immediately after the Iraqi invasion in September 1980, was given the responsibility for determining the essential commodities to be rationed, the quantity of each item in coupons, and the monitoring of retail outlets, both private and cooperative, for proper distribution of rationed commodities. At first, a few items were rationed, but as the war escalated and supplies dwindled, as many as 15 items at one time were made subject to purchase by coupons at controlled prices in government outlets. Rationed products included cigarettes, cooking oil, sugar, soap, detergents, eggs, chickens, rice, milk, meat, butter and cheese. Until the end of the war with Iraq, gasoline, kerosene and motor oil were also rationed.[7] Rationed items were sold mostly in a vast network of small private shops and some state-owned cooperative stores under the supervision of the Center. While the rationing system was nationwide, there were significant differences between urban and rural areas and from city to city. For example, a smaller number of rationed (and subsidized) goods were available through coupon books in villages and small cities.

The Government Trading Company (GTC), affiliated with the Ministry of Commerce, had the responsibility for the domestic procurement and importation of most of the essential goods and their distribution among retail outlets. The company was responsible for the purchase, importation and domestic shipment of the subsidized items while private sector outlets engaged in daily transactions at the retail level.

Subsidies to a number of basic staples and to certain essential farm inputs were instituted in the early 1980s in order to help the poor and the fixed-income groups, to encourage crop production, and to keep inflation in check. There were also price subsidies for some items consumed by special groups in the population (e.g. infants and the elderly). The OPCP was given a portion of import duties on certain commodities to be used for subsidizing domestic goods. A large part of public subsidies comes from this source, and is not included in the national budget.

As could be expected under the circumstances, the rationing system created a number of fresh problems. Since the rationed portions of nearly all items fell short of standard family needs, rationed goods were not always available at designated intervals, and coupons were not always issued on time. Therefore, a parallel free (or black) market came into being almost immediately. Those who wished to avoid long lines, inconvenient distribution centers, low quality products, and occasional disappointment could always buy rationed items in the open market at higher prices, often with no limitation. Ration coupons were openly (albeit not legally) bought and sold by those who were not initial or rightful recipients. Also, rationed goods were not always sold in official distribution centers, but found their way into private shops through a network of black-marketeers specializing in coupons.[8] Greater availability of rationed goods in cities and urban centers encouraged a further exodus of farmers. There were charges of graver offenses committed by individuals in the rationing process.[9]

Throughout the 1980s, the government tried to fight inflation through strict and stiff legislation against price gouging, hoarding, and speculative transactions. In the Musavi administration, under *ta'azirat-e hokumati*, heavy fines and long prison terms, in addition to the cancellation of business licenses, were approved by the *Majles* against so-called 'economic terrorists'. Ayatollah Khomeini's own exalted authority and religious *fatva* was invoked to punish wrong-dooers and control distribution channels. In January 1990, the *Majles* passed a bill making wealth accumulated through hoarding and over-pricing subject to Article 49 of the 1979 Constitution. Accordingly, such wealth could be classified as 'acquired through illegitimate means' and, therefore, subject to outright confiscation.[10]

Price controls were reduced in 1990/91, and except for essential commodities that were still imported by the GTC or other public agencies at the official exchange rate, all other imported items were allowed to fetch their prices in the open market. Rationed items were reduced. Producers were also allowed to sell a certain percentage of their output in the free market instead of being obliged to sell them all to the government at controlled prices. As a result, a new wave of price rises ensued. The government itself, as part of the new adjustment process, increased the prices of many staples and services (including gas, telephone, transport fares, and others).[11]

In short, the government's anti-inflationary stance throughout the 1980s targeted symptoms rather than causes. Unlike the situation in many other inflation-plagued countries, the Iranian case shows an essentially simple and uncomplicated link between rises in liquidity and increases in the price indices. Between the years 1977/78 and 1990/91, the M2 money supply soared from Rls 2,098 billion to Rls 22,969 billion, or nearly 11 times. During the same period, GDP (at factor cost) in constant 1982/83 prices actually declined from Rls 12,851 billion to Rls 12,045 billion, or nearly 4.5 per cent. In the classical idiom of more money chasing fewer goods, the substantial inflation of the post-revolution period should not be surprising. There could hardly have been a different outcome. Elemental factors leading to the annual rises in liquidity were different and complex. But larger volumes of money in circulation, with its velocity remaining fairly stable, acted as the ultimate cause.[12] The impact of wage and price movements on different groups in society is discussed in Chapter 15.

NOTES

1. For a reference to some of these methodological shortcomings, see M. R. Ghasimi, 'The Iranian Economy after the Revolution', *International Journal of Middle East Studies*, 24, 1992, p. 611.

2. According to a *Majles* deputy, while the CPI rose by 637.5 per cent between 1978/79 and 1990/91, government employees' salaries and bonuses went up by only 142 per cent. Since the irreducible minimum annual expenses of a two-member urban family in 1990/91 was estimated to be Rls 152,327, more than 90 per cent of public servants had regular salaries that placed them below the poverty lines. *Kayhan Havai*, January 15, 1992, p. 24. No details are cited for the sources of data and methods of calculations. The inferences, therefore, seem somewhat questionable.

3. Some unofficial estimates put the annual rates of inflation at 30 to 60 per cent higher than Bank Markazi figures. See, for example, *The Economist Intelligence Unit*, 'Iran: Country Profile' for the years 1989 to 92. The foreign press has regularly reported an annual inflation of 60–100 per cent accompanied by 25–40 per cent unemployment. See *The Wall Street Journal*, April 30, 1987 and May 12, 1990.

4. Bank Markazi's consumer price index covers eight basic categories: food, clothing, housing and utilities, household goods, transport and communications, health care, education, and miscellaneous items. The first three categories carry nearly 70 per cent weight in the total index, which is based on a sample of more than 400 items in 78 cities.

5. Although the *official* consumer price index for the two years, 1979/80 and 1980/81, showed rises of less than 11 per cent on average, an informal survey of 20 daily necessities conducted in mid-1980 (and other private estimates) placed the actual rise in CPI at about 50 per cent over the two-year period. See *The New York Times*, June 1, 1980.

6. Private estimates place the annual rate of inflation during the 1980–88 war with Iraq at 30 per cent on average. See *MEED*, March 1, 1991, p. 9.

7. Rationed items reportedly accounted for less than 25 per cent of the weight in the consumer price index.

8. As frequently reported in the local press, some of the items sold by government centers at low fixed prices were immediately resold in the market at 7 to 10 times the price.

9. See, for example, *Iran Focus*, October 1988; *Echo of Iran*, 'Political Bulletin', October 13, 1987; and 'Economic Bulletin', July 28, 1987 and 18 August 1987; *Ettela'at-e Siasi-Eqtesadi*, 1, No. 10, Tir 1366.

10. See *Iran Focus*, January 1990, p. 14.

11. For this reason, the government's claim of having reduced annual inflation in 1990/91 to less than 10 per cent has been challenged by businessmen and diplomats who believe the figure in that year was close to 60 per cent. See *The New York Times*, April 9, 1991, p. A10.

12. *Additions* to M2 money supply in just two years of 1989/90 and 1990/91 were actually larger than the entire *stock* of money at the end of 1977/78.

IV
NATIONAL
ECONOMIC POLICIES

7

National budget and fiscal policy

Iran's public sector under the Islamic Republic has been far more extensive and dominant than it was under the previous regime. Bucking the worldwide trend toward marketization and private enterprise in the 1980s, the role of the Iranian state in the economy greatly expanded after the revolution. Initially, the fundamentalists' penchant for radical economic restructuring called for the nationalization of foreign trade and the break-up of large land holdings. The shaky position of the private banking system and the depressed condition of industry at the time pushed the government into the wholesale takeover of private banks and large manufacturing establishments. The confiscation of the properties of people associated with the previous regime, on the grounds that such wealth was 'illegitimately' acquired, brought hundreds of firms in mechanized farming, manufacturing, mining, transportation, construction, real estate, trade, and engineering consultancy under public ownership and control. The outbreak of the war with Iraq served as an additional impetus for state involvement in the economy. Finally, the need for the completion of mammoth projects started during the previous regime in such high technology fields as metals, petrochemicals, electronics, transportation, and defense equipment helped to widen the scope of public investment in industry. Before the crucial policy reversal in 1988/89 in favor of liberalization and privatization, the state had enlarged its presence and activity in every sector of the economy, directly or indirectly, through regular government agencies or via parastatal organizations or the so-called 'revolutionary foundations'. The latter's control over the assets and revenues of confiscated firms, while expanding the nominal size of the public sector, has, however, been outside the national budget and legislative accountability.

The Islamic Republic's public sector consists of the central and provincial governments, public enterprises operating in the agricultural, industrial and services sectors, and semi-public 'foundations' (or revolutionary units) engaged in both public and semi-private economic activities. The central government functions mainly through 23 ministries headquartered in Tehran with provincial offices and more than 100 public agencies throughout the country. Provincial governments operate in 25 provinces on behalf of the central government, receiving their finances from Tehran. There are more than 500 municipalities, run by city councils which, with a few exceptions in economically depressed regions, are financially self-sufficient. There are about 220 public enterprises (including 9 banks, 4 insurance companies, and 4 pension funds) which operate independently of the ministries and public agencies, but whose budgets (revenues and expenses) are included in the government's comprehensive national budget. Several hundred business corporations under the supervision of the National Iranian Industries Organization (NIIO), although technically in the public domain, have their own separate accounts. So do many companies and agencies owned and operated by a number of hybrid charitable foundations and organizations called *bonyad*. Although privately run and partly self-financed, these agencies receive various kinds of financial assistance from the state.

Before the revolution, total public sector employment (including government enterprises and the armed forces) was estimated at 1.6 million (with 1.2 million as regular government employees). In 1990/91, thanks to the earlier nationalization of major industries, banking and insurance, as well as the creation of new revolutionary institutions, and the decentralization of certain public functions at the provincial level, the estimated size of public sector employment reached 4.7 million. Of this total, the regular government's workforce numbered about 2.2 million. Also, while there were only 19 ministries before the revolution, the number gradually rose to 23.

Despite extensive involvement in almost all aspects of the Iranian economy, the Islamic government's fiscal share in GDP – measured in constant prices – has been smaller than before the revolution.[1] The dramatic expansion of the state's role in the economy has manifested itself primarily through larger ownership of national wealth and a vast array of new regulations concerning economic activity. That is, the regular government's fiscal responsibility has relatively declined over the years, or has been shared with a host of semi-private institutions, while its distinct regulatory functions have greatly increased.[2] There has also been a carefully calculated decision by the Islamic leadership not to abolish, or even drastically restructure, most of the public ministries and agencies inherited from the Shah's regime, but to establish parallel organizations to perform similar functions under 'revolutionary' command and control.

As a result, the Iranian public sector in 1992/93 included administrative, financial, commercial, industrial, agricultural and service agencies and enterprises under various budgets, management, and supervision. Basic financial data on some financial public agencies (Bank Markazi and the nationalized commercial and investment banks) are readily available, as are the general accounts of the central government and the net fiscal position of ordinary public enterprises. But detailed information on the operation of the non-financial public sector (e.g. nationalized industrial enterprises and particularly the semi-public foundations) are lacking. For this reason, neither the consolidated budget of the whole public sector operations, nor the actual magnitude of the public sector's overall fiscal balance (e.g. the annual budget deficit) can be reliably ascertained.[3]

PUBLIC FINANCE

The Islamic Republic's fiscal position has been determined primarily by annual oil revenues, reliance on domestic financing, and attention to revolutionary promises. Throughout the decade, attempts were made to adjust expenditure to anticipated changes in oil receipts in order to keep the budget deficit in check. Non-oil revenues, particularly tax revenues, continued to play a limited role. Armed conflict with Iraq added significantly to the fiscal burden, directly through additional war expenses, and indirectly through reduced revenues, including oil revenues. The policy of limiting foreign indebtedness resulted in nearly total dependence on domestic bank financing, particularly borrowing from the central bank. Under the revolution's populist philosophy the state increased its welfare outlays for the poor through subsidies and other payments, but it was not able to 'soak' the rich.[4]

BUDGETARY PROCESS AND OBJECTIVES

Despite the new regime's spirited criticism of the budgetary process under the Shah, neither the basic structure nor the method of budget preparation, nor even the format of the annual budget document presented to the *Majles* underwent major changes. The budget bills have invariably projected larger total revenues (particularly oil revenues) than were realized;[5] routinely underestimated total expenditure; and regularly contained a sizeable deficit, expected to be financed by: unspent appropriations during the fiscal year; funds returned from previous year's unspent appropriations; and borrowing from the banking system (that is, the central bank).

As in the Shah's time, all revenue collection and public spending had to have prior parliamentary approval within the annual national budget. The first budget of the Islamic Republic for the Iranian year 1358 (1979/80) was (belatedly) approved by the Revolutionary Council in the summer of that year.[6] The first post-revolution budget submitted to the *Majles on time* (in other words, before the start of the Iranian new year on March 21) was for 1361 (1982/83). The budget document listed among its 30 or so objectives such goals as: meeting the armed forces' needs for victory in the war with Iraq; expanding farm output; rebuilding war-ravaged areas; launching employment-creating projects; opening new rural schools; financing the needs of heavy industries; increasing non-oil exports; supporting small productive units; assisting various cooperatives; and stockpiling strategic goods for national needs. In presenting the budget to the *Majles*, the prime minister acknowledged that the economy was suffering from recession, unemployment, inflation, excess liquidity, and shortage of foreign exchange. The responsibility for the country's economic plight was attributed to past mistakes and misfortunes. The Islamic Republic was said to be the heir to a century of exploitation by the superpowers. The old regime, Prime Minister Musavi claimed, was under the thumb of American capitalists and multi-national corporations which engineered the oil price rise in 1974 and made Iran more than ever dependent on them, and subservient to their interests. Inappropriate fiscal, monetary, and trade policies followesd by the old regime had resulted in a substantial waste of national resources, inflationary pressures, maldistribution of income and wealth, excessive rural migration, a decline in the productive labor force; the rise of consumerism; an imbalance among economic sectors; and a socio-economic crisis.[7]

In presenting his 'comprehensive' 1362 budget[8] to the *Majles* – the first planned budget with a 20-year perspective and a five-year plan – the prime minister again presented a litany of the problems and difficulties facing the nation: inadequacy of technical cadres; uncertainties regarding land tenure; shortage and maldistribution of construction materials; unavailability of spare parts; paucity of foreign exchange; external sabotage in procurement of imports; lack of relevant statistics; and the incongruity of the inherited bureaucratic machinery with the revolutionary government's Islamic commitments. The two outstanding features of the new budget were declared to be its consistency with new development planning and its anti-inflationary orientation. The government's fiscal policy, embedded in the budget, repeated some of the previous goals, and added: the need for reduced consumption and increased investment; emphasis on agriculture as the development pivot; enhancement of overall productivity; distribution of investment credit in favor of hitherto deprived regions and groups; augmentation of non-oil revenues and non-oil exports; and improved industrial management.[9]

For 1363, the 'comprehensive' budget included for the first time not only projected revenues and expenditures for regular government ministries and public agencies, but also the fiscal position of public enterprises and corporations. The document was also supplemented, for the first time, by a 'foreign exchange' budget designating sources and uses of foreign exchange. The pattern established in the budget document during the first four years of the revolution was repeated in all the subsequent budgets submitted to the *Majles* in later years. Objectives were always the same. Budgetary shortfalls were attributed to the same factors. Deviations of projected figures from the actual in previous budgets were blamed on unforeseen circumstances.[10] The need for improving budget preparation and tax collection was routinely emphasized every year. Monetizing the budget deficit was seen as the only real alternative for filling the gap.

The post-ceasefire budget, 1990/91, was the first to be part of the new five-year plan. It was supposed to be more focused, realistic, and anti-inflationary. Appropriations for current and development expenditures were distinctly separated. Its objectives were to conform to those of the plan. It provided for a presidential commission to supervise and control the budgets of state enterprises and review their financial condition. Nevertheless, the 'Rafsanjani budget' was still not without its critics in the *Majles* and elsewhere. In its format and structure, it was found to be no different from previous bills submitted to the parliament. In substance, too, the budget deficit was criticized for being too high; current expenditure, instead of going down, actually increased; and scant attention was paid to such issues as agricultural self-sufficiency, rising unemployment, and excess liquidity.

The 1990/91 budget's evident 'bias' in favor of the free market (e.g. the gradual elimination of consumer price subsidies, the refusal to absorb the losses of public enterprises, the introduction of competition among producers, and the withdrawal of privileges of special interests) was bitterly denounced by the *Majles* hardliners. These critics deplored the drift toward a 'capitalistic' economy; renewed dependence on industrial countries; new hardship for low-income groups; and the widening gap between the haves and have-nots. The new trend was attacked by the government's opponents as contrary to Ayatollah Khomeini's wishes and views.[11] The 1992/93 budget emphasized reconstruction of the economy, restructuring of the production base, increased agricultural and industrial output, harnessing inflation, and reducing public sector deficit.

Under the new economic reforms, since 1989/90 fiscal objectives have become less ideological and more concrete. Thus, the goals of the 1993/94 budget have included: the reduction of budget deficit and government borrowing from the Bank Markazi in order to contain liqiudity expansion and inflation; a cut in public expenditure through larger participation of the private sector in the provision of education, health care, and municipal services; larger public investment in infrastructure in the depressed regions of the country; sales of public enterprises to the private sector; special attention to the reconstruction of war-torn areas; low-cost (subsidized) loans to the cooperatives and the private sector for investment in productive activities; and purchase-price guarantees for basic farm products.[12]

The budget bill approved by the *Majles* in February 1993 is credited with three new characteristics. First, borrowing from the banking system is terminated as the rial is officially devalued and the budget deficit is financed by the sale of oil export proceeds at the 'unified' floating exchange rate. Second, the foreign exchange budget is confined to some $3,800 million earmarked for the importation of essential needs by the government itself at the old official exchange rate. And, third, there is greater transparency in the budget document, including the provision for repaying foreign loans, and subsidies for essential items.

The total budget of Rls 54,180 billion consisted of Rls 25,426 billion for the regular government, and Rls 34,732 billion for public enterprises, agencies, and banks. More than 67 per cent of the Rls 23,538 billion revenues was to come from the sale of oil and gas; 23 per cent from taxes; and 10 per cent from non-tax sources. Total expenditure of Rls 23,713 billion was divided between Rls 13,903 billion for ordinary outlays, and Rls 9,810 billion for development activities. The regular budget total was more than twice the previous year's, and its projected revenues from oil and gas, more than three times.[13] Although nominally conforming to the First Plan Law in terms of eliminating the budget deficit, and need for borrowing from the banking system, the 1993/94 budget figures are generally regarded as largely unrealistic. Oil export volumes and foreign exchange revenues are considered optimistic. Non-oil revenues are viewed as unattainable. And, the provisions for repaying foreign debts are not specifically funded. Direct and indirect reliance on oil and gas revenues for more than 80 percent of public revenues in an uncertain and weak global oil market makes the budget document even less credible.

FISCAL DEVELOPMENTS

Table 7.1 presents a summary of fiscal developments since the revolution. In the first two years, projected revenues and expenditures were reduced, but a deficit still emerged, and this had to be financed by the new issues of the 2–7 year treasury notes. The inability to use the funds appropriated for public investment helped to reduce budgeted expenditure, but projected revenues also fell short of targets. The outbreak of the Iraq war in September 1980 significantly affected the fiscal balance, thereby reducing actual revenues to only 57 per cent of the budget estimate. The deficit was financed mainly by borrowing from the central bank (71 per cent), and the new issue of treasury notes was used solely to replace maturing securities during the year. Public revenues improved in 1981/82, but actual receipts were still 28 per cent short of the projected figure. A larger portion of the deficit was financed by borrowing from the banking system (78 per cent), while returns of the principals from foreign loans, and advances on future oil sales financed the rest. New treasury notes were again issued to redeem previous obligations. The increase of the annual budget deficit over the projected figure, and measurable deviations of realized values from budget estimates, continued through 1985/86. The gaps between income and expenditure were also financed by borrowing from Bank Markazi by as much as 85 per cent in some years. New treasury notes were also issued to meet the commercial banks' obligations to purchase these assets, and to service the public debt.

The fiscal crunch occurred in 1986/87 when the Rls 1,490 billion projected revenues from oil exports turned out to be no more than Rls 417 billion, and the oil share in total revenues dropped from 62.5 per cent in 1982/83 to a mere 20.6 per cent. The budget deficit peaked to a record high of Rls 1,440 billion, four-fifths of which had to be financed by the central bank. The unprecedented budget gap in that year also raised the government's general net debt to the banking system to a record level. Despite a notable improvement in oil revenues in 1987/88, the new record deficit of Rls 1,472 billion was again 21 per cent larger than projected, and some 94 per cent of the new gap had to be financed by central bank credits. The year 1988/89 further added to the government's fiscal woes when another record budget deficit of Rls 2,188 billion was, for the first time, larger than *general* revenues. The budget gap (which neared 9.5 per cent of GDP) was more than 95 per cent financed by Bank Markazi.

The 1989/90 budget showed a marked recovery, after four years of consecutive deterioration, largely due to non-oil, non-tax revenue, following the government's decision to sell foreign exchange earned from oil exports in the free market at free-market rates. Thus, while total expenditure was relatively unchanged, total revenue was enhanced by 45 per cent and the budget deficit was almost halved (i.e. *de facto* devaluation of the Iranian rial). In 1990/91, a 45 per cent increase in oil export revenues, combined with increased tax revenues, and new massive sales of foreign exchange by the government in the free market, almost doubled total revenues. And, while total expenditure also rose by more than 48 per cent, the deficit was brought down by nearly 35 per cent from the year before.

The budgets for 1991/92 and 1992/93 were prepared under the mandates prescribed by the First Five-Year Plan Law of 1989. The law, approving a new medium-term plan (see Chapter 9) required the government, *inter alia*, to: limit increases in the annual budget's current expenditures to 6.6 per cent, and raise development expenditures by 17.3 per cent a year; to reduce the government's dependence on oil income to 24 per cent, and raise revenues from taxes to 44.8 per cent of total revenues; to cut the annual budget deficit gradually from 51 per cent of the total budget to 1.4 per cent by the end of the plan period (and from 9.6 per cent of GDP to 0.2 per cent); to amend the direct taxation law with a view to directing private investment into productive activities; and to establish a unified civil service, with public employee salaries adjusted and streamlined according to 'administrative justice'. Through these measures, the law was expected to reduce the ratio of public outlays to GDP; raise the ratio of total revenues to total output; double the ratio of tax revenues to GDP; increase the ratio of tax receipts to current expenditures from less than 29 per cent to nearly 68 per cent; and, finally, enhance the share of development expenditures (public investment) by more than 50 per cent.

The post-ceasefire budgets have aimed at: reducing the deficit in line with planned targets; shifting public expenditure toward capital outlays; and increasing non-oil revenues through expanded tax coverage, reduced tax exemptions, and reformed tax administration. Yet, success has been small and slow in coming. Nearly 70–80 percent of the total revenue is still directly or indirectly tied to oil export revenues.[14] The budget deficit as a percentage of GDP has been reduced as mandated by the Plan Law, but allegedly through some budgetary legerdemain.[15]

THE REVENUE STRUCTURE

The central government's total revenue is derived from three main sources: oil and gas revenues; non-oil revenues; and special revenues. Oil and gas income accrues from the export of crude oil and natural gas in which the state has a monopoly. Non-oil revenues consist of tax receipts and non-tax earnings. Taxes are levied on income and wealth; on production and consumption; and on international trade.[16] Income taxes extend to public and private corporations, individual wage and salary earners, and the self-employed. There are also levies on 'wealth' (i.e. gifts, inheritance, and real estate transactions). Taxes on production and consumption are in the form of moderate excise taxes on such revenue-generating items as cigarettes, beverages, oil products, and domestically produced automobiles. There are also high taxes on 'luxury' items to limit demand. The relatively smaller significance of excise taxes in public revenues stems from their specificity and inelasticity – relying on fixed rates on a limited number of items rather than a broad-based levy. Taxes on international trade include statutory (and fairly stable) customs duties approved by the parliament; variable taxes called a 'commercial profit' levy proposed each year by the Council of Ministers for parliamentary approval; registration fees for opening letters of credit as regulated by monetary authorities; and other charges (e.g. a 30 per cent surcharge on imported automobiles in effect in 1990). Non-tax revenues consist of receipts from state monopolies, sales of public goods and services; 'profits' from the sale of foreign exchange; exit and passport fees; stamp duties; and income from foreign investment. Special revenues are earmarked for specific tasks, and are always equal to special expenditure.

Under the Islamic Republic, annual government revenues gradually declined from more than 34 per cent of GDP (at market prices) in 1977/78 to about 10.5 per cent in 1988/89, before turning up again to about 31 per cent in 1992/93. A sharp drop in oil and gas revenues, a fall in tax receipts, and the sluggish rise in other sources of income were largely to blame. Excluding petroleum revenues, the government's tax receipts fell from the already low level of 7.5 per cent of GDP in 1977/78 to 4.7 per cent in 1990/91 – probably one of the world's lowest ratios – before heading up to 6 per cent in 1991/92, owing to the expansion of the tax base, reduction and exemptions, and improved tax collection. Only non-tax revenues achieved a slight increase over the years. And only the sale of foreign exchange in the free market at the free-market rate (i.e. indirect oil revenues) boosted receipts from this source after 1989/90.

The fall in oil revenue was partly the result of the limited volume of crude exports caused by the war-related damage to the oil facilities and the depressed price of oil in some years. But the main reason for the declining oil-GDP ratio was the government's deliberate policy of calculating the value of its petro-dollars at an artificially overvalued (and increasingly unrealistic) official rate of Rls 70=$1.[17] The decline in tax revenues in real terms was caused by a sharp drop in foreign trade taxes due to a reduced volume of imports, a shift in the composition of imports from high- to low-priced items, foreign exchange shortages (and rationing), and the use of over-valued exchange rates which reduced the tax base.[18] There was also a decline in taxes on production and consumption due to the lack of a broad-based excise tax.

Broadly viewed, total government revenues after the revolution were adversely affected by the inelasticity of the tax system; increased tax exemptions given to government wage and salary earners; numerous tax holidays granted to certain agricultural and industrial activities, and to nearly all semi-public charitable foundations and their affiliate enterprises; liberal deductions allowances (of up to 30 per cent of individual and corporate incomes) for contributions to charity; significant weaknesses in tax collection; and, finally, a slowdown in economic activity, and changes in income distribution.

Under these circumstances, direct oil revenues accounted for a large, albeit fluctuating, share of public revenues over the 14-year period, peaking at 62.5 per cent of total revenues in 1982/83, but falling to 21.5 per cent in 1986/87 before rising to 67 percent in the 1993/94 budget. Tax and non-tax revenues both increased their shares of total revenues. In the tax group, the best performance was shown by income taxes, and the poorest by import taxes which showed substantial relative declines, largely because of the use of the official exchange rate for custom calculation. Non-tax revenues increased their share, mostly due to the profit from the sale of dollars at free-market rates. Corporate tax receipts accounted for about half of tax revenues from income and wealth; the largest part of corporate taxes were paid by public corporations (mainly Bank Markazi) and the enterprises under the supervision of government ministries and agencies. Individual income taxes provided only one-third of total taxes. Despite import duties and surcharges of as much as 500 per cent on certain items, the contribution of trade taxes to tax revenues remained low due partly to under-invoicing, placement of imported items in lower duty categories by customs inspectors, and the conversion of foreign exchange invoices into the Iranian rial at the official exchange rate. Excise taxes – the most effective (albeit regressive) means of taxation in Third World countries – were always an insignificant part of the Iranian tax system due to their narrow base, small amount, specific nature, and, particularly, the low (controlled) prices of the goods on which they were levied. The unusually high top marginal tax rate, applied to corporations as well as individuals, often served as an incentive for tax evasion. Finally, the government's inability to collect legitimate and reasonable taxes from domestic economic activity was routinely deplored not only by outsiders, but by *Majles* deputies and government authorities themselves.[19]

The income tax code was thoroughly revised by the 3rd *Majles* in early 1992. The new rate schedule ranges between 12 and 54 per cent on income from wages, salaries, rent, and corporate profits. Generous tax exemptions were granted to government employees and low-wage workers. Most of the provisions of the new code deal with a long list of tax exemptions, deductions, and holidays granted to the export of handicraft and industrial wares, non-oil traditional exports, domestic farming, petrochemicals, educational and sports facilities, and others.

COMPONENTS OF THE EXPENDITURE

Public expenditure is divided into regular and special outlays. Regular expenditure consists of standard government expenses (covering law and order, welfare, and development). These are divided into *current* (or ordinary) expenses of running the state's basic functions, and *capital* (or development) appropriations for investment in public development projects. Current expenses include general government services; national defense; social services (e.g. education and health); and economic services (e.g. agriculture, water resources, energy, manufacturing, transport and communications). The development budget is also divided into these four categories. Special expenditures are financed by special levies, and are always equal to special revenues. Subsidies are part of regular expenses.

During the 1980s, despite a costly and devastating war, the influx of refugees, and a rapidly rising and more demanding population, the government managed to contain public expenditure within tolerable limits. But the compression was achieved mainly through: cuts in public investment, and non-completion of projects started under the previous regime; a moderately successful wage restraint policy; and a gradual shift of many public services to the private charitable foundations and semi-private social services organizations.

Public expenditure thus registered a significant decline under the revolution from 46.5 per cent of nominal GDP in 1977/78 to less than 19.5 per cent in 1991/92. Total public outlay increased in the first four years of the decade in line with increases in oil revenues; they fell in the subsequent three years following the sharp reduction in petroleum receipts. With the end of the war, and the beginning of reconstruction, all public outlays began to rise rapidly.

Current outlay fell from 26.6 per cent of nominal GDP in 1977/78 to about 12 per cent in 1991/92, while capital spending was down to about 5 per cent from nearly 20 per cent during the same period. The share of defense expenditure responded to the exigencies of the war, and ranged between 12.5–15 per cent of total expenditure, peaking at the height of hostilities.[20] While the share of social services (education, health, housing and welfare) in total expenditure increased over the period, the share of economic services decreased slightly. There was also a slight decline in the share of general services.

The figures presented in Table 7.1 do not include substantial private financial contributions to the war effort, thus limiting increases in the disclosed defense budget to merely 4 per cent a year on average. There is also an item in all the annual budgets called 'other expenditures' which runs as high as 20 per cent of the total in some years. These unclassified outlays are unexplained in their composition, thus preventing an evaluation of their changes over the years. Total government expenses are also somewhat understated, as non-financial public sector outlays incurred by public enterprises, foundations and non-government agencies engaged in public services are not always included in the total figure.

The breakdown of total current expenditure into various components in each category is not available. By some estimates, more than 60 per cent of total outlay in recent years was absorbed by the wage bill (consisting of wages, salaries, bonuses, fringe benefits and pensions). Purchases of goods and services accounted for about 20 per cent. The rest consisted mostly of grants and transfers to public entities. Since there is no interest charged by Bank Markazi on government borrowing, the interest payments on public debt have been relatively insignificant. Despite several increases in the rates of return on other financial instruments, the rates of charges on government securities still range from 4 to 7 per cent depending on maturity, but are invariably below corresponding rates for other assets. Capital expenditure commonly consists of the acquisition of capital goods and land, and various outlays in services, labor training, consultancy, etc., the breakdown of which is not published.

Part of the annual public expenditure also consists of budgetary transfer to various public sector enterprises in order to make up for their financial losses. Public enterprises receiving budgetary transfers include: the Agricultural Bank; Iranian National Air Line (Iran Air); Iranian Postal Company; Iranian Radio and Television; National Grain Board; IRNA News Agency; Organization for Promotion of Agricultural Cooperatives; Organization for Procurement and Distribution of Seeds; Organization for Promotion of Children's Education; regional water authorities; and others. In 1991/92, these transfers were estimated to reach Rls 250 billion. More than half of the total was earmarked for the national airline (20 per cent) and the state radio-television (35 per cent). The subsidies that are included in the national budget amount to about 1–1.5 per cent of total government expenditure. Subsidization of essential consumer goods is carried out through the Organization for the Protection of Consumers and Producers, and is not totally reflected in the general budget. The OPCP receives part of its resources from the government and another part from the price differentials between imports and the domestic output of certain commodities. Total subsidies effected through OPCP are estimated at about 1.6 per cent of GDP in 1992/93.[21] Government subsidies paid to producers and distributors included outright cash grants to the Fertilizer Distribution Company, the Consolidated Bus Company, and the Farm Machinery Expansion Agency; bonuses to dairy farmers; transportation facilities to the Central Organization of Rural Cooperatives, assistance to defray gasoline costs of taxi drivers; indemnifying agri-business company losses; paying for free school meals; and, of course, lowering the price of staple foods (wheat, sugar, vegetables oil, and others). Table 7.4 shows a brief summary of public subsidies through OPCP. OPCP plans to reduce fertilizer and sugar subsidies by 20 per cent a year starting in 1992/93. Milk subsidies are to end by 1994/95. Wheat subsidies, however, are targeted to rise due to larger government procurements from farmers, and higher procurement prices.

No consolidated account of public subsidies for all goods and services is available. Private estimates vary considerably.

According to President Rafsanjani's report to the *Majles*, as part of the 1993/94 budget bill, 21 per cent of the total government expenditures in 1991/92 constitutes public transfer payments. Per capita public subsidies out of the general budget in 1991/92 amounted to Rls 45,000 as compared to Rls 18,000 in 1988/89. 'Hidden' subsidies in the form of reduced prices of bread, water, electricity, fuel, and other essential items sold to the public by government agencies also were on the rise. The per capita subsidy for bread alone in 1992/93 was Rls 20,000; for fuel, Rls 167,000.[22]

BUDGET DEFICIT AND FINANCING

Overburdened by the cost of conducting the war, handicapped by the difficulties of collecting taxes under exceptional circumstances, and committed to reducing the tax burden on the poor, the Islamic Republic experienced a continuous, and often large, fiscal deficit in every year after the revolution. Starting with a budget deficit equal to about 8.5 per cent of GDP in 1977/78, this jumped to 14.6 per cent in 1980/81 before falling to 4.1 per cent of GDP in 1985/86 thanks to a rise in oil revenues and a similar improvement in non-oil revenues. With a sharp drop in oil prices in 1986/87, the escalation of the war, and the accumulated effects of increasing economic isolation, came a new deterioration in the government's fiscal position. The gap began to widen once again, reaching more than 9.8 per cent in 1988/89 – raising the yearly average for the ten-year period to about 7.7 per cent. With the cessation of hostilities in 1988, the recovery of oil prices, and increased domestic economic activity, the overall fiscal deficit moved downward to 6.6 per cent of nominal GDP in 1989/90. The authorities' decision to sell a significant volume of foreign exchange earnings in the free market at near free-market rates after 1989 suddenly and substantially boosted the government's non-tax revenues, and reduced the deficit to about 2.3 per cent of nominal GDP in 1991/92. Without the sale of foreign exchange in the open market, the figure would have been 7.5 per cent.

The actual magnitude of the *total* public sector deficit, however, is believed to be larger than these figures. The discrepancies existing between the published fiscal and monetary accounts have led to the conclusion that the overall budget deficit shown in Table 7.1 relates only to the *non-financial* public sector. That is, the reported general government deficit excludes the cash losses generated in central bank operations (such as, bad loans and unpaid interest on the central bank loans to the government), the imputed cost to the banking system of their subsidized loans to public enterprises, and the public agencies' accounts of their own shortfalls. If the deficit of the *financial* public sector (the central bank and nationalized banks) are added to that of the government's, the total public sector gap might average about 9.8 per cent of GDP per year in the 1980/81–1988/89 period, and 3.5 per cent thereafter.

The annual public sector deficits (both of the general government and of the public agencies and enterprises) after the revolution were virtually all financed by the domestic banking system, and in reality by the central bank itself. In some years, when public agencies were assisted in repaying part of their loans to commercial and specialized banks, the central bank in fact supplied more than 100 per cent of total bank finance. National accounts show that during the 1980s, the budget deficit was also regularly financed in a very small way with an external net transfer from abroad (e.g. interest and principal repayments on previous loans and investments). Foreign financing provided less than 1 per cent of the total gap.

THE FISCAL POLICY STANCE

The government's current resolve is to: reduce the budget deficit to less than 2 per cent of GDP through a reduction of public expenditure to below 20 per cent of GDP; emphasize capital outlays at the expense of current programs; and increase the share of non-oil revenues – both taxes and non-tax incomes – in the total receipts. For the near future, however, the planned increases in total revenues are based mainly on larger oil revenues, including income from the sale of foreign exchange. And the reduction in the budget deficit is to be realized from exchange depreciation rather than a significant cut in non-essential current expenditures, or a substantial increase in tax revenues. An increasing reliance on oil income, in turn, would make government finances more vulnerable to fluctuations in the world oil market, and make a hash of program budgeting.

For this reason, the authorities plan to take a series of measures aimed at reducing or eliminating a broad range of tax exemptions and subsidies, and to diversify non-oil revenue sources through the establishment of a broad-based consumption tax, more realistic real estate valuation, and more effective tax collection. In addition, steps are expected to be taken toward import-tariff restructuring, and the readjustment of the import-valuation exchange rate. The gradual sale of money-losing public enterprises to the private sector should also reduce total annual expenditure while bringing in some welcome receipts.

APPENDIX: PARASTATAL FOUNDATIONS

Iran's post-revolution public sector has included a number of parastatal organizations in the form of semi-public foundations, frequently under the direction or influence of religious leaders. These 'revolutionary' institutions – *bonyads* – currently own hundreds of private companies, farms, hotels, theaters, newspapers, and other properties confiscated from wealthy pro-Pahlavi Iranians who were arrested, imprisoned, executed, or who fled the country during or after the revolution. These organizations are responsible for a variety of economic and social functions ranging from publishing daily newspapers to providing housing for the poor. They commonly operate as an executive arm of the government in many nationalized or confiscated companies. Most of these 'charity' organizations are in effect responsible to no one but themselves for their institutional accounts, the use of their revenues, or the efficiency of their operation. The total budget of these foundations in 1992/93 was estimated at Rls 6,000 billion, or nearly half of the government's national budget. Of these *bonyads*, the following are of special significance due to their far-flung economic activities.[23]

Bonyad Mostazafan va Janbazan (Foundation for the Oppressed and the Disabled) was created in March 1979, ostensibly to take over and manage 'the wealth of the Pahlavi family' and those connected with the royal court who had allegedly amassed 'illegitimate' wealth. The resources of the new foundation were to be used to improve 'the living conditions and the housing needs' of the oppressed. The organization was to operate on a 'not-for-profit' basis, using the revenues from its own holdings and fresh private contributions to finance its welfare activities. Although a semi-private agency, the foundation was exempted from both taxes and public accountability, i.e. from the rules and regulations of the General Accounting Law to which all public organizations are subject. By 1983/84, the foundation reportedly owned or had interests in: 64 small and large mines; 5,000 small productive units; 20,000 real estate properties; nearly 150 industrial enterprises (in metals, plastics, textiles, construction materials, food, chemical, electrical, ship building, and ornamental objects); 140 construction firms; 250 commercial and trading companies; and three of Tehran's leading newspapers – in addition to unspecified numbers of farms, parcels of land, houses, theaters, and over $280 million of personal property (including carpets, automobiles, jewelry, antiques, and other valuables). In 1992, the foundation had become a vast conglomerate, employing more than 65,000 people and running an annual budget of $10 billion, nearly 10 per cent of the government's own budget.[24]

Bonyad-e Shahid (the Martyr Foundation) was established in March 1980 in order to administer veteran affairs, and to provide for the needs of the martyrs' families as well as of the disabled. The resources of this foundation are obtained from a special allocation in the general budget, private contributions, and expropriated wealth and properties placed at its disposal. In 1991/92 the foundation owned 150 companies in agriculture, mining, construction, and trade, with over Rls 160 billion of estimated annual sales.

Bonyad-e Mohajerin-e Janq (Foundation for the War Refugees) was created by an act of the *Majles* in June 1981 as an adjunct to the Ministry of Interior. Its responsibilities were to centralize the socio-political, economic, and health affairs of war-ravaged areas, assist refugees in their temporary resettlement problems, and help plan the reconstruction of war-torn areas after the war in order for the refugees to return to their homes. The resources of the foundation were provided by a special appropriation in the general budget, gifts of cash or kind from private sources and agencies, and income derived from investment in various projects entrusted to it.

Bonyad-e Maskan (the Housing Foundation) was set up in June 1979 as a not-for-profit, semi-public organization to house the poor, particularly in rural areas. The foundation's main duties were to construct and repair low-income housing units directly, or to provide interest-free loans to the poor to do the same; encourage and direct investment funds to the economically deprived and depressed, as well as tribal, areas of the country; and cooperate with other agencies in planning, research and studies in housing construction, building materials, rural environment, and housing education. Financial resources were to come from private contributions to a Bank Melli account called 'Account #100 of the Imam', assistance from the Foundation for the Oppressed; appropriation from the government's development budget for 'rural housing'; borrowing from the banking system; and income from production and distribution of building materials. By the last count, the Foundation had more than 200 branches in the provinces.

The *Jehad-e Sazandegi* was established in the summer of 1979 by a group of unemployed Islamic graduate students to find work and help the rural population improve their farm and livestock production. The service was later extended to include better rural social services, build and maintain rural roads, expand water resources and maintain irrigation canals, and improve health, education and welfare of rural inhabitants. The *Jehad*'s budget was to be provided by the central government, provincial governments, self-help contributions, and its own revenues. This foundation was later made into a full-fledged ministry. (See Chapter 11.)

There are several other similar institutions now in full operation, of which *Bonyad-e 15-Khordad*, and *Komiteh-e Emdadi-ye Imam* are the most prominent. Under the new privatization drive, some of these foundations have agreed to sell part of their companies and properties to the public directly, or through the Tehran Stock Exchange.[25]

As part of the new reform process aimed at fiscal realignment, and better demand management and resources allocation, the government is reportedly prepared to review the status of these foundations and their operation. As a first step, designed to place public and private enterprises on an equal footing, these foundations are to lose their preferential import licensing, their access to foreign exchange at the advantageous basic rate, and their tax-exemptions, as of the beginning of 1992/93.

NOTES

1. The government's per capita expenditure in real terms is estimated to have declined by 70 per cent between 1976/77 and 1992/93.
2. While the regular government budget was Rls 25 trillion, the budget of public enterprises amounted to Rls 37 trillion, and that of charitable foundations around Rls 7 trillion.
3. Of the 2300 'public' enterprises in 1992/93, only 230 were under *direct* government control. Yet, even some 45 per cent of the enterprises under direct control did not bother to submit their budgets for parliamentary approval and escaped auditing by the General Accounting Office. *Kayhan Havai*, January 20, 1993.
4. Between 1978/79 and 1982/83, three consecutive laws were passed by the regime to change tax rates for wage and salary earners in the private sector, presumably in the direction of progressivity. See *Barrasi-e Tahavolat-e Eqtesadi-ye Keshvar Ba'ad Az Engelab* (Review

of Post-Revolution Economic Changes) Tehran: Bank Markazi Jomhuri-ye Islami-ye Iran, 1984.

5. In some years, 1986/87 for example, only half of the projected total revenues and a scanty 40 per cent of the anticipated oil revenues, actually materialized.

6. The minimum salary for government employees was raised to Rls 25,000 a month. Up to Rls 30,000 a month of salaries became tax exempt. The gap between the lowest and highest salaries was reportedly reduced from 60 times to only 6 times. See *Ettela'at*, 25 Tir, 1358.

7. See statement of Prime Minister Mir Hossein Musavi in submitting the 1361 (1982/83) budget to the *Majles*, *Ettela'at*, 6 Bahman 1360, p. 5.

8. In the 'comprehensive' budget, the main document included transfers from the treasury to public enterprises for their current or investment outlays as well as transfers made by those enterprises to the treasury in the form of income tax payments, dividends and other payments. Thus, while the budget did not give a detailed account of the enterprises' operations, it did reflect their net fiscal position vis-à-vis the treasury.

9. *Ettela'at*, 5 Bahman 1361.

10. For example, the 1988/89 budget was initially expected to borrow only Rls 1,338 billion from the banking system, but ended up with a loan of Rls 2,146 billion by the end of the year.

11. *Iran Focus*, April 1990, pp. 9–10.

12. *Kayhan Havai*, December 11, 1991, and October 14, 1992.

13. *Kayhan Havai*, December 23, 1992, pp. 14–15.

14. See *Kayhan Havai*, January 29, 1992 and February 12, 1992.

15. *Kayhan Havai*, December 11, 1991, p. 9. The Rls 623 billion budget deficit for 1992/93 – the ceiling mandated by the Five-Year Plan legislation – was considered fictitious by a *Majles* deputy who accused the government of having inflated the projected price of oil (and oil revenues) in order to keep the budget gap within the prescribed limit. *Kayhan Havai*, January 8, 1992, p. 24.

16. A one-time tax on wealth of over Rls 100 million was imposed after the ceasefire in 1988 to help pay for reconstruction costs. According to a *Majles* deputy, however, no more than 10 per cent of the intended revenue was collected before the law's expiration in 1992. *Kayhan Havai*, January 15, 1992, p. 24.

17. The conversion of only 20 per cent of foreign exchange received from oil exports in 1988/89 at the prevailing free market exchange rate of Rls 1400 = $1 would have almost totally financed the government's (post-revolution record) budget deficit.

18. For example, customs duties on an import invoice of $1 million for an imported item, which might have cost the importer Rls 600 million at the 'competitive' exchange rate (Rls 600=$1), were calculated on the basis of only Rls 70 million at the official rate (Rls 70 = $1), and taxed at the corresponding tariff schedule. In such cases, the duty paid

to the government, say 20 per cent *ad valorem*, would amount to a small fraction of true import cost. A small adjustment of this practice was made in 1991 under which goods brought in by travellers were assessed (and taxed) at the *competitive* rate, and later at the floating rate.

19. It is estimated by the authorities that only 50 per cent of taxes due are collected annually, and the other half are variously evaded.

20. The war budget, according to some reports, was regularly understated at around 13 per cent of the total budget, whereas in reality, some 35–46 per cent of state expenditure was probably devoted to the war. See *The Economist Intelligence Unit*, 'Iran: Country Profile 1991–92', p. 37. See also *Echo of Iran*, 'Economic Bulletin', 17 March 1987, regarding statement by some public officials putting these expenditures at between 30 to 40 per cent of total outlay. Cf. *Kayhan Havai*, January 3, 1988.

21. Subsidies to agriculture throughout the 1980s averaged less than 5 per cent of the government's annual budget deficit – not a significant fiscal burden at face value. But, since the $2–$3.5 billion of foreign exchange spent each year on food imports (and other farm inputs) are calculated at the official (and enormously overvalued) exchange rate of about Rls 70 = $1, the true cost of food subsidization may be understated by a factor of 10 to 15.

22. *Kayhan Havai*, December 23, 1992. The figures cited by the president are presumably notional.

23. See *Barrasi-ye Tahavolat* (1984), pp. 268–280. For a critical evaluation of these welfare organizations, see Bahram Tehrani, *Pajuheshi dar Eqtesad-e Iran 1354–1364* (Study on the Iranian Economy 1975/76–1985/86) (Paris: Khavaran, 1986), pp. 453–529. See also 'Clergy Capitalism', *The Wall Street Journal*, May 5, 1992.

24. See *Ettela'at*, 17 Bahman 1362; *Kayhan Havai*, January 22, 1992; and *MEED*, April 24, 1992.

25. See *Iran Focus*, February 1990, p. 16.

8

Banking and monetary policy

The Iranian banking system under the Islamic Republic consists of the Bank Markazi (central bank) in charge of the normal functions of a central monetary authority; six commercial banks; three specialized investment credit institutions; and several non-bank financial institutions.

By law, all banks and insurance companies are nationalized, and operate under government direction. The impetus for the nationalization of financial institutions in 1979 was provided by both the Islamic Republic's ideology of controlling the economy's commanding heights, and the necessity of rescuing many private banks on the verge of collapse due to revolutionary turmoil, physical damage, massive withdrawals, and the exodus of many of their owners and managers. Foreign bank representative offices in Iran were all closed by February 1980, but some were later re-opened for limited operations.

The Banking Nationalization Act involved the regrouping and reorganization of all existing banks, and the takeover of the new banking network by the state.[1] As a result, 22 of the 26 commercial deposit banks were merged, while 4 were allowed to continue to operate independently, albeit under government supervision. Thus, the new Bank *Mellat* (People's Bank) and the new Bank *Tejarat* (Commerce) were formed from the merger of all other commercial banks.

In the specialized banking field, the new Industrial and Mining Bank took over five existing industrial institutions. The old Agricultural Bank (Bank *Keshavarzi*) acquired the Argicultural Development Bank of Iran and all other credit agencies affiliated with the old Ministry of Cooperatives and Rural Affairs. The new Bank *Maskan* (Housing bank) was formed by the merger of several banks involved in savings and loan activities. Three regional development banks – Azarbaijan, Khazar, and Khuzestan – were merged with Bank *Saderat-e* Iran which, along with Bank *Melli* Iran, Bank *Refah-e Kargaran*, and Bank *Sepah*, provided a network of major commercial banks.

In the wake of the revolution, all insurance companies, with the exception of the government's Iran Insurance Company, were privately owned and operated, many under joint ventures with international companies. The nationalization of the insurance industry affected seven companies that were joint ventures, with foreign interests ranging from 20 per cent to 35 per cent. Altogether, a dozen private companies were involved. In 1988, nine nationalized insurance companies (Arya, Omid, Pars, Tehran, Tavana, Hafez, Sakhteman va Kar, Sharq, and Melli) were all merged into Dana Insurance Company to function along with three other large insurance corporations, namely Alborz, Asia and Iran. The supervision of these state corporations was entrusted to the Central Insurance Agency, within the Ministry of Economy and Finance.

The Western-style Iranian banking system was changed by the *reba*-free (no interest) Banking Law of August 1983 which went into effect on March 20, 1984. The objectives and functions of the (interest-free) banking system were declared to be: the establishment of a monetary and credit system based on righteousness and justice with a view to systematizing a proper issuance of money and credit for a healthy and progressive economy; the use of monetary and credit tools to promote the objectives, policies, and economic programs of the Islamic Republic (including the creation of a just and equitable society, the elimination of poverty, and attainment of national self-sufficiency); and thirdly, the preservation of the value of money, creation of balance-of-payments equilibrium, and promotion of commercial exchanges.[2] In practice, the interest-free banks were expected to become partners, rather than mere creditors, in development projects. This partnership was also to serve the interests of the so-called neglected sectors (such as, agriculture, the under-developed regions, and small-scale undertakings) at the expense of previously favored activities (such as, large-scale industries, real estate development, and 'non-productive' services).

ISLAMIC MODES OF BANKING

Under the current Islamic banking system, there are essentially ten separate ways through which banks can make use of recourses (such as deposits) in financing personal needs, trade and business requirements, and longer-term investment.

1. *Qarz ol-hasaneh*, or interest-free loans to individuals, for the purpose of meeting the objectives of paragraph (b) and (i) of Article 43 of the 1980 Constitution (e.g. providing tools of trade for workers who lack these means; meeting urgent and unexpected needs of individuals; and facilitating production of agricultural, livestock, and industrial goods). The expenses of making such loans are borne by borrowers as fees or charges.
2. Partnership (*mosharakeh*) with individuals or corporations in industrial, commercial, or service undertakings, whereby the bank takes a share in the enterprise's equity in either direct or portfolio form, and receives part of the profit.
3. Direct investment in profitable projects, with at least 40 per cent of total required outlay to be provided out of long-term deposits at the bank's disposal, subject to the central bank's supervision as to the nature of the product (i.e. not 'luxury' or non-essential goods).
4. Limited trade partnership (*mozarabeh*) whereby the bank provides initial capital to commercial traders, both individuals and companies, preferably cooperatives, who engage in trade and business (other than imports). Profits from the undertaking are divided under specified terms at the end of the contract.
5. Forward purchases (*salaf*) of goods from productive enterprises with a view to providing them with working capital, under specific rules and regulations approved by the Council of Ministers. Thus, instead of lending medium-term money, or discounting an enterprise's notes, the bank buys part of future products at a fixed price, takes delivery of the goods later, and sells them in the market to recoup its outlay.
6. Instalment sales (*agsati*), whereby the bank undertakes to assist prospective producers (or home buyers) with needed funds by first purchasing machinery, equipment, tools, spare parts, raw materials, and other needs of enterprises in industry, farming, mining and services (or housing units needed by individuals); and then selling these items to applicants on instalment at cost plus profit under specific regulations.
7. Leasing with obligation to buy (*ejareh be shart-e tamlik*),

under which banks buy real estate or other assets needed by enterprises or individuals and lease these properties to them, for a profit, and with an irrevocable proviso that the lessee must purchase the property at the end of the contract and receive the deed, subject to specific rules. This differs from (6) in that there the deed is transferred at the time of the signing of the contract, with the bank holding a lien on the property, whereas under (7) the title is transferred at the end.

8. Service contract (*joaleh*), or an undertaking by the bank or the customer to pay a specific sum or service fee in return for a service as specified in a contract. Thus, the bank providing customary banking services (money transfers, cashing commercial paper, or handling other transactions) is entitled to a service fee. In practice, all regular banking services not carried out under other titles are performed under this category.

9. Farm leasing (*mozara'eh*), whereby banks lease their farm lands to farmers, or provide the latter with seed, fertilizer or cash, for a specific period, with the harvest divided in a specified ration between the two sides – but, again, without asking a specific, fixed sum as part of the contract.

10. Orchard letting (*mosaqat*), whereby orchards owned (or at the bank's disposal) are leased to fruit growers or other farm entrepreneurs. Alternatively, the banks provide cash, kind or service in return for a share of the produce at harvest time, with no fixed sum obligation on the part of the borrower.[3]

Table 8.1 shows the use of these modes by the banking system in the 1980s. Overseas branches of commercial banks are exempt from observing the Islamic banking rules.

STRUCTURE OF THE ISLAMIC BANKING SYSTEM

Bank-e Markazi-ye Jomhuri-ye Eslami-ye Iran, or the Central Bank of the Islamic Republic, is, by law, in charge of improving the performance of the country's monetary and credit system. In the discharge of this duty, the bank is empowered to use a number of tools and instruments. Broad guidelines are set forth each year by the annual meeting of the bank's shareholders (key economic ministers in the cabinet with the approval of the Council of Ministers) who also prescribe credit policy and short-term facilities. Long-term credit policy objectives (five years or longer) must be submitted to the *Majles* for approval. The Council on Money and

Credit, composed of public officials and private sector representatives, act as the central bank's policy board.

Short-term policy instruments at the bank's disposal consist mainly of credit ceilings, minimum reserve requirements prescribed for commercial and investment banks, and operations in government notes. Several new tools, introduced by the 1983 Islamic banking law, give the bank additional and more specific regulatory power. Of these, four discretionary instruments are the most effective. First, the central bank has the power to set the minimum rate of return (i.e. interest charged by banks) in regular or limited partnerships in each sector; these rates effectively elminate marginal and sub-par projects. Second, by determining the profit-sharing ratio between the banks and their clients in each sector of the economy, Bank Markazi can influence the amount of credit allocated by banks to various sectors. Third, by regulating and changing the rate of services fees (i.e. interest) charged by banks on forward transactions, instalment sales, and lease-purchases, the central bank can regulate the allocation of credit financing for these trades. And, fourth, Bank Markazi has the power to establish maximum limits for participation by banks in capitalization of long-term investment projects; it thus has the power to influence the allocation of investment funds to different sectors of the economy.[4] Table 8.2 shows the monetary accounts of the Bank Markazi.

Commercial banks accept two types of deposit: interest-free *demand* deposits (*qarz ol-hasaneh*), in the form of checking, time or savings accounts; and *investment* deposits, for a minimum of three months (short-term) or more than one year (long-term). There is no guaranteed, fixed-rate, payment-on-demand deposits. But in order to attract such deposits, banks offer depositors periodic prizes in cash or kind, reduction of service charges on bank transactions, and priority in utilizing banking facilities (e.g. credit). Private investment deposits constitute a special relationship between depositors and banks. Unlike the common practice in most other countries, investment depositors are not merely a bank's creditors, but actually its partners in investment (i.e. lending) activities. Banks use these deposits, as the agent of depositors, in various forms of partnership or joint ventures. Profits made in such transactions by banks are shared with depositors according to the volume and duration of the deposits. No fixed amount, or rate of return, can be guaranteed to the depositors in advance. 'Profits' are distributed *ex-post*.

Commercial banks, of which Bank Melli is the largest in terms of assets, are regulated by Bank Markazi. In addition to their reserve requirements with Bank Markazi, commercial banks have been required to buy government notes (of one-year maturity) at periodic intervals at an effective rate of return of 4–7 per cent. Bank Melli receives roughly 40 per cent of its funds from sight and time deposits and 60 per cent from investment-term accounts. It also serves as the government's agent for handling current obligations of the private sector, and thus holds a sight-deposits account for the government. The effective rate of return (lending rate) and the effective rate paid to depositors (in the form of prizes or profit share) vary according to type and duration of transactions. Minimum and maximum rates charged, or paid out, for each category of commercial bank activity are determined by Bank Markazi's Council on Money and Credit in accordance with rules approved by the Council of Ministers.

Specialized investment banks – the Agricultural Bank, the Housing Bank, and the Industrial and Mining Bank – deal mainly in long-term projects of five-year or longer duration in the form of debt financing or equity participation. These banks can and do accept investment-term deposits from the private sector. They are allowed to maintain government-insured checking and savings accounts at no fixed interest, but with possibilities of participating in the bank's net profits. However, with the exception of the Housing Bank, these banks have been unable to attract sizeable deposits. Typically, their main sources of finance are low-cost, long-term government funds, or advances from Bank Markazi. Investment banks are exempt from the obligation to buy government bonds as part of their assets. These banks are, in effect, development finance agencies that are supported by the state to promote fixed investments in prioritized sectors. They offer more attractive terms to their borrowers than commercial banks. In turn, they provide lower-cost and longer-term funds to their customers than the commercial banks. Specialized banks are assisted and appraised by the government on the basis of implicit returns on their investments. The lowest rate is accorded to agriculture in order to help the bank to lower its charges. All rates charged by these banks were below the corresponding inflation rates until 1990/91. Table 8.3 shows the consolidated accounts of commercial and specialized banks.

A very large number of private financial institutions under the name of Islamic 'interest-free loan funds' – so named to avoid nationalization by the government – have also been active in the domestic credit market alongside the nationalized banks.[5] Engaged mainly in domestic and foreign trade, brokerage activities, and services, these private institutions for many years escaped banking regulations and hampered the monetary authorities' attempts at controlling private liquidity and price levels. The funds, particularly those affiliated with the Islamic Economy Organization (originally the Islamic Bank which changed its name in order to evade nationalization), have been able to attract saving deposits from powerful high-income groups in the *bazaar*, and to effectively operate as an independent private bank outside the banking system.

Constant pressures by hardline radicals, and repeated reports of embezzlement and fraudulent activities in the domestic press, finally prompted the government to limit the powers of these organizations. In March 1989, the central banks' Council on Money and Credit issued new regulations concerning the establishment, operation, and financial reporting of these institutions. The funds had to operate as non-trading and not-for-profit units, and were restricted in their operations.[6] As expected, the Coordination Unit of Interest-Free Loan Funds has criticized the new measures as un-Islamic and unconstitutional.

Competing for private sector deposits with nationalized commercial banks and interest-free funds have been the limited partnership companies that promise much higher returns in clearly riskier (and often questionable) activities.[7] These private companies – called *sherkatha-ye mozarabe'i* have been operating on the basis of short-term partnership, in specific commercial projects. These financial companies or investment funds have reportedly been able to offer 36–48 per cent 'profit' a year on deposits, and to successfully compete with regular banks that until recently normally paid no more than 6.5–8.5 per cent a year on short- and long-term deposits. Despite intensive public campaigns in the press and on television against such profiteering, the practice has continued. Although they have lately been somewhat adversely affected by the revival of the Tehran Stock Exchange,[8] they constitute an integral part of the country's financial network.[9]

MONEY AND CREDIT POLICY

The Islamic Republic's monetary and credit policy since the revolution has been virtually dictated by the public sector's financial requirements. The monetary authorities' obligation to finance annual budget deficits, and their statutory mandate to preserve the value of the Iranian rial, have overshadowed all other considerations. Bank Markazi has almost obsequiously lent money to the central government each year to meet its expenses, and has enjoined the banking system from unauthorized credit expansion.

For almost the whole of the 1980s, the principal policy instrument employed by Bank Markazi to control the overall annual expansion of credit, as well as its sectoral allocation, were: quantitative quotas assigned to each bank; and administrative guidelines regarding the composition of credit to the various sectors. Within the aggregate credit limit for the year, commercial banks were given a credit ceiling based on their sources and uses of funds. Banks were also advised to observe an order of priorities in the use of their assigned ceilings. For most of the 1980s, until 1988/89, the highest priority was accorded to agriculture, followed by housing and industry, while credit for the services sector was frozen.

Under the current five-year plan (1989–94), the order of priorities was changed in favor of industry, followed by housing and construction, agriculture, and services. After March 1990, bank-specific credit ceilings and quantitative sectoral allocations were terminated, and banks were allowed to lend to the private sector as much as their deposits warranted. However, banks were required to conform with plan priorities on the distribution of their annual loans (investments). Accordingly, in 1993/94, industry was to receive 36 per cent of total credit; housing and construction, 30 per cent; agriculture, 19 per cent; trade and services 8.5 per cent; and exports, 6.5 per cent.

With the change in credit policy from administrative controls to market determination, the effective use of indirect instruments, such as minimum reserve requirements, came into vogue once again. For the first time since 1983, legal reserve ratios were changed in 1991/92. Ratios for demand and short-term investment deposits were raised from 27 per cent to 30 per cent; one-year deposit ratios were left unchanged at 25 per cent; and medium and long-term investment deposits (2–5 years) had their ratios reduced to 15 per cent from 25 per cent. Ratios for specialized banks were left the same at 17 and 15 per cent.

In order to reduce liquidity in the market and to prevent commercial banks from lending beyond the guidelines, banks were required as of the first day of 1991/92 to hold – in addition to their reserves with the central bank – the equivalent of 36 per cent of their demand and sight deposits in the form of government securities. This latter provision was later relaxed.

The 'investment deposit' rates (that is, interest paid out by banks) have varied according to maturity. In the second half of the 1980s, there were short-term deposits (less than a year) receiving 6 per cent annually, and long-term (one-year) commanding 8.5 per cent. In early 1990, three new types of deposits were introduced with maturities of 2, 3 and 5 years. The one-year rate was raised to 9 per cent, with correspondingly higher rates for longer maturities (for example, 13 per cent on five-year deposits). All rates were raised in 1991/92 in order, partially, to compensate for inflation. In March 1992, the rates announced by the central bank – ranging from 7 per cent for short-term balances and 14.5 per cent for five-year deposits – were labelled 'minimum'. Commercial banks were allowed for the first time since 1983/84 to offer market-determined extra dividends and bonuses to depositors, retroactively at the end of the year, if their own individual profits so allowed. Declared rates were to be considered 'interim, expected, profits'. As of March 1993, all bank rates were raised to a range of 7.5 to 15 per cent.

Rates of charges on bank loans (investments) were determined by Bank Markazi for most of the 1980s according to the type of project and sectoral priorities. Thus, between 1984/85 and 1989/90, the rates in the agriculture sector were set at 4–8 per cent annually; and services, 10–12 per cent. Beginning in 1990/91, these rates were raised to a minimum of 6–9 per cent for agriculture, and a maximum of 17–19 per cent for trade and services. As of March 1991, the rates for the latter two sectors were allowed to be market-determined – reaching 24 per cent in April 1992. The rates of 9 to 16 per cent for other sectors also represented the minimum payable, and were to be calculated retroactively after the end of the year according to market conditions. Money lenders in the *bazaar* were reportedly charging 30–50 per cent in mid-1992, and 'investment houses' were offering similarly high rates to 'deposit participants'. With effect from 1992/93, all loans and deposits rates are to be determined by individual banks on a competitive basis.

As of March 1992, state commercial banks were authorized to open letters of credit directly for the private sector, and offer their own guarantees for credits from abroad. Because some banks exceeded their monthly hard currency quotas set by Bank Markazi, some delays in payments occurred in June and July 1992 and continued into 1993.

The continuation of arrears resulted in a temporary cessation of new short-term credit from foreign official credit agencies. Negotiations were held during early 1993 for the postponement of maturity dates.

MONETARY AND CREDIT DEVELOPMENTS

In the second half of 1978/79, amid growing political unrest in the country, a major panic erupted in the financial market, and a massive run began on the banks. Withdrawals from banks in September 1978 were three times the normal amount. Between September 1978 and January 1979, commercial banks lost Rls 295 billion in deposits, all of it in the form of currencies and coins in individuals' hands. Only a massive injection of credit into the banking system (Rls 334 billion) by the central bank saved the banks from total collapse. After the establishment of the Provisional Government, a good portion of the withdrawn deposits returned to the banks.

The relative political stability of 1979/80 caused the banking system's net foreign assets to increase sharply, but public sector debt rose by more than twice the private sector's borrowing. With the passage in the summer of 1979 of the bank nationalization decree by the Revolutionary Council, the Council on Money and Credit set the 'minimum guaranteed profit return' (interest) for savings and time deposits at 7–8 per cent. No interest was to be charged on loans and credits to private borrowers. Instead, a 'service fee' and a 'contribution to the guaranteed profit' were to be received, the rate of which differed according to purpose (for example, 4 per cent for housing, farming and manufacturing; 8 per cent for services).

Due mainly to the rising government deficit – caused by depressed private sector activity, and, later, by war-related expenditure – private sector liquidity increased by an average of 22 per cent a year during 1979–82. Despite drastic changes in economic conditions in the early years of the revolution, there were no major changes in the monetary and credit policy. While private deposits with the banking system increased more than 90 per cent between February 1979 and July 1982, bank loans to the private sector rose about 40 per cent, reflecting a stagflation in the economy, and an explosive inflationary potential. To prevent such an eventuality, the Council on Money and Credit in 1982 raised the legal reserve requirements from 12 to 17 per cent (for the first time since the 1978/79 banks' rescue operation) and placed ceilings on bank loans to various sectors. Nevertheless, commercial banks' excess reserves continued to mount due to government budgetary deficits, expansion of private deposits, and depressed conditions in the private sector.

The threat of rising prices led the monetary authorities to raise the minimum reserve requirement on sight deposits from 17 to 27 per cent in the summer of 1983. Private sector liquidity was brought down to an annual growth rate of 17.2 per cent. The slow growth of the banking sector further intensified in 1984/85 (when the conversion of all operations to the new interest-free banking was completed) partly due to unfamiliarity of lenders and borrowers with the new system. As part of the implementation of the new banking law, the Council on Money and Credit established the 'minimum expected profit' in various economic sectors for lending or direct investment by the banks. These rates – ranging from 6 per cent (in agriculture) to 12 per cent (in trade) for lending, and 4 per cent to 8 per cent for investment – replaced previous interests charged by banks.

Until the ceasefire in 1988, the central government's borrowing requirements were the major reason for the credit expansion as claims on the government rose year after year. Due to a reduction of budget deficits in the two post-ceasefire years – resulting from the sale of foreign exchange at market-related rates – the rate of expansion of the banking system's claims on the government was reduced to 11 per cent in 1989/90, and turned negative in 1990/91. The overall net domestic credit expansion reflected mainly the government's budget shortfalls. Bank Markazi's claims on the central government progressively rose from 28 per cent of its total assets in 1979/80, to 83.6 per cent in 1989/90, before declining to 77.8 per cent in 1990/91.

Due mostly to credit restraints imposed by the central bank, claims on the private sector during 1980–88 grew modestly. However, during the following three years, the annual growth of such claims rose considerably, reflecting expanded private sector activity due mostly to economic liberalization and the relaxation of credit controls. Claims on public industrial and commercial enterprises also grew sharply at the beginning of the 1990s due to higher effective costs of imports, following the shift to a more depreciated rial rate. Under the new credit policy, facilities granted to the non-government sector rose, while the government's share declined. The government's cut in its subsidies and grants to public enterprises, and the latter's resort to bank borrowing in order to cover their losses, were the principal factors in this shift.

Net foreign assets remained largely stable for most of the 1980s, although undergoing yearly changes due to the improvement or deterioration in external balances and the government's foreign exchange payment obligations. There was a substantial increase in such assets in 1990–92, due to a temporary rise in oil prices and the repayment of previous obligations by the United States and France.

Under the government's new structural adjustment program – and the so-called domestic oil price rationalization (the valuation of oil export proceeds at free-market rates) – significant changes have taken place in the creation of domestic assets and private sector liquidity. As the financing requirements of the budget were reduced through the sale of foreign exchange in the free market, bank credit was diverted to the private sector during 1990/91. A good portion of this credit went to public enterprises whose output prices were still fixed, but their imported inputs now had to be paid for at the *competitive* exchange rate of Rls 600=$1, instead of the much lower official rate. The trend continued in 1992/93, and accelerated in 1993/94 when all non-essential imports had to be paid for at the devalued floating exchange rate through letters of credit issued by the banking system.

As shown in Table 8.4, broad money (M2) increased during the periods of largest public sector borrowing from the central bank. The broad money base was raised by Bank Markazi through periodic increases in the minimum reserve requirements of commercial and specialized banks, as well as through resort to the use of its net foreign assets. Larger reserve requirements not only supplied additional sources of finance to the central bank, but also more inflation-tax revenues stemming from a larger money base.

Bank Markazi's expansionary monetary policy, made necessary by the perennial budget deficits, induced a number of shifts in monetary aggregates. First, there was a notable shift in the composition of private sector liquidity from currency holdings and sight deposits to savings and time deposits. The shift reflected confidence in the Islamic banking system, and more attractive returns on term deposits. The ratio of quasi-money to broad money that stood at 44.4 per cent in 1981/82 rose to 51.2 per cent in 1990/91, while the share of currency holdings decreased from 26 per cent to 18 per cent, and demand deposits were largely unchanged. Responsibility for increased personal savings also lay with price controls and widespread shortages that left consumers with few alternatives. Second, the ratio of broad money to nominal GDP, that had fallen to 58.2 per cent in 1983/84 went up to 63.2 per cent in 1990/91, indicating a decrease in money velocity and an increase in banking activity. Third, due to the existence of a 'free market' in foreign currencies, private sector savings found an opportune outlet in foreign-currency-dominated assets which gave them higher real returns and also a good hedge against inflation. Real estate was virtually the only rial-denominated asset that gave asset-holders both of these guarantees in some measure. Fourth, the portfolio shift in favor of foreign assets contributed to further devaluation of the rial exchange rate in the free market, and, thus, to further declines in the demand for rial-denominated holdings. Finally, the government's tax collection in real terms declined due to the time lag in tax collection when prices were on the rise.

ISLAMIC BANKING IN PRACTICE

Within the limitations set in place by the monetary authorities, the banking system implemented its mandate by: providing low-cost loans to the agriculture sector for seeds, fertilizer, machinery and crop insurance; by offering incentives for the development and expansion of a viable cooperative sector with a view to launching 'innovative' industrial projects and 'domesticating' imported technology; by participating in large industrial projects (for example, the Mobarakeh Steel Project in Isfahan and the underground Metro System in Tehran) in partnership with the government; by reducing credit to the services sector, and to producers and importers of non-essential items in favor of liberalizing credit for making or importing capital goods; and finally, by helping low-cost housing, small-scale productive enterprises and cooperatives with interest-free loans without onerous collateral. Despite all this, the banking system's performance in the 1980s was anything but vibrant. Encumbered by a maze of regulations, restrictions, and prescriptions, the nationalized banking system operated largely as the regime's financial record-keeper and accountant instead of serving as an engine of growth as prescribed by the Islamic banking law.[10]

A realistic evaluation of the effect of Islamic banking on the post-revolution economy is hindered by several factors. To begin with, as has been pointed out by domestic and foreign analysts, the true financial position of the Iranian central bank and those of the nationalized banks have not always been clear from their annual reports or their profit-and-loss statements due to their operational and accounting methods. Bank Markazi, for example, incurs a 'quasi-fiscal deficit' in its cash flow operations each year as a result of: interest-free loans to the general government; unreported non-performing assets; and statutory advances made to the Treasury at cost mandated in the annual budget. However, the central bank also benefits from the appreciation of the official foreign exchange rate which enables it to pay back the public debt in depreciated rials in the free market (for example, with smaller volume of its foreign assets). Furthermore, the nationalized banks also routinely subsidize public enterprises under their own supervision and other privileged clients (such as, semi-public foundations) by providing them with low-cost loans and credits at negative (below inflation) rates of charges and fees (in lieu of interest).[11] Yet these subsidies are not recorded as bank losses because depositors are not guaranteed any *ex ante* return on their assets, and there is no fixed interest rate on deposits. Depositors are promised a share in the bank's 'profits' each year, and are thus paid according to the rate of return the bank obtains on its assets, whatever it may happen to be in the year past.

Finally, until the government's post-ceasefire economic liberalization, the banking system as a whole was the least active sector of the economy, with a stagnant or negative annual rate of growth. Impediments to expansion and vibrancy stemmed from: early dislocations caused by the revolution and subsequent reorganization and nationalization; the declining trend in private sector activities and investment under an environment of uncertainty; and, most significantly, limitations imposed by Bank Markazi on the use of bank resources. These limitations ranged from the mildly effective higher minimum legal reserve requirements and obligatory government bond purchases, to highly restrictive stiff limits on credit to various sectors and on the type of transactions. Thus, despite a growing volume of private sector deposits (due to rising government expenditure), the banks were unable to increase their lending. Commensurate profits were also limited due to rising idle resources, and because charging and paying rates by banks were both strictly regulated. Yet, while the net rates of return on short- and long-term deposits throughout the 1980s were, with rare exceptions, persistently negative (falling below annual rates of inflation), depositors still found commercial banks to be the safest place to keep their liquid funds for short-term durations. (Table 8.3 shows foreign assets and liabilities of the banking system.)

Due to the heavy concentration of the banking assets on short-term deposits, and the private sector's reluctance to commit funds for long-term financing, bank loans were also mainly utilized to finance short-term trade transactions (for example, hire purchase, instalment sales, limited partnerships, forward purchases, and service contracts). Long-term partnerships for project financing, and direct investment by the banking system in long-term undertakings, constituted a very small percentage of the total operations. In addition to many uncertainties regarding private ownership rights, and the very role and responsibilities of the private sector in the Islamic Republic, the government's own financial requirements pre-empted the use of deposits for long-term financing until the beginning of the 1990s. Iran's commercial banks are also, by international criteria, generally undercapitalized. Bank Melli, for example, as the largest domestic bank and within the world's top 100 banks in terms of assets, had a capital/assets ratio of only 0.43 per cent in 1991. Bank Saderat's was 2.48 per cent. Under the economic liberalization program launched after the ceasefire in 1988, two noteworthy changes have occurred in the banking system. First, banks have been permitted to determine the rates of return on bank deposits, and charges to borrowers, on a competitive basis within broad guidelines. Quantitative credit ceilings on bank lending have been removed, and discretionary power in the allocation of credit has increased. Second, in order to promote private capital investment in long-term projects, Bank Markazi has called for the establishment of 'non-bank credit institutions' in the private sector to engage in a broad range of banking activities.[12] Previously, the absence of opportunities for either self-financing, or using non-bank private sources, led public enterprises to rely exclusively on banks for their investment needs, and this led to rising inflation. The new credit institutions are expected to fill this gap. Awaiting the clarification of some issues regarding the legal status of these entities (e.g. the need for parliamentary approval), four commercial banks have already set up their own investment companies and introduced new products like travellers' cheques and credit cards.

In an apparent (albeit not acknowledged) break with formal Islamic modes, Bank Markazi announced in October 1991 the entitlement of foreign currency deposits in Iranian banks at home and abroad to a fixed 'yield' whose rate was to be announced every day by the central bank. Unlike rial deposits, whose rate of 'profit' was never fixed, and determined *ex post* by banks according to guidelines set by the Council of Money and Credit, foreign currency deposits would evidently enjoy a fixed daily rate called TIBOR, which would be slightly higher than LIBOR (for example, 7.2 per cent on October 22, 1991 versus 6.9 per cent).[13]

The new liberalization move may actually revive the dormant banking enterprise. So far, the regime's claim that Islamic banking has worked without a hitch, and created no turmoil in domestic trade and business, is essentially valid. But the benefits claimed for the new system by its supporters (and the expected advantages enumerated in the 1983 law) have not yet materialized. By all accounts, the banking sector under the Islamic Republic has been the least active sector of the economy. The shift of the traditional system from an interest-bearing basis to a 'profit-and-loss sharing' basis has been smooth, but not visibly productive. In view of the difficulty of creating non-interest-based instruments for financing government deficits, the central bank has been reduced to the proverbial printing press, monetizing the public debt at zero cost to the state. Foreign borrowing and on-going lending have also escaped the Islamic rule.

However, the most important effect of Islamization thus far has been a non-market-oriented approach to the pricing of capital. By restraining banks from competition with one another in negotiating rates of return, the government has denied state financial institutions the flexibility required by changing market conditions, and inadvertently encouraged unsupervised private lending operations at the former's expense. By fixing, until recently, both credit ceilings and returns, and making them unresponsive to energizing economic circumstances, the authorities have severed the link between money rates and inflation, thus hurting both the depositors and the banks. By restricting the use of government bonds, an important monetary control mechanism has been left idle.

To be sure, Islamic banking has worked, but at a high cost. With the annual increase in the (official) consumer price index during 1978–91 hovering at around 18 per cent a year on average, and the rate of return on bank deposits not exceeding 10 per cent a year on average, depositors lost about 8 per cent of their assets' purchasing power each year. With the cost of borrowing money – 6 per cent to 20 per cent for different purposes – almost always below the rate of inflation, bank borrowers received hefty subsidies paid by bank depositors. Those borrowers who bought foreign exchange at the official or competitive rates (below the open-market rate) had an additional windfall profit at the expense of savers and consumers. At the same time, private money lenders in the *bazaar* and *mozarabeh* funds that paid high returns on borrowed capital became the largest segment of the country's most active financial market, ostensibly within the Islamic modes, but in fact flouting the law's spirit.

APPENDIX: THE TEHRAN STOCK EXCHANGE

The market for industrial shares began in February 1968 with a limited annual transaction volume of Rls 15.3 million. During the late 1960s and the early 1970s, the market showed a dramatic rise in volume of transactions. In 1977/78, the value of the shares of 105 companies (industrial, financial, and others) traded in the market amounted to Rls 44,417 million, of which Rls 19,488 million was related to corporate equity shares, and Rls 24,929 million was in government and state-guaranteed bonds. The stock exchange turnover in 1977/78 equalled about one-third of total private sector liquidity. After the revolution, such factors as bank nationalization and the public takeover of industrial enterprises reduced the number of companies listed on the stock exchange to 56. Public debates regarding the religious legitimacy of interest on government securities also cut into demand for these instruments. After the passage of the interest-free banking law in 1983, interest payments on both government and private securities were banned by the religious authorities. No new bonds were issued thereafter.

The decline and rise of the stock market after the revolution were influenced by a number of different factors. Political turmoil during 1978/79 slowed down the activities of the Tehran Stock Exchange by 23 per cent compared to 1977/78, largely due to a sharp decline in the volume of government securities traded in the market. The shares of 105 corporations (24 banks and 81 industrial companies) listed on the stock exchange, however, were more actively traded. The government's decision to nationalize banks and insurance companies in 1979/80 drastically reduced market transactions in both government securities and corporate shares. Total volume of Rls 4,100 million was 88 per cent less than the previous year. In 1980/81, the downward trend continued, with total volume down by 87 per cent, and still no transactions on equity shares. Total activities, amounting to Rls 538 million, were limited to existing government securities. The situation worsened again in 1981/82, with no activity in industrial stocks and a paltry Rls 49 million in other securities – a 91 per cent decline from the previous year. In 1982/83, there was a modest recovery in the market when total volume rose to Rls 50 million, of which a small Rls 2.1 million was spent on industrial securities for the first time after a two-year hiatus. In 1983/84, the volume of transactions dropped to a record low of only Rls 9.2 million, an 86 per cent decline from the previous year. 70 per cent of total transactions, however, involved industrial shares due to the better performance of industrial enterprises. The year 1984/85 saw a reversal of the stock market's doldrums, and the volume of transactions rose to Rls 1,168 million – a post-revolution record high – almost entirely consisting of industrial shares of 23 enterprises (since interest-bearing government bonds were considered unauthorized). An increase in dividends, high returns in some companies, and the brokers' renewed zeal accounted for the increase. Equally effective was the stock exchange's new requirement that all member companies trade their shares exclusively in this market rather than in the *bazaar*. The record for annual transactions was again broken in 1985/86 with a total volume of Rls 1,211 million – almost totally consisting of industrial shares. A 43 per cent increase in the volume of transactions in 1986/87 pushed the value of the shares of stocks of 37 industrial enterprises traded in the market to Rls 1,735 million. There was no trade in government securities. The three-year upward trend in the stock market boom came to an end in 1987/88 when the volume of transactions fell nearly 3 per cent to Rls 1,690 million, all of which related to the shares of 38 corporations. There was no activity around government securities. The volume of trade in 1987/88 was only equal to 0.01 per cent of total private sector liquidity as compared to 33 per cent in 1977/78.

The ceasefire in the Iran–Iraq war, the return of confidence in the investment market, and the relative normalization of private economic activity in the second half of the year, gave a sudden boost to the stock market in 1988/89. Nearly 2 million shares changed hands, belonging to 39 (out of 56) member corporations, and with a total value of Rls 10 billion. The approximately five-times increase in the volume of transactions over the previous year gave the market its all-time record high in the post-revolution period. A new and favorable income tax law also helped the market. The boom continued in 1989/90, with 65 companies listed on the stock exchange, and the shares of 56 actively traded in the amount of Rls 11 billion involving 3.9 million shares. In 1990/91, the total number of shares of 95 companies traded in the exchange reached 13.3 million, worth Rls 65 billion. During 1991/92, the market experienced an extraordinary surge, with some 62.6 million shares of 121 companies worth Rls 478 billion traded, and a new post-revolution record set.[14] The number of companies listed rose to 261 in 1992/93 but the shares of only 107 companies were traded in the exchange at a total value of Rls 352 billion – considerably less than the previous year.

In 1991/92, the National Iranian Industrial Organization, the state banks (especially the Industrial and Mining Bank), the Organization for Promotion and Renovation of Iranian Industries, *Bonyad-e Mostazafan*, and *Bonyad-e Shahid* were among top agencies offering shares of stock of the companies under their supervision on the stock exchange.[15] Volumes ranged from 28 million shares worth Rls 200 billion for NIIO to 191,000 shares worth Rls 1.7 billion for *Bonyad-e Shahid*. NIIO planned to offer all of its shares to the public in 1992–93.[16] Foreign investment is restricted (except in the free trade zones) to 25 per cent of the shares of companies traded on the Tehran Stock Exchange. Portfolio investment, however, does not yet enjoy the legal protection that is afforded to direct investment.

NOTES

1. At the time of bank nationalization in the summer of 1979, the banking system consisted of 36 banks – 26 commercial, 7 specialized, and 3 regional. There was one joint venture government bank, and

one wholly-owned foreign bank. There were 8,274 bank branches of which 2,167 were in Tehran.

2. For the English text of the law, see *MEED*, April 13, 1984, pp. 57–59.

3. For the more elaborate definition of these various modes and their nuances, see Z. Iqbal and A. Mirakhor, *Islamic Banking*, (Washington: International Monetary Fund, Occasional Paper 49, 1986).

4. For most of the 1980s, the minimum and maximum rates of 'expected' return for the various sectors remained unchanged.

5. These so-called *Sherkatha-ye qarz ol-hasaneh* reportedly existed before the revolution in small numbers, but mushroomed after 1979 to some 3,000 companies holding some Rls 1,000 billion of private savings in 1987. See Amirahmadi (1990), pp. 141–142.

6. For details of these restrictions, see *Iran Focus*, April 1989, p. 11 and *Iran Yearbook '88*, p. 238.

7. See *Echo of Iran*, 'Political Bulletin', 9 and 22 September and 6, 13 and 20 October 1987; and *Kayhan Havai*, 27 Mehr and 4 Aban 1367.

8. See *Iran Focus*, December, 1989, p. 14, and January, 1990, p. 11.

9. As of March 1993, Iran's commercial banks included Bank Mellat (People's Bank); Bank Melli Iran (National Bank); Bank Tejarat (Mercantile Bank); Bank Saderat (Export Bank); Bank Refah-e Kargaran (Workers' Welfare Bank); and Bank Sepah (Armed Forces' Bank). Specialized banks consisted of Bank Keshavarzi (Agricultural Bank); Bank Maskan (Housing Bank); Bank Sanat-va-Madan (Industrial and Mining Bank); and Bank Toseeh Saderat (Export Promotion Bank). There were also certain non-bank financial institutions such as insurance companies; pension funds; *qarz ol-hasaneh* funds; *mozarabeh* companies (mutual funds); Iran National Investment; National Industrial Investment Group; Alborz Investment; and Behshahr Industrial Development. The provincial branches of Bank Saderat operate as Bank Ostan. By last count, the commercial banks had 8,681 branches inside Iran and 61 branches abroad, belonging mostly to Bank Saderat and Bank Melli. The specialized banks had 740 domestic branches.

10. A Bank Markazi official recently complained to a foreign correspondent about the central bank's lack of independence to 'act as guardian of the rial' and 'ensure the long-term stable growth of the country'. He continued, 'When there is a law compelling us to meet requirements of the government, then we cannot contain the money supply'. See *MEED*, November 15, 1991, p. 6.

11. A bank official recently explained that the reason the bank's fee (interest) for some industrial loans was 23 per cent a year was because the bank had many statutory obligations that did not produce any profit, and had to be made up through other loans. *Kayhan Havai*, January 29, 1992.

12. See *The Banker*, November 21, 1991.

13. *Kayhan Havai*, October 30, 1991, p. 1.

14. See *MEED*, November 15, 1991, p. 4, and *Kayhan Havai*, December 18, 1991, and April 29, 1992.
15. According to foreign press reports, there have been allegations of false accounting procedures and fabricated profits on the part of some companies – taking the gloss off the stock market's boom. See *Euromoney*, October 1992.
16. A company must show rates of return of over 10 per cent – among other conditions – in order to be listed on the exchange.

9

Planning and development policy

The Islamic Republic's planning concept and machinery were entirely inherited from the Shah's regime, and continued in almost the same fashion afterwards. The idea of accelerating economic growth through medium-term plans came into fashion soon after World War II, when it was thought that a careful husbanding of domestic resources in the service of economic revitalization and national welfare required a structured approach. Pre-revolution planning eyed essentially the public sector, and was only indicative for the private sector. It was often ignored by both, and its exact contribution to Iran's remarkable postwar economic progress was never clearly established.

In the populist and leftist environment of the early revolutionary period, planning's political appeal was at its zenith, and the imperative of orderly economic development through five-year plans was easily inserted in the 1979 Constitution as one of its major provisions. Planning machinery was kept almost intact under the Plan and Budget Organization (briefly as the Ministry of Planning), and the old planning culture and mission largely prevailed. Ironically, while the Iran-Iraq war years were the most critical for careful domestic resource mobilization, central planning was practically moribund; it was revived only after the ceasefire.

Iran's economic planning under the Shah was widely criticized by the opposition for its 'defective' formulation, and its oil-reliant financing. Periodic plans were said to be unduly based on foreign trade instead of domestic products. The Shah's development planning was further accused of emphasizing only the quantitative aspects of growth at the expense of broader social considerations and an equitable distribution of income and wealth. The objective of acquisition and increased material possessions was blamed for the propagation of Western consumerism; the exodus of rural population to cities for work in assembly plants or urban construction; feverish land speculation; and non-productive activities. Harmful economic dependence on foreign markets was claimed to have favorably affected the fortunes of only certain privileged groups. The favored few were said to have monopolized bank credits in order to expand assembly-plant operations, import consumer goods, and offer luxury services. Foreign dependence presumably ushered in foreign inflation which raised internal wage and price levels.

To remedy planning deficiencies and neglect, shortly after the formation of the Provisional Government, the Office of Revolutionary Projects began to prepare a new development program for the establishment of a social, political, and economic system based on the teachings of Islam and directed toward a classless society of 'divine unity'. Both of these social conditions were defined in vague theological and socialist terms. The program, however, was subsequently abandoned after Bazargan's resignation and the dawn of the new constitution.[1]

The 1979 Constitution explicitly made Iran's economic system contingent upon orderly and appropriate planning. According to Articles 3 and 44, 'the *planning* of a "correct and just economic system" in accordance with Islamic criteria is one of the goals of the Government of the Islamic Republic'. In the implementation of this provision, the government of Prime Minister Bahonar asked the Plan and Budget Organization (PBO) to prepare a new plan. By August 1981, a national system of planning was established, and the first five-year plan (1983/84–1987/88) was subsequently submitted to the *Majles* as the first part of a 20-year (1361–1381) perspective. The plan's general orientation was toward 'economic independence', 'social welfare', and 'propagation of the Islamic culture'.

Within the purview of a 20-year endeavor to raise Iran's GDP four times and its per capita GDP two-fold, the Five-Year Plan set a 9 per cent real growth as its basic annual *quantitative* target. A more equitable distribution of annual income in favor of neglected regions and disfavored social groups was its *qualitative* goal. With a view also to redirecting the structure of the Iranian economy away from its alleged dependence on the West, the planners singled out agriculture as the sector to be totally self-sufficient within 10 years. To achieve industrial independence, a significant share of machinery, parts and materials needed in this sector was to be produced at home. Other goals called for reducing the share of oil in the total energy supply from 80 per cent to 50 per cent by using more gas and hydroelectric power. It was planned to cut oil's contribution to the GDP from 20 per cent to 10 per cent, and reduce petroleum's contribution to public revenues. Public expenditures were to be shifted into prioritized sectors (e.g., agriculture, irrigation, education, research, and mining). Public service efficiency was to be enhanced. In addition to these broad objectives, the plan had a series of detailed quantitative and qualitative targets for the two basic sectors: *social* (education and health); and *economic* (agriculture, irrigation, industry, hydrocarbons, transport and communications, and housing). Needless to say, this plan – like those under the Shah – was not a command-type, Soviet-style, allocative blueprint for the economy where various parts supported each other and were supposed to be integrated in a whole. Rather, it was a medium-term 'investment budget' or a list of development projects for the public sector, and an *indicative* guidepost for the private sector. In the view of critics, it was basically a wish list.

The so-called 'economic, social and cultural' development plan for 1983–1988 was presented to the nation under the banner of 'changed priorities' and new policies. The overriding goal of the new plan was declared by the government's spokesman to be a change in the direction and structure of the Iranian economy from a 'bankrupt' position to a 'healthy' state. National self-sufficiency in agriculture within ten years was to crown such a dramatic transformation. Other salient features of the plan were claimed to be the contribution of more than 5,000 'committed and energetic' technicians to its preparation rather than the brain child of a few 'so-called experts'; allocation of larger investment to irrigation, agriculture, education, and mining; extension of urban social amenities to rural areas; the elimination of public subsidies to government enterprises (e.g., telephone and telegraph lines); and termination of government borrowing from the central bank for deficit financing. Finally, the plan was to set prices in such a way as to encourage production, and help the private sector to increase non-oil exports.[2]

Total investment in the plan was expected to be about Rls 12,985 billion ($166 billion). Total outlays were divided between public investment (Rls 7,500 billion) and private fixed capital formation (Rls 5,485 billion). During the plan period, the government's capital outlays were to rise more than 13 per cent a year on average; current outlays were to go up by an average of only 5 per cent per year. Quantitative targets were aimed at an average annual overall real growth rate of 9 per cent derived from an unprecedented 7 per cent annual expansion in agriculture; 14 per cent in industry; and 10 per cent in construction (promising to provide a home for each household by the year 2001). Since foreign borrowing was still anathema to the new regime, the main financing for planned investments was to be provided by oil and non-oil exports. Petroleum exports were assumed to be 2.2–2.5 mb/d of crude at $29 a barrel. Non-oil exports were to increase by 49 per cent annually.

The plan's ambitious growth targets, unrealistic financing assumptions, and politically controversial aspects did not give it much chance for quick approval by bickering *Majles* deputies. With the escalation of war with Iraq, a depressed world oil market, and internal political squabbling within the clerical leadership, the plan bill lingered for two-and-a-half years in the *Majles* committees, and was never put into effect. A revised version, approved by the *Majles* in 1986, dispensed with quantitative targeting altogether, and limited its purview to a number of qualitative generalities, including the completion of existing projects.[3]

Shortly after the Iran-Iraq ceasefire in August 1988, Ayatollah Khomeini, at the formal request of the heads of the executive, legislative, and judicial branches of the government, outlined the basic principles of the country's economic reconstruction. The supreme leadership reiterated the 'neither West nor East' doctrine to still be the overriding principle of the Islamic government. Reconstruction had to be pursued free from dependence on either superpower. Beyond this general edict, the Ayatollah called, *inter alia*, for: maximum assistance to the families of the war 'martyrs', and priority in employment for veterans; the strengthening of the country's military and defense capability and the rebuilding of the arms industry; continued primary emphasis on agricultural self-sufficiency as the guarantor of the independence of other sectors; the expansion of scientific research centers and support of the experts who were 'committed' to the advancement of the most economically relevant science and technology, free from Western or Eastern bias; and appropriate planning, within Islamic precepts, for 'balanced' public welfare. Special attention was paid to the fight against consumerism; encouraging domestic production; the expansion of exports; the reduction of reliance on oil income, and freedom of foreign trade under state supervision with respect to quality and price of imported goods.[4]

The Council of Policy Making for Reconstruction, headed by the then President, Ali Khamenei, made the Ayatollah's recommendations the basis for a new postwar economic plan. The directive on the Comprehensive National Reconstruction Plan was given to the Musavi government to establish special priorities for the oil and gas sector; power generating facilities; agriculture; construction materials and residential housing; industrial enterprises that were labor intensive, quick to renovate, and needed little foreign exchange; and village reconstruction. This directive was subsequently used for further revision of the previous plan into the so-called Musavi Plan. The latter, in turn, was later revised by the new president, Hashemi Rafsanjani, and sent to the *Majles* in August 1989 for final ratification.

The first (post-ceasefire) five-year plan, 1989/90–1993/94, was approved by the *Majles* in January 1990, estimating a total expenditure of Rls 29,316 billion. The plan's comprehensive current scope encompasses such objectives as: restoration of the country's defense capability; reconstruction and development of war-damaged areas; improvement in government administration; population control; and promotion of economic growth. Specific goals of the plan refer to the increase in per capita output; attainment of productive full employment; reduction of economic dependence on the outside world, self-sufficiency in strategic products; the fight against inflation; provision of the citizens' minimum basic needs; and the design of a proper consumption model in line with the people's essential requirements for material and spiritual progress, dignity and freedom.

The plan's total investment of Rls 29,316 billion is to be underwritten by regular government agencies (Rls 8,189 billion), public commercial enterprises (Rls 5,667 billion), and the private sector and the banking system (Rls 15,460 billion). Funds are earmarked, in each sector, for unfinished projects, new projects, and supplementary projects (see Table 9.1). The plan is to be financed largely from domestic sources: public budgets (40 per cent); private savings (27 per cent); and domestic bank borrowing (25 per cent). Foreign financing is limited to $27.4 billion (7.5 per cent), divided into joint-venture arrangements ($10 billion), and foreign borrowing ($17 billion), mostly for power generation, manufacturing projects, petrochemicals, and natural gas.[5]

At the macroeconomic level, the plan aims at fundamental changes in certain aggregate variables: that is, population control, economic structure and growth, public finance, price stability, foreign trade, and sectoral employment. The rate of growth of population is to reach 2.9 per cent a year by the end of the plan period in 1994 (down from 3.9 per cent), indicating an urban growth of 4.4 per cent and rural expansion of 1.2 per cent a year. The plan expects to create nearly 2 million new jobs. Thus, while the country's population is expected to increase by nearly 17 per cent during the five-year period, GDP is estimated to rise by 51 per cent.

A total of $120 billion in foreign exchange is earmarked to be spent during the plan. Oil and gas revenues from exports are forecast at slightly more than $83 billion. Non-oil exports are expected to bring in about $17.8 billion. The Plan Law authorized Bank Markazi to underwrite and guarantee nearly $17.5 billion of foreign borrowing to finance various projects in agriculture, irrigation, industry, petrochemicals, and oil and gas. Another $10 billion was also authorized for borrowing by the manufacturing and mining sectors on a buy-back basis (where lenders would receive principal and interest in the form of product exports). For details, see Table 9.4.

Quantitative growth targets set for different sectors are shown in Table 9.2. Compared to the previous plan, the new targets are more realistic, but still not easily within reach in certain categories (e.g., agriculture, non-energy exports, and housing). The projected magnitude of public and private investment for each year is shown in Table 9.3. The structure of production is to shift towards a larger share for investment, and larger responsibility for the private sector.

The ratio of aggregate investment to GDP is to rise to nearly 17 per cent in 1993/94 (from about 12 per cent in 1988/89). Total consumption is expected to rise half as fast as yearly investment. The government's share in total investment is projected to be 47.2 per cent. As a result, the share of private consumption in GDP is to decline from about 66 per cent in 1989/90 to less than 53 per cent in 1993/94. Given the projected rates of investment and growth, notable changes in the share of major sectors in GDP are to be expected. Thus, the relative share of agriculture in the total product is to decline from 24 per cent to less than 21 per cent; that of services from nearly 52 per cent to 50 per cent. By contrast, the share of manufacturing, mining, water and power, and construction are to increase (Table 9.2).

In the public sector, the principal objectives of the plan are to reduce the size of the government, state expenditures, and budget deficits. These goals are to be reached through: increased tax revenues, limiting public outlays, cost-cutting, and better tax collection; a reduced number of government employees and the transfer of some public activities to the private sector; the maximizing of oil production and exports to increase earnings; a revision in the price of public goods and services and user fees; and a shift of resources from consumption to investment, increased productive capacity, and better utilization of existing plants and equipment. Total revenues are projected to grow from about 12 per cent of GDP in 1988/89 to some 17 per cent in 1993/94, reflecting a substantial average annual growth of public revenues. The ratio of taxes to GDP is to rise to 8.4 per cent. Budgetary expenditures relative to GDP are estimated to fall to 17.3 per cent, reflecting mainly the reductions in current expenditure, and a shift in current development outlay in the latter's favor. The budget deficit is estimated to decline from 51 per cent of total expenditure to only 1.4 per cent by the end of the plan period. As a percentage of GDP, the budget gap is to decline from 9.6 per cent to a mere 0.2 per cent. Public borrowing from the banking system is to decline each year, reaching zero by 1993/94.

With substantial declines in the budget deficit, borrowing from the banking system, and private liquidity, the rate of annual inflation is to subside. Liquidity growth is to be limited to 8.2 per cent a year on average during the plan period (compared to 15 per cent a year in the previous five years) reaching 3.5 per cent by 1993/94. The consumer price index is to fall from about 28.9 per cent in 1988/89 to only 8.9 per cent by the end of the five-year period. A decline in inflation is to redress the balance-of-payments.

In the area of foreign trade, the plan expects 2.2 mb/d of crude export, and total exchange earnings of slightly more than $120 billion ($83 billion from oil, about $18 billion from non-oil, and $19 billion from other sources) over the five-year period. Total imports are estimated at about $115 billion (including $9.5 billion of defense-related items), with consumer goods being gradually replaced by intermediate and capital goods.

Finally, on employment, the plan expects to create nearly 395,000 new jobs every year; to lower the unemployment rate; and to increase labor productivity. During the plan period, 1.9 million people are expected to join the active labor force, which will increase to about 15.5 million. Unemployment is to decline from 2.1 million in 1988/89 to 2.07 million by 1993/94, that is, from 15.9 per cent to 13.4 per cent of the labor fource. Employment in agriculture, industry and mines, and services is to change to 25.4, 29.1, and 45.5 per cent, respectively, of the total labor force.

The principal objectives of the new plan in agriculture are self-sufficiency in food grains and improvement in irrigation. Food security, as one of the country's overriding priorities since the revolution, is once again underscored. In particular, the wheat crop is to increase through improved dry farming and better water use as well as the construction of several new dams. Farm technology is to be enhanced with the twin objectives of increasing both output and yields, mostly through expanded research and extension service. Major increases of 52 to 100 per cent in output over the five years are projected for feed grains, oil seeds, wheat, and sugar beet and cane. The principal aim in this sector is to increase the area under cultivation and to convert close to one million hectares of dry farming to irrigated cultivation. Agricultural imports, 30 per cent of national consumption in 1988/89, are expected to be replaced by domestic production. The sector is also expected to have sizeable surplus for export. Additional water for irrigating expanded acreage is to be provided by as much as 50 per cent from existing dams and the other 50 per cent from the construction of a number of new dams and better husbanding of water currently flowing under traditional irrigation networks.

The plan relies heavily on the expansion of oil and gas production and exports as a major source of contribution to GDP and also as a major foreign-exchange earner. In the oil sector, total production capacity is projected to steadily expand from 3.3 mb/d in 1989/90 to 4.1 mb/d in 1993/94. Daily output of crude oil is to remain at 85 per cent of capacity, reaching 3.5 mb/d by the end of the plan period. Oil exports are estimated to increase from 1.7 mb/d in 1988/89 to 2.3 mb/d in 1993/94. Total refining capacity is expected to rise to about 1.5 mb/d by mid-1994, opening the possibility of exporting surplus refined products for the first time since the Iran–Iraq war. The plan also encompasses some 10 large petro-chemical projects, including the completion of the Iranian Petro–chemical complex at Bandar Imam Khomeini as well as others in Arak, Isfahan, and Tabriz. Natural gas is expected to replace an increasing part of oil consumption as a source of power and fuel for industrial, commercial, and household use.

The major objectives of the industrial sector are to rehabilitate damaged infrastructure; complete unfinished projects; raise capacity utilization; upgrade the technological base; reduce dependence on foreign inputs and technology; increase non-oil exports; and improve industrial management. Within the sector, the plan calls for a shift away from consumer goods industries towards intermediate products (for example, iron and steel, non-ferrous metals, paper, synthetic fibers, and fertilizer), and capital (machinery, transport vehicles and power generators). Only about 10 per cent of total investment in this sector is allocated to consumer goods, compared with 70 per cent to intermediate, and 20 per cent to capital goods. The plan's $20 billion projected foreign exchange investment in industry by public agencies is divided between consumer, intermediate, and capital goods in shares of 21 per cent,

42 per cent, and 30 per cent respectively – with the rest earmarked for rural industries. Another $8 billion in foreign exchange investment is to be carried out by the private sector. A large part of industrial growth is expected from an increase in capacity utilization. The use of existing capacity is projected to rise from an estimated 40 per cent in 1989/90 to about 62 per cent at the end of the period.

The plan specifies an expansion in the role of the private sector, but the government will still maintain control over more than 60 per cent of total investment in industry and also two-thirds of large industrial enterprises. Private sector activities are still largely limited. Privatization efforts involve mostly medium-sized enterprises (such as car manufacturing and petrochemical products). The plan envisages an average growth of 15 per cent a year in the mining sector through utilization of existing capacity. A major expansion of output is envisaged in iron, coal, and copper – by two to three times over the period. Provisions are also made for comprehensive geological mapping, and a large exploration program.

The current plans expect steel output to be increased to a total volume of nearly 9 million tons a year by 1996 through the completion of the Mobarakeh steel's five furnaces, the renovation of the old Isfahan mill, and the improvement of the Ahwaz steel plant. Japan's Nippon Steel Company, and Mexico's Hylsa, are to assist in the expansion and completion of these plants. Aluminium production at Arak and Bandar Abbas is to be aided by Czechoslovakia's Technoexport and Pechiney of France. Automobile manufacturing capacity is expected to rise with the help of British Rover, French Peugeot-Talbot, and other foreign companies. Pulp, paper and cement plants are to be constructed with the help of Austrian, Bulgarian, Canadian, Danish, and German companies. Germany's Lorenz and Siemens will be engaged in upgrading the country's telecommunications network with the goal of installing 12 million telephone lines by 1996. Korean and Norwegian companies are active in other aspects of telecommunications. Plans are underway to double the electricity generating capacity to 35,000 MW in ten years; GEC Alsthom is contracted to provide some 14,000 MW generators to the state's Tavanir Company. Nine new dams under construction in various parts of the country provide hydroelectric potential.[6]

A cursory look at the plan document suffices to show that, despite a new mandate under the 1979 Constitution and the Islamic Republic's promise to change past practices, the nature and quality of planning has hardly improved since the revolution. The new plan is still only a wish list of investment projects and growth targets, with no input-output calculations or consistency. The quantitative relationships within the plan still leave many questions unanswered. And the role of non-governmental players is still murky and unco-ordinated.

As implicitly acknowledged in the plan law, obstacles to the realization of planned targets remain: a shortage of foreign exchange and lack of skilled workers; the under-developed nature of industrial research and development; a multitude of non-qualified industrial managers; lack of co-ordination among industrial policy-makers; a low ratio of industrial investment to GDP; inadequate access to modern technology and, above all, the prevalence of certain political and ideological taboos inimical to a technical/scientific culture.[7]

A MID-TERM REVIEW

The prospects for the successful execution of the new plan were considered uncertain even at the time of its ratification due to a number of political imponderables and economic hurdles. Impartial observers believed that a serious attempt at the reconstruction of war-damaged installations, combined with the repair and rehabilitation of physical infrastructure and industrial capacity, required a fundamental change in the regime's attitude toward foreign capital and economic cooperation and a friendlier treatment of the domestic private sector – a policy shift for which the political climate was not quite ready.

Some of the specific targets also seemed rather far-fetched. For instance, the construction of 2.5 million housing units in five years, financed largely by the private sector, appeared to be somewhat utopian. Keeping annual increases in real imports down to 2–3 per cent in the face of extraordinary needs for the reconstruction of the war-torn economy seemed unrealistic. Doubling tax revenues to more than 8 per cent of GDP without a fundamental reorganization of the tax-collecting machinery looked problematic. Increasing non-oil exports to $3.6 billion annually seemed questionable in the light of past experience. Achieving a sharp and sustained reduction in the rate of inflation in the midst of immense pent-up demand and excess liquidity was obviously a daunting task. Even the reasonable objective of expanding oil production capacity to 4.1 mb/d required considerably larger volumes of investment in the oil fields than had been contemplated in the plan. In short, the attainment of the plan's multi-dimensional objectives required the elimination of many structural deficiencies and financial distortions for which neither the political will nor the administrative expertise seemed to exist.

As could be expected, the plan law did not enjoy smooth sailing in the *Majles*, although it was finally approved. The political and economic objectives of the moderate and pro-business faction, embodied in the plan legislation, were greeted by fierce opposition from the hardline radical faction. The plan's critics took issue with: the priority given to industry over agriculture; the benign neglect of Islamic social justice in development planning; the new reliance on foreign assistance and finance; the possibility of increasing external debt; and the re-introduction of 'Westernization' to the detriment of Islamic culture. There were bitter complaints in the press and on the streets about public subsidies being reduced, prices of public goods being adjusted upward toward their real costs, the foreign exchange rate being effectively devalued through new import regulations, and the old industrial private sector revitalized.

As was clear during the *Majles* debate (which took almost a year, and absorbed nearly a quarter of the plan period) the quarrel was not so much about planning as it was about ideology, instincts, and motives. Subsequent events seem to suggest the futility, if not the irrelevance, of those debates. Published government reports show that the five-year plan has, so far, deviated from almost all of its quantitative targets: it has either exceeded, or fallen short of, initial projections.[8] In the first three years of operation, the goals of slowing down the rate of growth of population, raising employment and the value of the national product, reducing fiscal deficit, and increasing the share of capital outlays in the national budget, were more or less achieved – although not to the level of projected targets. On the other hand, the goals regarding certain other major variables such as housing construction, mineral exploration, lower inflation and non-oil exports were barely reached.

According to preliminary official data, in the first three years of the plan, population growth was reduced from 3.2 per cent to about 2.7 per cent a year. GDP grew by 8.1 per cent as contemplated in the plan. As shown in Table 9.5, the growth in total real investment (and particularly the private sector's share) fell short of projections. At the same time, both private and public consumption soared past their targets, threatening new imbalances over the course of the plan. The government's fiscal performance was mixed. The budget deficit was kept within prescribed limits thanks mostly to the sale of foreign exchange on the free market at highly devalued rial rates, and partly through the reduction of subsidies to money-losing public enterprises. However, the heavy reliance on oil and gas revenues vastly increased. In contrast, tax revenues, that were supposed to provide some 44 per cent of public revenues, were far behind. The approved 1992/93 budget expenditure was 77 per cent larger than mandated by the plan law, and 22 per cent larger than that of 1991/92 (instead of the prescribed 4.5 per cent). The nearly 50 per cent increase in civil service salaries over 1990–1992 was not anticipated in the plan. Neither was the surge in military expenditure in 1990–1992 at the expense of the productive sector, or the doubling of subsidies in the 1992/93 budget.[9] The treasury's resort to bank borrowing was measurably reduced because of lower budget deficits, but substantial borrowing by public enterprises (to cover losses no longer underwritten by the treasury) made up the difference. The volume of credit supplied to the private sector by commercial banks (no longer under quantitative ceilings) also surpassed its target. In the aftermath of the so-called exchange rate unification in April 1993, the money supply growth which was to be cut to 3.8 per cent in 1993/94 is now projected to rise upward of 30 per cent. And the CPI which was to go down to less than 9 per cent is forecast to exceed 30 per cent.

In foreign trade, imports exceeded the target beyond all expectations, and non-oil exports (particularly in the industrial, mineral, and pharmaceutical categories), although on the rise, lagged markedly behind targets.[10] Among major sectors, the most disappointing performance was that of agriculture, where the annual average growth rate fell short of the 6.1 per cent target. On the other hand, the growth rate in services was close to its target, while oil, power, and transport and communications jumped ahead of planned projections.

The regime's success in obtaining foreign financing is not known. The exact amount of foreign credit so far obtained to carry out the plan objectives is not published. In a press conference in late August 1992, Bank Markazi's governor reported that, of the $17.5 billion loans mandated by the plan law, some $15 billion had already been committed, and $6–7 billion disbursed. Foreign press reports put the total access to medium and long-term loan packages at no more than $12 billion. Even by the government's own account, the total foreign funds that have been utilized up to the middle of the fourth year of the five-year period amount to less than 25 per cent of planned borrowings, and there were no indications that the rest could be made up in the remaining years.

An assessment of the first three years of the plan by President Rafsanjani, points to a mixture of leads and lags. References are made to progress in repairing and expanding infrastructural facilities, enlarging basic industries, increasing non-oil exports, extending the gas-distribution network, reconstructing war-torn cities, and augmenting the volume of food and other commodities.[11]

Doubters and critics in and out of Iran are legion. Expatriates and foreign analysts tend to minimize the significance of the achievements by pointing out the regime's failures in areas such as unemployment, inflation and environmental deterioration. They also accuse the Islamic Republic of following the current Chinese model where economic growth is obtained at the expense of human rights and individual liberties. Domestic critics follow a different line. In a commentary of Rafsanjani's three-year administration by a hardline critic, the president is called to task for an undue dependence on the world economy; inordinate emphasis on economic issues at the expense of revolutionary objectives and values; excessive attention to 'expert' opinion; disregarding Islamic culture; a resolution of economic problems exclusively through economic means (such as relying on incentives instead of controls); an inadequate fight against corruption; and general deviation from genuine Islamic principles.[12]

Stung by these sharp attacks, and concerned about the forthcoming presidential elections in mid-1993, Mr Rafsanjani seems to have decided to go slow on the intended reforms. Defending the new structural adjustment policies of his administration in a mid-1992 speech, the president vehemently denied following a Western economic model, and termed the Iranian economy a 'mixed, Islamic economy' totally consistent with Islamic principles. Symptomatic of this politically cautious policy are the proposed re-establishment of price control over certain commodities, an increase in certain consumer subsidies, and a slow-down in the pace of privatization.[13]

In all, the economy's performance in the post-ceasefire phase of consolidation and adjustment has shown considerable progress over the second half of the 1980s, although the transition from the command economy to one of deregulation and privatization has seen both successes and setbacks. Understandably, the government wishes to put the highest gloss on its considerable achievements, while the opposition tries to turn the spotlight on obvious failures. What is not considered in this ongoing controversy is the apparent independence of these uncontested accomplishments and shortfalls from the planning process itself. Successes have not necessarily been the result of the planners' foresight, and setbacks have emerged despite optimistic projections. Iranian-type planning has yet to prove its role and relevance in the country's future course of development.

Discussions are already underway in the Plan and Budget Organization for the preparation of the second five-year plan

(1994/95–1998/99). First indications suggest more of the same framework and process. The planners hope, however, that by the beginning of the next plan, the government's current reforms in the area of privatization, taxation, exchange unification, and control over independent foundations will be completed, preparing the grounds for the private sector to play the dominant role as a principal force for expansion of productive capacity. The general theme is expected to be the continuation of the current plan and the completion of projects remaining unfinished.

At this juncture, the new plan stands a greater chance of realization than did the previous one, because planners have learned a good deal from past experience and are reportedly seeking advice from abroad in this new exercise. However, impediments to successful planning remain as powerful as ever. The break-up of the command economy in a rational and constructive manner will not be easy due to strong resistance by vested interests, and hesitation on the part of private entrepreneurs. Moreover, the implementation of even a good plan is likely to be hampered by inadequate physical infrastructure, shortage of trained labor, lack of proper coordination, and management inefficiencies. Most significantly, the leadership's commitment to abide by the plan's discipline, and its ability to adhere to specific targets, may not be kmuch greater than shown in the first plan.[14]

Table 9.5 shows some preliminary comparisons between projected and actual performance of the current five-year plan. Preliminary reports by the Plan and Budget Organization itself detail some of the major deviations from projected targets. The growth of labor productivity, for example, has so far fallen substantially below projections in industry and services, and has been minus 4.5 per cent in the construction sector instead of the 4.3 per cent plus target. By contrast, GDP at factor prices has grown at 8.3 per cent a year in real terms, slightly higher than the projected 8 per cent, on average. At the same time, non-oil exports, in both absolute terms and as a percentage of total imports, have dragged considerably behind targets. Public sector employment has exceeded projections more than three times. Detailed discussions of all other sectors show that none has behaved as planned.[15]

NOTES

1. See Sohrab Behdad, 'The Political Economy of Islamic Planning in Iran', in Amirahmadi and Parvin (1988), Chapter 7; and Hooshang Amirahmadi (1990), pp. 109–114.

2. For details of the new planning *process* see *Nezam-e Barnameh Rizi-ye Keshvar* (The system of national planning) (Tehran: Plan and Budget Organization, 1981).

3. For details of the 1983/84–1987/88 plan see *Barnameh-ye-Avval-Eqtesadi, Ejtema'i, Farhangi-ye Jomhuri-ye Eslami-ye Iran, 1362–1366* (The first economic, social, cultural development plan of the Islamic Republic of Iran, 1983/84–1987/88) (Tehran: Plan and Budget Organization, 1362 [1984]).

4. See *Kayhan Havai*, October 12, 1988.

5. For details see *A Summarized Version of the First Five-Year Economic, Social, and Cultural Development Plan of the Islamic Republic of Iran, 1989–1993* (Tehran: Plan and Budget Organization, May, 1990).

6. For details see The Economist Intelligence Unit, 'Iran: Country Report', No. 4, 1991; and 'Country Profile', 1992/93.

7. With a population of nearly 59 million in 1991, Iran reportedly had only about 5,000 engineers and technical analysts engaged in scientific research, while South Korea, with about 43 million inhabitants, boasted nearly 51,500. *Mahnameh-ye Barrasiha-ye Bazargani*, December 1991.

8. *Gozaresh-e Egtesadi-ye Sal-e 1369* (Economic Report for 1990/91) (Tehran: Plan and Budget Organization, January 1992). See also *Kayhan Havai*, January 9 and 29, 1992.

9. *Kayhan Havai*, February 5, 1992; and *MEED*, 21 February 1992.

10. For more details, including the president's state-of-the-economy message, see *Kayhan Havai*, March 18, and April 1, 1992.

11. *Kayhan Havai*, September 2, 1992, pp. 14–15.

12. See *Kayhan Havai*, September 9, 1992.

13. Of the nearly 500 public enterprises destined to be turned over to the private sector during 1992–93, no more than 100 were reportedly sold.

14. The Economist Intelligence Unit, 'Iran: Country Report', No. 1, 1992; and *MEED*, 'Iran', February 21, 1992. See also *Kayhan Havai* March 10, 1993.

15. See *Gozaresh-e Eqtesadi 1370* (Economic Report 1991/92) (Tehran: Plan and Budget Organization, February 1992).

10

Foreign trade and exchange policy

Iran's foreign economic relations and policies under the Islamic Republic were influenced by five factors: the early revolutionary ideology; diplomatic disputes with the United States and the West; the war with Iraq; instability in the global oil market; and domestic political uncertainties. Ideology produced protracted wrangling on the conduct of foreign trade. Quarrels with Washington resulted in the freeze on Iran's dollar reserves held abroad, and international sanctions on Iranian imports and exports. The Iran-Iraq war reduced oil exports and increased war-related imports. Oil market fluctuations played havoc with the country's export earnings and the government's budgetary planning. Political uncertainties encouraged capital flight, and impaired access to world capital markets.

Confronted with these internal and external challenges, the authorities' response was a pragmatic mixture of controls, restrictions, and *ad hoc* regulations. As a result, the Pahlavi regime's relatively liberal exchange system gradually became restrictive, bilateral, complex, and inefficient. Trade became vastly restricted and regulated, and the exchange system became multiple and controlled. Imports became a virtual state monopoly for most of the 1980s.

IDEOLOGICAL LEGACY

The victorious revolutionaries argued at first that Iran's large land area, a good variety of climatic conditions, excellent productive capacity, and ample mineral and marine resources provided a solid base for self-sustained growth. An enlightened and caring leadership, it was held, could unleash the nation's actual and potential capabilities. Under proper planning and with judicious use of technology and education, self-sufficiency in agriculture, industry, and business management could be attained. It was maintained that the previous regime's allegiance to 'imperialist' powers, and the economy's heavy dependence on oil had turned the country's economic direction against the interests of the poor and the deprived. It was claimed that none of the major economic sectors – industry, mining, construction, services, agriculture, and livestock – could operate efficiently without imports of raw materials, semi-processed goods, and capital machinery. There was thus a pressing need for a structural reorganization of the economy, and particularly of foreign trade and exchange.

In line with this ideological penchant for basic self-sufficiency and inward-oriented growth, a strong faction within the leadership hierarchy pressed hard for the nationalization of foreign trade, and the strict public management of imports and exports. Control over foreign trade thus became a major issue between the conservative right and the radical left among top policymakers. As mandated by Article 44 of the 1979 Constitution, a bill designed to place Iran's imports and exports totally in the government's hands was passed by the first *Majles* in April 1981. The Foreign Trade Nationalization Act required the government to submit enabling legislation within two months in order to properly implement the constitutional provision. A subsequent bill, duly proposed by the government within this time, envisaged a virtual government monopoly over foreign trade. Specialized public agencies in charge of imports, exports, commercial services, and other trade activities were to be established in the public sector. In support of its comprehensive trade nationalization bill, the government's brief argued that foreign trade in the private sector's hands was against the national interest for four reasons: it failed to meet national social needs due to the private profit motive; it harmed domestic *economic* interests by allowing the importation of non-essential goods, the proliferation of middlemen, unfair competition with local industry, and personal enrichment; it encouraged the surge of unsavory practices such as non-payment of taxes, illegal transfer of foreign exchange from the country, and fraud; and it sacrificed the country's *ideological* interests by neglecting political and doctrinal principles for the sake of private profit.[1]

The Foreign Trade Nationalization Act of 1981, when duly reviewed by the Council of Guardians, was rejected as both un-

Islamic and unconstitutional. The 12-member Council, citing Articles 4 and 72 of the 1979 Constitution, ruled that the inclusion of foreign trade in the public domain by the founders of the Constitution was not meant to be an absolute state monopoly over all imports or exports. The scope of state ownership and operation within the purview of Article 44, according to the Council, was clearly circumscribed by four distinct conditions: that no other provision of the Constitution should be breached by such public stewardship; no Islamic law should be violated by public operation; national welfare should be promoted by such undertakings; and society should in no way be harmed. The Council's conclusion was that the trade act was un-Islamic because it would deprive exporters of the fruits of their endeavor by forcing them to sell their wares to the state at state-determined prices. The legislation was also unconstitutional because the state bureaucracy could simply not handle some 200,000 import items every year in a manner that would promote economic progress or serve the public interest; and the trade monopoly would turn the state into 'a giant employer' – an eventuality that was ostensibly prohibited by Article 44 (2).[2]

To meet the Council's objections, the *Majles* approved a revised version of the bill in 1984, abrogating the state's *total* monopoly over imports, but assigning four-fifths of the import trade in all 'essential' goods to the government, to be implemented within four years. Non-governmental importers had to be approved by the Ministry of Commerce and were to proceed within a system of quota allocation and price supervision. Exports were also to be placed in state hands within four years. The objectives of the revised law were declared to be: freedom from foreign domination and independence from politico-economic polarity; expansion of trade with Moslem and Third World countries; protection of home industries; redirection of imports from conspicuous consumption to Islamic patterns; improvement of quality and diversification of exports; and balance-of-payments equilibrium. The new law was duly reviewed by the Council of Guardians, and was once again vetoed. No further legislative action was subsequently taken on the issue. Dominance and control over external trade by the government was later achieved through the allocation of foreign exchange and the annual regulation of imports and exports.

Over the following years, the government became in practice the prime importer of goods and services, gradually replacing the private sector. The administrative apparatus that had been set up earlier in anticipation of a foreign trade takeover was retained under the wartime exigency powers. As a first step toward the nationalization of foreign trade, a legal decree had previously been passed by the Revolutionary Council in mid-1980 to set up a number of Centers for the Procurement and Distribution of Imports within the Ministry of Commerce. The centers' task was to supervise and control the provision of national import needs and the distribution of imported goods through proper channels at controlled prices. The centers had an exclusive monopoly over the import of metals, textiles, pulp and paper, machinery, spare parts, electrical equipment, foodstuffs, plastic materials, chemicals, and electronic wares. All importers had to go through the centers in order to obtain authorization to open letters of credit with banks; they also had the obligation to sell at least 30 per cent of their imports through the centers. The centers could also import those goods on their own and distribute them to various consumer cooperatives, guilds, wholesale outlets and licensed retail stores. Goods imported directly by the centers or authorized by them had to be sold at the invoice cost plus 5 per cent profit. In practice, the centers' own direct imports and direct distribution were overshadowed by their control and regulation authority over all importers.

THE TRADE SYSTEM

The trade system that gradually evolved within the framework of the Islamic Republic's administration possessed four essential characteristics. It was quantitatively restrictive, and protective of domestic industries; anti-consumerist in intent, and against luxury imports in practice; selective in the choice of foreign trade partners; and increasingly controlled by the state. Imports for commercial purposes were allowed under import licensing, and were subject to customs duties, a commercial profit tax, a tax on letters-of-credit registration, a surcharge on certain items (for example, private automobiles), and various fees and charges earmarked for specific purposes. Quantitative restrictions on imports were exercised essentially through foreign exchange allocation. For both ideological and practical reasons, certain items that were regarded as luxuries, harmful, or non-essential were not legally allowed entry into the country. Deliberate attempts were made to divert trade away from the United States and towards Third World countries. And, through a vast array of laws and regulations, an increasing portion of import trade was transferred from the private sector to the state.

TRADE POLICY

In addition to specific prescriptions contained in the annual Rules and Regulations of Imports and Exports published by the Ministry of Commerce, the broad aspects of foreign trade policy were enunciated through official pronouncements and policy-makers' periodic declarations. Based on these signals, Iran's foreign trade policy was anchored on the following criteria: a policy of non-alliance, non-dependence, and relative self-sufficiency vis-à-vis both East and West; procurement of the country's import needs on the basis of mutual respect and healthy bilateral benefits; diversification of sources of imports both politically and geographically so as to minimize harmful over-reliance on any foreign power for supplies; close ties with Islamic, non-aligned, Third World, and oppressed nations; and the acquisition of high technology and modern technical skills and know-how from countries that were politically sympathetic to the Islamic Republic, not hostile to Iran's interests, and willing to establish bilateral relationships on the basis of mutuality of treatment and equality of status.[3]

These fundamental criteria for establishing economic relations with foreign countries admittedly favored politics first and economics second. The closeness of relations depended on the partner's 'ranking' with respect to politics, ideology, Islamic affinity, and economic advantage in that order. By these criteria, Iran's trade direction, which had previously been concentrated on Western industrial countries at the alleged expense of the Third World and the Eastern bloc, had to change.[4] In line with this declared policy, the Islamic Republic gradually concluded a dozen or so bilateral and trilateral trade agreements with Third World and socialist countries, some of which were still in effect in 1992.

In addition to considerations regarding *political* aspects of trade, the Islamic Republic's policy encompassed a complicated range of tariff and non-tariff regulations. Tariff rates, approved by the *Majles*, ranged from 5 to 100 per cent of import values. The 'commercial profit tax', imposed annually by the Council of Ministers, commonly had a spectrum of 5 to 400 per cent on top of customs duties.[5] Actual levies collected as the percentage of total imports, however, were quite modest – 30 per cent on average – due to generous exemptions granted to a number of importing agencies. Non-tariff barriers included outright prohibitions, quantitative allocations, various conditions attached to the importation of specific products, and, until recently, review by the public agencies concerned. Effective protection against foreign competition was enjoyed by industries where there were security or welfare considerations (for example, industries manufacturing food and beverages, chemicals, apparel, heavy machinery, motor vehicles, and assembly-type products). Protection was also offered through input subsidies to prioritized sectors, and rebates to non-oil exports. By assigning different rates of exchange to different categories of imports, the government was also able to regulate both the amount and the relative cost of different imported goods. Essential goods could be imported more cheaply by obtaining foreign exchange at the official (and highly overvalued) rate, while importers of less basic wares had to purchase foreign currencies at various higher rates. On the export side, non-oil exports were subject to regulations, inasmuch as they were required from time to time to surrender part or all of their export proceeds to the banking system at designated foreign exchange rates. Until late in 1989, exporters were also required to obtain permits for basic industrial exports in order to prevent domestic shortages.

A series of trade liberalization measures was adopted in the aftermath of the ceasefire, and the launching of the new five-year development plan. Foreign exchange licensing for private sector imports was virtually eliminated, and limits on payments for invisibles were liberalized. As from January 1991, importers no longer needed a *specific* import license or prior approval from the relevant procurement and distribution centers. In July 1991, importation of 'authorized' items was freed from quantitative restrictions if no foreign exchange was to be provided by Bank Markazi. At the same time, private importation of all motorized vehicles (banned, or heavily restricted, since 1979/80) was once again authorized as long as no foreign exchange had to be supplied by the government. The Council of Ministers' decree included passenger cars, trucks, buses, minibuses, vans, tractors, and construction machinery. Further import liberalization measures were put into effect after exchange-rate 'unification' in 1993.

TRADE DEVELOPMENTS

The volume of trade, which, in 1973, began on an upward trend that continued for five years, slackened towards the latter part of 1978. The downward slide in imports was accelerated in 1979 due to revolutionary turmoil, flight of capital, the multiplicity of power centers, falling confidence in the private sector, and lack of fiscal and commercial direction.

On November 14, 1979, ten days after a number of US diplomats in Iran were taken hostage by the so-called 'Moslem Students

Following the Imam's Line' – with the implicit backing of the Revolutionary Council – US Treasury officials in Washington learned that Tehran was planning to withdraw Iranian funds from American Banks in the United States and abroad.[6] Such an action posed an imminent threat to the already weak dollar, a potential loss to major American banks that kept Iranian deposits as collateral on their sizeable loans to Iranian enterprises, and a possible blow to international financial stability. Consequently, President Carter signed a freeze order blocking Iranian assets in the United States. Some branches of American banks in Europe contested the application of Washington's decision outside the United States. The Iranian government took the matter to the Executive Board of the International Monetary Fund as a violation of the Fund's Articles of Agreement. However, the latter declined to take any action.

The freezing of Iran's assets did not involve confiscating Iran's holdings, imposing a trade embargo, or a trade blockade. In fact, Washington insisted that the freeze was not designed to 'impair normal commercial relationships' between the two countries. The action also affected assets of the Iranian government and its agencies or agents, but not those of private Iranian citizens or private corporations. The initial Washington reaction to the taking of American hostages in Tehran was limited to the suspension of military exports and a ban on the import of Iranian oil. It did not involve an embargo on food shipments. Iran at the time was importing nearly 3 million tons of farm products – 30 per cent of its total needs – much of it from the United States. But, on November 13, 1979, the International Longshoremen's and Warehousemen's Union announced that it would refuse to handle cargo bound for or coming from Iran. In a sharp departure from its usual stand against the use of food as a political weapon, the American Farm Bureau Federation also announced on November 15 that it would support an embargo on US food exports to Iran.

With the severance of diplomatic relations between Iran and the United States in April 1980, a trade embargo was imposed by Washington against Iran. President Carter banned all imports from Iran and all exports except food and pharmaceuticals. Later on, European Community foreign ministers agreed in May 1980 not to allow any new contracts (again exempting food and medicine) to be signed after November 4, 1979, when the American hostages had been seized. But Britain and France decided to exempt a variety of services, such as engineering consultancy, insurance, transport, and tourism, from sanctions. Other countries also found it useful not to follow a common policy. Consequently, many transactions slipped through the net, or took place through intermediary countries. (Dubai and Abu Dhabi, in particular, played a crucial role in such transactions.) As a consequence, Iran was not really deprived of its absolutely essential needs (including some arms), but had to pay higher prices to procure them.

Early attempts by Washington to rally support among European allies for an effective trade embargo against Iran were therefore not very successful. Lukewarm reaction to US approaches was rationalized on the grounds that sanctions would be ineffective. Furthermore, there was uncertainty as to the willingness of the Soviet Union and perhaps even Japan to join in such action. A trade embargo could work only if Iran's income from oil was cut. But, apart from the difficulties of enforcing such a ban, a successful outcome meant the withdrawal of Iranian oil supplies from the world oil markets, and a further rise in the price of oil. This was an extra new burden for the whole world, particularly poor countries, that no one wished to undertake. The European Community and Japan lifted their trade embargoes as soon as the hostages were freed on January 1, 1981. But the British, French and West German export-promotion agencies refused for a while to extend credit to the Islamic Republic as a matter of risk assessment. In 1984, when Iran was named by the United States as a supporter of international terrorism, a new set of sanctions was imposed under the Arms Export Control Act and the Export Administration Act. On October 6, 1987, the US Congress called for the prohibition of Iranian imports, and later, President Reagan banned nearly all imports from Iran. The Foreign Relations Authorization Act of 1988 and 1989 prohibited the shipment of arms to Iran. Finally, the Iran–Iraq Arms Non-Proliferation Act of 1992 tightened the various prohibitions on technology transfer to Iran. Under US pressures, Japan, the United Kingdom, and other G7 industrial countries also imposed new restrictions on exports to Iran of a wide range of items in early 1993.

VOLUME AND COMPOSITION OF FOREIGN TRADE

Drastic changes in the magnitude and mix of foreign trade were promised by the new regime. As far as possible, the economy had to become self-reliant. Imports had to be restricted to capital and intermediate goods, and turned away from consumer wares particularly 'luxury' items. The intention was to reduce not only 'non-essential' imports, but also aggregate consumption in order to shift resources towards increased productive capacity. Non-oil exports had to be stimulated so that the country's nearly total reliance on oil exports would be progressively diminished.

Under the banner of anti-consumerism and anti-profligacy, a ban was announced on 'luxury' imports (including cosmetics, toys, costume jewelry, furs, food delicacies, crystal, designer clothes, and certain wood and leather items). In the foreign exchange budget, priorities were granted to essential imports. Non-oil exports were aided in a number of different ways. These policies, however, were thwarted by certain exogenous factors.

The magnitude of imports was affected by political turmoil and fluctuations in foreign exchange earnings. The revolution itself cut deeply into foreign trade in 1978/79 and 1979/80, reducing total value of imports by an average of 18 per cent a year as GDP and oil revenues reached lower levels. With the resumption of oil exports at much higher prices and the gradual improvement in economic conditions, imports resumed their pre-revolution upward trend in 1981/82, amounting to more than $1 billion a month on average. With war needs on the rise and oil revenues growing, total import values reached a post-revolution peak in 1983/84, partly due to higher prices (caused by sanctions, hikes in insurance and transport rates in the Persian Gulf, and the increased commissions of middlemen). Thereafter, the collapse of oil prices in the mid-1980s, and damage to oil installations and facilities, triggered a sharply downward movement in imports. Foreign purchases in 1988/89 were only about 59 per cent of the 1983/84 level, and 64 per cent of that of 1977/78 – despite considerable price increases in the meantime.

Generally speaking, the magnitude of Iranian imports for most of the 1980s was influenced mainly by the availability of foreign exchange, namely the revenues from oil exports. With scant willingness on the part of the Islamic Republic to go into foreign debt (and little opportunity to do so), the authorities' main concern was to contain losses of foreign reserves. Accordingly, import controls and exchange restrictions were periodically intensified or eased in response to foreign currency supplies. As oil and gas export revenues increased from $11.7 billion in 1980/81 to over $21.1 billion in 1983/84, merchandise imports were allowed to rise from nearly $11 billion to $18 billion in the same period. With a downward trend in annual oil export earnings after 1984/85, and the dramatic drop in oil income to only $6.2 billion in 1986/87, a commensurate brake was applied to imports, and the volume of foreign procurement was gradually reduced to $10.6 billion in 1988/89. Since then, an improvement in the foreign exchange position has helped liberalize import controls, and merchandise imports headed toward $25 billion in 1991/92 compared with the planned target of $16 billion. Tables 10.1 and 10.2 show the value and composition of imports and exports over the years.[7]

The *composition* of imports under the revolution has shown no appreciable change from earlier years. Rapid rise in population and the sluggish performance of GDP (particularly in the manufacturing sector), coupled with war-related shortages, stimulated the demand for imported consumer goods. Despite the government's professed intentions, the share of consumer goods in total recorded imports did not measurably alter. For much of the 1980s, while the value of annual imports experienced sharp fluctuations – soaring by 44 per cent between 1982/83 and 1983/84, and then plummeting by 42 per cent between 1983/84 and 1988/89 – there were similar changes in the import structure. Consumer goods, which accounted for about 18 per cent of total imports in 1977/78, surged to 23 per cent in 1981/82, before falling back to 18 per cent in 1989/90. Capital goods and intermediate items underwent corresponding fluctuations (see Table 10.3). Thus, despite a declining standard of living during the 1980s, the much-criticized dependence on the importation of consumer goods in the pre-revolution period continued unabated. According to the Center for Procurement and Distribution of Foodstuffs, in 1990/91 some $3.5 billion worth of foods were imported from abroad (including meat, cheese, butter, and cereals).[8] Private analysts believe the figure was $4–5 billion.[9]

The regime's intention to sharply increase non-energy exports was also thwarted by unfavorable circumstances and ineffective policies. Non-oil exports had a depressed market at the very beginning, but gradually improved their performance (see Table 10.2). Volume rose by about 8 per cent a year on average between 1978/79 and 1991/92. The value of non-oil exports declined by 25 per cent between 1977/78 and 1985/86, but began to rise after 1987/88 and registered a remarkable growth after 1990/91. Chiefly responsible for the post-ceasefire rise in non-oil exports have been such factors as: a realistic valuation of exports; the exporters' freedom to sell their foreign exchange proceeds on the free market; official recording of exports that were previously smuggled out of the country to avoid selling the proceeds to the government at less than free market rates; and the lack of access by productive enterprises to favorable exchange rates, making them seek independent sources of foreign exchange for their needs through exports.

Despite the dramatic improvement in foreign sales, however, the objective of changing the composition of non-oil exports, from traditional items to industrial goods, is still far from being realized.

The upward trend in industrial exports that had begun in the mid-1970s was reversed in the mid-1980s, and the composition of non-oil exports shifted toward traditional goods and raw materials, and away from industrial wares. While industrial goods (such as chemicals, detergents, apparel, shoes,and construction materials) accounted for nearly 22 per cent of total non-oil exports in 1977/78, this ratio fell to less than 14 per cent in 1990/91, largely due to the depressed conditions in the domestic industrial sector for most of the 1980s. Carpets continue to be Iran's largest non-oil export. Between 1978/79 and 1991/92, Iran exported some $4.5 billion worth of carpets. But strong competition from neighbouring countries (where a large number of carpet-makers had migrated after the revolution) cut into Iran's lead in this item. According to a Commerce Ministry official, Iran's share of the international handmade carpet market had dropped from 90 per cent in 1980 to about 25 per cent in 1990.[10] The press reports on the value of carpet exports in 1991/92 − nearly five times the average figure during the 1980s − seems to suggest that they have bucked this downward trend, assuming that the figures prove not to be a fluke. Pistachio exports provide the second largest non-oil export earners with an estimated $365 million. Caviar exports constitute the bulk of the 300-ton annual production, worth $90 million.

In addition to the change in composition, the terms of trade also turned against Iran during the 1980s. With some 150 per cent increase in the total volume of annual exports between 1979/80 and 1989/90, the total value rose by less than 100 per cent. Moreover, in view of the substantial increase in Iran's imports price index during the 1980s (estimated at a cumulative 138 per cent), the purchasing power of exported goods was down to only 42 per cent in real terms. Part of the reason for this reversal was the increasing share of raw materials in total exports when those items faced a depressed global market. The government's policy of holding down domestic prices was also partly responsible. However, the obligation of exporters to sell the proceeds of their exports to the government at less than free-market exchange rates was probably the chief factor.

As indicated in Chapter 9, the current five-year plan forecasts $17.8 billion of non-oil exports − or about 15 per cent of total foreign exchange revenues. To remove the impediments that kept these exports at low levels during the 1980s, the government has decided to make full use of existing capacity, standardizing quality, and using modern technology; and to remove harmful bureaucratic and customs regulations, freeing exporters from selling their proceeds to the government at fixed rates, and expanding international marketing through trade fairs and other means.[11] These measures, on top of the removal of quantitative restrictions, highly generous tax exemptions granted to incomes from non-oil exports, and the ability of non-oil exporters to sell their proceeds at the *floating* rate, have been highly effective, although only 69 per cent of the planned export target for the first three years has been achieved.

To further help promote non-oil exports, the establishment of an Export Expansion Bank, with an initial capital of Rls 50 billion, was announced in August 1991. The bank aims to assist exporters of industrial and traditional goods, as well as foreign buyers, with their cash or foreign exchange needs, information regarding foreign markets and potential customers, and advice on how to improve the size and quality of exports. Under the 1992 income tax law, exports of carpets and industrial handicrafts are 100 per cent exempt from taxation, and non-oil traditional exports enjoy 50 per cent exemption.[12]

DIRECTION OF TRADE

The *direction* of external trade under the Islamic Republic has reflected the regime's ideological preferences as well as certain harsh economic and political realities. As indicated before, the choice of Iran's trade partners was supposed to be made on the basis of their political and doctrinal affinity with the Islamic regime. This distinct inclination for expanding economic relations with Moslem and Third World countries was subsequently given an additional boost by Western trade sanctions. In order to combat these sanctions, and reduce diplomatic isolation, the embattled Iranian government in 1981/82 began to send a score of delegations to 'friendly' countries in Asia, Africa and Latin America to solicit diplomatic and economic support. Cooperation with neighbors – the Soviet Union, Turkey and Pakistan – was particularly intensified. Due to war-related difficulties in Persian Gulf shipping, transportation by trucks, rail and sea through Turkey and the Soviet Union was also markedly enhanced. Trade with Israel and South Africa was officially banned.

Reflecting the regime's own preferences, and its externally imposed restrictions, the direction of Iran's external trade thus underwent considerable changes. A comparison of the lists of the top 25 exporters to Iran in 1977/78 and 1990/91 reveals some noteworthy differences. First, the United States, as the third largest exporter of goods and services to Iran before the revolution, lost its position, and its overall trade with the Islamic Republic became negligible. Second, such countries as Finland, India, Kuwait, Sweden and Taiwan, on the list in 1977/78, were replaced by newcomers like Argentina, Brazil, Canada, and Denmark. Third, the United Arab Emirates replaced the United States as the third largest exporter to Iran at the end of the decade – mostly as a convenient conduit, and a third-party trans-shipper. Fourth, imports from the Soviet Union and other former socialist countries decreased slightly, while some countries like Syria and Yugoslavia, which previously had negligible trade with Iran, became more active traders. Fifth, while Germany and Japan retained their top ranking positions, their share of exports to Iran fell considerably. Finally, the share of the United Kingdom, and that of France, was measurably cut, while Turkey's share rose from a negligible 0.2 per cent to 3.9 per cent during the period. In the second half of the 1980s, the newly industrialized countries such as Argentina, Brazil, South Korea, Thailand and Yugoslavia increased their share of exports to Iran at the expense of Japan and the European Community. By 1992/93, Germany, with a reported $5 billion of exports was Iran's number one trade partner, followed by Japan and Italy.

On the export side, during the period under review, the US, Israel, Iraq, South Africa and Afghanistan reduced their imports from Iran to zero or a negligible amount. Saudi Arabia and Kuwait, who were the fourth and sixth most important customers for Iran's non-oil products in 1977/78, failed to make the list of the top 19 countries in 1990/91. The United Arab Emirates, on the other hand, rose from 9th to 2nd position, while the Soviet Union lost its number one position, and fell to 9th. In the second half of the decade, the European Community increased its share from 40 per cent to 54 per cent (essentially due to Germany's increased purchases). The Federal Republic remained the number one purchaser of Iran's non-oil products after 1978/79, although on a reduced scale, while the United Arab Emirates replaced the United States as the second largest export destination. Italy, Japan, Switzerland and the United Kingdom raised their shares while France and the USSR lost part of theirs. Sales to South Asia and the Pacific fell, but exports to OPEC members (excluding Iraq, Kuwait and Saudi Arabia) increased.

Trade between Iran and the US, which peaked in 1977/78 with American exports of $3.7 billion and imports of $2.9 billion, plunged in 1980 to sales of merely $23 million and purchases of $458 million (mostly oil). American exports edged up to $95 million in 1982 and $200 million in 1983; imports (mostly oil) reached more than $1 billion in 1983. Before the revolution, practically every major US corporation in world trade was involved in Iran. None was directly active after 1979. After the end of the war with Iraq, trade sanctions were somewhat relaxed, and some US oil companies were allowed to buy crude oil directly from Iran on the provision that they deposit the proceeds in the special account of the US–Iranian Claims Tribunal so long as the account was under the required minimum of $500 million. According to press reports, the United States became Iran's fourth largest supplier of goods in 1992/93, with $750 million of direct sales, and indirect supplies of well over $1 billion.[13] In 1993, US oil companies replaced Japanese firms as Iran's main customers.

During the 1980s, Australia and New Zealand became large exporters of lamb, wheat and wool to Iran, while, in Europe, Austria, Spain and Sweden became favored trading partners. Trade was also increasingly diverted toward socialist countries, and conducted on a bilateral basis until 1990/91.

FOREIGN ECONOMIC RELATIONS

Since the end of hostilities with Iraq, the Islamic Republic's foreign economic stance has encompassed five principal dimensions: a difficult and tendentious position vis-à-vis the United States: amicable but fragile links with the European Community and Japan; correct but tenuous ties with the Gulf Cooperation Council members in the Persian Gulf; ambitious and far-reaching designs in Transcaucasia and Central Asia; and friendly and cooperative relations with most Third World countries.

Relations between Iran and the USA have been restrained ever since the revolution. Nearly all imports from Iran have been prohibited. A variety of non-sensitive, non-military exports have been permitted from time to time. Nevertheless, trade between the two countries has continued directly or through third countries. Contacts between American oil companies active in the Middle east and Iran's NIOC have been reported in the press. Washington has been effective in blocking exports of certain dual-use items to Iran from other countries.

In the Persian Gulf area, relations with Saudi Arabia have remained tenuous despite repeated attempts at reconciliation. In addition to conflicts within OPEC on price and output policies, there has also been a rivalry between the two countries over the Islamic fundamentalists in other areas. Indeed both countries have been involved in passing money and support to them. Iran's establishment of 'free trade zones' on Qeshm and Kish islands in the Persian Gulf has also been in competition with GCC members. At the same time, a number of bilateral cooperation agreements have been signed between Iran and Dubai, Oman and Qatar involving air and sea traffic, customs preferences, and joint ventures. Abu Dhabi has continued to serve as a conduit for trade with the United States.

With respect to the relations with the Commonwealth of Independent States – the former Soviet Union – Tehran has pursued a multi-pronged strategy aimed at consolidating Iran's position with the Russian Federal Republic, and expanding its economic and trade ties with Moscow; taking maximum advantage of economic opportunities presented by the new republics outside Russia; and promoting Iran as an economic and trading gateway to the Transcaucasian and Central Asian republics. A series of overlapping regional initiatives have been undertaken through both multilateral and bilateral arrangements. Multilaterally, the Regional Cooperation for Development (RCD), founded in 1964 with Pakistan and Turkey, and dormant since the revolution, has been revived and renamed the Economic Cooperation Organization (ECO). Since November 1992, six former Soviet republics – Azerbaijan, Kazakhstan Kirgizstan, Tajikistan, Turkmenistan and Uzbekistan – plus Afghanistan have joined ECO to make the new group, (amounting to 300-million people) the biggest economic bloc after the European Community. The expanded group's major objectives are to remove tariff and other trade barriers between members; expand trade, banking and tourism; integrate rail, road and telecommunication networks; and ultimately to establish an Islamic common market. Since February 1992, another grouping under the name of the Caspian Sea Littoral States Cooperation Organization (composed of Iran, Turkmenistan, Azerbaijan, Kazakhstan and Russia) has been formed to exploit the resources of the Caspian Sea, and cooperate in conducting research on environmental issues affecting the littoral states.

The Islamic Republic has also signed a long series of bilateral agreements with the former communist states. In early 1982, Iran and the Soviet Union signed a protocol for accelerated economic and technical cooperation, involving several projects in power generation, steel mill expansion and irrigation dams. In mid-1987, a new economic understanding was reached between the two countries involving oil pipelines, shipping in the Caspian Sea, and rail linkage. Under another agreement signed in 1989, the export of natural gas was to be resumed, previous joint projects were to be completed, and Iran's new military build-up was to be assisted through the sale of Russian MiG29 jets, SU24 aircraft, missiles, submarines, and other equipment.[14]

With the other republics on both sides of the Caspian Sea, Tehran has been anxious to reassert historic, cultural and religious links. Thus, a number of bilateral agreements have been reached with Armenia, Azerbaijan, Kazakhstan, Tajikistan, Turkmenistan and Ukraine involving oil, gas, rails, roads, trade in consumer goods, and joint industrial projects. The landlocked Central Asian republics have particularly welcomed Iran's initiatives as a means of re-routeing their transport and communication links to the Persian Gulf via Iran, and gaining gradual economic independence from Moscow.

Economic relations with the European Community and Japan have been rooted in such objectives as securing the largest portion of Iran's needs for foreign financing from European and Japanese sources, obtaining modern technologies for oil and other basic industries, and isolating and marginalizing Washington's influence on European and Japanese trade and investment in Iran. Despite repeated Washington appeals to Japan and the European Community to end normal commercial relations with Iran and adopt a common 'containment' policy, the US partners' reaction has been rather cool. Western European countries are among Iran's main trading partners and are naturally reluctant to lose a lucrative market in Iran. A long-term concessionary loan agreement – the first after the revolution – was signed in May 1993 between Tokyo and Tehran for a $343 million, 25-year Japanese loan at 3 per cent annual interest rate for the construction of a 1000 MW hydro-electric power plant on the Karun river in the southwest of Iran. Two further loans totalling about $1000 million were to follow.

Finally, Iran has been active in expanding and strengthening economic ties with Third World countries in Asia, Africa and Latin America directly and bilaterally or through such organizations as UNCTAD, IFAD, the Islamic Development Bank, and the ASEAN group.[15] Among those countries outside the multilateral orbits already mentioned, China, Brazil and Syria have forged special relationships with Tehran. In addition to using World Bank credit for domestic development projects, Iran has also benefited from grants and loans from the Islamic Development Bank, and has applied for loans from the International Fund for Agricultural Development.

Since January 1989, the Islamic Republic has also reached 'agreement in principle', or signed trade protocols, with a large number of other foreign countries (Australia, Bahrain, Belgium, Canada, France, Germany, Great Britain, Italy, India, Japan, Libya,

Malaysia, Netherlands, New Zealand, Romania, South Korea and Sweden, among others) for joint economic cooperation and development in such fields as automobile assembly, construction materials, electric power generation, housing, iron and steel production, oil and mineral exploration, offshore drilling, gas and oil refining, petrochemicals, storage facilities, ship building, atomic research, and others. Tables 10.4 and 10.5 show the distribution of imports and non-oil exports by countries.

THE BALANCE OF PAYMENTS

For most of the years since the 1979 revolution, the Islamic Republic has experienced a deficit in its external accounts.[16] These deficits were mainly caused by reduced volumes of crude oil exports; the fall of oil prices in the mid-1980s after a hefty rise in 1979/80; additional import needs because of the war with Iraq; the detrimental impact of Western trade sanctions; flight of capital; and the government's policy of paying back external debt, shunning foreign loans, and rejecting foreign investments.

Developments in the external accounts since the establishment of the Islamic Republic are summarized in Table 10.6. As in the pre-revolution period, trade and current balances were mainly shaped by oil export receipts. During 1978/79, crude oil exports were down to 3.5 mb/d on average, and oil export receipts down to $18.1 billion (from 4.8 mb/d and $21 billion, respectively, in 1977/78). But due to a slowdown in economic activity caused by political unrest, and reduced total imports, the balance of payments on both current and overall accounts produced only a small deficit. In 1979/80, there was a steep decline in foreign payments due to reduced imports and new exchange restrictions. Foreign receipts, however, remained high due to sharp and sudden increases in the price of crude oil. As a result, the overall balance of payments showed a sizeable surplus of about $5.6 billion – the largest annual figure in the post-revolution period. In 1980/81, the government policy of reducing oil exports to the level of 'essential' national needs, together with the effects of the assets freeze and war with Iraq, resulted in a steep decline in foreign exchange receipts. At the same time, war-related needs and higher prices paid for import needs due to the trade embargo helped increase foreign payments. The result was a net current account deficit of some $2.4 billion and an overall deficit of $9.7 billion, wiping out the previous year's surplus. The unprecedented rise in the deficit on the capital account was due to the Bank Markazi's treatment of Iran's frozen assets as capital outflow.

The behavior of the balance-of-payments in subsequent years was influenced by such diverse factors as: the resolution of the American hostage crisis through the Algiers accord; fluctuations in oil export volume and prices caused by the war and foreign demand for OPEC oil; appreciation of the US dollar (in which oil income is received) in the first half of the 1980s and its fall in the second half; and the price of Iranian crude. In 1986/87, when foreign exchange receipts from oil exports plummeted to the record post-war low of $6.2 billion (a 54 per cent drop from the previous year), the government introduced an austerity Plan for New Economic Conditions. This *ad hoc* plan established strategic and critical priorities among various sectors, programs, and projects for the purchase of foreign exchange from Bank Markazi.

In the years following the revolution up to 1991/92, the overall balance of payments registered a total deficit of about $5.7 billion. Iran had a negative trade balance with most of its trading partners, and especially with the two top exporting countries, even when oil was included in the trade accounts. A not insignificant portion of the negative overall balance was due to a relentless flight of capital from the country through over- and under-invoicing of imports and exports.[17] Despite heavy penalties for unauthorized foreign exchange transactions, the authorities were unable to stop capital transfers throughout the decade. As a result, a large volume of the country's inherited foreign assets was drawn upon to finance the overall deficits.

The services account was affected in a number of different ways during the decade. On the receipts side, there was a decline in investment income due to reduced net foreign assets and the freezing of some foreign exchange holdings abroad. But there was an inflow of remittances from Iranian workers in some Persian Gulf countries, offsetting the balance. On the payments side, there was also a substantial reduction in debt servicing, due to reduced long-term foreign debt, and stringent restrictions on the allocation of foreign exchange for travel, study, medical treatment, etc. On the whole, the services account has remained in large deficit in every year since the revolution. Thus, despite a surplus in the trade account (including oil) in 9 out of the 14 years under review, the balance on the current account experienced a deficit for 10 of the years in the 14-year period.

The capital account in the 1980s showed the effects of several criss-crossing developments: the early repayment of Iran's long-term debt; the freezing of Iranian assets abroad; the gradual settlement of financial disputes under the Algiers accord; the repayment of principal and interest on the loans to foreign countries obtained during the Shah's regime; improvements in bilateral trade arrangements; and periodic resort to short-term borrowing and suppliers' credit. Reflecting these varied influences, the cumulative balance in the capital account registered a surplus of more than $1.9 billion. In the last seven years up to 1991/92, the almost persistent annual deficit on current account (due largely to growing imports as well as the gap in the services account) was more than offset by a surplus on the capital account (i.e., the use of suppliers' credits or advanced sales of crude oil). The capital account thus remained consistently in surplus during the seven-year period. The long-term account improved after 1985/86, largely because of the release of part of the frozen assets abroad, and the settlement of claims with France and Japan. The short-term account also registered a surplus due to the improvement of Iran's bilateral balances with East European countries and a substantial increase in short-term trade credits.

Foreign exchange received by Bank Markazi from the proceeds of non-oil exports in the first two years of the revolution showed a decrease from 1977/78 due to domestic inflation, depressed output, high domestic demand, and the disposal of exchange earnings in the free market. Despite increased incentives offered by the government, the value of non-oil exports further declined, due partly to the loss of traditional export markets, recession in the industrial countries, and 'unauthorized' sales (that is, non-recorded sales in search of a better exchange rate). In 1982/83, non-oil exporters were allowed to use the proceeds of their foreign sales for the direct importation of goods instead of remittance through the banking system. Nevertheless these exports declined by 16 per cent, reaching only $284 million, the lowest since the revolution. The situation considerably improved in 1983/84, although total sales still amounted to a relatively small sum. In 1984/85, non-oil exporters were further allowed to sell their proceeds freely to authorized importers in the private and cooperative sectors in addition to receiving other bonuses and incentives. Nevertheless, total non-oil foreign sales did not significantly improve. Continued promotional incentives given to non-oil exporters in 1985/86, including exemption from surrender requirements (the sale of proceeds to the banking system for certain goods), increased their sales to $465 million. The granting of a whole new set of bonuses and incentives raised non-oil exports to $915 million in 1986/87 and a record $1.1 billion in 1987/88. Part of the reason for the hefty increase was a bonus of Rls 350 over the official rate for each dollar of non-oil export. Due to further incentives such as bonuses, exchange of imports for exports, and preferential rates, non-oil exports steadily grew in the next three years. The recorded share of non-oil exports in total exports amounted to about 6 per cent.[18]

Trade liberalization, exchange reforms, and the shift in the origin of GDP growth from services to the commodity-producing sectors greatly impacted foreign trade. Total imports of goods and services rose from slightly more than $13 billion in 1988/89 to a record high of more than $30 billion in 1991/92. As a result, the current account, which had achieved a small surplus in 1990/91, deteriorated to a record post-revolution deficit of nearly $8 billion (Table 10.6). The deficit was financed mainly through borrowing and a drawdown on official reserves and foreign assets. Borrowing included forward sales of oil, short-term trade financing, and suppliers' credits. Iran also made a reserve tranche purchase of SDR 71 million ($100 million) from the International Monetary Fund in 1988, and sold SDR 200 million of its total SDR 244 million net cumulative allocation in 1992. The central bank governor referred to some 'payment problems' in August 1992 – giving substance to foreign press reports of Iran's difficulties in paying its letters of credit maturing that summer. As widely reported in the foreign press, the arrears totalling $2–3 billion continued past March 1993.

The breakdown of the balance of payments into its main components leads to four broad observations. First, the trade balance was determined essentially by the value of *oil exports* and the consequent volume of merchandise imports. Second, the services sector, perennially in deficit, was largely short in the freight and insurance account, and long in investment income from Iran's pre-revolution loans and investments. Third, principal activities in the capital account related largely to the freezing and the release of Iranian assets, as well as the use of short-term (suppliers) credit. And, finally, non-oil exports played a relatively insignificant role in the overall balance.

FOREIGN RESERVES AND EXTERNAL DEBT

Data on the Islamic Republic's foreign exchange reserves and external debt are not officially published. Figures given by international organizations, as well as private estimates, are based on a good deal of guesswork. Invoking national security considerations during the eight-year war with Iraq, the monetary authorities were reluctant to divulge the size of reserves or debt. High government officials have, from time to time, made fleeting references to the reserve figure without giving any details.[19] The figures cited have been mostly designed to reassure the public of the adequacy of foreign currency supplies. In May 1993, gross official reserves (excluding frozen assets) were estimated to be about $5–7 billion (or the equivalent of three months of imports).

Figures published by Bank Markazi put the net foreign assets of the banking system at the end of 1357 (March 20, 1979) at Rls 989 billion ($13 billion). The estimate for the end of 1369 (March 20, 1991) was Rls 1,316 billion ($18.8 billion). With the composition of the latter assets still unpublished, their true worth cannot be realistically appraised since it partly consists of money lent out, or invested abroad, by the Shah's regime, involving several developed and developing countries, the status of which is not presently clear.[20]

Furthermore, there are several conceptual and statistical questions raised by foreign analysts concerning the interpretation of data supplied by the central bank. First, there are differences between the annual overall balance in the balance-of-payments table and the change in net foreign assets. That is, the deficits or surpluses in the annual current and overall accounts are not always matched by changes shown in the net foreign assets of the banking system. Second, changes in net foreign assets are not broken down into its main components with the result that it would be impossible to know, for example, how much of a decline in assets is used to finance a deficit in the current account. Third, there is questionable methodology involved in: (i) the treatment of frozen funds as a decline in foreign assets and their release as an increase; (ii) computation of foreign balances held by Iranians as foreign assets in the assets accounts, but not as such in the balance-of-payments accounts; and (iii) periodic revaluations of gold held by Bank Markazi at market prices, and recalculations of dollar holdings against the Special Drawing Rights. Finally, *positive* entries shown by Bank Markazi under the rubric of 'errors and omissions' in the annual balance of payments (indicating capital *inflows* into Iran) during most of the 1980s seem hard to fathom because the rather unfavorable economic and financial environments of war, internal political uncertainty, and other disincentives were likely to encourage capital flight rather than capital repatriation.

Data on external debt are equally hard to verify. Estimates vary, and the breakdown into short-, medium- and long-term indebtedness is not available. By unofficial estimates, in the summer of 1979 Iran had $14–15 billion in foreign exchange assets held outside the country. Against these assets, the country had an estimated $7–8 billion of debt ($1.4 billion to commercial banks; $1 billion in short-term commercial debt; $1.5 billion in long-term debts; and $3–4 billion worth of project loans outstanding). Other private estimates put the external obligations at $9 billion, much of it owed to US banks.[21] Foreign analysts believe that the Islamic Republic used part of its foreign exchange reserves inherited from the previous regime to pay back its long-term foreign debts, and to finance its current account deficits. Most significantly, Iran replaced its medium- and long-term public sector debt with short-term obligations.

In one of his Friday sermons, President Rafsanjani indicated that Iran had accumulated $12 billion of short-term debt before the ceasefire with Iraq in August 1988.[22] The country's outstanding foreign public debt in early 1992 was placed by the government at $5.6 billion, of which $2.3 billion was made of medium- and long-term obligations. The total outstanding external debt in mid-1992 has been differently reported. The Bank for International Settlement puts the total in December 1991 at just over $13.6 billion. A *Majles* deputy has given the total figure of external debt at $30 billion in February 1993, up from $12 billion in 1989. Most of the debt was presumably in the form of short- and medium-term credits. Iran's long-term borrowing from the World Bank as of May 1, 1993 stood at $847 million – consisting of $250 million for earthquake damage reconstruction; $77 million for Tehran's water drainage system; $57 million for Sistan River flood control; $157 million for agricultural irrigation; $141 million for primary health care and family planning; and $165 million for upgrading electric power generation. There was another $800 million in project loan proposals in the pipeline for a sewerage system, a basic education program, vocational training, and gas-flaring reduction.[23] Offsetting these debts were the funds owed to Iran by foreign suppliers, joint-venture partners, and official debtors. Table 10.7 presents a summary of external debt's stocks and flows.

THE FOREIGN EXCHANGE SYSTEM

Iran's foreign exchange system under the Islamic Republic went through several stages of transformation in the direction of restrictions, quantitative controls, and a multi-rate structure. Following the Iraqi invasion of Iran's territory, the exchange regime was centrally managed and tightly controlled until 1989/90. It was also exceedingly complex – in sharp contrast with the system prevailing in the days preceding the revolution.

In the last four years of the Shah's regime, while Iran had an official and a free-market rate of exchange in its 'commercial' and 'non-commercial' markets, the two rates were very close. Active intervention by Bank Markazi (that is, the sale of US dollars in the free market) disallowed any lasting disparity. During this period, the central bank reportedly, sold about $7 billion in the free market to support the rial, a large part of which was used to settle certain invisible services and capital transactions (including private investments abroad).[24] Thus, for all intents and purposes, Iran had an effective unitary exchange system and a virtually convertible currency.

For a number of reasons, the situation changed after the revolution. Although the country's annual oil revenues during the first five years of the Islamic Republic were nearly equal to the petrodollar income during the last five years of the monarchy (i.e., an annual average of $16.8 billion before, compared to $16.2 billion after), several new developments disallowed the exchange system to remain free or liberal. A radical and interventionist streak that permeated the revolutionaries' thinking at the time called for foreign exchange control as a means of reducing 'economic dependence' and cutting off the multinationals' undue influence on the Iranian economy.[25] Bolstering this ideological tendency were the deterioration, and ultimate severance, of diplomatic relations with the United States, the freezing of assets, the war with Iraq, and Western economic sanctions – all calling for greater controls, and added restrictions to be imposed on the use of foreign currencies.

The first symbolic act of defiance was to declare the de-linking of the Iranian rial from the US dollar – an arrangement that had been in effect since the mid-1970s.[26] Despite the new declaration, the official rial/dollar exchange was left unchanged at Rls 70.5 = $1 for a few months after the revolution. In May 1980, the use of the US dollar as the sole intervention currency was abandoned, and the rial/SDR peg was changed to Rls 912.2984 = SDR 1, with no margins on either side. Daily buying and selling rates were announced by Bank Markazi for 15 major foreign currencies, instead of just the US dollar.

Due to both ideological and practical considerations, the maintenance of a free exchange market, inoperative since shortly before the revolution, was totally terminated, and a dual exchange rate system immediately followed. By August 1980, the rial exchange rates had grown in number. For example, foreign currencies repatriated by Iranian workers abroad were given a bonus, and were puchased by the banks at Rls 115 per US dollar, and later at Rls 150. Non-oil exporters were required to sell their proceeds to the banking system at a preferential rate of 11 per cent higher than the official rate in order to prevent a re-emergence of a free market. All foreign exchange transactions were subjected to specific documentation. Gradually, a growing list of items, both goods and services, that were considered 'non-essential' were denied the benefit of the official (low) rate, and were shifted to other (higher) rates of exchange in a full-blown multiple-rate regime.

After the outbreak of war with Iraq, the grip on foreign exchange was tightened. Available foreign currencies were allocated each year through the foreign exchange budget among various uses and users. A substantial increase in imports during 1980/81 (due mostly to war-related requirements, reduced domestic supplies, and shortages of basic goods) led the government to establish a Foreign Exchange Allocation Commission to appropriate foreign currencies for 'essential' needs. The allocation was made by a special interdepartmental committee composed of representatives from different economic ministries and agencies. An annual foreign exchanges budget had now to be approvd by the *Majles*. Bank Markazi was responsible for the administration of the exchange quotas.

Exchange regulation went hand-in-hand with trade restrictions. Alarmed by the increasing demand for foreign exchange (including capital flight), Bank Markazi imposed new restrictions on purchases of foreign currencies at the official rate for non-commercial purposes (e.g., travel, medical treatment, and study abroad). Imports by the private sector were also severely restricted. All foreign purchases were made subject to regulation by various government agencies, as well as by the Center for Procurement and Distribution and the Organization for the Protection of Consumers and Producers. The latter agency had the responsibility of checking the declared prices of imported goods, their quality, their retail mark-up, and their distribution through the centers. After 1981/82, all basic imports were rationed, and all import letters of credit were subjected to prior approval by the central bank. In the following years, trade restrictions were tightened or relaxed according to the availability of foreign exchange. Until the end of the war, various restrictions were kept on payments for both current and capital transactions. After the ceasefire with Iraq, certain items previously banned as 'non-essential' were again authorized for importation.

During the eight-year war, the monetary authorities tried to increase the supply of foreign exchange in any way they could. To this end, banks in 1981/82 were authorized to open foreign exchange accounts in the name of individuals if the funds came from abroad. Balances in these accounts were entitled to the same rate of return applicable to individual savings accounts in rials; they could be freely expatriated, or sold to domestic banks at the preferential rate applying to non-oil exports. These privileges were later extended to non-residents as well.

Regulations governing import payments and non-oil export receipts were significantly liberalized after the ceasefire, in line with the first five-year development objectives. Before 1991, importers needed to have a license from the Ministry of Commerce before opening a letter of credit in the banks; a foreign exchange allocation voucher by the concerned ministry or agency; and an approval from a procurement and distribution center. As of January 1991, imports by the private sector at the floating exchange rate required none of the above. Only goods covered by the *official* or the *competitive* rates (whose importation was assigned to the private sector) were subject to specific import licensing and exchange allocation by the relevant organization under its own foreign exchange budget. There were also other liberalization measures. In mid-1991, some 30 per cent of total imports were subject to the basic official rate (as compared to about two-thirds before); about 10–15 per cent used the *floating* rate, and the rest were covered by the *competitive* rate. Most payments for invisibles were also covered by the *floating* rate.

Under the 1991 reforms, regulations concerning non-oil exports and the surrender of export proceeds were largely revamped. As in the case of imports, only a general trade registration (rather than a specific and quantitative export license) was henceforth required. Exporters' previous obligations to negotiate their 'reference' export prices and to surrender to the banking system at least 89 per cent of their earnings at incentive rates were all abolished. Export proceeds could be sold to the banking system at the *floating* rate, or in the free market at the exporter's discretion. The individual 'reference' pricing for each export shipment was also replaced by a 'category' pricing mechanism as an indicator of likely export earnings rather than a determinant of the surrender sum. In addition, 50 per cent of income tax on export earnings was to be refunded to exporters as an extra incentive.

Up to 1989/90 the Islamic Republic practised an elaborate and complicated system of 12 different exchange rates. The basic *official* rate of Rls 9.23 = SDR 1 applied to oil export revenues, most 'essential' imports, military items, some invisibles, and official capital transactions.[27] There were two basic *incentive* rates (i.e., the official rate plus Rls 270 and Rls 350 per US dollar) applicable to the surrender proceeds for non-oil exports. Two other specific *preferential* and *competitive* rates (Rls 420 and Rls 800 per US dollar) existed for the importation of raw materials used in the production of 131 domestic products. There was a *service* rate (Rls 845) charged for certain invisibles (for example, study or health care abroad). There was an *intervention* rate at which the free market was fed by the banking system. And, finally, there was a *free-market* rate for all other private transactions (fluctuating between Rls 1200–1400 per US dollar) in the latter part of the 1980s.[28] In practice, this complicated system was further compounded by a series of either incentives or disincentives within each category. For example, non-oil export proceeds were sold at various rates depending on the category of items and their 'reference' export prices. Importers who could not obtain a foreign exchange license from a government agency with limited exchange allocation were allowed to resort to the free market, and so on.

Effectively, all public sector imports and all goods considered essential (for instance, defense procurements, staple foods, medicine, certain raw materials, and some capital goods) were entitled to obtain foreign exchange at the *official* rate. Some raw materials and spare parts for the production of consumer durables could be imported at *preferential or competitive* rates. All other 'permitted' imports would come in at the fluctuating *free-market* rates. Limited amounts of foreign exchange at the official rate were also sold for authorized services such as study or travel abroad. The total supply of foreign exchange changing hands in the free market is estimated to have been about $1.5 – $2 billion a year, or about 10–15 per cent of annual foreign exchange dealings. Income transfers on the part of foreign nationals working in Iran, and the repatriation of foreign capital invested in the country as well as their profits could be effected at the official exchange rate under certain limitations, regulations, supervision and/or certification of origin.[29] Under the post-ceasefire reforms discussed below, all future foreign direct investments will be given freedom of repatriation of profits and principal at the original rate of conversion into the Iranian rial.

Under the post-1991 reforms, the exchange rate structure was drastically simplified, but the multiple-rate system, and some restrictions on payments, for both current and capital transactions, were maintained. The 12 different exchange rates detailed above were reduced to three.

As of May 1992, the procedures for foreign exchange allocation were as follows. First, there continued to be the *basic* official rate at Rls 92.30 = SDR 1. Receipts from oil and gas exports, official capital inflows and invisibles fell into this rate category. Payments at this basic rate were authorized for specific imports, and for certain capital and invisible transactions. Privileged imports included essential food, spare parts, raw materials, defense-related items, and inputs for strategic national projects – all covered out of the foreign exchange budget, and requiring prior approval by the Ministry of Commerce and the ministry with allocated foreign exchange. Capital and invisibles included official debt, repatriation of dividends on certain foreign direct investment, part of the salaries of 'essential' foreign workers, and limited payments for authorized services such as study or medical treatment abroad.

Second, a *competitive* rate of Rls 600 = $1[30] applied to sales by embassies to meet local expenses, and to scores of specific imports needed by domestic industrial enterprises. These imports included raw materials, spare parts, and consumer products, and still required prior approval and allocation. Certain medical and transportation expenses were also entitled to receive foreign exchange at this rate. A large number of intermediate and capital goods and certain invisibles, which had previously enjoyed the basic rate, were subject to this rate. As part of the government's intention to unify the exchange rates eventually, a number of items in this category were moved to the floating rate.

Third, the *floating* exchange rate replaced the old intervention rate, and applied to all ordinary transactions including those not covered by the other two rates. This rate was variable, and announced daily by Bank Markazi – slightly below the free-market rate at about Rls 1440. Receipts in this category included: proceeds from non-energy exports; foreign direct investment inflows; tourist expenditures, and all other foreign exchange offers. Payments applied to all authorized imports with no restrictions, but subject to pre-registration with a Procurement and Distribution Center and a commercial bank, or an additional 10 per cent commercial profit tax. Capital and invisibles transactions in this category covered repatriation of principal and dividend; limited allowance not eligible for cheaper rates; and transfers from individual foreign currency accounts.

A *free-market* rate, determined solely by free forces, and free from any restrictions, has continued to exist alongside the other three. This rate is determined by the developments in the global foreign exchange market, seasonal fluctuations in the local demand and supply of foreign currencies, and other relevant variables (including psychological reactions to domestic and world events). The rate is also itself influenced by the daily sales of foreign currencies in the open market by Bank Markazi and commercial banks. These daily injections of funds by Bank Markazi have kept the free rate from excessive rise. Foreign exchange has been bought and sold at this rate on a no-questions-asked basis. Purchases in the free market could be transferred abroad through the banking system.[31]

Transactions at the basic and the competitive rates had to be included in the annual approved foreign exchange budget.[32] The share of transactions at the basic rate in total import payments in 1991/92 was 61 per cent; that of the competitive rate 19 per cent; and for the floating rate and the free rate, 15–20 per cent. Bilateral payments arrangements that existed with Eastern European countries and the former Soviet Union were all terminated in 1991 and 1992. These arrangements remained active with only Algeria and the Syrian Arab Republic by mid-1992.

The exchange regime was further modified as of March 21, 1993 in the direction of additional rial devaluation and exchange unification.[33] The country's projected $19.5 billion of foreign exchange receipts in 1993/94 were to be offered to the private sector and most of the public enterprises at the 'floating' exchange rate except for $3800 million set aside for the government's own imports of basic food, fuel, pharmaceuticals and defense needs at the official rate of 70 Rls to the dollar. Public entities and enterprises which had enjoyed specific foreign exchange allocation in previous years were instead budgeted Rls 1,000 for each previously allocated dollar, and were directed to purchase their foreign exchange needs in the open market at the floating rate. The foreign exchange budget was effectively terminated.

The official 'floating' exchange rate at Rls 1538 to $1 announced at the start of the Iranian new year indicated a *de facto* devaluation of 95.6 per cent. The Iranian currency was declared 'fully convertible' in mid-April 1993 at Rls 1648 to the dollar. The latter rate, however, was revalued slightly several times during mid-1993 to about Rls 1600 to the dollar in late July. Nevertheless, experts believed that a successful stabilization of the currency at the new level would require simultaneous introduction of a series of monetary, fiscal and welfare measures for which a good deal of political will, technical expertise and ample compensatory resources would be needed. Without such a comprehensive financial scheme, a drastic overnight devaluation of the rial (a kind of shock therapy) would be bound to dry up the sources of income for many established interest groups; push prices of public-enterprise products through the roof; raise the price of imported foodstuffs and other subsidized imports; and create a destabilizing financial panic. The authorities, aware of these dire eventualities, have talked about a 'safety net' of subsidies and other measures to cushion the impact of rising prices and economic hardship on the poor.[34]

FOREIGN INVESTMENT

The current five-year development plan clearly anticipates foreign participation in financing some development projects to the sum of $27 billion under different arrangements. While not specifically emphasized, the spirit of these arrangements suggests that the government is ready to welcome foreign private investment under certain conditions. The framework for attracting foreign participation is still the old law of November 28, 1955.[35] On the eve of the 1979 revolution, Iran had an estimated $1.57 billion of foreign investments, up from $56 million in 1971/72. As a result of political upheaval and the government's new policy, those investments fell to less than $550 million in the following year. There were virtually no major or new foreign investments in Iran after the revolution except for Rls 12 billion by the Japanese in their petrochemical joint venture in the south.

For a while, it was not even clear whether foreign capital could legally be invested in the local economy. The radical hardliners relentlessly invoked Article 81 of the 1979 Constitution which 'absolutely' forbids the granting of 'concessions' to foreigners for establishing companies or engaging in trade and business in Iran. In 1981, the Council of Guardians interpreted the constitutional prohibition to mean only monopolistic rights rather than 'legal contracts' properly concluded with Iranian government agencies. In May 1985, the Council of Ministers also resolved that joint ventures under the provision of the 1955 investment law were not a contravention of Article 81. Under these accepted interpretations, foreign capital can be invested in Iran in the form of partnerships or joint ventures where Iranians, private firms or state-owned enterprises, hold various share percentages, and the activity does not fall under exclusive government ownership and operation.

In mid-1992, the High Council on Investment, a cabinet-level group, announced its readiness to consider applications for foreign private investment in Iran with no limitation on ownership or management control. Such investment was to be guaranteed a free return on capital and profit to investors' home countries, and of compensation in hard currencies in case of future nationalization or confiscation.[36] Hardliners in and out of the *Majles* have subsequently denounced this new policy as contrary to Articles 81, 153, and 43(8) of the 1979 Constitution, which ban foreign concessions and prohibit foreign control over national resources.[37] While the government seems to have prevailed in its decision, no application for notable long-term private foreign investment was reportedly in hand by September 1992.[38] One reason for this lack of interest may be the uncertainty as to whether a simple government directive is sufficient for lifting the 49 per cent ceiling on foreign stakes, or whether a *Majles* act is needed – a requirement which the government is evidently reluctant to follow. Other reasons cited by prospective investors range from bureaucratic hurdles and frequently changing regulations to the volatile exchange rates and high-cost labor.

APPENDIX: IRAN–US CLAIMS SETTLEMENT

On November 14, 1979, ten days after the American Embassy staff were taken hostage in Tehran, Finance Minister Abol Hassan Bani-Sadr threatened to withdraw all Iranian deposits from US banks. President Jimmy Carter immediately ordered the US Treasury, under the International Emergency Power Act of 1977, to freeze all Iranian assets held by the US government or by US banks and companies at home or abroad. The total amount of Iranian funds blocked by the US was estimated to be $12 billion. Twelve large American banks held the lion's share of Iran's frozen assets.[39]

On the day after the Treasury action, the Chase Manhattan Bank – the leading partner in a twelve-bank, $500 million, syndicated loan to the Shah's government – failed to receive a $4 million interest instalment due on the loan because the assets were frozen. The New York bank thus immediately declared Iran in default. Chase's action set off a chain of legal moves by other banks and companies to protect their outstanding loans by attaching Iranian properties in US courts. Some 300 lawsuits, attaching about $6 billion of the Iranian assets, were soon filed.

As part of the negotiations for the release of the US hostages, the Iranian government demanded $14 billion from the United States as the value of Iranian gold and other assets claimed to have been frozen by Washington or otherwise under 'attachment' by the US government. In addition, Tehran asked for a cash guarantee equal to $10 billion as a percentage share of the properties of the Iranian people allegedly 'plundered by the deposed Shah and his relatives'. Among the $14 billion of frozen assets claimed by the Iranian government, $4 billion was listed as the deposits of Bank Markazi with American banks in London and Paris; about $875 million in deposits by various Iranian agencies in American commercial banks in the US; $1 billion worth of gold and $270 million cash with the Federal Reserve Bank of New York; $1 billion worth of US Treasury notes; $800 million deposited in the US Foreign Military

Sales Trust for military purchases; and $2.1 billion relating to oil delivered to US companies not yet paid for.

The US Treasury estimated Iranian assets in the United States in November 1979 to be 'no more than $8 billion', but gave no exact figure. Private estimates at the time reached as high as $13 billion. On the Shah's alleged assets in the United States, Washington neither ventured an estimate, nor took any step to freeze them. The Islamic government claimed that the Shah and the royal family had taken between $32 billion and (by some wild estimates) $72 billion out of Iran. But a spokesman for the family estimated the Shah's estate as worth 'less than $200 million', not all of it in the United States.[40]

In September 1980, Ayatollah Khomeini declared the unfreezing of Iranian assets a condition for releasing the hostages. A flurry of diplomatic efforts immediately began, and legal and finanical negotiations got underway to settle the matter. In what was termed the largest private financial transfer in history, an agreement was finally reached between Washington and Tehran, under Algeria's good offices, to release Iran's frozen assets in exchange for the release of the hostages.

Although at some point Iran had asked for a straight $24 billion as a condition for the hostages' freedom, the final accord involved a very different amount, and a more complex agreement. Briefly put, of the nearly $12 billion on the list of Iranian assets frozen on November 14, 1974, some $5.5 billion were found to be Iranian deposits in the overseas branches of US Banks; $4 billion was held in the US by banks or companies in the form of deposits or other assets; and $2.4 billion represented cash, securities, gold and down-payments for arms that were controlled by the US Federal government. In accordance with the Algiers accord, $7.977 billion of the total was transferred to an escrow account of the Algerian Central Bank at the Bank of England. This portion was then divided as follows: $3.76 billion was paid back to US banks and their international partners as the repayments of all syndicated loans they had arranged for the Shah's government; nearly $1.4 billion went into an escrow account to liquidate loans made by other individual banks to the Iranian central government, quasi-public entities, or Iranian banks; and $2.86 billion was paid back to Iran's Bank Markazi. The $4 billion of deposits in US banks' domestic branches was to be used to pay off some 4,000 legal claims by US citizens against Iran to be adjudicated in a nine-man international arbitration tribunal established in The Hague. Iran was expected to receive at least half of this amount eventually.[41]

By mid-1987, the special US-Iran Claims Tribunal in The Hague ordered some $858 million in American private claims to be paid by Iran, and $64 million in Iranian claims to be paid by Washington. At the same time, since Iran had paid off some loans to non-US members of banking syndicates (in addition to the $3.76 billion paid back to the Federal Reserve Bank of New York), the Tribunal ordered the US Treasury to return $454 million (loan repayments plus accumulated interest since 1982) to Tehran. Washington released $570 million of the assets in the fall of 1989 and spring of 1990. By January 1993, more than 3840 cases placed before the tribunal had reportedly been adjudicated.[42] A final agreement on compensation of $278 million to Iran from Washington for undelivered American-made military equipment purchased before the revolution was reported in November 1991.[43] Among Iran's still outstanding claims against the United States were compensation for the Iran Air passenger jet shot down by USS Vincennes in 1988 involving the death of 290 people and damage inflicted on four oil platforms in the Persian Gulf by US forces in 1987–1988.

Under the 1981 Algiers agreement, Iran was to maintain a security fund of $500 million at all times for the periodic settlements of US companies' claims. In 1991, the fund fell below $500 million, and Washington authorized over $200 million worth of Iranian oil to be directly imported into the United States (and exempt from the embargo) on condition that payments went into the security account. After payment of $260 million to two US oil companies in November 1992, the fund again contained only $250 million, or half the required amount, and Tehran was put on notice to replenish the account.[44]

Exactly how much of Iran's funds in the United States still remains frozen is a matter of dispute between the two countries. The Iranian press frequently mentions $12–20 billion without giving details or evidence.[45] Some private American analysts put the figure at less than $2 billion. A more reliable informal estimate of the blocked assets gives a figure of $11 billion.[46]

NOTES

1. *Gozaresh-e Towzihi-ye Layeh-e Dowlati Kardan-e Bazargani-ye Khareji* (Explanatory Report on Foreign Trade Nationalization Bill) (Tehran: Ministry of Commerce, April 1981), pp. 34–41.
2. For details of the Council's ruling see *Ettela'at*, 6 Azar, 1361.
3. See 'Iran's Foreign Economic Policies', *Ettela'at*, 31 Bahman 1362, p. 5.
4. Four years into the revolution, Third World and Moslem countries

acquired a 25 per cent share of total Iranian trade, and socialist countries accounted for 11 per cent, with the West's share reduced to about 65 per cent (compared with pre-revolution percentages of 10, 5, and 85 respectively). The US portion was down to a trickle.

5. This tax was tantamount to the share of the profit made by importers to which the state was entitled since it had a 'monopoly' on foreign trade under a law enacted in the early 1930s.

6. Earlier, on November 9, Washington had announced the suspension of deliveries of about $300 million of military equipment and spare parts to Iran.

7. The breakdown of imports into military and civilian items is not available. It is estimated that by 1985/86 some 30–40 per cent of all imports were military equipment, not separately identified. Some items were also believed not to be included in official import data. See The Economist Intelligence Unit 'Iran: Country Profile 1991–92', p. 40. For these and other reasons, the figures for total imports in Tables 10.1 and 10.6 do not always match.

8. *IRNA* broadcast in English, June 16, 1991. Iran's import of wheat in 1989/90 was officially put at 5 million tons. *Kayhan Havai* August 29, 1990.

9. *The New York Times*, April 9, 1991, p. A10.

10. *Iran Focus*, July 1990, p. 10.

11. For details see *Iran Focus* May 1990, p. 8.

12. *Kayhan Havai*, March 11, and April 1, 1992.

13. *MEED*, November 15, 1991, February 21, 1992 and July 9, 1993; and *US-Iran Review*, April 1993. US trade regulations impose a nearly complete embargo on imports from Iran. But sales of US products to Iran are allowed for non-strategic, non-military items (e.g. oil-field equipment, spare parts, construction machinery, and medical products).

14. The most noteworthy element in the 1982 trade was the Soviet purchase of 2.2 million tons of Iranian oil for the first time ever.

15. In July 1992, Iran raised its share of capital in the Islamic Development Bank from 2.5 million to 177 million dinar units.

16. Balance-of-payments data published by Bank Markazi often show sizeable differences from customs data, and from those appearing in international publications. There are also frequent revisions year after year in the original figures.

17. From 1979 to 1986, the fund outflows were estimated at $10 billion. See *U.S. News and World Report*, March 17, 1986.

18. By contrast, in 1991, 70 per cent of Mexico's exports represented non-oil sales, with 55 per cent from the manufacturing sector alone. *The Wall Street Journal*, February 21, 1992.

19. For example, the reserve figure at the end of March 1980 was put at $10 billion by the then President Bani-Sadr, and at $4 billion at the end of March 1981. *Ettela'at*, 9 Farvardin 1360. Or, the Bank Markazi governor was quoted as claiming that Iran's foreign exchange

reserves amounted to $9.72 billion on March 20, 1990. *Reuters,* August 23, 1990. See also the *Middle East,* January 1993.

20. Iran's foreign assets on the eve of the revolution are estimated to have been $15 billion, and its foreign debt $7.5 billion. See *Institutional Investor,* December 1984, p. 126. The assets figure in both official and private publications evidently excluded a good part of Iran's loans and investments abroad, as these were never published in detail before the revolution. The figure also excluded sizeable private holdings of Iranian citizens abroad.

21. See *The New York Times* July 31, 1979 and November 24, 1979; and *Business Week,* January 5, 1979.

22. See *Kayhan Havai,* August 14, 1990, p. 9; and *World Debt Tables* (Washington: The World Bank, 1992).

23. See the *Economist Intelligence Unit,* 'Iran: Country Report', No. 1, 1993; and *MEED,* November 27, 1992, February 5, and April 9, 1993.

24. *Barrasi Tahavollat* (1984), p. 325.

25. For an impassioned defense of this policy, see Ebrahim Razzaqi, (1988), ch. 13.

26. In February 1975, the Iranian rial was pegged to the IMF's Special Drawing Rights at Rls 82.2425 = SDR 1, and the US dollar became only the intervention currency. A margin of $2\frac{1}{4}$ per cent on both sides of the new rate was established for allowable daily fluctuations before intervention became necessary. However, as deviations from the margins exceeded the limits, the government was reluctant to change the rial/dollar rate, and the margins were widened to $7\frac{1}{4}$ per cent on each side. Subsequently, the rial remained effectively fixed on the US dollar.

27. Through the years, the dollar/rial equivalent of the SDR rate fluctuated within a wide range of Rls 68 = $1 to Rls 91 = $1 as the SDR/dollar rate underwent daily changes. See Table 10.6.

28. By the summer of 1979, the free-market rate of the Iranian rial (which was close to the official rate of Rls 70) reached Rls 115 per US dollar. By mid-November 1979, after the hostage crisis, the value of the US dollar rose to as high as Rls 170. By December 1982, the rate was close to Rls 400. The rate climbed to Rls 620 in December 1984; Rls 815 at the end of 1986; Rls 1100 in 1987; Rls 1450 in 1989; and Rls 1660 in early 1993. For details of yearly fluctuations see the *World Currency Yearbook* for each year.

29. If foreign investment had taken place at the free-market rate, then repatriation was also effected at the same rate.

30. The *competitive* rate of Rls 800 = $1 was reduced to Rls 600 = $1 as prices of imported products and domestic items surged upward.

31. The free-market rate hovered around Rls 1450–1500 = $1 for most of 1992.

32. This budget for 1992/93 was $19.8 billion, compared with $20 billion for 1991/92.

33. The unreality of the official rate can best be understood by the fact

that, while private liquidity rose some 23 times between 1972/73 and 1991/92, the rial/dollar rate remained fixed at about Rls 70 = $1.

34. For details of the Iranian exchange system, see *Exchange Arrangements and Exchange Restrictions Annual Report 1992*, (Washington: International Monetary Fund, 1992).
35. *Law & Regulation Concerning the Attraction and Protection of Foreign Investments In Iran* (Tehran: Ministry of Economic Affairs and Finance n.d.). See also *MEED*, February 21, 1992.
36. See *The New York Times*,June 29, 1992, and *Kayhan Havai*, June 17, 1992. For details regarding the application of the law, see *Iran Business Monitor*, September 1992.
37. For the opposition's arguments, see *Jomhuri Eslami*, 15 Khordad 1371 (June 5, 1992).
38. *Kayhan Havai*, September 2, 1992, p. 14.
39. The actual size of the assets has, to this day, been a matter of dispute and has never been authoritatively determined.
40. *The New York Times*, December 22, 1980.
41. For details of the accord, see J. A. Westberg, *Case Law of the Iran-U.S. Claims Tribunal* (Washington: International Law Institute, 1991).
42. *Kayhan Havai*, January 29, 1992, p. 11.
43. *The New York Times*, November 28, 1991.
44. *MEED*, November 27, 1992.
45. *Kayhan Havai*, May 20, 1992.
46. For further details about the dispute and its adjudication, see Warren Christopher, *American Hostages in Iran* (New Haven: Yale University Press, 1985).

V
MAIN ECONOMIC
SECTORS

11

Agriculture: farming, fisheries and forestry

Iran's geography presents extremes of temperatures, humidity, rainfall and wind. Vast contrasts in topography and hydrology affect both the climate and variety of soils. Frequent droughts, floods, sudden temperature changes, and earthquakes limit both the area under cultivation and product varieties. Due to relatively scant rainfall, most cash crops have to be irrigated. Several large dams and a vast network of traditional underground canals — *qanats* — serve as the main water supplies. A half-dozen small dams were completed after the revolution. But water remains in critical shortage.

Iran's agricultural endowments and development potential are subject to different estimates among experts. Some analysts believe that all essential factors — climate, water and land — are weak except in certain tiny areas.[1] Others argue that substantial under-utilized resources in water and soil and significant potential for increases in yields, still remain to be tapped. For example, an additional 1 million hectares of land are said to be cultivable through improved irrigation efficiency. Yields in rain-fed areas can also be substantially improved.

In the absence of an updated soil survey (reportedly under preparation), estimates of arable and cultivable land also vary considerably. By all accounts, Iran's total land area of about 165 million hectares is more than 52 per cent (82 million hectares) desert and wasteland. By some estimates, over 17 per cent of the total (28 million hectares) consists of pastures, forest and scrub-lands. This leaves about 30 per cent of the whole territory, or about 50 million hectares, as potential cropland. But expert opinions differ on the size of cultivable land. Conservative estimates place the land available for arable farming at about 10 per cent of the country's surface area at best, and 7.5 per cent or less at least. More generous estimates go as high as 12–13 per cent.

The latest official statistics show the total arable land at about 17.8 million hectares, of which about 5.4 million hectares remain fallow. The 17.8 million hectares of cultivated area is divided between rain-fed (10.5 million hectares) and irrigated (7.3 million hectares). Of the total irrigated land, 1.2 million hectares consist of orchards.[2] These estimates leave some 17–18 per cent (or nearly 30–32 million hectares) as marginal uncultivated land which might be potentially capable of reclamation if water were available. The area under permanent crops is less than 1 per cent of the total. Of the 900,000 hectares below major dams, only 300,000 hectares are used.

Expansion of cropland thus depends mainly on the amount of rainfall and partially on the better utilization of surface water sources and dams. In terms of its average annual rainfall (17 to 20 inches, or one-third of the world average) Iran is commonly characterized as a semi-arid country. More significantly, some 52 per cent of the total rainfall occurs in the Caspian littoral which constitutes only 25 per cent of Iran's area. Nevertheless, by some estimates, about 40 per cent of the country's water capacity (i.e., 50 billion cubic meters) remains unutilized or under-utilized. Some agronomists even argue that, with efficient utilization of its existing supplies, Iran is *not* a water-short area. By some estimates, 60 per cent of Iran's rainfall is usually evaporated and unutilized; 15 per cent goes underground; and only 25 per cent remains on the surface, of which almost half pours into lakes and rivers. Only 12.5 per cent of rain water is thus used for irrigation, largely by traditional and inefficient methods. A good number of the country's *qanats* that used to irrigate some 40 per cent of all villages have now gone dry or are in disrepair due to earthquake damage, or the need for collective maintenance that is not practical under small land-ownership. Mechanization, although highly encouraged by both the previous and the present regime, is still not well developed.

The agriculture sector includes farming, livestock, forestry and fisheries. On a yearly average, farming constitutes some 50–60 per cent of the value added in this sector, followed by 30–40 per cent from livestock, 2 per cent from forest products, and less than 1 per cent from fishing. Agricultural productivity is found to be one-third of the level of developed countries. Annual farm output is considerably below the country's potential. The average weight of cattle and calves, as well as the average milk produced per cow, is considerably below world averages.

According to the latest estimates published by the Iranian Statistical Center, in 1988/89 there were some 41 million sheep, 22 million goats, and 6.4 million cattle in Iran.[3] Livestock raising is conducted by nomadic tribes, traditional farms, and a small number of modern establishments near major urban centers. Iran is believed to have over 80 varieties of fish (including the caviar-bearing sturgeon) in the Caspian Sea and over 200 species in the Persian Gulf. More than 176,000 hectares of land surface in Iran are forest – mainly oak, ash, elm, beech, poplar, pine, cypress, maple and walnut.

Food grains currently use more than two-thirds of the total area under annual cultivation, with wheat representing 46 per cent, and barley 18 per cent. Nearly two-thirds of food grain crops are rain-fed. Rice, cotton, sugar beets, oil seeds, potatoes, and forage occupy most of the remainder of the cultivated lands. (Table 11.1.)

BREAK WITH THE PAST

The Islamic Republic's assessment of pre-revolution agriculture was one of total disapproval, if not outright condemnation. Agricultural growth was found slow in comparison with that of industry and services, and the share of farming in the domestic product fell between 1973/74 and 1977/78. Dependence on imports for food items was seen as unduly large. The country's agricultural potential in both land and water usage was judged insufficiently utilized. Terms of trade were said to have moved against the rural sector.

Slow growth, sluggish productivity and stagnant rural income were blamed on a host of factors, all presumably rooted in the old regime's allegedly scant attention to agriculture, emphasis on rapid urbanization, and pro-industrialization policies. Low agricultural productivity was blamed on the maldistribution of credit in favor of large farmers; high cost and insufficient use of machinery; and paucity of proper seeds, fertilizers and pesticides. Stagnant real income was attributed to increasing inflation and rising production costs; a multiplicity of middlemen; inadequate price support by the government; forward sales of crops at low prices; and rising costs of the farmers' industrial and service needs. The lure of urban life, food subsidies offered to city workers by the government, and new problems created by the Shah's land reform program were said to have expedited rural migration and aggravated the plight of the rural population. In short, Iran's development under the previous regime was found to be superficial because economic planning neglected agriculture and failed to support farmers and livestock growers (who constituted half of Iran's population).

The Shah's land reform program (1963–1974) was criticized for the following reasons: land was not distributed among all farmers but only to renters and sharecroppers; the size of the plot given each family was less than the minimum necessary for subsistence; the initial 'land-to-the-tiller' policy was subsequently reversed in favor of state farm corporations and large private agribusiness; and the program was not adequately assisted with necessary financial and technical backstopping. The result, the critics claimed, was increased rural poverty, mass migration, dependency on imports, and the decline of farming as a share of the gross domestic products. Another charge repeatedly made by the revolutionaries was that the previous regime ruined Iran's traditional agriculture, making the country dependent on imported food for about 25–30 per cent of its national needs in wheat, soya beans, vegetable oil and rice.[4]

Shortly after the revolution, the Provisional Government decided to end its direct participation in agricultural production, and to limit its involvement to the provision of farm credit, training, technical services, and price support. To this end, a large number of state farm corporations were dissolved and their assets returned to their farmer-shareholders.[5] Steps were also taken to liquidate large state agribusiness enterprises. Simultaneously, the government raised the previous price support levels for certain crops, and reduced interest rates on farm loans. A land reform law was also enacted to distribute farmlands among potential cultivators. In 1981/82, rice was added to wheat and barley as crops purchased by the government at guaranteed prices.

Determined to undo the old regime's 'mistakes', and to put Iran's agriculture on a new path of regeneration and eventual self-sufficiency, the Islamic Republic introduced a detailed and elaborate agenda as part of its first five-year plan (1983/84–1987/88). The list of objectives included ultimate self-sufficiency within ten years through increased output, and moderation in consumption of farm products within physiological, nutritional and traditional requirements; the conservation of natural resources, and replacement of oil and gas for wood burning needs; the improvement of rural income through enhanced opportunities for output and employment, and expansion of cottage industries; the improvement of traditional water systems, and expansion of new irrigation networks; the cultivation of barren and abandoned land; the reform of the land tenure system; and the expansion and improvement of fisheries.

To these ends, the government obligated itself to institute appropriate programs for, firstly, the provision of material and technical needs of the farm sector such as selected seeds for irrigated and rain-fed lands, infrastructural services, credit, instruction, research in the area of combining farming with animal husbandry, proper cultivation and harvesting methods, and pest control; secondly, the determination of costs and prices for different products in different parts of the country for the purpose of minimum price support; and thirdly, the adequate supply and proper distribution of farm credit, particularly credit in kind, and supervision of its use.

The new path toward agricultural rejuvenation envisaged a mixture of private operation and state regulation. As part of this basic strategy, the system of land ownership was destined to change. The latter, under the original 1962/63 land reform program, had shifted toward the establishment of a small peasant proprietor class, but after 1964/65 drifted away from that objective, and from 1967/68 onwards turned toward large scale agribusiness and farm corporations. It now had to come full circle. Following the revolution, the traditional small and medium-size farms were favored once again in a land reform bill submitted to the *Majles* in 1980.[6] Although the bill was not passed as submitted, the Land Allocation Boards proceeded with parcelling out 'ownerless' as well as state-owned lands among small peasant cultivators. Under the post-ceasefire reforms, however, it was decided once again to allocate some farm lands to large investors in single plots rather than having them split into several small ones. Investors were to be provided with irrigation water and other facilities to create big agro-industrial farms.[7]

EMERGING DILEMMAS

As outlined earlier, the Shah's Land Reform Program and his agricultural policy in the 1960s and 1970s were among the opposition's primary points of contention. Ayatollah Khomeini and his bourgeois supporters blamed the Shah for the sluggish growth of agriculture, low yield, depletion of rural population, and the country's growing dependence on food imports.[8] Left-wing followers and their theoreticians criticized the Shah's farm policy as 'the groundwork for transforming Iran into a dependent capitalist state'.[9] There was strong political pressure on the revolutionary government to give agriculture reform high priority. A more compelling factor, however, was the breakdown of law and order in the countryside and unauthorized land seizure by peasants, former landlords and revolutionary units in many parts of the country.[10]

Farmers and farm workers expropriated large holdings abandoned by their owners (particularly along the Caspian Sea and in the Turkaman districts in the North) invoking the revolution's promises of Islamic equity and justice. Former resident landlords began to claim their distributed lands on the grounds that the Shah's program was un-Islamic. Revolutionary committees and local courts ordered confiscation of the landholdings of those accused of cooperation with the monarchy, and placed them at the disposal of the *Bonyad-e Mostazafan*.[11]

In September 1979, the Revolutionary Council passed a bill for the Transfer and Revival of Land, calling for the distribution of *mawat* (barren land) and arable estates confiscated from associates of the previous regime. After the ratification of the Constitution, an amended draft of the law was passed by the Council in April 1980 under the title of Land Allocation and Rehabilitation. The new act, sanctioned by three leading ayatollahs, aimed at large-scale land redistribution and reform. It limited landholdings to 2 to 3 times the acreage locally considered sufficient for the maintenance of a peasant family. This provision effectively reduced the largest single farm to less than 30 acres. Implementation of the law was entrusted to the seven-member Land Allocation Boards made up of central and local representatives.

In practice, the new law proved to be a nightmare for the authorities. Overzealousness by land committees resulted in more turmoil in the countryside and widespread new land seizures through arbitrary decisions by run-away local boards. Opposition to the law arose among farm specialists who saw a ruinous break-up of efficient, mechanized farms; middle-level commercial farmers and landowners (through well-organized local 'agricultural councils'); and five leading ayatollahs (declaring the law to be in violation of Islamic principles). In November 1980, six months after the passage of the bill, Ayatollah Khomeini ordered its suspension. By that time, some 35,000 hectares of arable land (mostly the lands in the government's hands) had been transferred to the peasants. Some 800,000–850,000 hectares had also been 'leased' to peasants on a temporary basis (*kesht-e movaqqat*) because their owners had challenged the law's constitutionality.

A new draft of the land reform bill presented to the newly elected *Majles* in 1980 brought the infighting among the post-revolution leaders to the surface. A radical group, calling themselves *Moja-*

hedin of the Islamic Revolution (not to be confused with the
Marxist *Mojahedin-e Khalq*), lobbied for the bill's passage as the
cornerstone of Iran's economic recovery program. An influential
group of clerical landowners, trustees of endowed landed estates,
and other religious conservatives opposed the legislation. In June
1980, the *Majles* passed a compromise law for the nationalization
of unused urban land, but the Council of Guardians refused to
approve it on the grounds that such confiscation was un-Islamic.
Upon Ayatollah Khomeini's personal intervention, and the substitution of 'purchase' for 'confiscation', the Council approved the
bill for a limited duration.

In December 1982, the *Majles* approved yet another rural land
reform law, retaining the 1980 law's upper limits on farm ownership, but calling on landowners to lease the extra acreage to local
peasants under various Islamic provisions (for example, rent,
partnership and sharecropping). This law was again vetoed by the
Council of Guardians on the grounds that it went beyond Islamic
law in scuttling private property rights for the good of the
community. In October 1986, the *Majles* passed special legislation
regarding the 800,000–850,000 hectares given to farmers for
temporary cultivation. It provided for all land already in the hands
of non-owner cultivators to be permanently transferred to them
provided they were poor, lacked other sources of income, and were
local residents.

According to the central headquarters for the Land Allocation
Boards, by December 1990, some 1.25 million hectares of barren,
agricultural, industrial and 'temporary' cultivation land had been
distributed among 220,000 rural families. Of the 850,000 hectares
temporarily occupied by peasants, some 130,000 hectares were
transferred permanently to 20,000 farmers by January 1990, and
400,000 hectares were scheduled to be ceded to their occupiers by
1992.[12]

Due primarily to the basic ideological rift between the two main
clerical factions, ambiguities regarding private ownership of much
confiscated and distributed land continue to this day.[13] Uncertainties concerning property rights in the Islamic Republic have not
been cleared up yet, and private investors still shy away from long-
term commitments on that account.

INSTITUTIONAL BASE

On the eve of the revolution, farm lands in Iran were cultivated by
several different modes. Following the Shah's land reform, some

1.6–1.8 million farm families (totalling an estimated 12 million people) had become small-scale owner/operators of more than 8 million hectares tilled in traditional fashion.[14] The second mode consisted of commercial farming, using farm machinery. Mechanized farming typically took place in irrigated areas of from 50 to 400 hectares owned by prosperous landowners who used deep water wells and produced mostly cotton and sugar beets. In exceptional, cases, the mechanized farms belonging to very large landholders ploughed several thousand hectares of irrigated lands thanks to large credits from agriculture banks and the use of modern farm practices.

Farm corporations, consisting of large entities established to consolidate small and unprofitable holdings that belonged to new peasant/proprietors, were the third mode. In these farm corporations, new landowners were required to exchange the land titles received under land reform for shares of stock. A variant of these farm corporations were the production cooperatives where farmers pooled their resources in large-scale operations, without giving up the title to their land. These modes covered some 300,000 hectares of farms, involving about 130 units, and some 75,000 families. To encourage mechanization, and promote mixed commercial farming in areas arrigated by large dams, the Law for Development of Agricultural Poles in 1975 had devised a still different mode or pattern, called agribusiness (or agro-industry), which consisted of integrated farm enterprises to which farmers sold their lands and became farm workers. Several hundred projects, involving several thousand hectare tracts, were approved by the government, but only a small number of Iranian-owned, or joint-ventures with foreign interests came to fruition. The latter were not very successful.

Finally, there were several public regional development enterprises (in Qazvin, Jiroft, and Sefid Rud) that were managed by the Ministry of Agriculture as large-scale farm operations in areas classified as public domain.

These arrangements were subjected to certain reformulations after the revolution, but were, for the most part, *de facto* recognized. Only the religious endowments' properties (*owqaf*) which had also been included in the old land reform program were taken away from the tillers' ownership by *Majles* laws in 1983, and 1992, and leased to them instead. Some farmlands, managed by farm corporations or production cooperatives, were returned to their shareholder participants, and corporate installations and equipment were used as rural service units. Public agribusiness joint-ventures rid themselves of foreign partners, and continued operation as public enterprises.

SECTORAL MANAGEMENT AND CONTROL

Administratively, Iranian agriculture under the Islamic Republic has been supervised by a number of public agencies and institutions. The main responsibility for this sector has rested with the Ministery of Agriculture. The Ministry of Water and Power is also peripherally involved in agricultural issues concerning irrigation (mostly the construction of high dams). The Ministry of Agriculture is in charge of the general farm policy formulation and application, crop supervision and development, research and extension services, management of public agri-business corporations, and control of marketing organizations. The Soil and Water Research Institute and the Plant Improvement Institute are the two major technical units with several hundred scientists and experts working on hundreds of research projects. Extension and service centers offer training, and facilitate technological transfer, including guidance for raising crop yields. A number of marketing boards for grain, meat, and milk are supervised by the ministry, as are several food processing plants.

The Ministry of Jihad, starting in June 1979 as *Jihad-e Sazandeqi* (Construction Crusade), was initially a semi-religious, semi-revolutionary institution. It was set up as a volunteer agency with the task of revitalizing the allegedly neglected rural sector. Its basic responsibilities were to increase food supplies and to improve the farmers' standard of living.[15] Assisted by voluntary local contributions of resources and manpower, the Jihad began with rural road building, irrigation works, and electrification. Later, it spread out into extension and training, research, water mobilization, and seed distribution. Still later, it added on the management of fisheries, small rural industries, and local construction. By 1991/92 the originally small, self-help, voluntary organization had a staff of some 55,000 (rivalling the Ministry of Agriculture's 74,000 employees). The bulk of its resources consisted of public funds, appropriated under the national budget for agricultural development. The ministry was in essence a hybrid of planning and execution at the village level. Since 1990, this ministry has focused its responsibilities on livestock development, leaving farming largely to the Ministry of Agriculture.

Farm credits are supplied to farmers by the Agricultural Credit Bank, in conformity with Islamic banking tenets, under three main arrangements: short- and medium-term 'interest-free' loans with a small 'service fee' depending on the borrower (for example, cooperatives or individuals) and the amount; instalment sales of machinery, equipment, or other inputs where the borrower pays the bank in instalments for the cost of the item plus a 'mark-up' at a fixed rate; and thirdly, forward purchases as a form of working capital loans with buy-back arrangements. The bank is supervised by the Ministry of Agriculture.

Crop insurance is provided by the government (90 per cent) and voluntary contributions from farmers (10 per cent). Coverage is extended to wheat, rice, soya beans, cotton and sugar beets against such hazards as locust invasion, storms, fire, frost, and other natural disasters. A 'catastrophe' fund against floods is financed entirely by the government.

Other agricultural services and aids are provided by various types of cooperative. In 1977/78 there were 2,942 rural cooperatives in the country with 3 million members and Rls 9.4 billion capital. The number of units and their membership increased every year following the revolution, reaching 3,117 in 1987/88 with a membership of 4.1 million, and a total capital of Rls 57 billion. In October 1991, the *Majles* passed a law placing all cooperative organizations in the country under the supervision of a new Ministry of Cooperatives. Under the law, within six months, the Rural Cooperative Organization, the Central Organization of National Cooperatives, the Central Organization of Mining Cooperatives, Centers for the Promotion of Productive Activities, and other bureaux in each ministry dealing with cooperatives, were to be transferred to the new ministry.[16]

By some private estimates, in 1991/92 there were some 3.1 million agrictural units in Iran, of which 2.6 million were in farming, and 498,000 in animal husbandry. Some 88 per cent of cultivated land was tilled by owners, 6 per cent was leased, and 6 per cent run on the share-cropping basis. Of the total production units, some 863,000 (or 27 per cent of total) had less than one hectare of land to work on, and more than one million (or about 33 per cent) possessed between one hectare and less than five hectares. Only 56,000 units (or about 2 per cent) operated on 25 hectares or more. Average holdings per cultivator was about 6 hectares. Due to this extreme fragmentation, 60 per cent of units were believed to be uneconomical, making management and modernization difficult and cumbersome. Holdings of fragmented and non-contiguous parcels unamenable to mechanization were incapable of meeting the financial needs of a rural family without supplementary occupation or income although some small farms were able to purchase 'mechanized services' from machinery owners.[17]

STRATEGIES AND POLICIES

The Islamic Republic's initial agricultural strategy was based on the assumption that agriculture alone was the pivot for economic expansion and growth. All other economic policies and programs had to be formulated in direct relation to agriculture. Industry itself was primarily to serve agriculture's needs for light and heavy machinery. Other sectors also were to support agricultural production towards self-sufficiency. To serve this strategy, the policy measures pursued by the government included subsidies at the producer and consumer levels, price controls, import restrictions, export promotion, and free-market incentives.

Subsidy to producers – in addition to low-price (and below-cost) water and electricity – has taken the form of guaranteed prices established by the government for wheat, rice, potatoes, meat, sugar beets, cotton and oil seeds. These prices were set by the High Economic Council, largely based on input cost, inflation rate, and certain welfare considerations. The guaranteed price was occasionally augmented with additional incentives. The cost of transportation from the field to the government purchase centers was paid by cooperative societies. This scheme enabled the government to successfully procure several million tons of local wheat each year, and to virtually eliminate the role of private marketing in wheat. The Central Rural Cooperative Organization (CRCO) within the Ministry of Agriculture was in charge of procurement from the farmers. Storage and further distribution to processors or consumers were made by CRCO, or by another specialized agency (Sazman-e Ghalleh) in the case of wheat. The share of the government procurement in total supply varied according to products (for example, 85 per cent for wheat, but only 10 per cent for milk). The state's success in its near monopoly of wheat purchases may be attributed to a number of factors among which the relatively attractive guaranteed purchase price plus other premiums played a primary role.[18] In addition to guaranteed prices, the government also systematically subsidized agricultural inputs such as fertilizers, pesticides, seeds, and farm machinery.

At the consumer level, the Islamic Republic has followed a four-pronged policy of: heavily subsidizing basic staples (particularly wheat); establishing price ceilings for a number of products; issuing ration coupons for basic necessities to all citizens; and allowing a free market legally to operate alongside state distribution. While the state-guaranteed price of flour to farmers and millers amounted to Rls 210 per kilogram, the government sold the flour to bakeries at Rls 12 per kilogram in order to keep the price of bread unchanged, and its supply not subject to rationing. The resulting bread subsidy to consumers has been put at Rls 1,200 billion a year.[19] For all other rationed products, there was a two-tiered market where a limited quantity of each item was available to all at fixed (and subsidized) prices against coupons, and additional quantities could be purchased at free-market prices depending on supplies. Open market prices for meat and milk were often four to five times higher than rationed prices – roughly corresponding to the amount of the subsidies. For non-basic staples (including fruits, vegetables, barley and sometimes rice) there was no price control or subsidy.

State intervention in the agricultural sector has also involved import restrictions (through quantitative quotas or foreign exchange rationing) of 'luxury' items (e.g., exotic fruits, coffee, chocolate, etc.). Production and exports of traditional items, in turn, were encouraged by allowing exporters to sell part or all of their foreign exchange earnings in the free market (at rates that were often several times higher than the official rate) or to import scarce items without foreign exchange permits.

These incentives, and a number of other officially-sanctioned 'safety valves', served the interests and objectives of the authorities exceedingly well as they kept both the rich and poor reasonably satisfied. By permitting private channels to operate fairly openly, the free market for foodstuffs was ample most of the time – albeit sometimes via smuggling and extra-legal means – helping to keep the affluent content and complacent. An unlimited supply of bread (at one-tenth of its real cost), and a minimum of other rationed and subsidized basic staples, also kept the poor in line.

Shortages of individual food items occurred from time to time, but there was never a critical dearth of life-sustaining staples, even in the worst years of the war, thanks partly to oil-financed food imports. In order to supplement domestic production, the government regularly imported such foodstuffs as wheat, sugar and meat, among others. Starting from slightly more than 1 million tons, wheat imports surpassed 3 million tons in 1983/84 and reached 5 million tons in 1987/88 before being reduced to 2.5 million tons in 1992/93 when domestic crops reportedly reached 10.3 million tons. Of the total domestic supply, some 27 per cent is reportedly lost in process. There were sharp increases in other food imports as well.

As indicated earlier, the regime's policy on agriculture and food subsidies began to undergo marked changes after the ceasefire. In 1989/90, the government's farm policies shifted toward price decontrol and market deregulation. Farmers were generally freed from the obligation of selling their produce to the state purchasing centers. Of all farm commodities, price controls were kept on only 20 products, including wheat. Price adjustments were also allowed in the case of farm machinery, both locally produced and imported, with a view to raising prices of many agricultural products to international levels.

DEVELOPMENTS AND PROBLEMS

As indicated in an earlier chapter, the farm sector performed relatively better than the rest of the economy during the 1980s. The respectable showing of domestic agriculture reflected the high priority granted by the government to increased wheat output; the relative independence of farming from reliance on oil revenues and imported inputs; smaller damage to this sector by the flight of capital, skills, and management; virtual stagnation of output in the base year, 1980/81; greater affinity and familiarity of the new ruling establishment with farming through past management of religious endowments; and, most significantly, the vast and solid infrastructure (multi-purpose dams, irrigation networks, agricultural equipment, machine-building capacity, and an accommodating land-tenure system) available in the country at the time of the revolution.

According to government data, the area under cultivation in both irrigated and dry farming was expanded after the revolution through greater ultilization of pastures and fallow land, and more extensive mechanization, but also because of larger land area occupied by new farmers.

Almost all major crops experienced a steady growth between 1980/81 and 1990/91. For most, however, output growth was both relatively slow and erratic. Except for tea, tobacco and onions, where acreage under cultivation remained nearly constant, all other food grain and non-food crops expanded their area – with oil seeds and barley experiencing considerable expansion.

Progress in output growth during the period, however, was mainly due to expanded acreage, as well as increased use of machinery, fertilizers, pesticides, and higher-quality seeds, rather than improvements in basic productivity. Total fertilizer consumption (at subsidized prices) increased by nearly 65 per cent over the

1979–87 period from 1 million tons a year to 1.65 million tons. The number of tractors used rose from 78,000 in 1979/80 to 135,000 in 1988/89. The number of tillers and combines also increased by 15 per cent. Despite massive and concerted efforts to raise farm productivity, however, the yield per hectare of cultivation changed relative little over the years and remained generally low. Assuming the accuracy and reliability of offical data, the yield per hectare of wheat crop (which was the focus of government attention and effort) rose only slightly between 1978 and 1992. For other crops largely free from state control, (e.g., barley) the percentage increase in yields was considerably higher (Table 11.1).

A careful appraisal of the Islamic Republic's agricultural policy by neutral international observers points to the following conclusions. First, output technology, particularly in the case of food grains, did not improve, and yields remained relatively stagnant. Iran's economic isolation from the Western world caused the country to fall behind in the acquisition of new technologies. Domestic research expenditures were cut drastically in the first three years after the revolution, and even after recovery in 1984/ 85, research outlays were only 42 per cent of the 1976 level. Extension service is also judged to have been fragmented and weak. As a result, the average index of food production per capita in 1987–89 was only 87 per cent of 1979–81; that of 1988–90 was only 104.[20]

Second, the intensive and continued input-subsidization policy (water, power, fertilizers, machinery and credit) failed to obtain the intended results, and turned out to be a rather inefficient method of raising output (compared, for example, with price deregulation and free-market incentives). Due to the shortage of locally produced fertilizers after the Iran-Iraq war, a part of the country's fertilizer needs had to be imported.

Third, the government's farm price policies caused considerable distortions in relative input and output prices with the result that too many scarce resources were allocated to a few low value-added products such as food grains. Wheat, for example, which occupied about 45 per cent of the area under annual and permanent crops (but accounted for 24 per cent of total crop value), lagged in real price and profitability behind other agricultural prices (as well as the consumer price index). Within the farm sector, barley commanded a much higher price than wheat because the price of bread had been kept artificially low by the government, and there had been no profitable private market for wheat. Barley (mainly used as animal feed) benefitted from the high price of meat in the open market. Similarly, the price of bran was higher than that of flour.

Farmers sold their wheat crop (even the portion that was normally retained for their own consumption) to the government purchasing centers at high guaranteed prices, and bought back their daily bread from government-supplied bakeries at much lower costs. Price disparities also resulted in increased consumption of bread at the expense of higher protein products such as meat and fresh milk. Data on rural/urban terms of trade are at best conjectural and unreliable. There are unsubstantiated claims in the popular press that farmers have been shortchanged, and that their purchasing power has persistenly declined during the five years ending in 1992.[21] The prevailing impression, however, is that the farm sector presumably benefitted from better terms-of-trade vis-à-vis manufacturing, but at a very high, and perhaps unsustainable, cost to the government. Input and output subsidies also introduced many distortions into the system, of which the vested interest of urban consumers in perpetuating public assistance has been the most evident.

Fourth, the government's farm support policies were not accompanied by a corresponding capital expenditure for agriculture and water resources. In fact, the government's gross fixed capital formation in this sector declined during the 1980s. After 1983, nominal increases in public capital expenditures did not even compensate for inflation, with the result that the figure for 1989 was one-third of that of 1983. There has been inadequate attention to agricultural infrastructure, and there remains a large backlog of deferred maintenance (particularly in water dams that suffer from heavy siltation).[22] According to a senior government official, soil erosion in Iran amounts to 2 billion tons a year of the most fertile land, resulting in the addition of 800,000 hectares to the desert category, and reducing the efficiency of 100 million square metres of dam waters due to sedimentation – costing the country an estimated Rls 1,000 billion.[23] Thanks to increased availability of agricultural credit throughout the period, private fixed capital formation in this sector's superstructure began to rise after 1983/84.

Fifth, there was little or no coordination among the various agencies dealing with agriculture. Imprecise terms of reference and scope of responsibility between the Ministry of Agriculture, the Ministry of Energy, and the Ministry of Jihad resulted in duplication, overlapping, confusion, and uncertainty in many policy areas, particularly in extension and research, irrigation planning and maintenance, and water charges. Pricing of farm inputs and products was handled by the Ministry of Commerce without effective coordination with agricultural ministries. The High Economic Council was theoretically the coordinating body, but the exercise left a good deal to be desired.

The consensus among observers is that agriculture's more noteworthy achievements were largely hampered by such factors as political disputes over land reform, uncertainty about private property rights; recurrent droughts; and reduced public investments. Ironically, some analysts argue that agriculture's suboptimal performance was due to the fact that the much-publicized emphasis on rural regeneration was in fact *urban-oriented*. Subsidies and incentives given to farm production are said to have been designed ultimately to assist city dwellers, not small farmers.[24] The Islamic Republic's lack of a comprehensive policy for rural infrastructural development, water use, soil management, training and extension work, credit allocation, and price support, are cited as evidence.[25] Furthermore, there were other growth-inhibiting factors, such as wastage of both water and farmland, inefficient use of land in regard to crop suitability, lack of proper training of farm specialists, the poor state of extension work, and the shortage of farm machinery. Livestock and fisheries also had their problems. Animal husbandry was hampered by inefficient breeding and maintenance methods. Fisheries suffered from lack of investment and attention, falling short of their potential by close to 50 per cent. And large areas were converted from high-value, long-term, cash crops to short-season, low-value cereal cultivation.[26]

As a result of all this, the country slipped further into food deficit. With domestic food output lagging behind demand, and foreign exchange in short supply for food imports, the country was perennially faced with shortages of some food products (e.g., meat, eggs, butter, rice). As the regime's domestic critics have charged, not only has Iran remained dependent on foreign suppliers for machinery, fertilizers, pesticides and technology, it has also turned from a partial food exporter to a net food- (and feedstock-) importing country.[27] As Table 10.1 shows, the average annual cost of food imports during the 1978/79–1989/90 period amounted to $2,150 million, as compared with $1,850 million in 1977/78. Table 11.2 portrays the rising volume of food imports, in both absolute and per capita terms, after the revolution. Foreign observers have questioned the government's plans to boost wheat production by expanding irrigation to increase yields by 50 per cent in some 400,000 hectares of new farmland. Valuable water supplies are urged to be diverted to other and more profitable irrigated crops where output falls short of domestic demand.[28]

A recent evaluation by researchers not unsympathetic to the Islamic regime concludes that despite 'remarkable' increases in the use of fertilizers and farm machinery, and despite the government's emphasis on agricultural self-sufficiency, the sector has had 'weak performance' in the post-revolutionary period. Among the causes of this weakness, reference is made to increased labor costs, 'lopsided' control of farm prices, and reduced funds for investment and research.[29] Other analysts believe that without a thorough reform of the current agricultural institutions, and considerably larger annual investment in this sector, Iran may become dependant on imports for more than a third of its annual food consumption (and a larger percentage of feedstock) for years to come. Increasing conversion of farm land to urban use, growing desertation of pasture land, soil erosion, and deforestation are largely at fault.

NOTES

1. See, for example, Keith S. McLachlan, *The Neglected Garden* (London: I. B. Tauris, 1988).
2. *Kayhan Havai*, July 15, 1992, p. 10.
3. For different estimates see Food and Agriculture Organization, *Production Yearbook 1989/90*.
4. For a partial list of more recent criticisms see Hooglund, (1982); McLachlan (1988); A. Farazmand, *The State, Bureaucracy and Revolution in Modern Iran* (New York: Praeger, 1989); and Cyrus Yeganeh, 'The Agrarian Structure of Iran', *State, Culture and Society*, vol 1, 1985.
5. Out of 93 joint-stock companies engaged in farming, 88 were dissolved.
6. See Cyrus Salmanzadeh, *Agricultural Change and Rural Society in Southern Iran* (Canterbury: MENAS Press, 1981), Postscript.
7. See *Iran Focus*, May 1990, p. 11.
8. Ayatollah Khomeini's speech at *Behesht-e Zahra* Cemetery, February 2, 1979.
9. M. Parvin and M. Taghavi, 'A Comparison of Land Tenure in Iran under Monarchy and under the Islamic Republic', in H. Amirahmadi and M. Parvin, *Post-Revolutionary Iran* (Boulder: Westview Press, 1988).
10. *The New York Times*, June 1, 1980.
11. For details of these developments, see Ahmad Ashraf, *Dehqanan, Zamin va Enqelab* (Peasants, Land, and Revolution) in *Masa'el-e Arzi va Dehqani* (Problems of Land and Peasants) (Tehran: Agah Publications, 1361 [1982]); Bakhash, *The Reign of the Ayatollah* (London: I. B. Tauris, 1985), Ch. 8; Bashiriyeh, (1984), pp. 139–143; and Amirahmadi (1990), ch. 2.
12. *Kayhan Havai*, December 19, 1990, p. 10.
13. An experimental cadastral survey of private ownership in three areas

– Khorramshahr, South Tehran, and Qeshm Island – was announced in the summer of 1991. See *Kayhan Havai*, July 3, 1991, p. 10.

14. At the time of the land reform, there were an estimated 2.4 million farm families in Iran, of which some 600,000–800,000 were owner/operators or part-owner/lease holders, and the rest were landless share-croppers, farm workers and others.

15. Initial responsibilities of the Construction Crusade were to improve farm production and animal husbandry; construct and maintain public buildings in rural and tribal areas; build and maintain rural roads; provide and maintain water resouces and electric power; and assist in health services. Its resources were to be derived from the general budget, private contributions, and revenues from its own projects.

16. *Kayhan Havai*, October 23, 1991, p. 10.

17. *Kayhan Havai*, November 13, 1991, p. 13.

18. For example, wheat farmers were allowed to use part of the proceeds of their deliveries to the government for the purpose of scarce items (sugar, tea, household goods, farm machinery, transport vehicles) at official (and substantially below market) prices.

19. President Rafsanjani's budget speech before the *Majles*, reported in *Kayhan Havai*, December 18, 1991, p. 11.

20. *World Development Report 1991* (Washington: The World Bank, 1991), p. 211, and *WDR 1992*, p. 225.

21. See *Ayandeh Eqtesad* (Mirror of the Economy), Ordibehesht-Khordad 1371.

22. Sefid Rud dam has reportedly lost 50 per cent of its capacity in 18 years.

23. *Kayhan Havai*, July 24, 1991, p. 11.

24. K. S. McLachlan, paper presented before the M. Group's Center for Strategic Studies (Geneva, 1990), p. 14.

25. Amirahmadi (1990), p. 152.

26. See *The Economist Intelligence Unit*, 'Iran: Country Profile 1991–92', p. 24.

27. *Kayhan Havai*, May 1, 1991, p. 18

28. *The Economist Intelligence Unit*, 'Iran: Country Report', No. 4, 1991.

29. A. Mojtahed and H. Esfahani, 'Agricultural Policy and Performance in Iran: The Post-Revolutionary Experience', *World Development*, (June 1989).

12

Industry and related services: manufacturing, construction, water and power, transport and communications

This chapter discusses the industrial sector, which, in the Iranian context, includes manufacturing, construction, electric power, and mines as well as transport and communications, which, in the Bank Markazi's national accounting system, are categorized as services.

No sector of the Iranian economy in the Shah's regime came under more blistering attacks from the opposition and the victorious revolutionaries than the industrial (mainly the manufacturing) sector.[1] The standard indictment was that Iran's pre-1979 industrialization was pushed forward without due regard to either domestic resource endowments and capabilities, or society's basic needs. As a result, industry allegedly failed to meet the country's basic requirements. Excessive protectionism, unwise availability of tax exemptions and easy credit, inappropriate use of foreign technology and expertise, and the reliance of domestic enterprises on foreign technicians, raw materials and processed goods, were said to create a system of assembly-plant operation and fragile 'dependent capitalism' at the mercy of external crises.[2] In short, industry was blamed for failing to meet agriculture's needs for heavy machinery, the oil sector's requirements for exploration and refining, and even its own needs for spare parts and raw materials.[3]

The target of these indictments was principally the manufacturing sector that was concentrated on consumer goods, particularly big-ticket items consumed by the well-to-do (passenger cars, household appliances, leisure products and the like).

EARLY ATTEMPTS AT INDUSTRIAL REORGANIZATION

From its inception, the Islamic Republic was bent on radically altering the Shah's industrialization drive. But, unlike other major sectors, industry was beset by many incapacitating problems of its own which defied political or ideological solution. In the wake of the revolution, manufacturing enterprises experienced an accelerated decline in capacity utilization, due mostly to disruption of supplies and a drop in sales. Essential problems involved private industrial enterprises whose owners or managers had left the country; colossal debt owed by these companies to the faltering banking system; labor agitation; confusion regarding ownership and administration of abandoned units; constant threats by new managers to shut down operations and dismiss workers unless assisted by the government; and the intrusion of Islamic *komitehs* in the enterprises' decision-making process.

To combat these problems, the Provisional Government immediately offered a Rls 85 billion line of credit in early 1979 to reduce industry's financial woes. But no more than Rls 25 billion was taken up by the end of the year. The crucial difficulty turned out to be not so much the credit shortage, but political uncertainties and poor economic management. In addition to these impediments, the freezing of Iranian assets and Western sanctions caused the slowdown or stoppage of operations in many industrial enterprises, cutting off access to raw materials and spare parts. The problems finally led to the government's takeover of the establishments in distress.

The Islamic Republic's short-term industrial policy placed its main emphasis on two principles: encouraging industrial activities with quickest, high-value possibilities; and supporting enterprises with the highest domestic content, and least dependence on foreign exchange. The overriding long-term criteria were industrial self-sufficiency and independence, and the redirection of the industrial sector towards the implementation of the Constitution's clause 43, requiring the government to ensure the provision of food, clothing and housing needs.[4]

A bill for the Protection and Development of Iranian Industries, passed by the Revolutionary Council in July 1979, had the following six diversified objectives: determination of workers' pay according to Islamic tenets; deliverance of Iran from foreign economic dependence; the expansion of employment opportunities and expertise; the expropriation of properties belonging to agents of the (previous) autocratic regime; the avoidance of state domination over the economy; and protection of the private sector against unfair foreign competition.

The 1979 legislation divided existing industrial enterprises in Iran into four categories: basic and strategic industries (including oil, gas, railways, fisheries, electric utilities, automobile manufacturing, ship-building, aviation, and basic metals); mining and industrial units belonging to individuals deemed to have been acquired or expanded by illegal or illegitimate means; factories, firms, or enterprises which owed the banks more than the value of their assets; and, fourthly, enterprises not classified under the previous three categories. The first category enterprises were to be placed under public ownership and operation; their legitimate owners were to be compensated for the net worth of their holdings. Some 200 firms and units under the second category were to be confiscated and transferred to the government. Another 200 or so enterprises under the third category were to be placed under the (nationalized) banks' trusteeship, and to be run, or liquidated, on behalf of their public or private creditors. Enterprises not included in the above categories were recognized as legitimate private enterprises protected by law.[5] The claims of owners of confiscated properties were to be settled through legal channels.

A new National Iranian Industries Organization (NIIO) was established to administer all entities under the first three categories. A total of 580 companies were thus taken over from the private sector, of which 450 were placed under the trusteeship of the NIIO.

THE STRUCTURE OF MANUFACTURING

Iranian 'industries' include handicrafts, small rural and urban workshops, large-scale consumer-goods enterprises, and modern heavy industries. Handicrafts have historically represented Iran's magnificent creative and artistic endeavors: Persian carpets; silk, cotton, felt and wool textiles; embroidered cloth; colored glassware; gold, silver and copper metalworks; inlaid woodworks; enamelled items; and leather goods. These products have traditionally met domestic demand, and earned foreign exchange by their export. An estimated 90 per cent of raw materials used in these crafts is home-grown, and an adjunct to agricultural activities.

Small industrial workshops – those employing 9 individuals or less – dot both the rural and urban landscape. Rural cottage-level industries are nearly all household units where mostly female members provide their service communally without formal or regular remuneration. A majority of these units are engaged in hand-made carpet weaving and textiles, and the rest in food and other activities.[6] Total value-added by this subsector to the non-oil GDP is low. Urban small workshops (of fewer than 9 workers) consist of such units as bakeries, blacksmith shops, carpentries, shoe-making and the like. These shops, using modern tools, equipment, and technology, are engaged mostly in textiles and carpets, food processing, metal work, and others. Total value-added by these activities to the non-oil GDP is also modest.

Medium and large-scale manufacturing enterprises, employing at least 10 (and upward of 1,000) workers, comprise 9 major categories: food, beverages and tobacco; textiles, apparel and leather; lumber and wood products; pulp and paper; chemicals and petrochemicals; non-metals and minerals; basic metals; machinery and transport equipment; and others. In 1990/91, while there were an estimated 352,000 urban industrial units in Iran, no more than 13,000 were classified as medium or large enterprises. Despite their relatively small number, however, medium and large companies accounted for the lion's share of value-added in manufacturing. (Manufacturing accounted on average for about 50 per cent of value-added in the industrial sector.)

Of an estimated 1.5 million workers engaged in manufacturing workshops, some 740,000 were employed in 328,000 small enterprises of less than 10 workers, and 237,000 in 108 establishements with workforces of over 1,000. Some 64 per cent of all manufacturing workshops were in consumer goods; 28 per cent in intermediary products; and 8 per cent in capital goods. All of these industries were heavily dependent on imported inputs (65 per cent for consumer products, 70 per cent for intermediate goods, and 85 per cent for capital goods). The vast majority of industrial workshops were in the hands of private individuals and families. They accounted, however, for less than 30 per cent of industrial value-added. Less than 15 per cent of all units were owned or managed by the public sector. Yet almost all large manufacturing enterprises and a vast majority of medium-size firms were run by state agencies, parastatal organizations, semi-private 'foundations', and a few cooperatives. While these enterprises have constituted a relatively small percentage of total industrial units, they were responsible for more than 73 per cent of value-added, 72 per cent of employment, and 65 per cent of investment in their category.[7] Table 12.1 shows output, employment and wages in large manufacturing enterprises during 1980/81–1990/91.

ADMINISTRATION OF THE MANUFACTURING SECTOR

Manufacturing activity under the Islamic Republic has been carried out, supervised, and regulated by several different agencies, institutions, and owner/manager establishments in a complex (and not always coordinated) fashion. In 1981, the Ministry of Industries and Mines was divided into two new ministries, Industries, and Mines and Metals. In 1982, a separate Ministry of Heavy Industries was established. As of March 1993, these three ministries were in charge of the direction and supervision of medium and large-scale enterprises. The Ministry of Industries is broadly responsible for industrial development and policy coordination. It is in charge of issuing required licenses for the establishment or expansion of eligible projects; it makes industrial surveys and, through the National Iranian Industries Organization (NIIO), it oversees a large number of nationalized firms. According to official data, in 1992/93 some 93 per cent of all industrial workshops, 79 per cent of industrial employment, and 80 per cent of manufacturing value-added were covered by the Ministry of Industries, as was about 10 per cent of GDP.

Originally, a total of 450 industrial establishments with a combined workforce of 170,000 workers were entrusted to NIIO. Gradually, however, several dozen companies were transferred to the direct control of other ministries or returned to the private sector. Of the enterprises in NIIO's hands in 1992/93, over two-thirds were in manufacturing and the rest in the service sector. At the time of the original takeover in 1981, the nationalized companies had a negative net worth.

The NIIO has a board of governors composed of the ministers of industries, commerce, labor, finance, and agriculture and the head of the Plan and Budget Organization. Its director is a deputy minister of industries. Enterprises under the NIIO's trusteeship are divided into 10 different functional groups, each with a director who appoints each enterprise's chief executive officer, selects the enterprise's board, and determines the firm's administrative, financial, marketing, production, expansion and technological policies. The groups consist of chemical, shoes and leather, textiles, construction, cement, pulp and paper, pharmaceuticals, food and beverages, household appliances, and trade and commercial establishments.

The Ministry of Heavy Industries (MHI) is in charge of planning and management of heavy engineering enterprises. Since its formation in 1982, the Organization for Promotion and Renovation of Iranian Industries (originally established in 1967 to undertake the formation of high-priority industries in the public sector, and offer guidance and management training to private-sector industries) was annexed to this ministry as its main executive body. In 1992/93, there were some 120 industrial units under MHI, of which 30 per cent were leased out to private contractors. The majority of units in six specialized categories – transport vehicles, machine tools, cutting and drilling machinery, construction machinery, iron casting and steel rolling, and ship-building – are directly managed. Passenger cars, buses, tractors, combines, cranes, lift-trucks, compressors, distillation towers, pressure tanks, boilers, pipes, locomotives, discs and other such products are among the output of the companies under MHI. In 1992/93, Iran also had small ship-building and railway freight car factories. Many of the units supervised by this ministry have reportedly been operating at a loss.[8]

Under the current five-year plan, the ministry has moved to reactivate its vehicles division (automobiles, wagons, trucks, tractor, ships, bicycles and motorcycles) through joint-ventures with foreign manufacturers in France, Italy, Japan, South Korea and Sweden.[9] To expedite private investment in these industries, the ministry has announced its readiness to issue its 'agreement in principle' to every industrial project capable of exporting at least 30 per cent of its products. Industries so favored are motorized vehicles, rolled steel, aluminium profiles, and lift-trucks.[10] In January 1992, the government put all the shares of the state automobile factories on the Tehran Stock Exchange.

The new policy decision is significant in two major respects. First, it involves partial or total denationalization of the automobile industry. Second, it means a resumption of the (previously reviled) assembly-plant operation in certain industries as long as a portion of the final products (40 per cent) is made at home, and a share of total production (30 per cent) is exported – requirements similar to, or even less stringent than, those operating as an integral part of the assembly policy before the revolution. This apparent policy reversal is reportedly caused by sheer necessity. With automobile production down to only 15 per cent of the pre-1979 level, and the domestic (market) price of a home-assembled Peugeot 405 at Rls 29,000,000 ($48,333 at the *competitive* exchange rate), there was no way to bring the price down except by increased production through new investment and capacity expansion.[11]

The Ministry of Mines and Metals (MMM) has the responsibility for the conduct of geological exploration and mining surveys; it is also in charge of the operation and expansion of metallurgical industries. MMM owns and operates such large-scale enterprises as the Iranian National Steel Company, the Iranian National Copper Company, the Arak Aluminium Corporation, the Iranian Geological Survey Organization and others, totalling about 20 firms.

Iran's heavy industries are still the weakest link in the economy. Aluminium is a high-cost, high-energy-using operation, heavily dependent on foreign materials. Copper has little domestic use, and its exports are subject to fierce competition in the world market. Tractors and construction equipment machinery are still largely assembly-plant activities with insufficient domestic content.

According to the minister of mines and metals, Iranian steel production needs major restructuring in its equipment, technology and personnel. In 1991/92, for a total steel production of about 3 million tons in three main complexes (Isfahan Steel, Ahwaz Steel and National Steel), there were 70,000 people at work, whereas an Italian steel plant was producing 10 million tons of steel with a labor force of only 6,000. The minister also acknowledged that Iran's proven reserves of iron ore and coal were not sufficient for domestic production, and both had to be imported. Upon completion of the various steel projects already under way, domestic output would exceed internal demand, and export markets would have to be sought.[12] The major metal projects under way for the Ministry of Mines and Metals have been the expansion of Isfahan steel mill, Mobarakeh steel complex, expansion of Sarcheshmeh copper complex, Kavian heavy rolling mill and steel alloy, Zanjan lead and zinc projects, Ahwaz steel complex, Iran alloy steel near Yazd, and Nasr steel mill at Ahwaz.[13]

In addition to the three ministries, a number of other public agencies, banks, and semi-public foundations are involved in industrial management. The Oil and Gas Ministry handles, *inter alia*, petrochemical plants and oil refineries. The Ministry of Armed Forces and Logistics controls Iran's growing arms industry and related supplies. The Ministry of Jihad-e Sazandegi is involved in the development of rural infrastructure and small-scale rural industries and cottage-type activities. A large number of industrial units are also run directly by other technical ministries, or by specialized and commercial banks that had taken them over initially in lieu of their outstanding loans when their owners left the country after the revolution. A number of other industrial units confiscated from individuals who were tried in the revolutionary courts have also been managed by certain religious/revolutionary foundations (such as *Mostazafan, Shahid, 15th of Khordad, Saduqi*, and others).

MANUFACTURING SECTOR POLICY

Despite a clear provision in the Constitution, as well as a clause in the law for the Protection and Development of Industries, enjoining the government from state patrimony in the economy the Islamic Republic has so far been the dominant force in Iran's industrial development. Since the triumph of the revolution, the government has taken a number of distinct measures in the direction of its new industrialization policy. First, the responsibilities of the former ministry of industries and mines were divided into three new ministries in charge of mines and metals, consumer goods, and heavy industries.[14] Second, in an effort to move production sites away from the Tehran area (harboring 50 per cent of all industries), a bill was passed to create 50 industrial parks with adequate infrastructure (site, water, roads, energy and other services) in provinces outside Tehran. Finally, as part of the twenty-year long-range planning, the government required all new industries to be based on domestic raw materials; to contribute to economic independence; and to gradually increase the share of processing and capital goods industries at the expense of current consumer goods.

In order to achieve these objectives and policies, the industrial sector has been heavily protected not only by tariffs, but also by outright import prohibition of certain products; quantitative restrictions on imports of permitted items; annual foreign exchange allocations to importing agencies; and price regulation of industrial inputs and outputs. Since the end of the war with Iraq, and the launching of a new five-year plan, the government's industrial policy has taken a sharp turn towards deregulation and marketization. In a clear retreat from early revolutionary slogans (such as praise of agriculture as the focus of all development efforts), future hopes for the expansion of the economy have now been placed on rapid industrialization. The current five-year development plan places its main focus on the industrial sector. Two of the plan's ten general objectives are directly related to industry, and five others are indirectly linked.

Briefly stated, the order of priority for industrial development during the plan points to the following seven features: maximum utilization of existing industrial capacity; the establishment of needed new industries; the expansion of industrial exports; control of consumption patterns; the use of industrial activity for reducing poverty; improvement of international competitiveness; and protection of the environment. The industrial sector is expected to take a lead in the reconstruction and modernization of production

facilities; the expansion of output and national income; the creation of employment, reduction of economic dependence (through
self-sufficiency in strategic inputs); curbing inflation; and improvement of education, science and technology.[15]

In order to achieve these goals, the government has, since 1990,
embarked on a new liberalization and privatization policy. In the
manufacturing sector, for example, price controls have been
removed from a host of 'non-essential' manufactured products,
and the cost-plus approach to pricing domestic and imported
products has ended. This move has been followed by the lifting of
quantitative restrictions on exports and imports. Under the 'privatization' drive, several significant measures have been put into
effect. Some industrial enterprises have been returned to their
original owners (albeit with a much larger work force and much
worn-out equipment). Former industrialists have been encouraged
to return to Iran and reclaim their expropriated property through
the judicial system. The government has also declared its intention
to gradually divest hundreds of large-scale industrial enterprises
under its ownership or supervision or owned by nationalized
banks. These enterprises are to be privatized in a number of
different ways, including: sale of shares on the Tehran Stock
Exchange; negotiated arrangements with former owners or new
entrepreneurs; auctions; or joint management under one of the
many Islamic modes (for example, leases, and partnership). Private
entrepreneurs have also been permitted to invest in all but strategic
industries. The 1989 Regulations Concerning the Attraction and
Protection of Foreign Investment in Iran, updating a law passed
during the Shah's regime, guarantees freedom of repatriation of
profits and principal for all registered foreign investment. Under
the five-year plan, 'free zones' have also been established where
investors are exempt from many local laws and regulations,
including income taxes and the usual limitations on the percentage
of ownership.

RESULTS AND CONSTRAINTS

In the years immediately following the revolution, the manufacturing sector experienced some expected ups and downs, but for most
of the decade the sector went through a period of lack of direction,
neglect, decay, and poor performance. Throughout the 1980s, the
manufacturing subsector showed intervals of sporadic recovery,
but generally declining capacity utilization. Technological obsolescence and deteriorating international competitiveness followed

heavy domestic protection and exchange overvaluation. Growing state ownership, production, and regulation, combined with institutional weaknesses and legal confusion, resulted in a dwindling interest and participation on the part of private entrepreneurs. For the first few months after the revolution, some factories managed to survive by drawing down their stocks and spare parts, using their liquid assets, deferring their debts, and benefiting from the skill and experience of remaining managers and staff. But the passage of time, harassment by local *komitehs*, and labor strikes exhausted both the enterprises' resources and their managers' resourcefulness. Failing industries had to be taken over by the naitonalized banks, and their dwindling supplies replaced by imports. Average capacity utilization gradually came down for the sector as a whole, and fell to less than 25 per cent in some factories.

The poor performance of the manufacturing sector has been clearly the result of revolution-related difficulties; exogenous adverse developments, not totally unrelated to the revolution; and interruption in the ongoing process of Iran's industrialization process. Among the problems created by the revolution itself, were the disproportionate exodus of managerial skills and technical cadres, labor strikes and industrial dispute (workers councils' demands for higher wages), political and ideological interference with industrial management, and electric power shortages. The confiscation of private industrial firms, and growing anxieties regarding the status of private ownership, the direction of the government's industrial policy, and the safety of new ownership and investment, effectively discouraged a wholehearted rehabilitation of existing private units, and postponed investment in new ventures. An ideological hold on private industrial investment and management, a proclivity for controlling prices and incentives, excessive and complicated regulations, and the shortage of foreign exchange (needed to purchase imported inputs and upgrade the industry's technological underpinnings) contributed to inefficient allocation of resources and the discouragement of private sector initiatives. The cumbersome foreign exchange regime also played havoc with private investment, pricing, and output decisions.

Since prices of industrial outputs were frequently determined on a cost-plus basis, and wholesale and retail margins were also fixed by the authorities, enterprise managers lacked necessary incentives to cut production costs or increase their competitiveness. Moreover, since a considerable amount of the input needs of import-substituting enterprises were imported from abroad, and paid for with foreign exchange purchased from Bank Markazi at the highly overvalued official rate, enterprise managers had a vested interest in preserving this hidden subsidy. Any significant official devaluation of the Iranian rial would be confronting these key enterprises with eventual competitive demise. Still further, any realistic hope for the industrial sector to generate measurable non-oil exports was hampered by its inherent lack of international competitiveness. Given significant tariff protection and exchange subsidies, export prospects were fairly scant without further and concurrent government assistance.

The manufacturing sector also suffered from certain institutional deficiencies, among which the lack of a clear industrial direction and the absence of policy coordination seem to have been the most damaging. The division of responsibility between three principal ministries and a number of different agencies (and the application of these responsibilities to individual projects without a clear industrial policy framework) left a significant void. Not only was there no consistent approach to matters of operational efficiency and externalities, but also little or no attention was paid to the complementarity of a given industrial policy with pricing, trade and exchange-rate policies.

To some extent also, the legal confusion and bureaucratic restrictions accompanying revolutionary decrees and decisions played their part in discouraging private investment and initiative. Complaints routinely aired in local newspapers highlighted such factors as the government's exchange allocation below the foreign currency needs of industrial enterprises for full capacity operation; excessive length of order processing, and the latter's concentration in Tehran; limitations on loading and unloading at points of entry as well as transport limitations by rail or truck; difficulties in customs clearance of imported goods; delays and procrastination in obtaining needed working capital; and, above all, rising international prices of imported inputs without the enterprises' ability to raise prices on their finished products over the ceilings established by the government.[16]

Adverse *external* factors affecting industrial performance included Iran's initial public isolation from the international centers of industry and technology; the freezing of Iranian foreign exchange assets abroad after the American hostage crisis; Western economic sanctions affecting imports of vital machinery and spare parts; and, not least, the vicissitude of oil export volumes and revenues caused by the Iran-Iraq war and the behavior of the volatile global petroleum market.

By far the most vexing problem for the industrial sector, however, related to its extreme vulnerability to external shock, and its early-stage (and temporary) dependence on imported inputs of raw materials, spare parts, technology, talent, and even capital.[17] A survey undertaken by the Iranian Statistical Center after the revolution is often used by the regime's supporters as proof of this vulnerability. Among the large industrial firms, each having an 85 per cent or more share of the market, and each employing 50 or more workers (in all 415,000 employees) in 1979/80, none was operating at more than 70 per cent of capacity, and some were below 11 per cent. Four categories (paper, textiles and apparel, chemicals, and food and beverages) operated between 60 per cent and 64 per cent of capacity. Others (woodworking, machine tools, cement, glass, bricks, etc.) operated between 47 per cent and 57 per cent. Only basic metals operated at 70 per cent. On average, 57 per cent of raw materials needed by industrial units were imported from abroad. For some industries (such as pulp and paper, printing and binding) this dependence on imports of materials and spare parts was as much as 85 per cent. For equipment, machinery, machine tools and metal products, the need for foreign purchases approached 76 per cent. Food and beverage industries – the least dependent of all – still imported nearly 30 per cent of their primary materials, and 62 per cent of their spare parts, from abroad.[18] Excessive and troublesome as this foreign dependence was, however, it could not be solely responsible for the fall in capacity utilization, since Iran still had substantial revenues from oil exports at the time and could easily afford to pay for needed imports. Capacity under-utilization had many other reasons.

Among the latter was the absence of coordination among responsible agencies. For example, the Ministry of Industries was in charge of determining total national needs for the importation of equipment, machinery, parts, semi-processed goods, and raw materials. Import licenses, however, were issued according to a rationing system whereby each unit was allotted part of the aggregate foreign exchange budget. Centers for Provision and Distribution, within the Ministry of Commerce, were in charge of importing major items for local distribution. Bank Markazi had jurisdiction over the opening of letters of credit and placing orders for both the centers and licensed private importers. However, there was no coordinating mechanism to match national priority needs with decentralized imports.

To sum up, the Iranian manufacturing sector has suffered from years of negative growth, low capacity utilization, small-scale operation, aging technology, overstaffing, inexperienced management, lack of easy access to raw materials and parts, high cost of transport and warehousing, replacement of efficiency criteria by ideological considerations, excessive price and exchange-rate regulations, addictive and unhealthy protection against foreign competition, and the politico-economic crowding out of the private sector. External factors and structural handicaps – including exchange overvaluation and ineffective customs duties – have also played their part in keeping growth down.[19] But, after years of uncertain direction, stagnation, aging equipment, poor maintenance, and aging technological modernization, the industrial sector has now regained its priority status under the current five-year plan. Public ownership and management of non-strategic industries are to be gradually relinquished to the private sector. Private investment in the manufacturing and construction sectors is actively encouraged. However, import-substitution still seems to be favored over export orientation. While non-oil exports, and particularly industrial exports, are routinely emphasized, state officials frequently point to the way in which new industrial projects have contributed to the reduction of the import bill.

Indicative of this bias towards industrial paternalism, inward-orientation, external dependence, and protection against foreign competition is a report presented to the 4th *Majles* in late 1992 by the Minister of Industries. Summing up the progress and problems experienced in the first three years of the ongoing five-year development plan, the minister reported the growth of industrial output in the enterprises under his jurisdiction as going from 7.3 per cent of GDP in 1989/90 to 10.3 per cent in 1991/92. Continued growth of this magnitude, however, was said to be hampered by such impediments as: the shortage of allocated foreign exchange: inordinate volume of imports through regular channels as well as smuggling from the free-trade zones in the Persian Gulf; inadequate protection against foreign imports; the absence of a 'buy Iranian' policy in government ministries, agencies and the semi-public *bonyads*; and inadequate credit.[20]

The true weakness of Iran's manufacturing process, however, continued to lie in its dependence on oil revenues for the purchase of imported inputs; in its neglect of employment generation; and its nearly exclusive concentration on production for a soft home-market – a market weakened by a decline in the national standard of living as well as low capacity utilization. By official reckoning, during the industrial boom years of 1989–92 when the manufacturing subsector enjoyed annual double-digit growth, less than 10 per cent of the new entrants in the labor force was absorbed in this sub-sector. The result of this continued labor-intensive industrialization was the transfer of workers to low-productivity or technologically stagnant areas such as services and small industries.

ELECTRIC POWER

Eighty per cent of electric power generation in Iran is in the hands of the Ministry of Energy, and 20 per cent belongs to other public agencies and the private sector. Electricity is produced from steam, hydropower, gas and diesel generators. National production is shared between the Ministry of Energy's large power stations and small, private units.

In 1977/78, total installed power-generating capacity was about 7,105 megawatts (MW), producing nearly 18 billion kilowatt hours (kwh) of electricity, and selling more than 13 billion kwh. The priority given by the Islamic Republic to rural and small town electrification resulted in a steady growth of generating capacity during the 1980s despite the war impediments. According to data published by the Ministry of Energy, the country's total installed capacity in 1991/92 neared 19,000 MW of which over 93 per cent belonged to the Ministry of Energy. Of the ministry's share of power generation, 65 per cent was produced by steam engines; 15 per cent by gas turbines; 11 per cent by hydro power, and about 2 per cent by diesel motors. Due to the shortage of parts, the war damage, and other related problems, only about 60 per cent of installed capacity was utilized during most of the decade.

The country's total electricity generation reached 64.1 billion kwh in 1991/92, of which 6.9 billion kwh were produced independently. Of the nearly 57 billion kwh of electricity generated by the Ministry of Energy, only 49.2 billion kwh were sold, and the rest was internally used, or was lost in transmission. Both per capita production and consumption of electric power rose more than 70 per cent during the 1977–91 period.[21] Impeding even faster growth of power generation were, in addition to wartime constraints, such factors as shortages of skilled manpower, dependence on foreign equipment and machinery, costly investment requirements, and undue waste of energy in production and transmission.

The main contributor to the growth of the sector has thus been the extension of power lines to a growing number of villages, an accomplishment which the regime has widely and proudly publicized. In 1977/78, of the more than 66,000 villages scattered over the country, only 4,500 had access to electricity. With unprecedented rapidity, this number reportedly increased to more than 9,000 villages by the end of 1982/83. The trend continued, and according to a Construction Crusade Ministry report, by 1992/93, more than 12,000 were electrified.

In 1978/79, the industrial sector consumed more than 38 per cent of all electricity generated by the Ministry of Energy; agriculture had the lowest share with only 3.3 per cent. Households' share was 30 per cent, and commercial establishments' 24 per cent. After 1982/83, due to a slump in industrial output, the households' share surpassed both industrial and commercial use. However, this trend is now expected to be reversed in the current five-year development plan. In 1991/92, the total number of subscribers to the Ministry of Energy's power surpassed 10 million. Of the total electricity consumption of 49 billion kwh in 1991/92, some 39 per cent was used by private households; 28 per cent by commercial establishments; 22 per cent by industry; 8 per cent by agriculture; and 4 per cent by others.The high priority given to the reconstruction and renewal of war-damaged power plants, has resulted in blackouts being gradually reduced. Yet with a considerable level of suppressed demand, electricity use is believed to be supply-constrained for some time to come. The need for upgrading the existing capital stock is also great. According to certain estimates, by the turn of the century Iran will need some 34,000 MW of electricity for all its needs.[22]

Expansion of power-generation capacity has had one of the highest priorities in Iranian planning. The country was to have an installed capacity of 16,100 MW by 1987/88. As a result of war constraints and damage, however, Ministry of Energy's real capacity was merely 11,270 MW, generating nearly 43 billion kwh of power, and selling 36 billion kwh (over $2\frac{1}{2}$ times more than in 1977/78).

Like other energy sources under public ownership and management in Iran, the nominal cost of electric power generation in the official ledgers is said to cover less than its marginal production costs. Nor does the price charged by the government evidently account for its opportunity costs. Given the very large foreign exchange component of power generation in Iran, the official exchange rate that has been used for purchase of equipment tends to grossly underestimate the true scarcity cost. Even at this rate, the selling price of electricity in mid-1992 covered only 70 per cent of cost, with the remaining 30 per cent subsidized by the state.

In a detailed report to the *Majles* in September 1992, the minister of water and power indicated that a kilowatt hour of electricity, even at the highly unrealistic exchange rate of Rls 70 = $1 (charged for the equipment) cost the government Rls 14.50, while the average sale price was only Rls 10.50 per kwh (and the rate charged to the farm sector only Rls 2). Consequently, the power sector faced a deficit of Rls 200 billion each year. As to water rates, the official reported that some 75–80 per cent of Tehran residents paid less for water than it cost the ministry to supply them.[23]

As a result of financial constraints, managerial deficiencies, technical neglect caused by the war, the depletion of technical cadres, reduced investment and poor maintenance, Iran's power generation capacity has clearly failed to keep pace with the rising demand, and fallen short of efficient operation. Much of the capital stock is obsolete or in a state of disrepair. By some standards, nearly 17 per cent of installed capacity has been operating at less than 25 per cent of its potential. Blackouts and brownouts have been recurrent and lengthy – sometimes as long as 4–5 hours a day in Tehran. The frequent daily blackouts are blamed on shortage of thermal fuel, reduced water levels at hydroelectric stations, and a general deficiency of some 2,000–2,500 MW of generating capacity in relation to current demand.

In the current five-year plan, nearly 90 per cent of the needed funds for expansion is to come from domestic sales. However, if the real costs of the project are to be 90 per cent self-financed, a number of new sources (including higher electricity prices, borrowing, or private sector equity participation) are said to be needed. According to press reports, the government plans to extend the privatization program to electricity generation.

A good part of the needed capacity growth is to come from new hydroelectric dams. In 1978, there were thirteen large dams in Iran, with nine more under construction. Of these, six were finished by 1988. The three remaining, plus four new ones, were incorporated in the 1989–94 development plan and are currently under construction – with potentials for electricity generation of more than 5,000 MW. Plans are also being made to build twelve more dams in various parts of the country – the largest, Karoun 3 and Karoun 4, in southern Iran.[24]

With no more than three of Iran's 500-plus cities having sewer systems, and the government bent on privatizing city services since 1990, water and sewer companies have been set up in 20 localities, and plans are underway to establish similar entities elsewhere.[25]

NUCLEAR POWER

The rising price of oil in the 1970s, combined with the increasing need for electricity (particularly in energy-intensive industries such as basic metals and petrochemicals) led the Shah's regime to search for new sources of energy. The installation of 20 nuclear power stations with a total capacity of 23,000 MW was projected to be added to the existing oil-burning plants during a 15-year period. The Atomic Energy Organization of Iran (AEO) was established in

1974/75 in an effort to promote nuclear energy research and power production. Four initial power stations were to be located at Bushehr and Ahwaz, and four more later in Isfahan and Tehran. Projects for the Bushehr and Ahwaz plants were signed when the revolution occurred. Germany and France had won contracts to develop nuclear power in Iran. Iran had also invested in Namibia's RTZ corporation for producing uranium.

In May 1979, the Provisional Government decided to abandon the nuclear program on the grounds that Iran lacked the infrastructure, the sophisticated technology, and even the need for nuclear power. Massive reserves of gas and oil in the country, and hazards associated with nuclear plants, were cited as the reasons against such an expensive undertaking.[26] By that time, the AEO had signed a contract with Germany's Kraftwerk Union (a subsidiary of Siemens) for two nuclear power stations with a total capacity of 2,400 MW, and another contract with France's Framatome for two more stations of 1,800 MW. Work on the two 1,300 MW and 1,100 MW stations in Bushehr by KWU was about 80 per cent and 50 per cent completed, respectively, but all activities were stopped in 1979. These plants were heavily damaged during the war with Iraq. Iran had already made a down payment to Framatome, but construction was at the early stages, and the Provisional Government in May 1979 cancelled the contract.

After the ceasefire in 1988, interest in nuclear power development was intensified by the Islamic Republic, and KWU was invited to finish the Bushehr projects. The company, under various pretexts, refused to proceed, and the government sought to resolve the dispute through arbitration. Despite a subsequent ruling in Iran's favor, that KWU was obligated to complete the project, the German contractor is reportedly in the process of working out a different arrangement. The regime has vowed to finish the project in cooperation with other willing partners. China and India, with whom Tehran had reportedly been negotiating to acquire the necessary technology, have evidently shown reluctance to follow through with the sale of giant reactors.

The dispute with France dragged on for 12 years before it was reportedly settled in 1992. According to press reports, Iran in 1974 had made a $1 billion loan to France's Commissariat à l'Energie Atomique; a $163 million equity investment in the French-based Eurodif (a European uranium enrichment consortium); and a $47 million advance on nuclear fuel deliveries to Framatome. Tehran was demanding the return of these funds plus interest. In 1986 and 1987, France made two repayments of $330 and $300 respectively. Countering Iran's claims, Eurodif demanded $1,500 million in compensation for AEO's failure to honor its commitments as a shareholder to take deliveries of nuclear fuel. Framatome also claimed $700 million in compensation for the cancellation of its contract to build a power station near Ahwaz. The dispute was reportedly settled through an agreement whereby France agreed to pay Iran $1 billion of which $550 million was to be paid immediately and the rest within a year. No other details were released, but informed sources believe that Tehran kept its 10 per cent share in Eurodif, without the right to receive enriched uranium.[27]

After a lull in its activities until 1982/83, Iran's Atomic Energy Organization continued its research and exploratory activities related to the discovery of uranium reserves in central Iran, the building of power plants, and the purchase of uranium. It also began to explore new sources of energy, and even to look into the construction of water-desalination and heating plants using solar energy. The AEO has continued its research program with a 5 MW reactor supplied by the United States in 1960. China, in 1991, agreed to provide a small nuclear reactor for research and experimental purposes, as did India. Under an agreement signed in Beijing in early September 1992, China is to provide Iran with two 300 MW, nuclear power plants subject to international inspections for possible mis-use. According to foreign press, Russia has shown an interest in building two to four 440 MW nuclear power plants in Iran.[28]

HOUSING

This subsector had one of the fastest growth rates during the mid-1970s. Yet urban housing has been perennially in short supply. The Shah's regime was severely reprimanded by the opposition for neglecting the nation's housing requirements. Rising rents, and increasng lack of affordable homes in major urban centers, were said to have been one of the economic causes of the 1979 revolution. In 1976/77, the total number of dwellings in Iran was estimated by the official census to be nearly 5.3 million units (2.4 million urban and 2.9 million rural). The housing 'deficit' was estimated at 1.4 million units. By 1982/83, the deficit had reached 1.9 million units; by 1989/90, 3.7 million.

From the beginning, the Islamic Republic placed great emphasis and importance on housing and home ownership, particularly for the urban poor. Article 43 of the 1979 Constitution singles out housing as the overriding basic need of the Iranian people. In the first (post-revolution) five-year plan (1983/84–1986/87, two million housing units were expected to be constructed in urban (1.2 million) and rural (800,000) areas.

A number of domestic and externally imposed factors, however, did not allow the housing program to proceed as scheduled, and housing construction lagged behind its targets. Of these obstacles, the exorbitant rise in land prices, acute shortages of building materials, and the dwindling size of aggregate investment in this sector were the most important. Table 12.2 shows the number of houses built, as well as the magnitude of public and private investment in the construction sector. As can be seen from this table, the private sector provided the lion's share of investment in housing. Public sector investment, which constituted 23 per cent of the total in 1976/77, fell to only 5 per cent in 1986/87. Residential housing was responsible for nearly 62 per cent of investment in the construction industry during 1978/79–1987/88. The increased share of *housing* in the construction sector reflects the rapid decline of public sector investment in infrastructural facilities during the post-revolution period. The total number of housing units increased to 8.3 million by 1986/87 (4.7 million in urban and 3.6 million in rural areas) for a population that had reached 49.4 million.

In 1979/80, the government abolished private ownership of unused urban land in order to combat real estate speculation. The Housing Foundation was established to allocate nationalized land holdings among needy families; it appropriated Rls 115 billion of bank credit at 4 per cent 'charges' (interest) to approved applicants on long-term instalment bases. A new wave of rural immigration to Tehran and other major cities followed, and 'unauthorized' construction outside city limits expanded rapidly. The outbreak of the war in September 1980 put an end to the rise in housing activities in the first half of the year, bringing the annual expansion to a mere 3 per cent at constant prices. The government's deliberate policy of stopping rural migration through a larger allocation of public funds to small cities and towns resulted in a temporary decline of housing construction in Tehran and a corresponding rise in other urban areas. In 1981/82, the construction industry faced a new downturn due to war and a foreign exchange shortage, putting new pressures on prices. Public investment in construction was largely centered on dwellings for low-income groups.

To cope with the housing shortage and to fight price rises, the *Majles* passed a law requiring private purchase of dwellings in designated urban centers to be based on prior approval by the Ministry of Housing and Urban Development. Priority and permission to buy was to be granted to buyers who did not own a house, were married, and who had a ten-year residency in the city.

The government also embarked on the construction of 5,000 low-cost houses for the victims of the Tabas earthquake, and buildings in the war zones. The ban on the purchase and sale of urban land without government authorization, coupled with the shortage of building materials, aggravated the recession in residential construction. Available funds and bank credits were thus shifted towards purchase of existing homes. Urban real estate prices subsequently began to rise at an unprecedented rate.

The *de facto* nationalization of urban land in 1981/82 was followed by the establishment of a number of agencies called urban land organizations in various parts of the country. These organizations had the task of purchasing vacant lots within the city limits from their owners at government-determined prices and, along with ownerless plots, selling them to individuals or cooperatives under specific guidelines. In 1982/83, some 11,000 lots totalling 3 million square meters were distributed across the country. Several new bodies were also organized to cope with the reconstruction and renewal of war-torn cities and facilities.

The protracted recession in the housing sector came to an end in 1983/84. Rising real estate prices and the allocation of new lots for construction helped the recovery. Investment in new homes and housing units started during the year showed a more than 90 per cent increase over the previous year. Having acquired a total of 220 million square meters (sq/m) of urban land during the two-year period, the government transferred another 77,000 lots with a total area of 25 million sq/m among individuals, cooperatives, and building agencies. As a result of housing starts on the newly distributed land, construction costs shot up by 30 percent over the previous year. The recovery, however, was short-lived, and, while private investment showed no change, public investment was considerably smaller. The slump in housing construction that began in 1984/85 continued in 1985/86 due to the spread of recession to other sectors of the country. The 17 million sq/m of urban land offered to about 70,000 families in that year was 24 per cent less than the year before. Both private and public investment in this sector also declined. The slump continued with greater intensity in 1986/87 due to foreign exchange shortages needed for import of construction materials. Again, aggregate investment in this subsector fell by 20per cent compared to the previous year. Sharp declines in the importation of construction materials in 1987/88, shortages of local building supplies and their rising costs helped prolong the depression in the housing market. Value-added in the sector fell by 14.7 per cent, due in part to the reduced size of urban land (13 million meters) among fewer families (53,000), as well as reduced private sector investment. Public investment, however, showed considerable growth over the previous year. Despite the anticipated revival in the construction industry after the ceasefire, the slump continued in 1988/89 with private housing permits, investment, and finished dwellings all registering declines. The same was true of the acreage of urban land distributed (about 10 million meters) and recipient families (about 4,320). The urban housing shortage was more acutely felt due to increasing rural migration. By some private estimates, housing costs in Tehran and other large cities constituted no less than 50 per cent of some wage-earners' regular income. Some 20 million people (4.5 million households) lived in two-room units. In addition to the nationwide shortage (particularly in major urban centers due to growing rural migration), housing has suffered from exorbitant prices, poor quality, improper zoning laws, unenforced building codes, and environmental hazards (for example, seismic safety).

The current five-year plan again calls for the construction of some 2.5 million housing units over the period (1.7 million in urban areas, and 0.8 million in rural). Top priority is to be given to construction of apartment blocks of six to twenty storeys, as well as detached and semi-detached dwellings in the major cities (including 100,000 new homes). Construction of public buildings, libraries, police and military quarters are also part of the plan. So is the creation of fifteen new cities with a total population of four million under the supervision of the Supreme Council for Urban Development. The private sector is particularly encouraged to invest in high-rise residential blocks. In the first full year of the plan, however, only 116,000 housing units were built in the urban areas, and fewer in rural regions, bringing the total to an estimated 195,000 units – considerably below the plan targets.[29]

In the aftermath of post-ceasefire reconstruction efforts, the construction industry in Tehran and other major cities has begun to experience a mini-recovery, compared with its ten years of relative stagnation. Housing has again become a safe haven for investment in search of quick, sure profit. Responsible for the surge of activity in this sector are said to be such factors as steeply rising prices of housing and rentals.[30] By some private estimates, while post-revolution inflation was (officially) some 637 per cent in 1991/92, and the free-market rial/dollar exchange rate rose by twenty times, real estate prices in Tehran and some major cities increased by thirty times or more.

The significance of a housing shortage in Iran's current economic problems has been questioned by the government. A statement by President Rafsanjani, released in early October 1991, claimed that

75 per cent of the Iranian population enjoyed adequate housing, 10 per cent were itinerant (*khosh-neshin*), and only 14–15 per cent faced a housing problem.[31] According to the President, the government was ready to put one million lots in 200 places in the country at the applicants' disposal, but the real problem for the home seekers was lack of funds.[32] At about the same time, one of the country's labor leaders publicly complained that half of the 2.5 million industrial workforce in Iran did not own a place of their own in which to live, and that the larger portion of the workers' take-home pay was used for rent.[33]

TRANSPORT AND COMMUNICATIONS

The transport industry is divided into three sectors: public, private and cooperatives. Modes of modern transportation include railroads, surface roads, air, sea, and pipelines. In 1990/91, as in 1977/78, the country's domestic and foreign transport needs were far beyond national transport capacity. The expansion that took place after the revolution has been inadequate, and a good part of existing facilities that were damaged by the war and poor maintenance remains in disrepair. The system has also been unduly overloaded because the bulk of imports delivered at southern and northern ports of entry routinely goes to Tehran first, and from there the cargo is sent to other parts of the country and production centers.[34]

Road transport by trucks, buses, and other vehicles is the principal mode of transportation for both merchandise and passengers. It is responsible for some 85 per cent of the value-added in the transportation subsector. On the eve of the revolution, Iran had 63,000 km of roads, of which less than 14 per cent were asphalted main roads. In 1990/91, the road network outside of the cities comprised a total of about 170,000 km of roads of various quality: trans-Iranian highways, asphalt roads, feeder roads, and earth roads. Of this total, 860 km were four-lane freeways; 25,000 km were main roads; 41,000 km were secondary roads; more than 43,000 km were rural roads; and 60,000 km were access dirt roads. There were some 500 km of intra-city freeways.[35] Some 62 per cent of this road network was built after the revolution (including 29,000 km built in rural areas by the Construction Crusade in the form of rural as well as access dirt roads). The latter organization's priority has been to build more roads at the expense of properly maintaining existing ones. Due to war damage and lack of proper maintenance, the road system is badly in need of improvement. The division of responsibility for *building* rural roads (the Ministry of Jihad) and *maintaining* them (the Ministry of Roads) adds to the problem. Even under the current development plan, more roads are being constructed than properly serviced. The needed target of total roads is estimated at 250,000 km, or 50 per cent over the current level. The current plans call for the construction of 360 km of highways, 1,400 km of main roads, and 1,530 km of secondary roads.

As part of its new policy of invigorating the private sector, new freeways are now to be bank-financed without government help. They include Qazvin-Zanjan-Tabriz to the north; Tehran-Saveh; and Qom-Ksahan-Isfahan-Shiraz in the center.

In 1977/78, there were an estimated 1.7 million motorized vehicles in Iran, of which more than 63 per cent were private, personal vehicles (including motorcycles). By the end of 1990/91, the total reached nearly 2.8 million, of which 64 per cent were private means of transportation. Despite the Islamic Republic's opprobrium against consumerism and 'luxury' living, public passenger transportation by intra-city and inter-urban buses and taxis constituted only about 7 per cent of the total by the late 1980s.[36]

The relatively small fleet of public transport vehicles engaged in public transportation of people and freight are in the hands of some 2,000 road companies, of which less than 6 per cent are government owned. Urban transport is provided by buses, minibuses and taxis. Taxis are privately owned and operated under personal and corporate ownership. Mass transit is mainly operated by municipalities. Fares are regulated and are low by international comparison. Service is short; vehicles are old; traffic is congested; and pollution is uncommonly high. Traffic regulations are adequate, but generally ignored.

Railway traffic is managed by the Iranian State Railways, created by law in 1935 as a semi-autonomous agency under the overall supervision of the Ministry of Roads and Transportation. Some 4,600 km of main railways, and some 1,250 km of trunklines, connect Tehran with ports in the Persian Gulf to the south; Tabriz, Ankara, Baku, and Moscow in the north and northwest; and Mashad and the central Asian republics in the northeast. In 1991/92, railroads served 14 out of 24 provinces, with 8.2 million passengers, and about 17 million tons of freight – accounting for about 7 per cent of total passenger traffic, and 15 per cent of freight. Some 1,000 km of main rails are to be added to the network during the current plan, raising total yearly freight to 25 million tons, and passengers to 10 million.

The current five-year development plan gives high priority to railway reconstruction as the core of a new strategy for opening up markets in neighboring territories. It calls for the expansion of the network, including the much delayed completion of the 730 km double-track Bafg-Bandar Abbas rail link, and a new 165 km line connection Mashad to Sarakhs on the joint border with Afghanistan and Turkmenistan. Another line is planned from Mashad to link up with Bafg, to allow Turkmenistan direct access to the Persian Gulf. In the planning stage are also a short link to Pakistan, a Mashad-Ashkhabad railway, and double-tracking lines from Tehran to Tabriz and to Ahwaz.

All the country's major cities are scheduled to have their own urban rail transport networks. The only underground railway, in Tehran, is being built through financing by two commercial banks, Mellat and Tejarat. The Tehran project was initially talked about as far back as 1958. A contract for the construction of a 60 km line was signed with the French company, Sofretu, in 1970, and preliminary work began in 1976. After the revolution, the work was stopped until the mid-1980s when Tehran's overflowing population and worsening air pollution revived the idea, and the cabinet approved the resumption of operation in 1986.[37]

Rail transportation is heavily subsidized by the government. Revenues in recent years have covered less than 45 per cent of operating and maintenance costs – in contrast with some Third World countries, where state railways are a source of net revenue.

Air transportation in 1978/79 consisted of the publicly-owned Iran National Airline (HOMA) (operating on domestic and international routes), plus four private lines – Pars Air, Air Taxi, Dur-Aseman and Air Service – engaged in domestic passenger and cargo traffic. Iran Air had a fleet of 29 planes of various types and capacity. After the revolution, the four domestic airlines were merged into one, Aseman, engaged in regular and charter flights. Due to the difficulties of obtaining spare parts during the Iran/Iraq war, the country's operating passenger fleet was gradually reduced, while passenger traffic steadily increased – thanks in no small measure to the extremely low fares. In 1992, according to airline officials, only 40 per cent of demand for air flights was met by the available fleet, and the projection of traffic for the rest of the decade was for an increase of 100 per cent, requiring a fleet of 50–60 aircraft. As reported by a trade magazine, in addition to Iran Air and Aseman, there are three small private airlines, Saha Mahan Seyr and Kish Air, in regular domestic operation, and a first privately-owned cargo line, Safiran, which started in mid-1992. There was also Iran Air Tour Aviation, a private company equipped with 10 Tupolev aircraft leased from the Russian Republic to serve smaller towns and cities. According to press reports, in April 1992, Iran Air purchased two A-300 wide-bodied jets from Airbus, and later held talks with Boeing to purchase sixteen Boeing 737–400 aircraft, with an option on four more.

In 1993, there were 42 airports in operation throughout Iran, of which five – in Tehran, Isfahan, Mashad, Shiraz, and Bandar Abbas – were equipped for international traffic. Eleven others were suitable for large aircraft. These airports reportedly handled 7 million passengers in 1991/92, of which about 1 million were international travellers. They also processed some 70,000 tons of cargo, of which 33,000 tons were imports passing through Tehran Mehrabad Airport. The facilities in these airports, even at Tehran's Mehrabad, are considered substandard by international guidelines, and the capacity is also limited. Among the 21 new airports being built across the country, the new Tehran international airport, under construction since 1981, is only 10 per cent finished and requires new injections of funds. The airport, to be called Imam Khomeini International Airport, is a large complex involving various facilities (e.g., terminals, hotels, and commercial outlets) requiring $800 million in hard currency for its first phase. Once completed by the end of the decade, it is projected to handle 12 million passengers and 200,000 tons of cargo a year. In the meantime, twenty other new airports are being built across the country, while modernization is being carried out at existing ones. The government's efforts to obtain $1.15 billion in foreign credits have been hampered by the extremely low fares charged for flights inside Iran which, despite a hefty 81 per cent increase in July 1992, remain among the lowest in the world.

The government's Civil Aviation Organization is in charge of the operation, maintenance, and expansion of existing airports; the construction of new airports; and air traffic control and permits for civilian flights. Domestic fares – unchanged between 1985 and 1992 – are low and cover less than 70 per cent of current operating and maintenance costs.

While 20 per cent of Iran's external (non-oil) trade volume is normally shipped via rail, air, and surface roads, seaports still handle about 80 per cent. All cargo ports for non-oil products fall under the supervision of the Ports and Shipping Organization, established in 1960 as a semi-independent agency. In 1978/79, Iran possessed forty-two cargo ships with 525,000 tons capacity. There were eight ports, three of which were put out of commission by the war, at least partially and temporarily. In 1990/91, Iran's port facilities had a nominal capacity of 28 million tons per year, of which only 70 per cent was utilized due to lack of equipment and rail/sea coordination, and other problems (e.g., poor management and poorly trained workforce). Millions of dollars of demurrage charges are still being paid each year.

In 1990/91, four major cargo ports served the Persian Gulf traffic, of which Khorramshahr (once the largest) was destroyed by the war, and although it is now being rebuilt it cannot be fully operational until the Shatt-al Arab is cleared of the war wreckages. Bandar Khomeini (formerly Bandar Shapur) and Bandar Abbas were used during the war in lieu of Khorramshahr. Two small ports are located on the Caspian Sea for lighter traffic with Europe and the former Soviet Union. Only Bandar Khomeini and Khorramshahr have had links to the rail network. The bulk of Iran's exports of crude oil had been shipped from oil terminals in the Persian Gulf of which Kharg was the largest before the war, and promises to be soon again.

The current five-year plan projects an increase of nominal port capacity to 30 million tons a year. In 1991/92, the Islamic Republic Shipping Lines had a fleet of 71 vessels of various kinds – general cargo, bulk vessels, tankers, containers, refrigereated, passenger carriers, and others. The national cargo fleet of 110 vessels belonging to, or leased by, three companies (including ISL) had a total capacity of nearly 3 million dead weight tons. Traffic through Iran's sea ports reached 17.5 million tons in 1991/92, a 15 per cent increase over the year before. Sea ports handled 81 per cent of all the country's imports. Nearly 13.5 million tons of import cargo (65 per cent of total) were carried by domestic flag ships and other leased vessels.

By the government's own account, transportation has been one of the regime's crippling bottlenecks. Millions of tons of goods remained and were often ruined in ports, factories and farms year after year, due to the shortage of transport means. Existing motor vehicles are often inoperative because of the lack of spare parts and tyres, both of which were in short supply due to the foreign exchange crunch.

Post, telephone, telegraph, radio and television are owned and operated by the state. The Ministry of Post, Telegraph and Telephone is responsible for providing these services, internally and internationally, through two state-owned companies – Telecommunications Company of Iran and Post Company. According to official reports, since the revolution the number of automatic dialling exchanges has more than doubled, and installed telephone lines increased nearly three times. Some 320 towns and cities in Iran, and 137 foreign countries, are now connected by direct long-distance dialling. Yet both inter-city lines and installed telephone connections have fallen short of the targets set in the original plan. Telegraph and telex services have also expanded, as have radio and television broadcasts. *Seda va Sima-ye Iran* (Voice and Vision of Iran), as a separate government agency, is in charge of radio and television, both of which are used as a means of information and Islamic 'guidance'. Linkage with the outside world is also provided by several satellite stations already at work in Hamedan, Isfahan, and Bumehen, and four others are under construction. The existing three earth stations with 1,300 channels are connected through Intelsat with 39 foreign countries, and plans are to increase channels to 5,000 in three years.

The Post Company has 213 main offices which supervise 620 urban and 858 rural post offices. It handles annually some 317 million pieces of despatched domestic and foreign correspondence, and 325 million pieces of received. In addition, it handles 1 million parcels, and 12 million newspapers – all relatively small volumes by international standards.[38]

Communications and telecommunications in Iran are modern but admittedly inadequate. The country's legendary postal service, said to be instituted some 2,500 years ago by the Achaemenid kings, was joined by telegraph in 1858, telephone in 1885, radio in 1924, microwave in 1964, and satellite in 1969. Although all services have expanded since the revolution none has been able to keep pace with population growth or increase in demand. This is particularly true of telephone services, especially in Tehran, where obtaining a line may take several years, and existing lines are bought and sold as a valuable financial asset. In rural areas, inter-city telephone connections have nearly trebled during the 1980s, but meet only still one-third of projected demand.

According to official statistics, in 1990/91 there were a total of 2.2 million operating telephones in the country, up from 1.2 million in 1984/85. During the current five-year plan, some 2.5 million new lines are to be added to existing ones. In 1990/91, there were 138 AM and FM radio stations, and 706 television stations, including earth satellites.[39] The Telecommunication Company of Iran (TCI) as a subsidiary of the PTT ministry, is reportedly negotiating with foreign suppliers for the installation of mobile telephone systems, a geo-stationary satellite for domestic communications, small satellite earth stations, and a nationwide paging system.[40] Costs of most services are not presently fully recovered, and are a burden to the public budget. The current plan calls for self-financing within five years.[41]

MINING

Iran's mining potential is still largely unexplored. Some 20 metals and 30 non-metal minerals are believed to exist on Iranian soil. The sector's links with the domestic economy are at best peripheral and indirect. The share of mining in GDP hovered around 1 per cent throughout the 1980s. More than two-thirds of extracted materials usually go into construction, and the rest into industry. Major non-oil minerals consist of iron ore, copper, chromite, gypsum, salt, turquoise, coal, lead, zinc, bauxite, phosphate, tin, sulphur, uranium, tungsten, manganese, gold, silver and others. This sector has in the past suffered from relative inattention, small investment, and scant research. During the war with Iraq, a number of factors, including trade sanctions, export controls, and shortages of capital and skilled labor, kept mining activities in a depressed state.

Oil, gas, iron, copper, and uranium mines were all nationalized during the Shah's regime. Other mines, (for example, metals, quarry slabs, coal, salt and sulphur) could be developed by the private sector, with an 'ownership fee' to be paid to the government. With the establishment of the Islamic Republic's Ministry of Mines and Metals, and the Mining Law of 1983, national mines were divided into small and large categories. Large and strategic mines were to be state-owned, developed and utilized by the government and public agencies. Small mines also belong to the government, but can be leased to private entrepreneurs. In terms of content, mines were divided into four basic categories: construction materials; oil and gas; nuclear materials; and all other. Oil and gas reserves are managed by the Ministry of Petroleum. Radioactive materials are in the hands of the Atomic Energy Organization. Most other mines are handled by the Ministry of Mines and Metals. The provisions regarding ownership and operation are prescribed by the Mining Law of 1983.[42]

There were officially 1,344 active mines in the country in 1992/93, producing 43 types of ore. The majority were in the private sector. Some 95 per cent of the 166 mines in the public sector were under the jurisdiction of the Ministry of Mines and Metals, and the rest were managed by the Ministry of Jihad (3 per cent), *Bonyad-e Mostazafan* (1 per cent) and *Bonyad-e Maskan* (1 per cent). Nearly 43,000 miners were active throughout Iran in 1991/92, producing about 59 million tons of minerals worth an estimated $7 billion, of which some $168 million was exported.[43]

The Ministry of Mines and Metals claims to have discovered significant quantities of alunite, phosphates, borax, antimony, talc, cobalt, tungsten and bauxite in various parts of the country. Yet the number of active mines has considerably declined since the revolution, In 1991/92, the ministry had a number of projects under way involving iron ore, gold, copper, lead, zinc, and coal.

In line with one of the initial revolutionary goals of developing non-oil sources of foreign exchange, the government intends to invest some $5 billion in the mining sector during the current plan, with a view to lifting the sector's share in GDP to as much as 5 per cent by 1994. Favored to receive special attention is the $300 million alumina (bauxite) mine in the northeast with East European companies to supply domestic needs. Proven bauxite reserves are about 22 million tons with an average parity of 48 per cent. Production is to start with 280,000 t/y in 1994. Australian interests are also attracted to the Sangan iron ore in Khorasan with a $750 million credit for the purchase of Australian technology. The government intends to add about 10 million tons to the current annual output of 15 million tons. The mining sector was projected to have $2 billion of exports during the current five-year plan, but actual exports so far are considerably below targets.

Implementing the government's new privatization drive, the Ministry of Mines and Metals announced in mid-June 1992 its intention to sell shares in 29 mining companies under its jurisdiction to the private sector.[44] Japanese, French, Italian, Czech and other European firms have reportedly agreed to enter into joint-ventures to exploit reserves of coal, copper, zinc, lead and baux-ite.[45] In mid-1993, 85 per cent of Iran's active mines was exploited by the non-state sector.

APPENDIX: HEAVY INDUSTRIES

Iran's non-hydrocarbon heavy industries include steel, aluminium, copper, machine building, tractors, and pulp and paper. Among these, a few large complexes that have been the focus of attention under the Islamic Republic are worth cataloging here.

The Isfahan steel mill, a high furnace type, was built with Soviet help under the Shah's regime, and began operating its cast iron section in 1971, with an initial design capacity of 550,000 tons a year. In 1981/82, its second phase became operational. Since 1976, there have been concerted efforts to raise capacity to profitable levels. In 1992/93, the mill was expected to produce a record 2.4 million tons of steel (mostly low-grade construction beams). By the government's own reckoning, for each ton of steel, the mill employs 20 workers, while Japan's ratio is 1:1, and in some Western countries the ratio is even lower. Contracts reportedly signed with Japan's Nippon Steel and Italy's Danieli are designed to obtain foreign expertise and technology to raise production capacity to 4–5 million tons by 1996.

The Ahwaz steel complex, a three-unit direct reduction plant using natural gas, was commissioned in 1977 with a sponge iron capacity of 330,000 tons, and an ultimate design capacity of 1.5 million tons. For war-related reasons, the plant's output in 1991/ 92 was no more than 200,000 tons. Contracts for its repair and renovation and an eventual expansion of capacity to 2.5 million tons a year by the mid-1990s (and ultimately 3.8 million tons annually) have been signed with Mexico's Hylsa, Germany's Mannesmann, and Japan's Kobe steel.

The Mobarakeh steel complex, 75 km south of Isfahan, began under the Shah's regime and was in an advanced stage before the revolution. Planned to be sited at Bandar Abbas, it was moved to Isfahan to be closer to supplies of domestic iron ore. Currently, it is Iran's biggest industrial project completed after the revolution at a reported cost of over $5 billion. Situated on 35 square km of land, it has 28 plants, including a steel mill that is publicized to be the largest of its kind in the world. The complex has the original annual capacity of 2.5 million tons of hot and cold rolled plates. It consists of a steel manufacturing unit, foundry, cooling system, and ingot unit. Work on the complex was resumed in 1979 with the help of several foreign contractors, but completion was delayed because of foreign exchange shortage, war-related difficulties, lack of specialists, and non-delivery of supplies by foreign firms. The first phase of the plant was commissioned in late September 1991, scheduled to produce 200,000 tons of sheet. The project is to be finished by the end of the five-year plan, with part of its output designated for export. A two-unit 680 MW power station is to supply electricity to the complex. The first phase of a 200 MW thermal power station to serve the plant was inaugurated in July 1991. The complex, with an eventual workforce of 18,000, is considered highly labor intensive.

The Arak Aluminium Company was formed in 1967 as a joint-venture between Iran, Pakistan, and the US Reynolds Metals Company, holding a 70 per cent, 5 per cent and 25 per cent share respectively. The nominal capacity was 45,000 tons, to be later raised to 90,000 tons. Products were to be aluminium ingot, rolled sheets and billets for the production of profiles, cables, utensils, etc. In 1971, the plant started operation, and annual production reached 50,000 tons, while smelting capacity was planned to rise to 120,000 tons. The shortage of electricity later in the 1970s reduced output, but after the revolution the company's production was raised to 45,000 tons. The Arak aluminium factory is now capable of producing 45,000 tons of aluminium bars in its reduction unit, and 120,000 tons of alloys in its casting unit. Bar production capacity was to rise to 70,000 tons.

A contract for a second, $1.6 billion, aluminium complex, claimed to be the largest in the Middle East, was signed in December 1991 for the construction of an aluminium smelter at Bandar Abbas, called Al-Mahdi. The plant is expected to be commissioned in April 1994 with 220,000 t/y of initial output. The project is a joint venture between the Ministry of Mines and Metals and the Dubai-based International Development Corporation on a 60/40 equity basis. According to a government spokesman, this has been the first joint-venture project undertaken within the provisions of the current five-year development plan. The complex will include a 300–400 MW power station and a desalination plant. Fuel is to be provided by natural gas from the Qeshm island. Half of the total projected output is intended for export. The supply of raw materials for the plant is to be imported from Guinea. The plant's viability in the face of high initial cost, a highly competitive world aluminium market, and the absence of clear comparative advantage remains to be tested.

The Sarcheshmeh Copper Company started operation in 1983 with a capacity of 158,000 tons, and a potential for 240,000 tons. It uses Kerman's copper reserves, estimated at 750 million tons (and potentially 1,800 million tons), with a copper content of 0.5 to 1 per cent). The copper complex consists of an integrated process from extraction to refining. Products include blisters, cables, billets and their by-products. The plant is expected to produce 200,000 tons by the end of the current plan.

The machine-building industry is located in Arak and Tabriz. The Arak Machine-Building Company, with technical and financial assistance from the Soviets, was established in 1969, with a capacity of 20,000 tons, for the production of machinery, boilers, cranes, conveyer belts, and agricultural equipment. Operation began in 1972 and capacity was increased to 30,000 tons, but products were limited to steam boilers, spare parts for sugar and cement plants, and certain farm machinery. The Tabriz Machine-Building Company, with assistance from Czechoslovakia, designed to produce machine tools, electro-motors, and engines, was inaugurated in 1972 with a capacity of 10,000 tons. The Tabriz Tractor Company was established with technical assistance from Romania, and started an assembly operation of 10 units a day in 1969, reaching a total of 3,000 tractors in 1971. In 1974, the plant's model changed from the Romanian Universal to the Massey-Ferguson type. In 1978, a foundry was under construction. In 1983, a new line of Perkins motors was added to the company's products with a capacity of 20,000 tractor motors and 10,000 lift-trucks, air compressors, and generators. Later, a cast-iron unit with a 54,000 ton capacity was added. The company's output in 1991/92 was estimated at 7,500 units, twice the number of 1990/91.

Iran's large-scale manufacturing also includes defense industries whose products are not included in annual statistics. In the aftermath of the Iraqi invasion, the Western arms embargo, and the ensuing protracted war, an unexpected boost was given to Iran's defense industries. In addition to a wide variety of small arms (rifles, machine guns, and ammunition) which were produced domestically in the 1970s under the Defense Industries Organization, several new lines of activity were added to the existing facilities. Aided by international arms dealers and certain friendly governments, the Revolutionary Guards Corps set up its own military-industrial installations. At the end of the war, government authorities claimed that the Islamic Republic had access to 240 major arms factories and was supplied by some 12,000 private workshops around the world. Defense officials also claimed that the country was capable of producing missiles, mortars, aircraft parts, part for tanks and armored vehicles.[46] Recent reports in the popular press make repeated references to the regime's negotiations with many industrial countries for assistance in expanding and improving the country's defense industry.

According to press reports Iran's total steel output in 1992/93 was 3.5 million tons, and was expected to reach 4 million tons in 1993/94 – with a possibility of 300,000 tons in exports. Domestic steel consumption is estimated at between 3–5 million tons a year, depending on economic conditions.The country's copper production was estimated at 120,000 tons, and that of aluminium 120,000 tons.[47]

NOTES

1. See *Barrasi-ye Tahavolat* (1984), pp. 159–160.
2. By some estimates, as much as $20 billion was invested in manufacturing during the Shah's rule, of which two-thirds were in the private sector. More than 200 joint-venture companies were set up with foreign firms.
3. Ebrahim Razzaqi (1988), pp. 435–444.
4. See *Ettela'at*, 20 Azar 1362; and *Barrasi-ye Tahavolat* (1984), p. 161.

5. *Ettela'at*, 3 Bahman 1361, p. 4; and *Barrasi-ye Tahavolat* (1984), pp. 165–166.
6. There are reportedly more than one million carpetlooms in the country, providing income to some 8 million workers. *Kayhan Havai*, June 17, 1992, p. 2.
7. See *Comprehensive Industrial Statistics 1988/89, Statistics of Industrial Workshops 1987/88*, and *Statistics of Large Industrial Units under the Management of Public Sector in Iran* (Tehran: Iranian Statistical Center, 1985 and 1990); and for a summary, see *Iran Focus*, December 1989, p. 14.
8. *MEED*, November 8, 1991, p. 14
9. For details see *Iran Focus*, June 1990, pp. 12–13.
10. See *Kayhan Havai*, July 24, 1991, p. 13
11. The Bank Markazi governor told a stock exchange seminar in October 1991 that Iran was spending $700 million a year in foreign exchange to produce some 30,000 passenger cars under twenty-year-old technologies, whereas only $380 million could buy 50,000 automobiles built with modern technology. See *Kayhan Havai*, October 30, 1991, p. 11.
12. Interview with the minister of Mines and Metals, *Resalat*, 6 Azar, 1369 p. 8.
13. For details see *Iran Focus*, April 1989, pp. 12–13.
14. In January 1992, the government submitted a bill to the *Majles* to merge the three ministries once again into a single ministry of industries and mines. *Kayhan Havai*, January 15, 1992.
15. For a brief summary, see *Iran Focus*, April 1990, p. 14–15.
16. *Ettela'at*, 20 Azar, 1362.
17. The shortage of foreign exchange in the latter part of the 1980s, for example, reportedly resulted in the production of only 2,000 tractors and 90 combine harvesters domestically, while existing factories were capable of producing 35,000 tractors and 750 combines. Automobile production was down from more than 100,000 a year before the revolution to only 10,000 in 1987/88. See *Iran Focus*, March and May 1989.
18. See *Barrasi-ye Narasaíha va Vabastegiha-ye Kargahha-ye Bozorg-e Sanàti-ye Keshvar dar Sal-e 1358* (Tehran: The Iranian Statistical Center, 1359 [1980]).
19. The Government Auditing Office recently revealed that state-owned companies with Rls 40,000 billion in assets, were not even able to match the mere 5.24 per cent annual return on capital realized in the private sector, due to 'mismanagement'. Some have incurred losses year after year. See *Kayhan Havai* June 26, 1991, p. 11.
20. *Kayhan Havai*, November 25, 1992.
21. While electricity generation between 1977 and 1988 increased by a respectable 7.5 per cent a year on average, the average growth rate of power during 1962–77 was nearly 22.4 per cent a year.
22. See Bank Markazi, *Annual Review* 1991/92.
23. *Kayhan Havai*, September 2, 1992, p. 25.
24. *Iran Focus*, February 1990, p. 15; and *MEED*, October 25, 1991, p. 13.

25. *Kayhan Havai*, September 2, 1992, p. 25.
26. *Business Week*, June 25, 1979; and *Barrasi-ye Tahavolat* [1984], p. 154.
27. See *MEED*, November 8, 1991; and *Kayhan Havai*, November 6 and 13, 1991, and January 8, 1992.
28. *The New York Times*, September 11, 1992.
29. *Gozaresh-e Eqtesadi 1368 (Economic Report for 1989/90)* (Tehran: Plan and Budget Organization, 1990), p. 343. Private estimates put Iran's housing needs at 600,000 units per year.
30. See *Iran Focus*, May, 1990, p. 12.
31. The survey of urban family budget for 1369 (1990/91) shows 75.4 per cent of all city dwellers owning their homes. It indicates, however, that for some 14.3 per cent of total who were tenants, the rental cost was as much as 34 per cent of total expenditure in certain cities. See footnote 8, ch.4.
32. *Kayhan Havai*, October 16, 1991, p. 11.
33. *Kayhan Havai*, October 9, 1991, p. 10. According to a *Majles* law passed in January 1992, large industrial enterprises were now required to provide adequate housing for at least 30 per cent of their homeless workforce. *Kayhan Havai*, January 29, 1992.
34. See *Ettela'at*, 27 Azar 1362. The use of animals for local transportation is still significant in villages and small towns.
35. *Statistical Yearbook, 1990/91* (Tehran: Iranian Statistical Center, 1992), p. 354; and private sources.
36. In late 1989, Tehran reportedly had 1.7 million automobiles, 1,500 buses, 5,000–6,000 minibuses, and 16,000 taxis.
37. See *Iran Focus*, October 1989; *MEED*, December 7, 1990, and July 24, 1992.
38. For details, see Iranian Statistical Center, *Annual Statistics, 1990/91*; and *Iran Focus*, July 1989, pp. 12–23.
39. *Iran in the Mirror of Statistics*, no. 8, p. 151; and *Statistical Yearbook, 1990/91*, pp. 372–373.
40. *MEED*, October 25, 1991, p. 13. According to a *Majles* deputy, in January 1992 there were 2.5 million private telephone lines and 15,000 public telephone booths in Iran, and 500 cities had access to automatic dialling – all substantially up from 1978/79. *Kayhan Havai*, January 15, 1992, p. 25.
41. For details see *Iran's Telecom Strategy* (Cambridge: Pyramid Research, 1991).
42. For a summary of the law's provisions, see *Iran Focus*, March 1989, pp. 11–12.
43. *OPEC Bulletin*, June 1992, p. 56; and *Kayhan Havai*, August 19, 1992.
44. For the list of these companies, see *Kayhan Havai*, June 17, 1992, p. 10.
45. See *MEED*, September 25, 1992, p. 10.
46. See *Echo of Iran*, 'Economic and Political Bulletin', (February 23, 1989), and *MERIP Reports* (January–February, 1987).
47. *Kayhan Havai*, September 9, 1992, p. 15 and The Economist Intelligence Unit, 'Iran', No. 2, 2nd Quarter 1993.

13

Hydrocarbons: oil, gas and petrochemicals

The Iranian economy produces and consumes a vast variety of energy materials: oil, gas, coal, and traditional fuels such as wood, charcoal and animal waste. The discussion in this chapter is largely confined to oil and gas. Due to Iran's enormous resources of hydrocarbons, and comparative advantage in their derivative products, a section here is also devoted to petrochemicals, instead of discussing this as part of the industrial sector.

PETROLEUM

Iran is the oldest oil producer in the Persian Gulf region, with its first crude output going back to 1908. As of January 1993, the country's recoverable reserves were officially estimated at 92.8 billion barrels, or about 9.3 per cent of the world's total.[1] Proven reserves, however, were privately put at no more than 60 billion barrels – still making Iran fifth in the world after Saudi Arabia, Iraq, Kuwait, and Abu Dhabi. Most of Iran's oil consists of medium to heavy grade with a high sulphur content. Of the total proven reserves, nearly 90 per cent are onshore located in large fields in the Khuzistan and Fars provinces, and 10 per cent are offshore located in the Persian Gulf. In 1992/93, there were at least 800 free-flowing wells producing oil in more than 40 of Iran's 60 known fields scattered along a 700-mile stretch across the southern reaches. Dozens of rigs were drilling for new oil, with the aim of increasing production capacity to near pre-revolution levels.

Iran's oil industry was nationalized in 1951, but under a 1954 agreement, extraction and marketing were left in the hands of major oil companies which operated on behalf of the National Iranian Oil Company (NIOC). From 1973 onwards, the NIOC exercised total control over Iran's oil resources, but operated under a contract with a consortium of 14 major international oil companies who provided technical and managerial assistance, and marketed about 2.5 million barrels per day of the daily crude output. About 2.5 mb/d were also marketed by the NIOC itself through direct sales, barter trade with the Eastern Bloc, or other agreements, including some with jointly-owned refineries in Madras, South Korea, and Johannesburg. NIOC also had a number of pioneering offshore joint production ventures in the Persian Gulf and the North Sea in which it shared ownership with several foreign companies. The latter included Iran Pan American Oil Company; the Lavan Petroleum Company; the Iranian Marine International Oil Company; the Hormoz Petroleum Company; Société Irano-Italienne des Pétroles; and the French Sofiran. These joint-ventures were engaged in exploration, production, transportation and marketing of Iran's crude oil.

NIOC conducted some of its diversified activities through a number of fully-owned subsidiaries, each with its own specific task. These subsidiaries consisted of the National Iranian Tanker Company, handling a sizeable part of the country's crude exports, fuel imports and inter-terminal cargoes; the National Iranian Offshore Company, managing offshore activities; the National Iranian Drilling Company; and others for specialized functions. Iran's natural gas production and marketing were handled by the Iranian National Gas Company. Oil derivatives and petrochemicals were the responsibility of National Iranian Petrochemical Company (NIPC).[2]

ATTEMPTS AT POLICY REVERSALS

The 1979 revolution brought about significant changes in the structure and policy direction of Iran's hydrocarbon sector, particularly the petroleum industry. In fact, no other sector of the Iranian economy was as thoroughly affected by the 1979 revolution, and subjected to so many conflicting internal policies. Similarly, no other factor influenced the behavior and performance of the domestic economy as much as petroleum output and exports. The Islamic Republic's policies regarding production, export, marketing and pricing of Iran's crude oil during the 1980s were heavily influenced by the Iran–Iraq war, Western sanctions, and, not least, by Saudi Arabia and its Arab allies who openly or surreptitiously backed Baghdad against Tehran. The industry itself had to conform to a new revolution ideology; bear the brunt of the war; and adjust to a global oil market that went from boom to bust, and bust to boom. Within a 14-year period, crude oil prices tripled during the first year of the revolution, fell to one-fifth of the early peak in 1986, and shot up again to near the early 1980 level after the Persian Gulf war, before settling down to a mid-range between the two extremes.

Ideology was the oil industry's initial master. One of the opposition's fiercest attacks on the Shah and the Pahlavi regime involved Iran's post-Mosaddeq oil policy. The one issue on which all factions in the revolutionary coalition generally agreed was the charge that the monarch's relentless push for higher oil production and exports was injurious to Iran's interests. Precious petroleum reserves were said to have been depleted too rapidly; the proceeds of oil exports were wasted on 'useless' arms and grandiose projects; domestic industries were hurt by consumer imports; and the economy as a whole was made unduly dependent on the West and the United States.[3]

Bowing to political pressure generated by these charges, on February 28, 1979, NIOC announced the unilateral cancellation of the Consortium agreement whereby the Iranian Oil Participants Company was marketing Iranian oil, and the Oil Services Company of Iran offered a broad range of services. Both the NIOC leadership and the Provisional Government were anxious to have oil production and exports started up again on their own. In the waning days of the Shah's regime, the oil industry was all but immobilized, and by mid-January 1979, daily output was cut to only 700,000 barrels, or below domestic consumption – compared with 5.7 mb/d of production and 4.9 mb/d of exports as late as October 1978. The moderate elements within the government and the oil company were for increasing production to about 4 mb/d and exports to 3.1 mb/d. But there were two major obstacles to this modified production policy. First, the *ad hoc* workers' councils in the oil fields – the remnants of the old Tudeh party cells – had strong feelings against foreign staff who were needed for highly sophisticated operations such as gas reinjections and intricate processing. These leftist elements were demanding sweeping management changes. Meanwhile, in the heat of the revolutionary turmoil, most of the 650 or so top foreign employees and experts of the Consortium and joint venture companies had already left Iran. The second obstacle was that the radicals in the Revolutionary Council, with the tacit support of the religious leadership and other factions, insisted on keeping daily oil output at much lower levels in order to stretch the life of dwindling reserves, and move toward the creation of an 'oil-free' economy.

In September 1980, the Ministry of Petroleum was established to manage and direct the NIOC and its subsidiaries, the National Iranian Gas Corporation, and the National Iranian Petrochemical Corporation. The new ministry was put in charge of the hydrocarbon subsector in the broad energy sector. Within the NIOC, three subsidiaries were later created: the National Iranian Offshore Oil Company; the National Iranian Drilling Company; and the National Iranian Refining and Distribution Company. The Continental Shelf Oil Company took over offshore activities. Within the NIGC, one subsidiary, the Liquified Natural Gas Unit, was kept for exploring LNG potentials. NIOC has also established an oil trading company in London. In recent years, the aim has been to make refineries more autonomous and more competitive, and to give the private sector a bigger role in distribution.[4]

Revolutionary turmoil, strikes, and oil workers' demands reduced Iran's oil output from a peak of 6.1 mb/d in September 1978 to 1.4 mb/d in the first part of November. By December 1978, oil exports totally ceased, and were only partially resumed in March 1979. The war with Iraq after September 1980, continuous wrangling within OPEC, and Iran's need for foreign exchange, subsequently determined the oil industry's level of output and export. Following the substantial drop in Iran's oil output, and the rapid escalation of the official market price toward $34 from $12 in a short time, Saudi Arabia raised its production to more than 10 mb/d in order to make up the supply deficiency and keep prices in check. Increased Saudi exports, magnified by the 1981/82 global recession, threatened oil prices and forced Riyadh, as a reluctant 'swing producer', to cut daily lifting several times in order to support the official oil price at $34. By January 1983, the kingdom's production was down to 5.5 mb/d; by 1985, to as low as 2.2 mb/d amidst a chaotic and volatile petroleum market. Except for a short period of aborted cooperation in the mid-1980s, the Tehran-Riyadh relations in and out of OPEC were stormy, acrimonious, and hostile, affecting Iran's economy in many ways.

OIL OPERATION AND INVESTMENT POLICIES

The Islamic Republic's policy regarding oil production (and pricing) has gone through several phases since the revolution. After abrogating the Consortium in February 1979, the government directed the NIOC to assume all production, marketing and investment responsibilities. Accordingly, onshore production and exports were resumed immediately, and the first post-revolution cargo left Kharg Island on March 5, 1979. The four offshore joint ventures were subsequently merged into the Continental Shelf Oil Company as a single NIOC subsidiary. In September 1979, a new subsidiary, the Kala (goods) Company was formed to take over the purchasing functions of the former Iranian Oil Services, and to engage in the procurement of NIOC's foreign needs.

Next, in line with the prevailing xenophobic stance, the government in April 1980 moved to divest itself of its minority (17.5 per cent) share in a joint venture with French and South African partners in the Sasolburg oil refinery in South Africa, using Iranian crude supply. In July, NIOC's 50 per cent share in the (South) Korean-Iran Petroleum Company refinery in South Korea was sold to the Korean partners. However, the partnership in the Madras refinery in India, set up during the previous regime, was maintained.

Under the initial clamor to reverse the Shah's oil policy and to drastically reduce oil exports, NIOC's oil exploration budget was slashed in half to $1.9 billion from the previous year, reducing the number of exploration rigs from 50 to 18. This move, coming in the wake of disorder in the oil fields during the revolution and poor maintenance of oil equipment and installations, caused a reduction in sustainable production capacity to about 2.5–3 mb/d. The government's decision to suspend eight major gas reinjection programs also caused oil field pressure to decline, and output level to fall off. Some experts believe that declining reservoir pressures may have caused irreversible losses in recoverable reserves of as much as one billion barrels.

In the months immediately after the establishment of the Provisional Government, many radical factions in and out of the government were in favor of reducing oil production to less than 3 mb/d. Despite its radical appearance, this was in fact a moderate and rational policy. Production capacity had already been significantly reduced, making large output impractical. And crude oil prices had soared, guaranteeing large enough revenues out of smaller volumes of export. In the meantime, the government's financial needs were also expected to decline in the absence of huge arms procurement programs and ambitious development projects. In the twelve months following the first oil shipment in March 1979, average daily crude production stood at 3.4 mb/d, out of which about 2.6 mb/d were exported.

After the American hostage crisis, Washington imposed econ-

omic sanctions against Iran, with the European Community following suit shortly afterwards, along with Japan. Oil exports to these
countries from Iran were subsequently stopped. Official figures
released by Bank Markazi put crude oil production in 1980/81 at
1.48 mb/d on average, showing a massive 57 per cent decline from
1979/80. Crude exports amounted to 762,000 b/d on average – a
70 per cent drop from the year before. Part of the decline was due
to the government's deliberate decision to reduce overall oil output;
another part was due to reduced demand for high-priced Iranian
crude. Imposed Western economic sanctions played a major role.
On the eve of the Iran-Iraq war in September 1980, crude exports
stood at about 700,000 barrels a day.

After the damage inflicted by Iraqi bombers to Iran's main
export terminal at Kharg Island, oil liftings dropped to
100,000–200,000 b/d, before remedial measures were taken. In
February 1981, Iranian officials claimed a daily export of 1.5
mb/d – twice the immediate pre-war level – with private industry
sources in the West finding the true figure close to 1 mb/d. Some of
the shipments went to new customers (the Soviet Union, Spain and
India). The war, however, continued to limit oil puchasers' access
to Iran's oil terminals, and war damages naturally reduced production and export capacity below pre-war levels. Crude exports in
the first half of 1981 hovered around 1.0–1.1 mb/d, and in the
second half ranged between 500,000–700,000 b/d, making the
daily average for 1981/82 close to 830,000 b/d. Iran's share of
OPEC production in 1981 was about 6 per cent (down from more
than 17 per cent in 1978) while Saudi Arabia's was about 44 per
cent (up from about 28 per cent). Since at these levels of exports,
and in the face of falling oil prices, the government's foreign
exchange receipts trailed foreign exchange expenditures, the authorities in the summer of 1982 began talking again about a
production target of 2.5–3 mb/d and exports of 2.0–2.5 mb/d.

The oil-saving strategy was thus short-lived. A drastic fall in
industrial capacity utilization after the revolution, a decline in
overall output, rising budgetary deficits, loss of foreign exchange
reserves, and the threatening balance-of-payments deficit led the
government to rethink its priorities. The early promises of decou-
pling the economy from oil had proved impossible in the face of
inexorable economic realities. The war with Iraq made the
country's dependence on oil as a primary source of foreign
exchange more than ever unavoidable.

In the winter of 1982, Iran announced a production goal of 3
mb/d, more than twice its OPEC quota of 1.2 mb/d. At the time,
Iranian output was believed to run at 2.5 mb/d, of which 700,000

b/d was used in domestic consumption. By January 1983, under a highly discounted price strategy followed during 1982, Iran's oil production substantially turned around, and reached 3 mb/d. The escalation of Iraqi air attacks on Kharg Island and the Gureh pumping station in the fall of 1985 again reduced Iran's oil exports to a trickle. Twelve out of fourteen berths at the island had been put out of action by Iraqi raids, and Iran used the remaining two berths for oil shipment. But since Kharg had been designed to load some 6 mb/d, the two intact berths were still able to handle 1.5 mb/d. Several makeshift export terminals at Sirri, Larak, and Lavan Islands in the southern part of the Persian Gulf, out of reach of Iraqi bombers, were opened to handle cargo brought by tankers and other means for trans-shipment.[5]

In early 1986, Iran achieved a number of military victories against Iraq. Forces took the Iraqi port of Fao in February, and appeared ready to move on Basra, and eventually Baghdad. But Tehran's fortunes turned after August 1986 when Iraqi planes began regularly to hit refineries, power stations, petrochemical plants and particularly oil platforms and shifting lines. As a result, Iran's oil exports fell again to 600,000–700,000 barrels a day, compared with its quota of 2.3 mb/d. Although production and exports recovered later, average daily exports during 1986 still only amounted to about 1.5 mb/d. In July and August 1987, when Tehran took advantage of the halt in Iraq's attacks on Gulf shipping in response to a UN ceasefire resolution, Iran's daily oil output reached 2.8 mb/d (compared with its quota of 2.369 mb/d).

Since the ceasefire with Iraq in 1988, extensive and concerted efforts have been made by the NIOC to repair war damages to oil terminals, platforms and other export facilities. With the intention of expanding sustainable production capacity to 4 mb/d by March 1993, 4.5 mb/d by March 1994, and 5.5 mb/d by the turn of the century, a three-pronged plan was put into action. The first phase of the plan was to increase drilling activities, including the drilling of new wells and the repair of damaged ones. The number of rigs rose from 8 in 1989/90 to 50 in 1992/93 and was expected to reach 60 in the following year. In the second phase the number of oil fields was increased to 47 as mandated by the five-year plan, and the number of wells to 800. Finally, half of the new increased capacity was to be obtained through enhanced recovery methods (including more than 6 billion c/f of gas injection) in the onshore fields of southern Khuzestan province. The plan called for the drilling of 250 new wells, and 3000 km of pipes from those wells to the operating areas. As part of the effort to expand export capacity, an extensive repair and maintenance program aimed to increase the handling capacity of the Kharg Island terminal from 3 mb/d in 1990/91 to 5.5 mb/d by the end of 1992/93.

Thanks to these efforts, crude oil output increased steadily from 2.4 mb/d in 1987/88 to 3.2 mb/d in 1990/91. Iran benefited from the cessation of oil exports from Iraq and Kuwait in the aftermath of the Gulf War. For one week in mid-October 1992, the daily output of crude oil reached 4 m/b. But the average daily production for 1992 was estimated at about 3.44 mb/d (with 350,000 b/d from offshore wells). Average daily exports in 1992 hovered at around 2.5 mb/d, and reached as high as 2.8 mb/d.[6] While oil ministry officials insist that the country can produce 4–4.5 mb/d on a sustained basis, oil veterans believe that wartime neglect, damage to facilities from Iraqi attacks, and pushing output beyond prudent guidelines in the past have greatly reduced reservoir pressure, and made sustainable crude output above 3.6–3.8 mb/d exceedingly difficult without foreign help.

In 1991, Western oil companies were invited to invest in offshore exploration and development in Iran in exchange for long-term lifting contracts on favorable terms. While in some Western circles, these arrangements have been dubbed a *de facto* 'denationalization' of the petroleum industry, oil ministry officials have ruled out any equity or production-sharing agreements which are clearly contrary to existing laws. Even so, some of the joint undertaking between NIOC and foreign companies seems suspiciously close to equity sharing.

According to the Western press, Iran and several companies from the US, France, Britain, Italy and Japan have been negotiating to develop offshore oil and gas fields in the Persian Gulf. These negotiations, indirectly confirmed by the Iranian authorities, were part of the plan to boost Iran's output capacity with the help of foreign investment and technical assistance. In May 1991, a joint venture agreement was reached between the NIOC and France's Total to develop offshore oil fields in the Persian Gulf, around the Sirri area near the Strait of Hormuz, for an expected production of 100,000 b/d of crude. In September 1991, NIOC and Japan Petroleum Exploration Company (JAPEX) signed a letter of intent on the exploitation of oil fields in a 3,600 square-kilometer area of Bandar Abbas, according to which JAPEX would undertake by its sole risk and cost a multi-year, $1.7 billion project to produce an anticipated 80,000 b/d of oil in 1997. JAPEX is to receive payment in crude oil from the field through a guaranteed long-term supplies agreement. These agreements have not yet been finalized.

In yet another policy shift within the post-ceasefire reforms,

NIOC has been reported to be looking again for investment in downstream operations. In June 1991, the New York-based *Petroleum Intelligence Weekly* reported that NIOC would buy into a 15,000 b/d refinery in Canada near Quebec city. At about the same time, it was reported that NIOC would construct a joint-venture 120,000 b/d refinery at Port Qasim in Karachi with Pakistani participation. A similar deal has also been mentioned with Portugal and the Philippines.

MARKETING AND PRICE POLICY

As part of the post-revolution decision not to deal with former Consortium members and the world's oil majors, NIOC sold its first two cargoes on the spot market in March 1979 – reportedly at about $20 a barrel, considerably higher than the OPEC market price of $12.90. By the end of March, some 1.6 mb/d of crude was offered for sale through contracts with independent buyers. At the end of April, NIOC announced the conclusion of 35 long-term sales contracts for the exportation of 2.5 mb/d through the end of 1979 at prices ranging from $16.04 to $16.57 a barrel. Twenty-one of these contracts were with independent oil companies; six on a government-to-government basis; and eight were sales with the oil majors (including British Petroleum and Royal Dutch/Shell). The latter companies agreed not to press for immediate negotiations on their claims for compensation rising from the unilateral cancellation of their previous purchasing agreements with NIOC running up to 1993. Within a month or so, fifteen new agreements were also signed. While the price per barrel in these contracts was higher than the previous agreements with the Consortium participants, there were a number of disadvantages: the number of buyers was unduly large, contract sales were for small quantities (20,000 to 50,000 b/d), and contract duration was uncomfortably short (9–12 months).

The April 1980 US trade sanctions imposed on the Islamic Republic, followed by similar embargoes by the European Community in May 1980, caused Iranian oil to be increasingly diverted to the Soviet satellite countries and Iran's neighbors, often on a barter, counter-trade and net-back basis. A growing percentage of total sales was also transacted on the spot market. Lulled by a strong sellers' market, caused in part by a reduction of Iran's own oil exports, NIOC under a new leadership decided to embark on an aggressive price policy and a set of revenue maximization schemes. Iranian (light) crude prices had risen steadily from less than $14 a barrel in January 1979 to $35 a barrel within thirteen months. Projecting a continued surge in oil prices to $40 a barrel or more, and experiencing a notable improvement in the country's trade balance in 1979/80, the authorities initially opted for a high-price, low-production strategy, designed to keep foreign exchange receipts stable over time. In retrospect, this strategy proved to be counter-productive and short-lived.

Bani Sadr (and his like-minded oil-output minimalists) began to devise various formulae (premium, surcharge, and profit-sharing in the refinery margins) for raising the price of Iranian crude without regard to quality differentials. Soon after, Iranian prices acquired the reputation of being the most expensive in the world, and NIOC gained notoriety for being an unreasonable bargainer and an unreliable supplier. Iran had been able to raise its light crude prices from $13.45 a barrel in January 1979 to $23.50 in October, $28.80 in December, and $31 a barrel in February 1980. By January 1981, Iranian crude was officially offered at $37 a barrel (or $6–8 above comparable grade oils supplied by other Persian Gulf countries) even without the occasional surcharges of up to $3.80 a barrel.

Misjudging the underlying downward trend in the global oil market, the Iranian oil policy-makers stuck to their high-price stand. As Iranian prices remained the highest in the region, a buyers' resistance surfaced, and many prospective shipments were cancelled. With a production capacity of about 3 mb/d in the first half of 1981, Iran could not sell more than 1–1.1 mb/d. Weakened world demand for oil in the global recession of 1981/82, and the mounting over-supply of crude from new non-OPEC sources, exacerbated Iran's competitive disadvantages. Spot sales now had to be made at below offical OPEC prices. Price concessions had to be made, not only to attract non-Western customers, but also to underwrite the insurance premiums demanded for securing oil shipments from the war zone.

Early in 1982, Oil Minister Mohammad Gharazi publicly admitted that Iran had lost all its traditional markets. Once a price hawk within OPEC, Iran had to cut prices five times between February and April 1982 to $30.20 a barrel, undercutting OPEC's reference price of $34 a barrel. Some oil was sold on the spot market at around $26 a barrel. Some was bartered for goods from the Soviet bloc, Turkey and other Third World countries. The early 1982 price was a total of $7 less than a year earlier. This was considered the first time that a member state had openly undercut OPEC's consensual decision. With Iran unable to sell its oil at competitive prices because of the risks involved in its shipment, and thus taking the lead in breaching the official price, an informal downward price spiral developed among other members.

In February 1982, oil exports were reported to be around 500,000 b/d, only half of what they had been in November 1981. Further price cuts of $2 a barrel were reportedly offered in a Japanese spot purchase of 6–7 million barrels at $26 a barrel. Iran also put an end to the U.S. boycott by selling via the Geneva-based Gatoil International some 1.8 million barrels of crude to the U.S. Strategic Petroleum Reserve, reportedly at $29.51 a barrel – the first sale to the US since 1979.[7] Price discounts advertised in European newspapers boosted Iranian sales to the point where, by May 1982, the country was producing 1.5 mb/d – 300,000 barrels in excess of its March 1982 OPEC quota. After Syria closed Iraqi pipeline terminals at Banyas and Tripoli in sympathy with the Islamic government, Iran signed an economic agreement with Hafez Assad in April 1983 for the supply of 130,000 b/d (in excess of Syria's domestic needs) at undisclosed terms.[8]

The climax occurred in the early summer of 1982 when price-discounted oil exports took off dramatically on the spot market. There were reports that under the new aggressive market strategy (i.e., discounts of $5 to $10 a barrel below OPEC's official price) Iran could sell all it could produce, albeit part of it through barter deals. Bank Markazi officials claimed that Iran's foreign exchange reserves were rising by $1 billion a month.

During 1983 and 1984, Iran resorted to a number of different schemes to maintain oil sales. Discounts were regularly offered from the official OPEC prices to bring sale prices more in line with spot quotations. Some cargoes were sold partly at the official price and partly at spot rates. Each deal was negotiated separately with prospective buyers, while the official OPEC price acted as a reference. Bartering or counter-trade was stepped up during 1984, when an estimated quarter of Iran's imports was paid for by the sale of oil to Japan, the Soviet Union, COMECON countries, Turkey, China, the Far East, and other nations. The Ministry of Petroleum also entered into some 'netback' deals, whereby the oil price was linked to the final market value of the refined products made of the crude minus the costs of transportation, refining, and marketing. In a declining market which characterized OPEC's predicament in the first half of the 1980s, 'netbacking' meant a valid discount of several dollars from the official price.

By resorting to these marketing schemes, the Islamic Republic succeeded in raising its crude exports beyond its OPEC quota, keeping its foreign exchange earnings at near the peak level of 1979/80, and (along with other OPEC members) resorting to price discounts and over-the-quota production. These actions pushed down the Saudi output in mid-1985 to about a fifth of its 1980 level, while Riyadh tried to hold its official price until the fall of 1985. Internal political pressures on the Saudi ministry of petroleum to stop the country's fiscal hemorrhage and to regain the kingdom's market share led Minister Zaki Yamani – the architect of the 'swing producer' stance – to change course in December 1985. The new strategy adopted by the Saudis was to increase oil exports, flood the market, break prices, and drive marginal producers out. There were also rumors at the time that Iran's repeated victories in its five-year war with Iraq during 1985 frightened the House of Saud as Iraq's ally, and prompted the kingdom to drive oil prices down and deprive Iran of the main source of its foreign exchange revenues. As intended, the Saudi move resulted in a market collapse, with crude prices tumbling as low as $6–8 a barrel in July 1986 for some oil cargoes, down from a high of $28 in December 1985. Iran suffered enormously.

Subsequent accommodations with Saudi Arabia within OPEC helped restore crude oil prices to near pre-revolution levels, and a mildly upward trend began. Thus, the price of Iranian crude increased from less than $14 a barrel on average in 1986/87 to about $16/b during 1988/89. In the aftermath of the Gulf War, prices rose to $31/b before turning back to the high teens in early 1992. In 1992, Iran's crude was sold for spot, monthly, or long-term (one year or more) deliveries. Oil was shipped by NIOC tankers to destinations, and was also stockpiled in several places abroad. Some crude was sent for refining abroad and returned for domestic consumption.

Iran's active marketing program reportedly contemplated the formation of a state oil trading company, Naftiran, in London to engage in the sale of Iranian oil, and possibly non-Iranian crudes. NIOC had supply contracts with a number of foreign buyers in Japan, Sudan, Pakistan, Bulgaria, Yugoslavia, Hungary, and Poland for daily offtake of some 600,000 b/d of crude. Table 13.1 shows Iran's production, export, and domestic consumption of oil during 1977/78–1990/91.

IRAN AND OPEC

From the beginning, the Islamic Republic adopted a defiant posture toward OPEC (which it considered an agent of Saudi interests) and those of other enemies of the Iranian revolution. Joining the 'hawks' within the organization, Algeria and Libya, Iranian delegations took a routinely inflexible position in favor of restrained output, fixed official prices, and populist criteria for quota allocation and market-sharing. This radical stand served Iran's interests rather handsomely at first. The high official price was a convenient cover for NIOC to offer hidden discounts and curry favor with special customers. The total output ceiling for OPEC as a whole would keep the market tight, and individual quota allocations gave a smart member the chance to increase sales clandestinely without being caught, and with no great harm to the market. However, as other members discovered the benefits of non-compliance (a 'free ride'), cheating became widespread, and the organization's survival was seriously threatened. Tehran later changed course, and (as shall be seen below) became a constructive team player, and an influential member.

In the first OPEC meeting after the Iranian revolution, Iran was regarded by the majority of the membership as a pariah determined to politicize the 13-member organization in the direction of Islamic fundamentalism. Saudi Arabia was the effective leader to whom most other members turned for organizational cohesion and stability. But the Saudis' fundamentally different objectives and interests from those of many other members (and their alleged arrogance and heavy-handed tactics in OPEC meetings) gradually strengthened a nascent coalition among weaker members. Iran took up the challenge by the Saudis on both oil prices and production quotas, and volunteered to champion the cause of 'the oppressed members' against the 'rich and decadent' Arab sheikdoms.

Iran's seductive argument, strongly backed by Algeria, Libya, Nigeria, (and tacitly favored by Ecuador, Gabon, Indonesia, and even Venezuela), was that the relatively large-population, low-reserve countries in the majority should be given larger quotas and assured of high oil prices in order to develop their economies at a rapid pace. By contrast, Persian Gulf oil producers with few inhabitants, huge financial reserves, and scant opportunities for non-oil development at home, were asked to make greater 'sacrifices' in terms of lower output (and less exorbitant revenues) in order to maintain high oil prices in the world markets.

The global oil balance, however, did not favor Iran's position. Successful conservation measures adopted by industrial countries following the oil price explosion of 1973/74, and particularly after the second oil shock caused by the 1979 Iranian revolution, worked against Iran's wishes. The transformation of the global oil market from the OPEC-dominated conditions of the 1970s to the ascendance of non-OPEC suppliers in the 1980s reduced both the poignancy of Iran's 'sell less, charge more' policy, and the wisdom of challenging large-reserve Arab countries. The withdrawal from the market of close to 4—4.5 mb/d of crude in the wake of the Iranian revolution was more than offset by Saudi Arabia (which raised its output from 8.5 mb/d to more than 10 mb/d) and by non-OPEC producers. Pushing up oil prices in the midst of a world-wide recession, allied to the new interest in conservation measures and the emergence of alternative energy sources, had a devastating effect on OPEC. Due to a decline in demand, the free world's oil output fell from 48.6 mb/d in 1979 to 38.6 mb/d in 1985. OPEC's output went down from 30.9 mb/d to 15.4 mb/d during the same period. The difference was made up by production outside OPEC (excluding the centrally planned economies), which went up from 17.7 mb/d to 23.2 mb/d.[9]

The organization learned its lessons the hard way, as wrangling over prices, quotas, discounts, and differentials continued in semi-annual ministerial meetings throughout the 1980s and early 1990s. At OPEC's December 1978 meeting in Abu Dhabi, it was decided to raise the benchmark price of crude gradually by 10 per cent during 1979. Due to a sharp reduction in Iran's output, however, spot market prices soon surpassed OPEC's projected levels. In March 1979, the official base price was fixed at $14.55 for the Saudi light crude; but the radical faction (Iran, Libya and Algeria) obtained a concession from the group to add to the base price whatever 'surcharge' was warranted by the market. Iran's surcharge in June 1979 reached $3.80 per barrel. In the June 1979 meeting, the base price was raised to $18 a barrel and the total price (base plus surcharge) was fixed at a maximum of $23.50 per barrel. In the December 1979 meeting, the benchmark price was again raised to $24 a barrel, while the market price hovered around $30. Iran's attempts to raise the official price to $35 a barrel, to change the oil currency from the US dollar to a basket of currencies, and to coordinate members' output policies were not successful. In the June 1980 meeting, the marker crude was priced at $30 a barrel, but Saudi Arabia chose to retain the price at $28. In the December 1980 meeting, following the outbreak of the Iran-Iraq war, the two warring nations went along with the rest of the membership and raised the base price to $32 a barrel and the maximum to $36.

A relentless surge in oil prices had, by the time of OPEC's May 1981 meeting, cut the demand for OPEC oil. Spot prices had also started a downward trend. Thus, while the base price was kept at $32 a barrel (with the maximum raised to $41), the organization was for the first time faced with the need to restrain output in order to support the base price. A 10 per cent cut in total OPEC output was voted to take effect as of June 1, 1981. The growing absence of oil price unity among members – a policy that had been the backbone of OPEC's survival and success since 1973 – prompted members in their October 1981 meeting to agree on a unified price of $34 a barrel for the marker crude, to be observed by all from November 1981 to the end of 1982. A quality differential of $1.50 was approved for the North African countries.

In an effort to support OPEC's new 'unified' official price, and to reverse the falling demand for oil (particularly for OPEC crude), Saudi Arabia in March 1982 took the lead in proposing a pro-rationing program to limit the members' daily production to a pre-assigned quota, and the group's total output ceiling to 17.5 mb/d from an average daily output of about 20 mb/d. The quota-system, long advocated by some OPEC members, and always rejected by Riyadh during the organization's 22-year history, was approved for the first time by the entire membership. The Saudis assumed the role of a 'swing producer', raising and lowering their own output as market demand for OPEC oil exceeded the ceiling or fell below that level. Iran's quota was fixed at 1.2 mb/d – roughly half of its actual average daily production at the time. Tehran denounced its low quota as unfair and refused to restrain its production. The total OPEC ceiling was later raised to 18.5 mb/d in December 1982.

Faced with continued falling demand for OPEC oil, while spot prices were lowered to $5–6 a barrel below OPEC's marker crude rate by Western oil companies, OPEC in March 1983 lowered its official price to $29 per barrel, and its output ceiling to 17.5 mb/d after Saudi Arabia raised its production, forcing down the price. Iran's quota was raised to 2.4 mb/d. Tehran again faintly rejected its assigned quota, and protested against the reduction of the base price. In the meantime, while the Saudis were waging a diplomatic war against the oil majors, demand for OPEC oil remained weak, and OPEC members experiencing financial difficulties (including Iran and Iraq who were at war) began exceeding their quotas and giving price discounts, thus further weakening global oil prices. A further cut in OPEC's output ceiling to 16 mb/d was made in November 1984, and Iran's share was slightly reduced to 2.3 mb/d. As already mentioned, Saudi Arabia's self-imposed policy of operating as a swing producer resulted in the kingdom's output plummeting to as low as 2.2 mb/d in 1985. At the same time, by most estimates, 80 per cent of all oil produced in the summer of 1985 sold for as much as $2 per barrel below OPEC's official price. Saudi threats to flood the market with oil and drive down prices unless other producers – meaning the United Arab Emirates, Kuwait, and non-OPEC exporters – showed a willingness to cooperate fell on deaf ears.

By mid-1985, under mounting budgetary deficits, cuts in public spending, reduced subsidies, and elimination of new industrial projects, Riyadh threatened those OPEC and non-OPEC exporters who were engaged in larger sales at the kingdom's expense by relinquishing its 'swing' role and reclaiming its previous output of 4.35 mb/d. However, since increased sales in a depressed market for OPEC oil could be accomplished only through price discounts, and all prevailing discount schemes (spot sale, barter, and longer payments) were bound to be matched by other producers in a price war, the Saudis resorted to 'netback' deals. This mechanism helped minimize the purchaser's risk in a depressed market. The new scheme, put into effect toward the end of 1985, enabled the Saudis to increase their sales to 4.5 mb/d in early 1986, and close to 6 mb/d in the summer of that year.

In the OPEC ministerial meeting of December 1985, the four-year effort to prop up oil prices by restricting output was effectively abandoned, and the delegates voted only to have OPEC secure and defend a 'fair share' of the global market (considered to be 17–17.5 mb/d). Although the decision was unanimous, Iran, Algeria and Libya later rescinded their votes and argued that OPEC stood to lose more from an open 'price war' than by the alternative of keeping prices at higher levels. The December decision meant the end of the Saudis' self-imposed role as the sole 'swing producer'; the end of OPEC as the world's residual supplier; the end of restriction on members' daily production; and a *de facto* abandonment of unified pricing.

As non-OPEC producers ignored OPEC's plea for output reductions, and members increased their output towards a 'fair' market share,a glut of 2–3 mb/d soon developed. In early February 1986, crude oil prices both in Europe and the United States closed at their lowest levels in seven years. In mid-February, Iran, along with other OPEC members, adopted a formula under which its oil price declined automatically as free-market prices fell. Tehran also announced a production cut.

As total OPEC output surpassed 20 mb/d in June 1986 (against the ceiling of 16 mb/d), oil prices collapsed. At the end of June, Brent crude traded at around $8.55 a barrel, and the Saudi light netback values dropped to around $7 – the lowest in 15 years. Iran, who, with Algeria and Libya, had blocked the Saudi move to lower OPEC's official price by $1.50 a barrel in July 1985, was taught a costly lesson. Iran's own oil prices declined from an average of $25.50 to $8.50 a barrel in less than one year. By March 1986, the government's oil income had fallen to the lowest level since 1979, reflecting both reduced volume (due to new Iraqi assaults against Iran's oil terminals) and reduced prices.

Stung by the oil price fall from $28 a barrel to as low as $6 within eight months, and faced with the prospects of $4–5 a barrel, OPEC members desperately sought a way out of their predicament. In a major diplomatic coup that stunned world oil analysts, the Iranian delegation in the OPEC meeting of August 5, 1986, offered a formula that pulled members together on a surprise agreement. Soliciting and obtaining support from Saudi Arabia, its arch-rival, Iran proposed to limit OPEC production for September and October to a ceiling of about 16.8 mb/d, allocated among members in line with the 1984 quotas. The ceiling was nearly 4 mb/d below the organization's actual output, and required three-quarters of the cutbacks to be borne by Saudi Arabia, Kuwait, and the UAE. Iraq, which was in the midst of its six-year war with Iran and had recently suffered a series of battlefield defeats, objected to its 1.2 mb/d quota in the 1984 arrangements, and demanded a quota equal to Iran's 2.3 mb/d, (although its actual daily output was only 1.8 mb). To remove this major stumbling block, the Iranian delegation again captured everybody's attention by offering to exempt Iraq from any production restraint for the two-month duration, and let it produce as much as it could. This deal effectively fixed the ceiling for the other 12 countries at 14.8 mb/d. The conclusion of this short-term agreement immediately sent crude prices up toward $15–17 per barrel before returning to the $14–16 range. Some non-OPEC members also reportedly went along with export cuts.

Although all OPEC members (including the Saudis) were eager to compromise, in part because of a severe financial squeeze caused by falling prices, the pact was widely viewed as an immense political triumph for Iran for a number of reasons. First, the accord would mark the defeat of the Saudi-engineered price war to hurt Iran, drive marginal non-OPEC competitors out, and secure OPEC's leadership in output and price policies. Second, the new policy was a clear rejection of the December 1985 strategy to gain a given market share for OPEC at any price, a policy which Iran and its allies had denounced as counterproductive. Third, by isolating Riyadh not only from its neutral followers (e.g., Indonesia and Venezuela), but also its Gulf Cooperation Council members (i.e., Kuwait and UAE), Iran moved to re-establish its pre-1979 weight in future policy deliberations. Finally, the departure of Zaki

Yamani, the architect of OPEC's price war, from the Saudi cabinet confirmed the victory of the new strategy.

Originally advocated by Iran and its radical allies, and later accepted by the OPEC majority, the new strategy recognised that reasonably high and sustainable oil prices must be supported by production cuts. Iran's success in breaking the deadlock in the August meeting was due to political pressures felt by Saudi Arabia and Kuwait as a result of Iran's military advances in the war against Iraq, and potential threats to their own production and shipping facilities. Part of the victory was also the result of sensitive political contacts (and a new *rapprochement*) between Iran and Saudi Arabia whereby Tehran pledged to refrain from engaging in subversive activities against the kingdom. At the same time, in a major concession, Iran had to drop its original insistence on having the total OPEC ceiling reduced to 14.5 mb/d, and having its own share remain twice as large as Iraq's. A major reason for this capitulation was believed to be the report that by July 1986, Iranian profits on a barrel of oil had fallen to about $1, from $18 to $19 in 1985. Iranian foreign exchange receipts from oil were also expected to drop from $16 billion in 1985 to $6–$7 billion in 1986.

In the December 1986 meeting, OPEC ministers voted to cut total production for six months by 7.6 per cent to about 15.8 mb/d – the lowest level in the organization's 26-year history. The group also agreed to fix its prices at higher levels, averaging $18 a barrel starting January 1, 1987. Iraq again refused to sign the pact that gave it a quota of 1.54 mb/d. Iran at first demanded that Iraq be forced this time to join the rest of the group, or be ousted from OPEC for refusing to comply. Eventually, however, Tehran had to give in on both demands. Yet this was by no means a defeat for Tehran, as new tension was created between Iraq and Saudi Arabia, whose monarch was visibly annoyed by Baghdad's snub, and its refusal to go along with the majority's decision.

The June 1987 meeting raised the total ceiling to 16.6 mb/d for the second half of the year. This limit was a compromise between the Iran-led group which wanted to keep output down to 15.8 mb/d and the Saudi faction which advocated an increase to 18.3 mb/d. Iraq, expected to be producing about 2.5 mb/d, again refused participation in the quota allocation. With no new military victories to report in its war with Iraq in 1987, Iran began to lose its position. While Tehran still pushed towards $28 a barrel, the Saudis' desire for moderate prices around $18 prevailed. Iraq also continued its defiance of the organization's decisions without being restrained by either Iran or Saudi Arabia.

The brief period of relative Saudi-Iranian cooperation ended abruptly in July 1987 when demonstrations by Iranian pilgrims in Mecca resulted in a clash with the Saudi police, and a large number of deaths. The international oil price that had risen over $19 a barrel since the July 1986 accord was threatened anew as a result of Saudi-Iranian tension. A furious new political dispute erupted between Tehran and Riyadh, and the Saudis began seeking an Arab alliance against Iran.

A new embargo voted in September 1987 by the US Congress on purchases of Iranian oil, followed by some other Western countries, on top of the escalating 'tankers war' in the Persian Gulf, began to choke Iran's oil exports and strain its finances. By some estimates, the sale of about 400,000 b/d, representing a quarter of Tehran's oil exports, was lost as a result of the ban. Sales were reported down from 1.9 mb/d in October to as little as 1 mb/d in November. Iraq's resumption of attacks on tankers in September 1987 forced Iran to take extraordinary and costly measures to get its oil cargoes from Kharg Island to Larak, near the Strait of Hormoz, for on-shipment to Europe and the Far East. These measures included the charter of about 22 shuttle tankers, and a reported price discount of $1.5 to $2 per barrel.

Officially, however, Iran was still committed to an increase in OPEC's base price from $18 to $20. But the goal was highly elusive because OPEC members were already producing about 19 mb/d toward the end of 1987 (2.4 mb/d over the self-imposed ceiling), and also because the Saudis were opposed to any price increase. The average price of Mideast oil at the time hovered around $12–$15 a barrel. Since more than half of the excess output came from Iraq, Baghdad promised to cut its 2.7 mb/d output if its oil quota equalled Iran's. Tehran's conditions for acceding to Iraq's demand were two-fold. First, any increase in Iraq's quota must be offset by cuts among Arab members which supported Baghdad in the Iran-Iraq war. Second, Tehran wanted a base price increase to account for inflation and the decline in the value of the US dollar since the $18 base was established a year earlier.

In the December 1987 meeting, Iran accused Saudi Arabia and Kuwait of deliberately depressing oil prices to hurt the Islamic Republic. The Iranian delegation threatened to double its output and start a price war if Iraq were given a larger share of OPEC's total output. The threat, however, was not taken very seriously, as Tehran was not at the time capable of meeting even its own quota because of Iraqi attacks on its oil fields and tankers (and was selling a large portion of its output at discounted prices). In an astonishing turnabout from the 1986 victory, Iran found itself helpless in the meeting as several members favored a rise in Iraq's quota even if Iran refused to sign the agreement. Kuwait and Saudi Arabia also seemed pleased to see Iran made responsible for wrecking OPEC's shaky cohesion, and becoming futher isolated. Only Algeria, Libya and Gabon supported Iran's position at first, but they, too, backed off afterwards. In a weak and ineffectual agreement that was finally reached in mid-December, the $18 a barrel benchmark and the 16.6 mb/d ceiling were both left intact for another six months. Both Iran and Iraq failed to achieve their objectives. But, while Iraq's quota was not raised as requested by Baghdad, Iran was generally considered to be in retreat since it had threatened to secure a benchmark price of at least $20 a barrel at any cost. Meanwhile, Iraq continued to produce twice as much as its 1.5 mb/d quota; total OPEC output hovered about 2 mb/d over the ceiling; and world oil prices ranged from $1 to $2 below OPEC's benchmark.

Another acrimonious meeting in June 1988 finally agreed to extend the existing production and pricing accord for a further six months. Iraq, and this time the United Arab Emirates as well, excluded themselves from the pact. For the rest, the agreement was practically meaningless because many exceeded their quotas and sold their oil at discounted prices. Meanwhile, after five years of rightfully claiming the post of OPEC's secretary general and being rebuffed by the Arab group, Iran finally relented, and an Indonesian was elected to the post. Before the six months were over, the ceasefire in the Iran-Iraq war went into effect on August 20, 1988, and a new era began for OPEC, which had been torn apart by the eight years of intramural bickering between two of its founding members.

By the November 1988 gathering of OPEC ministers, oil prices had fallen by a third in 12 months, largely due to over-production by the Arab group. Without a new enforceable agreement, prices were destined to go below $10 a barrel. Iran again stood firm in refusing to share its historical number two position with Iraq, and accused the Gulf Cooperation Council of joint efforts to isolate and punish it. The Iranian oil minister vowed not to accept parity with Baghdad 'under any circumstances'. Yet, facing a financial squeeze at home, and the possibility of OPEC's break-up, he finally gave in. After several days of gruelling negotiations, the Iranian delegation finally agreed to Iraq's return, after two years, to OPEC's quota system at an output share equal to that of Iran. Under the new arrangement, signed by all 13 members, OPEC's production ceiling was raised to 18.52 mb/d for the first six months of 1989. Iran and Iraq each received a quota of 2.6 mb/d. OPEC's output at the time was about 22.5 mb/d – a seven-year high – since almost every member was in violation of its assigned quota.

In the June 1989 meeting, the ceiling was raised to 19.5 mb/d for the second half of 1989, with the possibility of increasing it again in September. The one million barrels of extra output were to be allocated among members on a pro-rata basis. The 'target' price of $18 a barrel was now called the 'reference' price. Iran received a daily quota of 2.783 million barrels. In November 1989, OPEC's output ceiling was raised to 22.1 mb/d, while the $18 reference price was maintained. Iran's quota was adjusted upward to 3.147 mb/d for the first half of 1990. During the first three months of the new year, Kuwait and the UAE exceeded their quotas by nearly 2 mb/d, and OPEC's output reached 24 mb/d in March 1990 – the highest average daily output in 8 years. Various attempts by Iran and Iraq to establish a quota discipline within the organization proved fruitless. The two old combatants now wanted the ceiling reduced, and the target price raised, in order to earn larger revenues.

In June 1990, OPEC ministers, under Iraqi pressure, approved a $3 per barrel increase in crude prices to $21 as a 'minimum reference price' for a basket of seven crudes (the first increase in almost four years). At the time the market price for OPEC oil averaged $17.5 a barrel, while OPEC's output was averaging 23.3 mb/d. The new ceiling was put at 22.5 mb/d. Iran had been pushing for a price of $20 a barrel. The move was seen as a triumph for the two old enemies who, after fighting a bitter border war, needed additional revenues to rebuild their economies. Interestingly, Saudi Arabia also fully concurred with the Iran/Iraq push for a higher 'reference' price. The meeting was clearly dominated by Iraq, as it forced Kuwait and the UAE to cut their output.

With the invasion of Kuwait by Iraqi forces in August 1990, and the UN oil embargo, the crude price soared from about $17.5 a barrel to nearly $30 as some 4 mb/d of OPEC oil was cut off from world supply. In late August 1990, OPEC ministers temporarily suspended output quotas, and authorized key oil producers to pump as much oil as they could to make up the shortage. Iran, joined by Libya and Iraq, opposed the decision, arguing that the international oil companies and Western governments should use their commercial and strategic stocks of oil before asking OPEC to increase production. Iran, at the time, was reported in the Western press to be producing some 3.3–3.5 mb/d – significantly over its quota of 3.12 mb/d.

In the regular ministerial meeting of December 1990, the Iranian delegation succeeded in obtaining a pledge from all members to reimpose output curbs when the Persian Gulf crisis came to an end.

At the time, industry sources believed Iran had as much as 50 million barrels of unsold oil in tankers at sea, and was trying, without much success, to induce other members to observe the self-imposed ceiling of 22.5 mb/d.

In a special meeting in March 1991, after the end of the Persian Gulf war, called to discuss postwar production and pricing policies, OPEC ministers decided to cut production by 5 per cent, or about 1 mb/d, and push OPEC's prevailing price of $17.74 a barrel to $21 a barrel. Iran and Algeria expressed their reservations, arguing that the proposed cut was not large enough to raise the price to the reference level. But the meeting, which was now incontestably dominated by Saudi Arabia, refused to entertain Iran's request for a 2 mb/d cut, to be made mostly by the Saudis. Iran's quota was set at 3.22 mb/d, while actual production was reportedly 3.4 mb/d.

With neither Kuwait nor Iraq being able to resume oil exports before the end of the year, the regular June 1991 meeting of OPEC ministers decided to go along with the Saudi/Iranian joint determination not to reopen output and quota issues for the time being, and to leave the group's ceiling at 22.3 mb/d. Meanwhile, in an international conference held in Isfahan to review petroleum's prospects in the 1990s, Iranian authorities, for the first time since the revolution, sided with the Saudis in favor of keeping oil prices stable.

In the September 1991 meeting, when OPEC oil output was running at 23.5 mb/d – 1.2 mb/d aove the self-imposed ceiling agreed earlier in the year – the division among members on production and prices surfaced once again. The Saudis, citing Soviet supply disruptions, the seasonal rise in demand for oil, and the possibility of economic recovery in the United States, wished to increase the group's output ceiling by 10 per cent in order to keep oil prices at their current moderate range of about $19 a barrel world-wide. Iran and Algeria, however, argued that the group should wait for the average price of OPEC's basket of seven crudes to reach the minimum target of $21 before deciding to increase output. All other members were also in favor of no increase in production, or very little, beyond the actual current level of 23.5 mb/d, just enough to accommodate the re-entry into the market by Iraq and Kuwait. After two days of uneventful meetings, the Saudis' proposal to raise the output ceiling to 23.65 mb/d (and give the kingdom an 8.5 mb/d share) for the fourth quarter of 1991 was adopted. The Iranian delegation, while still active in promoting the high-price objective, chose not to force a confrontation with the Saudis, and passively accepted the latter's upper hand in OPEC affairs for the time being. Iran's pricing strategy, although considerably mellowed from its hawkish posture of the 1980s, was still overwhelmed by the Saudis' predetermined position to preserve the stability of oil markets. The OPEC quota system, which was abandoned in late August 1990, remained suspended, and the 'free-for-all' approach continued. But, since all members except Saudi Arabia were producing at or near capacity, there was no need to discuss individual country quotas. At the time, Iran was producing about 3.4 mb/d.

The Tehran-Riyadh detente was further tested in OPEC's ministerial meeting of November 1991 where Tehran wanted some 'agreement in principle' that OPEC output would be cut if prices began to falter in the second quarter of 1992; but the Saudis adamantly refused to make any such commitment. The ministers decided to keep the ceiling on total production (23.65 mb/d) and the target price ($21) unchanged for the first quarter of 1992. In the three subsequent ministerial meetings of early 1992, Tehran's attempt to have OPEC's ceiling of 23.5 mb/d reduced by 1.5–2 mb/d to boost crude prices was decisively rebuffed by the majority. Although Algeria and Venzuela also pressed to have OPEC's actual production of more than 24 mb/d cut back to 22 mb/d (largely at the expense of the Saudis) the final agreement fixed the ceiling at 23 mb/d, and kept the reference price for OPEC's basket of seven crudes at $21 per barrel.

Conflict between Iran and Saudi Arabia began to surface once again during the February 1992 meeting and thereafter. The relative political harmony prevailing for a short time between the two turned into a new confrontational stance as OPEC output exceeded demand by close to 1 mb/d and prices began to falter. Over the 1990/92 period, the old disputes had diminished because both were able to produce at or near capacity – taking advantage of the 4 mb/d missing exports from Kuwait and Iraq. However, as Iran's production capacity increased under a massive investment program, and Kuwait entered the market with rising daily exports, quota allocation – suspended since the outbreak of the Persian Gulf war – once again became a divisive issue. Iran, Algeria, and smaller producers wanted the bulk of the output cut (needed to raise the crude price towards the $21 target) to be borne by Saudi Arabia; but the kingdom insisted on keeping its 35 per cent share (that is, no less than 8 mb/d) of OPEC's total sales.

Although the first-quarter ceiling of 23 mb/d was renewed for the second and the third quarter (plus whatever additional oil Kuwait could produce) OPEC's actual output in mid-1992 reached 24.5 mb/d – nearly 1 mb/d above the demand. Faced with internal pressures by individual members for higher shares, the concept of output 'ceiling' was abandoned in September and, against Iran's objections and its officially recorded dissent, OPEC's 'market share' for the fourth quarter of 1992 was raised to 24.2 mb/d. Nevertheless, the group's total production rose even further, to 25.3 mb/d towards the end of the year. Iran's own output gradually rose from 3.2 mb/d towards 3.8–4 mb/d. As a result, the price of OPEC's basket, which averaged between $19 and $20 a barrel during the summer, fell below $19 a barrel.

With the average OPEC oil price during the first half of 1992 remaining at about $18.26 per barrel and the US dollar weakening for much of the period, Iran again pushed for a lower output ceiling to raise the price toward the $21 a barrel target. But the majority, in the September 1992 ministerial meeting, decided to reject Iranian objections.

In order to stem the price slide, OPEC's November 1992 ministerial meeting set the group's new ceiling for the first quarter of 1993 at 24.582 mb/d. Kuwait still remained exempt from the limits. Ecuador was left out as it intended to leave the organization at the end of the year. Iraq under a UN ban was also not included in the quota calculations. After two days of gridlock with Iran insisting on having a quota of 3.8 mb/d, and Saudi Arabia rejecting any allocation below 8.4 mb/d, a compromise was reached whereby Iran's quota was raised to 3.5 mb/d – up from its previous share of about 3.2 mb/d. All other members were expected to abide by the quotas they had before Iraq's invasion of Kuwait. Under pressure from falling prices, OPEC's February 1993 meeting established a new ceiling of 23.6 mb/d for the second quarter of 1993. Iran's quota was slightly reduced to 3.34 mb/d (or about 4 per cent) as was every other member's.

At the start of 1993, Iran was both the second largest oil producer and petroleum exporter within OPEC, and the fifth largest supplier and number two exporter in the world. The Islamic Republic's position in OPEC had also changed from being regarded as the virtual pariah in 1979 to that of Saudi Arabia's major challenger. Nevertheless, the Saudis, by virtue of their immense reserves, enormous exports, and various Western alliances normally dominated the organization in the period from 1979 to 1993. Except for the July 1990 meeting when Iraq pulled its military weight, Saudi Arabia usually set both OPEC's periodic agenda and its major resolves. By contrast, Iran's influence was frequently neither comparable to its pre-1979 prominence, nor commensurate with its subsequent status. With one or two notable exceptions already cited, the Iranian delegation, supported by Algeria and Libya, was often only successful in making a point rather than achieving a major goal. Success was achieved only when Tehran's policy stand was not seriously opposed by Riyadh, and was close to the majority's mainstream position.

DOMESTIC OIL REFINING AND CONSUMPTION

The war damage to Iran's refineries left the nation with serious shortages of jet fuel, gasoline, kerosene, and other refined products. By April 1981, only three of Iran's six refineries were fully operational. In 1978/79 Iran possessed six refineries – Abadan, Bakhtaran, Lavan, Shiraz, Tabriz and Tehran – with a total capacity of 998,500 barrels per day. Of these, Abadan with a capacity of 630,000 b/d, and Tehran with 225,000, were by far the largest. Toward the end of 1980, with the coming on stream of the 240,000 b/d Isfahan refinery, the country's refining capacity was raised to 1.2 mb/d. Abadan's capacity in 1978/79 was divided into fuel oil (42 per cent), gasoil (18 per cent), kerosene (11 per cent), gasoline (9 per cent), jet fuel (7 per cent), and other. The refinery was badly damaged and stopped production altogether shortly after the Iran-Iraq war. At its peak, it provided 65 per cent of the country's refining capability.

Crude oil delivered to all refineries in Iran before the revolution averaged 784,000 b/d. In the first three years of the Islamic Republic (1978/79–1980/81), daily inputs averaged 751,000 b/d. With extensive war damage to Abadan, Bakhtaran and Lavan refineries, domestic refining dropped to 540,000 b/d on average during 1981/82–1982/83. To meet domestic needs, the government concluded a series of agreements with Italy, Spain, and Southern Yemen whereby Iranian crude was exported in exchange for the importation of refined products (190,000 b/d in 1993/94). After the outbreak of the war, the government's domestic fuel policy called for a reduction of private transportation and a mobilization drive toward energy saving. Reflecting this new posture, gasoline and home heating fuels were rationed. Gasoline prices were raised threefold (from Rls 10 per litre to Rls 30 for regular, and from Rls 12.5 to Rls 40 for high octane), but prices of other fuels were kept markedly below their opportunity cost at home, or compared to their international equivalents abroad. Through March 1986, the coupon price of fuel oil was Rls 1.2 per litre; gasoil, Rls 2.4 per litre; and kerosene Rls 2.5 per litre. Afterwards, these prices were raised to Rls 2.0, Rls 4.0, and Rls 4.0, respectively (until March 1991, when fuel oil price was raised to Rls 5 per litre). Gasoline prices by coupon were kept at Rls 30 (regular) and Rls 40 (high octane) until February 1991 when rationing ended. Thereafter, the pump (non-coupon) prices, that had run at Rls 60 and Rls 80 since March 1986, were reduced to Rls 50 and Rls 70, respectively. The free market (non-coupon) price of gasoil was Rls 10 per litre throughout the 1980s.

At these levels, the prices of kerosene, gasoil and fuel oil ranged between 10 per cent and 20 per cent of their international equivalents. Even the price of gasoline, which was deliberately kept higher to discourage consumption, lagged behind comparable prices in Europe and the United States when converted at free-market exchange rates. Although with the end of rationing in early 1991, gasoline prices were effectively raised by 50 per cent on average (except for urban taxis), the new prices were still less than the equivalent of $0.20 per gallon – one of the lowest in the world, and by some estimation below its true cost of production.[11]

Due to deliberately low administered prices of refined products, the rapid rise in population, and faster urbanization – and despite strict rationing – domestic consumption of oil products increased at an average annual rate of 8 per cent between 1980 and 1985. After prices were raised in March 1986, consumption growth continued at about 5 per cent a year, with the result that total domestic oil consumption reached about 950,000 b/d in 1992/93 – despite the growing share of natural gas use (estimated at about 285,000 b/d of oil equivalent).[12] (See Table 13.1.) At the same time, a substantial part of domestic and imported fuel products sold at subsidized prices in Iran were reportedly smuggled out of the country for sale in the neighboring countries at higher price.[13]

Before the Iraqi attack, Iran exported as much as 235,000 b/d of refined products a year. But due to repeated Iraqi raids on Iran's five major refineries and extensive damage to its oil installations, a deficit developed in 1983/84, and the country changed from a net exporter to a net importer. Since then, Iran has had to import considerable quantities of refined fuels, kerosene, gasoil, and jet fuel from abroad – in some years as much as 350,000 b/d. After the ceasefire and partial reactivation of Abadan, as well as improvements in other refineries, refined imports fell to less than 300,000 b/d in 1992/93. Allowing for these imports, Iran's *net* export of hydrocarbon products did not exceed 2 mb/d throughout the 1980s.

During the current five-year plan, the demand for refined oil products is expected to increase by more than 6 per cent a year due to the overall growth of the economy, rising household income and population growth. Holding domestic consumption to just below 1 mb/d is to be achieved by the gradual substitution of natural gas for oil products, and the government's declared intention to cut down on product subsidies. With partial restoration of Abadan to a new capacity level of 330,000 b/d by March 1994, the repair of other refineries, and the full operation of the newly inaugurated 150,000 b/d Arak refinery, Iran's total refining capacity in mid-1993 (about 900,000 b/d) may be short of domestic needs by only about 150,000 b/d. With the completion of the 250,000 b/d Bandar Abbas refinery in the mid-1990s, the country is expected to be virtually self-sufficient in refined products, and an exporter afterwards.

The government is also planning to expand its refining capabilities by building a second 130,000 b/d installation in Arak, and by acquiring refineries abroad through joint ventures. One such agreement has already been signed with Pakistan for a joint refinery of 120,000 b/d capacity at Port Qasim near Karachi. The refinery will process Iranian heavy crude, and 20 per cent of the product will be transported to Iran or exported to other countries. A 600 km pipeline from Bandar Abbas to Isfahan is to transport imported refined products for consumption in Rafsanjan, Kerman, Yazd and Isfahan.

NATURAL GAS

Iran's natural gas reserves in mid-1992 were officially estimated at 20 trillion cubic meters (693 trillion cubic feet), and considered to be about 15 per cent of total world reserves. Consisting of both associated and non-associated reserves, Iran's holdings are second only to that of the former Soviet Union. In mid-December 1991, the government announced the discovery of a new untapped reservoir of gas, gas liquid, and oil in the South Pars field, north of Qatar in the Persian Gulf. According to Iran's oil minister, the new field holds 100 trillion cubic feet of gas, and as much as 2.5–3 billion barrels of gas liquid, worth $200 billion. Total estimated gas reserves are equal in caloric value to about 113.5 billion barrels of crude oil. Based on gas output of 50 bc/f a year, the reserves are projected to last 400 years (compared with only 60 years for oil reserves at the 1992 production level).[14]

DOMESTIC USE

From the beginning of oil discovery and production in Iran at the turn of the century until 1970, a very small percentage of associated gas from southern oil fields was used in the oil fields and as a fuel for the Abadan refinery, and, later, as feedstock for the Marvdasht fertilizer plant near Shiraz. Some 90 per cent of the supply was flared. Since 1970, when gas exports to the former Soviet Union started, there has been growing use of gas for domestic and industrial fuel needs. Gas has also been utilized for injection into oil wells to stimulate oil extraction.[15]

In 1972/73, gas output stood at 44 bcm, of which some 8.5 bcm was exported, 9.4 bcm was used internally, and 26 bcm (60 per cent) was flared. At its peak in 1977/78, nearly 60 bcm of gas was produced: 9.2 bcm was exported; 24 bcm domestically consumed; and 26 bcm flared. After 1978/79, both annual production and internal consumption of natural gas declined. Output was down due to reduced oil extraction, and domestic consumption was less because of declining industrial and commercial demands caused by reduced economic activity.

A significant part of domestic use has been for electricity generation, but residential and commercial uses have been actively encouraged by the government. There are currently three main trunklines for internal distribution and export (IGAT I, Sarakhs-Neka, and Qeshm-Bandar Abbas). Domestic consumption of natural gas has followed crude oil output over the years. As oil production declined precipitously in 1980–1982, so did the associated gas output and domestic use. As Table 13.2 shows, natural gas consumption during the rest of the 1980s has grown at an irregular pace, except in the 1986/87–1990/91 period when the trend was distinctly upward. In comparison with the pre-revolution year, 1977/78, gross output in 1990/91 was slightly less (54.4 bcm compared with 59.5 bcm), but domestic consumption (excluding gas re-injection) was about the same. Natural gas exports to Russia, after a 10-year hiatus, were resumed in 1991 at about 23 per cent of the 1977/78 volume. The magnitude of gas flared as a percentage of output was down to about 17 per cent in 1990/91 from 44 percent in 1977/78, as production was lower in relation to crude oil output, and as domestic gas distribution, underway at the time of the revolution, was continuously expanded to new urban and rural centers. Total sales, however, were still much less.

Government plans call for an approximate doubling of domestic consumption as an alternative to oil products in both industrial and household uses. The number of gas-fired power plants is to increase from 15 to 23 between 1990/91 and 1994/95. Some 4,500 km of main gas pipelines are to be added to the existing 5,000 km, thus raising the number of cities connected to the gas grid from 147 in 1992/93 to more than 200, and benefiting some 2 million subscribers, compared to 1.2 million in 1990/91, only 200,000 in 1983/84, and 50,000 in 1979/80. By the end of the current five-year plan, domestic consumption of natural gas is to reach 26 bcm a year. The major source of supply for increased natural gas processing is to be the Nar-Kangan gas refinery near Bushehr, which was under construction at the time of the revolution, and was to be completed by 1980. The first phase has already been completed and is under operation. The second phase, which promises to be one of the largest in the world, is now under construction and is expected to be completed soon. Another gas refinery, Sarkhun, commissioned in May 1991, has a daily capacity of 550 million cubic meters and receives its supply from reserves near Bandar Abbas. The new refinery is to supply the gas requirements of Bandar Abbas thermal power station, Hormozgan Steel, Mahdi Aluminium and Bandar Abbas Oil Refinery. A new gas pipeline is to carry gas to Sarcheshmeh Copper Complex and residential areas in Sirjan, Rafsanjan, and Kerman City.

During the current five-year plan, power plants are expected to consume 51 per cent of the total, local industries will account for 26 per cent, while households and commercial units will take 23 per cent.[16]

GAS EXPORT

Under a 1966 agreement with Moscow for the exportation of Iran's natural gas to the Soviet Union, a 1,100 kilometer gas pipeline – Iran Gas Trunkline (IGAT) – was constructed from the Persian Gulf oil fields to Russia via Bid Boland, Saveh, Tehran, Qazvin and Astara on the Soviet border. The pipeline was capable of carrying 900 million cubic feet a day (cf/d) of natural gas to Russia. The initial price charged to the Russians was 18.6¢ per 1,000 cf. By 1977, along with the oil price increase, the gas price had gradually increased to 76¢ per 1,000 cf. The line's total capacity of 1.5 billion cf/d was partly used, through a series of spurs to Isfahan, Shiraz, Kashan, Qom and Tehran, for home and industrial use.

Meanwhile, in 1975, the National Iranian Gas Company concluded a series of agreements with West Germany's Ruhrgas, Gaz de France, Austria's OMV, and the Soviet Union, to build the IGAT II for the purpose of exporting gas from Nar-Kangan field near Bushehr in southern Iran to Europe via the Soviet Union. At peak capacity, IGAT II would carry some 27 billion cubic meters of gas, of which 17 bcm was to go to the Soviet Union. Of the latter, 13.5 bcm was to be delivered to Germany and 3–5 bcm to Czechoslovakia. Some 10 bcm of gas was to be distributed to various urban centers within Iran. At the delivery time in 1981, the price of this gas to Iran was to be 96¢ per 1,000 cf (based on the price of fuel oil at the German border). As part of the agreement, the Soviet Union was to build a 2,480 mile gas line from Siberia to the Czechoslovak border in order to supply the German, French and Austrian companies with gas from its own northern fields at prices ranging from $1.43 to $1.60 per 1,000 cf. The difference between the price paid Iran and those charged to the European countries was to be considered a transfer fee. Revolutionary upheavals in Iran put a stop to the IGAT II pipelines under construction, and gas export to Russia via IGAT I was stopped shortly after. Abandoned, also, was the Kalingas project designed to build an LNG plant to export liquid gas to Japan and the United States, as a joint venture with American companies.[17]

Gas exports to the Soviet Union were stopped after the revolution, both because of price disputes and a fall in the volume of associated gas resulting from declines in oil production.[18] Under a 10-year economic cooperation agreement signed between Tehran and Moscow in 1989, gas exports were resumed in April 1990 at a rate of about 3.1 bcm a year at an undisclosed price, paid partly through barter arrangements. In May 1990, a high government official said that the price was linked to international rates (that is, $1 for 10 cubic meters of gas). Proceeds of gas exports were to be kept in a special account from which the Russians were paid for their power, gas, mining and metal projects carried out in Iran. The Soviet side also agreed to let Iran export natural gas to six European countries, through its territories, via IGAT II pipeline, with a daily capacity of 80 mcm. The pipeline has already been extended from southern gas fields to Isfahan. Turkey has also shown interest in having the line go through its territory to Europe. In 1990/91, some 2.1 bcm of gas was exported to the Soviet Union with an estimated value of about $200 million. Following the breakup of the Soviet Union, Iran's gas exports reportedly consisted of 300 mcm to the Republic of Azerbaijan in 1992/3 in return for the provision of 100,000 tons of gasoil delivered to Iran's northern provinces.

A memorandum of understanding was signed with Pakistan in May 1991 under which Iran was to export 2 mcf of gas daily to Pakistan after 1995. Japan, South Korea, and Taiwan could also be buyers of Iranian gas. Export of LPG was also resumed in 1991 after a lapse of eight years. Japan is expected to be interested in investment in LPG production.

The Petroleum Ministry has been authorized to obtain foreign funds for exploiting South Pars gas field (at the median line between Iran and Qatar). Gas company officials hope to transport liquified natural gas by ship via the Red Sea to terminals in Europe. Three different routes for the export of piped gas to Europe are being studied for transshipment through Turkey. The $2 billion South Pars project is to be financed partly by foreign banks as well as the World Bank; it is to be completed in 1995 with a projected output of 35 million cm/d of gas for the Iranian market via IGAT II on the mainland, and 50,000 b/d of condensate for export. Oil ministry officials predict some 50 bcm a year of surplus gas eventually available for export.[19]

PETROCHEMICALS

In 1993, Iran reportedly had more than 10 per cent of total Middle East output capacity in petrochemical products. The 1992/93 production of 5.4 million tons is to reach 12 million tons by the end of the decade. According to official reports, there are eight major petrochemical complexes, producing 30 types of products. Some 40 more products are to be added by the end of the five-year plan.[20] Petrochemical products included fertilizers, pesticides, plastics, paints, rubber, detergents, PVC, construction materials, food additives, and textile fibers. With the export of 400,000 tons of sulphur in 1989/90, Iran was among the world's top 10 sulphur exporters. While Iran imported 1 million tons of fertilizers annually on average throughout the 1980s, it was to become self-sufficient by 1994, and an exporter from then on. The industry is expected to export 1.5 million tons of petrochemicals and 1 million tons of LPG by the end of the current plan.[21] Petrochemical exports in 1992/93 reached $150 million, according to press reports, up from $28 million in 1989/90.

Iran's petrochemical industry began with the Marvdasht Fertilizer Company near Shiraz in 1963, using natural gas from the Gachsaran fields. It was systematically expanded with the establishment of the national Iranian Petrochemical Company (NIPC) in 1965. The Shiraz Petrochemicals Complex has four units of which three were installed in 1963, 1972 and 1976, and the last one in 1985. Various products made in this complex include ammonia, urea, ammonium nitrate, soda ash, and nitric acid; they supply the domestic market. The Razi Petrochemicals Complex at Bandar Imam Khomeini (formerly Bandar Shapur) started producing fertilizer products in 1970 and was expanded in 1978. Products include urea, ammonia, phosphatic fertilizers, and sulphuric acid and sulphur. Operations were largely suspended during the war, and war damage repaired after the ceasefire. The plant was expected to export some 500,000 tons of sulphur annually, while satisfying about 50 per cent of domestic requirements of diammonium phosphate (500,000 tons).The complex inaugurated a new 1.9 million ton LPG project in 1991, 25 per cent of which was destined for export.

Abadan Petrochemical Complex near the Abadan refinery, came on stream in 1971, as a joint venture between NIPC and B. F. Goodrich, for the production of PVC, DDB, and caustic soda to meet domestic demand. Production capacity in 1975 was 57,000 tons a year. The NIPC acquired the 26 per cent Goodrich share in 1979. This complex was damaged during the war and stopped production. Reconstruction began after the ceasefire.

Kharg Chemical Complex was established on Kharg Island in 1969 as a 50–50 joint venture between NOC and AMOCO to produce propane and butane gas, with a capacity of 450,000 tons (with pentane and sulphur as byproducts). Like other plants, this complex was nationalized after the revolution, and was later damaged by the war. It is being reconstructed in three phases.

Iran-Nippon Petrochemicals Company, established in 1972 in Bandar Shapur as a joint venture between the NIPC and Mitsubishi, is situated near the Razi Complex in Bandar Imam Khomeini. Starting operation in 1972, with a capacity of 45,500 tons a year, the company's Japanese shares were later transferred to NIPC, and its name was changed to Farabi. The plant supplies raw materials for Iran's plastics and paint-making industries.

The Iran Carbon Company, a joint venture between the NIPC and Cabot Corporation started producing carbon black in 1975 with an ultimate capacity of 16,000 tons. The plant's output was used as a raw material for tires. The foreign share was acquired by NIPC after the revolution. Capacity was raised to 21,000 tons in 1982.

The privately-owned Polica Company at Karaj near Tehran was taken over by the NIPC in 1979. It has a capacity of 6,000 tons a year, and was designed to use Abadan's PVC for the production of hard pipes, cables and related products. Capacity was increased to 10,000 tons after the revolution. Due to the closure of the Abadan complex during the war, the company had to rely on imported raw materials. The Pasargad Chemicals Company was established in 1963 for the production of chlorine and caustic soda. After it was recaptured from the Iraqi troops early in the war, it was reconstructed and commissioned in 1985; its products include hydrochloric acid and Javel water. In addition to these units, there are four other smaller petrochemical companies, and several lubrication plants in operation.

As part of the Islamic Republic's 'independent' economic policy after the revolution, Iran's National Petrochemical Company proceeded to buy out its American and Japanese partners in four existing joint ventures in Khuzestan. Included in the takeover were the 50 per cent stake in Kharg Chemical Company owned by Amoco International, a subsidiary of the Standard Oil Company of Indiana; the half share of Boston's Cabot Corporation in the Iran Carbon Company; B. F. Goodrich Company's 26 per cent shares in Abadan Petrochemical Company; and the shares of Iran-Nippon Petrochemical Company owned jointly by Mitsubishi and Nissho-Iwai of Japan.

For political and practical reasons, the Iran-Japan Petrochemical Company's complex in Bandar Shapur (later Bandar Imam Khomeini) − a joint venture by NIPC and Japan's Mitsui group − was excluded from the takeover because it was not completed, and had to be finished by the Japanese who had all the blueprints. The venture was a 50−50 arrangement signed in 1973 with an initial design capacity of 3.8 million tons at the cost of $500 million, for the production of a range of petrochemical intermediates including ethylene and propylene derivatives, caustic soda, and benzene. Due to further design expansion, additional infrastructural facilities and other reasons, the cost of the 12-unit complex gradually rose by 500 per cent overrun after the Arab-Israeli war and the oil price explosion. On the eve of the revolution, some $2.8 billion had been sunk into the project which was only 85 per cent finished, and required another $500−600 million to bring it on stream. In the summer of 1980, a restart was begun by Mitsui when strikes, sabotage and threats by various revolutionaries subsided. But the onset of the Iran-Iraq war and bombing attacks by Iraqi planes again halted the project.

Initial efforts after the ceasefire to induce Mitsui (and its five partners) to finish the project were not successful because Iran could not guarantee a long-term supply of low cost naphtha and other inputs essential to profitable operation. The project was designed to produce 330,000 tons a year of ethylene and its derivatives as well as liquified natural gas. The Japanese, having already spent some $1.3 billion on the project, wanted Tehran to shoulder all future costs for its completion on top of the more than $3 billion that Iran had already spent. The cost had reportedly risen to $5.5 billion by 1988. After months of negotiations, the dispute was settled in the fall of 1989, and all the Japanese shares were transferred to the NIPC. In October 1989, the oil ministry announced the conclusion of an agreement with Dutch company Lummus Crest for further work on the three-phase complex.

In short, petrochemical production gradually came to a standstill following the outbreak of the war as most plants were located in the war zone. This led to shortages of fertilizers, polyvinyl, and chloride which had to be made up through imports. Iran also had to import raw materials for synthetic fibers produced by Isfahan's Polyacryl Company. The latter, approaching completion when the revolution came, was the largest single private investment in Iran, worth $350 million, by the Behshahr group in association with Dupont. Except for the Shiraz complex, all other petrochemical units were damaged or destroyed by the Iran-Iraq war. None had any output during the war. Since the war's end, extensive efforts have been made to repair and reconstruct the damaged plants.

Under the current five-year plan, several petrochemical projects are under way in Arak for the production of olefinic material; Bandar Imam Khomeini for the completion of stalled construction; Isfahan for aromatics; Tabriz for rubber and plastics; Shiraz for methanol and chloro-alkali; and others.[22] Estimated to cost $7.5 billion in foreign exchange, these projects are to be financed by appropriation from the plan sources as well as through joint-venture arrangements, buy-back deals, and foreign credit – all being sanctioned once again by the Islamic Republic. A number of petrochemical projects were offered to the private sector in 1991 and 1992 for direct investment or participation with NIPC.[23]

PROSPECT SUMMARY

Oil, gas, and petrochemicals occupy a privileged place in Iran's curent economic development. Oil production, officially reported to have reached 3.8 mb/d in mid 1992, promises to continue as new wells are brought on stream. Output capacity is still projected to reach 4.5 mb/d by the end of the current five-year plan. Exports, hovering around 2.5 mb/d, are officially expected to increase, partly through pre-payment deals with foreign customers (Japan, Ukraine, Romania). NIOC maintains its position as the second largest supplier of oil to the European Community from the OPEC group. Exploration and drilling activities are promised to continue in joint ventures or service contracts with foreign firms. The company has also entered into refining and downstream ventures abroad in Pakistan, Malaysia, and elsewhere. The South Pars gasfield is actively explored by Italy's Saipem and Technologie Progetti Lavori. The National Iranian Tanker Company has added an LNG tanker to its vessels for transporting liquid gas for domestic consumption in the country's coastal areas. The National Iranian Petrochemical Company claims success in obtaining foreign funds for investment, against future sales of products.[24]

Despite all this, the demand for oil products at home is still not fully met by domestic output. Kerosene has remained in short supply, and there were occasional shortages of other fuel products. The 1992/93 budget set aside some 280,000 b/d of crude export to finance imports of refined products. Part of the problem was, of course, related to the war damage to the country's oil refineries (particularly Abadan). But the continued shortage – four years after the ceasefire – has been due in part to the government's fuel price policies.[25] Heavy subsidies offered by the government on the household use of oil products, and on means of transportation (where fuel is a large part of cost) are directly responsible for both excessive demand and insufficient supplies. Without a change in policy, the shortage is likely to last even after the domestic refining capacity is increased.

NOTES

1. This estimate of Iran's reserves followed similar increases in petroleum reserves announced by Iraq, Kuwait, and the UAE. Some analysts interpret these 'sudden' discoveries as not unrelated to a move within OPEC to base daily production quotas on proven reserves.
2. For more detailed information on Iran's post-revolution oil industry, cf Fereidun Fesharaki, *Revolution and Energy Policy in Iran* (London: The Economist Intelligence Unit, 1980); Bijan Mossavar-Rahmani, *Energy Policy in Iran: Domestic Choices and International Implications* (New York: Pergamon Press, 1981); S. A. Schneider, *The Oil Price Revolution* (Baltimore: Johns Hopkins University Press, 1982). Factual data on capacity, output, and exports on a regular basis can be found in *OPEC Facts and Figures* (Vienna: OPEC); British Petroleum *Statistical Review of World Energy* (annual); *Petroleum Intelligence Weekly*; *Oil and Gas Journal*; *Middle East Economic Survey*; *Middle East Economic Digest*; London *Financial Times*; *Petroleum Economist*; and *Iran Oil News*.
3. For reference to these charges see Shaul Bakhash, *The Politics of Oil and Revolution in Iran* (Washington: The Brookings Institution, 1982), pp. 2–6.
4. See *MEED*, April 24 and September 25, 1992.
5. In addition to damage inflicted on Kharg Island, the demolition of a dozen oil platforms in 11 offshore fields reduced offshore output from 780,000 b/d before the Iraqi war to 180,000 b/d in 1989/90.

6. *MEED*, January 22, 1993; *The Wall Street Journal*, November 25, 1992; and The Economist Intelligence Unit, 'Iran', No. 1, 1993.

7. Technically, the US embargo against Iranian products was lifted by the Algiers pact of 1980, but American and other major oil companies abided by an informal decision not to buy from Iran.

8. According to press reports, 100,000 b/d were to be delivered at $25 a barrel, 20,000 b/d free of charge, and 10,000 b/d to be bartered for Syrian grains, phosphates, and cotton. See *The New York Times*, April 25, 1983.

9. *OPEC Annual Statistical Bulletin 1989* (Vienna: OPEC Secretariat, 1990).

10. It is interesting to note that despite OPEC's strenuous efforts to preserve its market share, and to protect its revenues, the price of OPEC oil at the end of 1992 was still lower than the 1974 price in real terms (when global inflation was taken into account).

11. In remarks to a group of clergy, President Rafsanjani said: 'We distribute 1.27 million barrels of oil and 50 mcm of gas every day among the Iranian population, the annual value of which is over $10 billion. But, not only do our domestic sales make no net contribution to the treasury, we spend additional huge amounts in freely distributing this wealth among the people'. *Vision of the Islamic Republic of Iran*, july 13, 1991 (broadcast).

12. *OPEC Bulletin*, July–August, 1992, p. 76; and The Economist Intelligence Unit, 'Iran', No. 1, 1993.

13. See *Kayhan Havai*, May 15, 1991, and January 1, 1992.

14. *Los Angeles Times*, December 18, 1991; and *MEED*, August 7, 1992.

15. Iran's crude output peaked in the 1974–76 period to near 6 mb/d. The government had a gas injection program to enhance secondary recovery and produce a larger percentage of oil in place. The average recovery factor of the Iranian fields was less than 20 per cent.

16. *OPEC Bulletin*, September 1991, p. 23.

17. *International Petroleum Times*, February 15, 1979.

18. From January 1977 onward, the price of gas exports was calculated at 76¢ per 1,000 cf. With a sudden jump in the international price of oil after 1979, Iran expected to receive higher prices for gas, but could not come to an agreement with Moscow. There was 3.5 bcm of export in 1978/79 and none thereafter until 1990.

19. *MEED*, November 15, 1991, p. 14; and *Financial Times*, February 8, 1993.

20. The eight complexes included Shiraz, Razi, Abadan, Kharg, Farabi, Iran Carbon, Polica, and Pasargad. Several other smaller plants (Polyacryl, Persepolis, Alyaf, and Parsilon) were also involved in petrochemical production. Seven of the eight major plants date back to the Shah's regime. A new plant in Tabriz is to produce tires.

21. *Iran Focus*, February 1990, p. 11; *MEED*, February 19, and April 9, 1993.

22. For details regarding products and design capacity, see *Iran Focus*, October 1989, pp. 10–12.

23. *Kayhan Havai*, May 1, 1991, April 1, 1992.
24. For more details, see The Economist Intelligence Unit 'Iran: Country Report', No. 4, 1991, and 'Country Profile', 1992–93.
25. In April 1992, a litre of gasoline was sold in Iran at the subsidized price of Rls 50, and a litre of gasoil at Rls 10. In neighboring Turkey, corresponding prices (at the free-market exchange rate) were Rls 1200 and Rls 1000 respectively. As a result, a good part of distributed fuel products was smuggled out of the country in search of profits. See *Kayhan Havai* April 22, 1992, p. 14.

VI
PERFORMANCE AND PROSPECTS

14

The economy's balance sheet

In the last seven chapters, aggregate economic trends and sectoral developments have been examined and analysed. This chapter attempts an assessment of the economy's overall performance.

As indicated in the Preface, a comprehensive evaluation of the Islamic Republic's economic record is not easy. Relevant information is often unavailable, inadequate, or inconsistent. Sectoral and aggregate numbers frequently elude reconciliation. Frequent revisions of official data disrupt the consistency of time series. Conclusions based on available information are therefore unavoidably partial and incomplete.

A brief reference to some of these deficiencies outlines the difficulties encountered in the evaluation process. In the national income accounts, the total value of output (and per capita income) is somewhat distorted by the conversion of oil export revenues into Iranian rials at the official exchange rate: if oil and other tradeable goods were valued at the true equilibrium rate for the US dollar, both nominal and real GDP in rials would be measurably different (that is, larger than official figures). At the same time, aggregate data's comparability over time is obscured by the large size and erratic yearly fluctuations of two recurring entities: 'changes in stock' and 'statistical discrepancy'. In certain years, the total sum of these two items amounts to 16–19 per cent of gross domestic expenditure – enough to change the growth of total output from positive to negative. Moreover, as has been noted by many analysts, yearly changes in these two rubrics do not always correspond to changes in other figures in the accounts. For example, in 9 of the 12 years between 1978/79 and 1989/90, the item called 'changes in stocks' shows an annual *increase*, in some years by as much as 10.5 per cent of GDP. Such positive changes in stocks generally reflect periods of depressed demand and recession where supplies are difficult to unload, and inventories accumulate. Yet, throughout the 1980s, the Iranian economy was faced with shortages, rationing, price controls, black markets, and other indications of effective unmet demand. There is no explanation for these inconsistencies in the official statistics. Wartime security considerations (or other political objectives) might have been the reason for the discrepancy, and a role may have been played by insufficient expertise in collecting and processing the raw data. The item called 'statistical discrepancy' is also often abnormally large and erratic in size, due to differences in calculating GDP from the income and expenditure sides.[1]

In addition to these ambiguities, there is also a lack of transparency in some other aspects of the economic record. Attention has already been drawn to the undisclosed fiscal status of semi-public foundations and so-called charitable organizations that account for a significant percentage of national income. There is also little or no information on such operations as debt management or foreign exchange portfolio placement by the Ministry of Finance or Bank Markazi.[2] Without such information, and other related data, the economy's balance sheet would naturally be flawed. There are similar difficulties and large discrepancies in individual sector data. In agriculture, domestic food production and food imports are shown to have risen during the 1980s (Tables 11.1 and 11.2), reflecting increases in the demand for food. This is evidenced by rising food prices ahead of the consumer price index (Table 6.1). The supply imbalance is also indirectly confirmed by the persistence of rationing, shortages, and black markets. At the same time, per capita real income has been on an almost steady decline (Table 14.1). This paradox may theoretically occur in two circumstances: if there is a significant internal redistribution of income in favor of low income groups who normally spend a larger share of their earnings on food; or if, at the same level of income, there is a shift in the population's expenditure pattern towards increased food consumption. Yet available figures show no meaningful change in income distribution, or expenditure pattern. A possible explanation may be that the rate of growth of population has exceeded that of domestic food output (requiring larger imports), and declining per capita real income has been made up by public subsidies (supplementary income). But there is insufficient data to support this explanation.

Information is similarly contradictory in other sectors of the economy. In the hydrocarbons sector, the figures published by the Ministry of Petroleum, the Bank Markazi, and OPEC on natural gas production and use do not correspond, and some of the figures on gas re-injection are questioned by private investigators. In industry, the average annual decline in manufacturing output during the 1986/87–1988/89 period of only about 8 per cent (Table 14.6) is hardly consistent with the reported idle capacity of some 50–60 per cent in large manufacturing enterprises. In the energy subsector, it is hard to see how the 'industrial' use of electricity (Table 12.3) between 1977/78 and 1990/91 could have almost doubled while the entire industrial sector's contribution to GDP was smaller at the end than at the beginning of the period. In services, there is a need to know how a mere 18 per cent rise in the sector's growth between 1977/78 and 1990/91 (Table 14.2) could absorb a nearly 90 per cent increase in employment (Table 5.1).

Despite these inadequacies in the basic data – some of which Iran shares with other developing countries – it is still possible to provide a broad, and reasonably accurate, picture of the economy's overall performance in the post-revolution period.

The Iranian authorities and their supporters claim that, given the previous regime's 'wrong-headed' policies, the considerable disruptions caused by the revolution, and the dislocations brought about by the 'imposed' war, the economy has performed better than expected.[3] Critics, in contrast, point to the regime's undeniable and acknowledged economic shortcomings to show that, despite the Shah's legacy of sizeable infrastructural resources, large production facilities, trained manpower, and ample foreign exchange reserves, the Islamic Republic has failed in all but a handful of its main economic objectives.[4] The contrast between the two appraisals reflects not only an evident partisan bias, but also a lack of agreement on the choice of performance criteria, the source and nature of supporting data, and the methodology of evaluation. A reconciliation of these conceptual and methodological differences is neither easy nor the object of this study. The procedure followed here is an accepted treatment of both *measurement* and *comparison*.

Broadly speaking, the overall performance of a national economy is measured by a combination of two common criteria: efficiency and equity. Efficiency commonly refers to the growth of real output, high employment, price stability, external balance, rising standards of living, and enhanced per capita real income. Equity is generally identified with fairer distribution of wealth and income, equality of opportunity, social welfare, and security. In the case of 'one-commodity' countries such as Iran, economic diversification is also considered a measure of economic progress.

There are also three principal methods by which a country's overall economic performance may be compared and evaluated. The first method – the time-series analysis – compares economic progress in a given country before and after a particular turning point (such as the 1979 revolution in the Iranian case). The second – the cross-section analysis – contrasts the behavior of major economic variables across several countries in the same or a similar stage of development during a given period (such as a comparison of Iran with some other nations since 1979). The third method is to assess a nation's economic achievements against its own national socio-economic agenda (such as measuring the Islamic Republic's economic performance during 1979–92 against its own revolutionary and post-revolutionary objectives).

Each of these methods has its own merits and drawbacks. The comparison of Iran's economic performance during 1979–1992 with, say, 1963–1987 – the alternative that is advocated by the regime's critics – would contrast the economic boom of the 1960s and 1970s with the relative stagnation of the 1980s. However, such a comparison is bound to be interpreted as a judgment on the revolution itself, and an invidious contrast between the new and the old regimes – a matter that is beyond the purview of this study.

The comparison of Iran's post-1979 economy with other similarly positioned economies – the alternative which is probably preferred by the regime's supporters – would be difficult to undertake because a consensus may not be found on the selection of countries and the similarity of underlying circumstances. For example, should Iran be compared with the 'upper-middle-income' countries, as the World Bank's *World Development Report 1991* suggests? Or should it be classified within the group of oil exporting countries, as the 1980 issue of the same report chose to do? Should it be compared with its neighbors – Turkey, Pakistan, and Iraq – or with other Middle East countries? What stage of development was Iran in during the 1980s? And which other countries were in the same stage? It is no doubt possible to compare the regime's economic record with those of a number of arbitrarily chosen countries, either within the Middle East region, or among OPEC members, or among other newly industrializing countries, in terms of two or three major indicators such as, growth, employment, and inflation. But to make such comparisons meaningful, it would be necessary to present the differences in underlying economic conditions in each case – a daunting task that would take the study far beyond its original objective.

For these reasons, a review of the economy's overall performance in the light of the Islamic Republic's own intentions, objectives, and promises would seem to be least biased. This approach examines the regime's record not in terms of recent history (the Shah's regime), or geographical comparison with other countries, but through introspection. Under this method – undoubtedly still not without its critics – the aggregate, as well as sectoral, performance of the Iranian economy will be reviewed against the Islamic Republic's socio-economic agenda as stated in the 1979 Constitution, the five-year development plans (I and II), the annual budget documents, and the leadership's declarations on various occasions.

BASIC GOALS OF THE ISLAMIC REPUBLIC

The structure and direction of the Iranian economy after the revolution were to undergo a systemic transformation, according to revolutionary Islamic ideology. As interpreted by Ayatollah Khomeini, this ideology was bent on creating an Islamic society that was economically egalitarian, puritanical, and self-reliant; and politically independent, non-aligned, anti-imperialist, and anti-Zionist. The principal socio-economic goals of this society were spelled out most prominently in the 1979 Constitution and in the texts of the two (post-revolution and post-ceasefire) development plans to which reference has already been made.

Briefly reiterated, these objectives consisted of five elements: economic growth for the purpose of raising per capita output, creating productive full employment, and reducing economic dependence on the outside world; the attainment of self-sufficiency in the production of strategic agricultural and industrial products for the purposes of national security; the curbing of inflation to ensure orderly growth; the fair distribution of income and wealth to secure the basic economic needs of the people; and the creation of a 'consumption model' free from profligacy and extravagance. In short, Iran's economic order had to be 'revolutionized' away from its hitherto dependence on the outside world through the creation of a thriving, equitable, and self-reliant economy.[5]

More specifically, the new regime was determined to reverse the economic course of action pursued in the old order, and to rescue the economy from past 'mistakes'. Among specific objectives, several areas were emphatically targeted. Planning was to become operationally disciplined and coordinated. The economy was to be freed from its undue dependence on income from oil exports. Agriculture was to provide a pivotal role in post-revolutionary development; to launch a proper land reform program; and to receive all its input needs domestically so as to increase its productivity and reduce the nation's reliance on food imports. The terms-of-trade between farm products and other goods and services had to be corrected so as to raise investment incentives in farming and achieve self-sufficiency in foodstuffs. Ardent efforts had to be made towards improving socio-economic conditions in rural areas. Income gaps between rural and urban populations had to be narrowed in order to check the harmful migration of farmers to urban centers.

Production and export of oil had to be determined, not, as in the past, by the energy policies and fuel needs of industrial, oil-consuming countries and major 'oil-cartels', but by a far-sighted national strategy, bent on conservation of this exhaustible resource for the sake of forthcoming generations. Oil output and export were to be substantially reduced to match only the 'real' foreign exchange needs of the country.

Restructuring and reconstruction of industry was another favored goal. The harmful and hazardous dependence of this sector on foreign markets for its inputs had to be reduced. The Shah's industrial stragegy – judged by the revolutionaries to be 'sham industrialization' – had to be revamped. The past strategy, considered neglectful of domestic resources and capabilities, inattentive to the economy's need for heavy industries, dominated by foreign-supplied 'assembly plants', and in constant need of state assistance, had to be reversed. The former emphasis on consumer goods, reliance on foreign technology, and dependence on monopolistic markets for inputs had to be altered. In short, the industrial sector's direction had to be shifted towards economic independence, self-sufficiency, and coordination with the basic needs and requirements of the domestic economy.

The housing shortage which, despite the old regime's varied efforts, had become chronic and alarming, was to be remedied, and high inflation was to be squeezed out of this sector. Speculation in urban land and residential dwellings had to be ended through strict regulation of real estate transactions and the public appropriation of unused urban lots. Affordable housing for all citizens had to be provided by the government as a matter of individual economic right. Luxury housing had to be stopped, low-cost dwellings encouraged, and, if necessary, supplied by the state itself.

The government's fiscal dependence on income from oil exports had to be substantially reduced. Oil export income had to be substituted by taxes on domestic products, and a substantial increase in internal tax revenues, particularly income levies. Regressive excise taxes were to be cut. Taxes due on the incomes of professional cadres and self-employed income-earners had to be assiduously collected in order to produce a fairer distribution of the national tax burden. Redundant public agencies and enterprises had to be eliminated in order to reduce public expenditure. In short, the 'unhealthy' structure of the public budget inherited from the previous regime had to be worked over in the direction of increasing public investment and reducing current administrative outlays. The budget had to be balanced.

Foreign trade and exchange policies had to be reconstructed with a view to curtailing dependence on the external world. The previous regime's tolerant attitude toward the import of consumer goods had to be shifted in favor of importing the country's 'real' needs such as non-consumer and basic items. The use of the nation's foreign exchange had to be carefully controlled, and directed toward 'proper' outlets. The basic necessity of all imported goods and services had to be approved by the government; their prices had to be controlled, and their distribution among rightful people regulated. Non-oil exports had to be encouraged and vastly increased. Foreign borrowing had to be avoided as far as possible.

The country's banking system had to be reformed. Ownership and management of commercial and specialized banks which were in the hands of a 'few major capitalists' powerful enough to ignore national money-and-credit interests had to be terminated. Financial institutions had to be restructed in such a way as to be able to facilitate the country's 'real progress'.

Finally, the Shah's hugh expenditure on an ultra-modern military in the 1960s and 1970s – considered by the revolutionaries a wasteful squandering of Iran's oil money on unneeded sophisticated weaponry – had to be stopped, and the country's arms expenditures had to be confined to those necessary for defense.[6]

THE REPORT CARD

The Islamic Republic's foregoing socio-economic agenda thus called for specific measures to enhance the economy's *efficiency* through productive full-employment growth; to ensure social *equity* through fair distribution of income; and to secure *balanced growth* through eventual self-sufficiency in strategic products.

Measured by these performance criteria, the economy's balance sheet for the 1979–92 period portrays a mixture of (some) successes and (many) setbacks. While state officials and the pro-government press and publications are usually replete with glowing reports of accomplishments in almost all aspects of the economy, the regime's economic woes have been too transparent and too overwhelming for anyone – including the leadership – to dispute.

In his Friday prayer sermon of August 9, 1991, devoted to a 'stock-taking' of the national economy, President Hashemi Rafsanjani gave a candid summary of the state of the nation. From the economic and material viewpoint, he declared, the country was in a very serious plight (the details of which he could not yet divulge). Gross domestic product had fallen precipitously since the revolution, with the result that per capita GDP was down by nearly 50 per cent. Due to a considerable fall in private investment, and the government's inability to undertake sufficient public capital formation, unemployment had increased at an alarming rate. Employment had shifted into middleman activities, smuggling, and illicit trade. Inflation had soared from less than 10 per cent a year in 1979/80 to nearly 29 per cent in 1988/89. The basic needs of almost 50 per cent of the people in society – water, electricity, education, health, roads, and employment – were still unmet, despite the government's repeated promises to give priority to depressed regions. While the country was impoverished during the 1980s, the new national poverty was not equitably shared; the government had been unable to prevent economic 'leeches' from amassing fortunes in the black market at the expense of the poorer strata in society. The deprived and disenfranchised had become, in reality, further weakened and impoverished. The government had incurred large foreign and domestic financial obligations. An estimated Rls 5 trillion of development projects inherited from the past regime were still unfinished. Infrastructural facilities had not been properly maintained. Five hundred municipalities had had to reduce public services due to lack of revenues. Factories were neglected and mostly obsolete. Warehouses were empty. And the people had to rely on government subsidies for their daily living.[7]

Implied in these frank statements is a tacit admission that *none* of the basic objectives of the Islamic regime has so far been achieved. Many have hardly been approached; and some have been unceremoniously set aside. Higher income growth, larger per capita income, and fuller employment have not materialized. Self-sufficiency in neither agriculture nor industry has been attained. Inflation has intensified. Income redistribution has not favored the poor. No Islamic consumption pattern has been established. And Islamic justice, virtue and brotherhood remain to be seen.

EFFICIENCY CONSIDERATIONS

As detailed in previous chapters, the Iranian economy during the post-revolution period suffered serious internal and external imbalances. Symptomatic of these imbalances were reduced output and per capita income, chronic unemployment and under-employment, double-digit inflation, perennial budgetary deficit, and a frequent balance-of-payments gap.

Iran's real GDP in 1989/90 was nearly the same as that of 1973/74. With an addition of 4.5 million workers to the country's total work force since the revolution, and an inflow of some $200 billion in oil export revenues, the real GDP in 1990/91 (Rls 12.045 billion) was still 6.3 per cent *below* total output in 1977/78 (Rls 12.851 billion). The per capita real income was 38 per cent less. Even at this low level, the official per capita figure probably exaggerated the true level of income because the deflator officially used did not reflect true inflation. The GDP figure itself, as the basis of per capita calculation, was also somewhat inflated by the significantly large contribution of the services sector as the latter partly reflected the salaries of semi-idle employees in the enormously enlarged bureaucracy. Furthermore, other such new social disamenities as long queues for rationed goods, increased air pollution (placing Tehran among the world's unhealthiest cities), more frequent power blackouts, occasional shortages of goods and services, and other daily irritants, should also be counted against the monetary figures.

Several major macro-economic trends further confirm the economy's poor performance. Despite large government subsidies on food, energy, utilities, transportation, housing and other necessities, annual consumer prices increased at a double-digit rate for most of the period. Almost one third of the new entrants in the labor force during the period could not find gainful employment, and the rest were nearly all employed either by the government, or were engaged in low-paying service jobs. And, despite substantial oil export revenues, drastic reduction in domestic investment, a sharp decline in per capita consumption, and severe import restrictions, the country's balance of payments on current account was in deficit two-thirds of the time.

Many of the specific institutional and sectoral objectives of the regime also experienced a fate similar to those of the basic indicators.

The economic planning and budgetary process that was often criticized by the revolutionaries as oblivious to the country's 'real' needs seems to have continued in the same fashion as before. The aborted first five-year plan (1983/84–1987/88) is judged even by a friendly analyst to have been 'merely an exercise in calculating numbers', with no attention paid to 'the existing economic structure', and with its growth target rates 'calculated from similar estimates in the previous (i.e., pre-revolutionary) plans'. Altogether, the early plan was regarded as 'no more than a fantasy'.[8] Another sympathetic analyst, writing about the regime's post-ceasefire prospects, calls the new five-year development plan highly ambitious in its growth targets, and totally 'non-credible'.[9]

In **agriculture**, the well-publicized objective of national self-sufficiency in food within a decade, as declared by the regime in 1979/80, still seems far from realization. Throughout the 1980s, annual food production lagged behind total demand as the population grew at a rapid rate, and government subsidies encouraged consumption of basic staples. Wheat consumption, for example, grew nearly 6 per cent a year during most of the 1980s, while wheat output experienced an annual growth of only 4 per cent. The gap in supply was made up by imports. Wheat imports doubled between 1980 and 1984 to 3.2 million tons, and remained in the 1.5–5 million range throughout the decade and into 1993/94. The 1992/93 wheat production, officially put at 10 million tons, was still below domestic demand. Interestingly, the domestic self-sufficiency ratio in food grains, which hovered around 87 per cent during most of the 1970s, is estimated to have declined to less than 74 per cent by the mid-1980s, and continued to trail the past record even in the early 1990s.

In an effort to meet rising demand for basic staples (wheat, rice, pulses, and others), a sizeable portion of foreign exchange earnings was annually earmarked for food imports (i.e., foodstuffs, live animals, beverages and tobacco). Exchange allocation for food imports grew from $1.98 billion in 1979/80 to $3.5 billion later in the decade, despite rationing of many food items.

The promises to substantially improve the terms of trade in agriculture's favor, and to reverse rural migration to the cities, have also yet to be fulfilled. Although agriculture's share in the gross national product rose during the 1980s (Table 14.6), the improvement was due partly to the fall in the overall real GDP, and the substantially reduced share of oil. In spite of the regime's 'agriculture first' policy, productivity in the sector remained low, as did rural incomes. Wide-ranging activities by *Jihad-e Sazandegi* (the construction of extensive village roads, provision of clean water, considerable rural electrification, improved health services, and increased literacy rates) were undoubtedly helpful in filling certain gaps in the standards of living between rural and urban areas. Nevertheless, the absolute living standards of the peasantry in comparison with urban households were not substantially raised.

The lack of data on farm-gate prices and industrial goods and services preclude any meaningful analysis of the rural/urban terms of trade. But rudimentary figures on rural/urban household incomes and expenditures (Table 14.2) provide some indications of changes in the trade terms. As the figures show, the ratio of urban to rural incomes, and urban to rural expenditures, declined between 1977/78 and 1987/88 (the last year for which information is available). These declines suggest a narrowing of the gap between living conditions in the cities and the countryside. There are also anecdotal observations to this effect. However, other facts warn against hasty generalizations. First, the average ratio of rural expenditures to rural incomes deteriorated from 124.6 to 127.7 during the period, reflecting further rural dissaving, as household expenses rose faster than household earnings. Meanwhile, the magnitude of urban expenditures as a percentage of urban incomes during the same period registered an even greater deterioration, from 97.7 per cent to 129.5 per cent. These figures seem to indicate that the narrowing of the urban/rural income gap was probably due to a decline in the living standards of the urban population rather than a notable betterment in the lot of the peasants. Also, lower ratios of urban to rural incomes, and urban to rural expenditures, toward the end of the 1980s may simply have resulted from a change in demographic nomenclature rather than a change in real well-being. Since the census bureau's threshold for a community to be classified as a 'city' is a resident population of over 5,000 inhabitants, every rural village that grew in size beyond that threshold automatically became a city (an urban center) without any change in its other characteristics. The 1986/87 census identified 194 such villages (called *abadi*) as 'urban' centers – thus reducing both the average urban income, and the urban/rural income ratio. Finally, the relative physical and financial difficulties of regularly supplying remote villages with rationed (and heavily subsidized) goods must have actually *increased* the imbalance between town and countryside, as the more accessible urban populations were favored over the rural populace.

The government has also failed to stem the flow of villagers to the cities. Rural migration has continued to be one of the regime's headaches during the entire period. In addition to the dislocations caused by the war, a number of other factors such as the lure of city jobs, and the expectation of receiving welfare benefits, have encouraged a continuous outflow of rural people from their villages. Despite the adoption of several policy measures designed to improve village life and redistribute social services in favor of less developed locations, rural migration has continued steadily. Other measures which have failed to stem this migration include: mandatory service obligation in the deprived areas by new government employees and professional cadres (such as, physicians, dentists, and teachers); significant wage and salary differentials favoring employment in underdeveloped provinces; special budgetary allocations for small rural and tribal projects; and special quotas for students from deprived areas in the country's universities. Not only have large cities continued to be a magnet for rural migrants (with Tehran absorbing close to 40 per cent of the total), but also a number of small population centers have acquired 'city' classification without being able to establish a municipality, or to provide regular city services.[10]

The regime's fundamental objective of making agriculture the 'axis' of all development efforts has been largely frustrated. An agricultural analyst, in fact, argues that the revolution did not greatly help Iran's farming because it was urban-based and urban-oriented, and its leaders had neither the necessary comprehension nor the enthusiasm for agricultural pursuits.[11] This observation seems to be substantiated by the fact that the annual growth of farm products in real terms during 1978/79–1990/91, estimated to be 4.7 per cent on average (Table 4.6), was no better than comparable rates of real growth achieved during 1960/61–1969/70 (4.4 per cent a year) or 1970/71–1977/78 (5.2 per cent a year).[12]

Above all, the primacy of agriculture in the Islamic Republic's economic planning – even though only an *ideal* objective – appears to have been set aside altogether in the current five-year development plan. The 12 per cent share of fixed investment earmarked for agricultural and water resources in the plan lags far behind the share for industry (including manufacturing, mines, power, transport, and communications), which is projected to be nearly 21 per cent of the total planned capital formation (Table 9.5). The share of agriculture in total GDP is also expected to fall from 24.5 per cent in 1989/90 to 20.6 per cent in 1993/94, as its annual growth is projected to be smaller than that of the industrial and service sectors.

In the **oil** sector, despite a strong early commitment to break the economy's dependence on foreign markets, and the promise of a genuine drive towards eventual economic self-sufficiency without oil, petroleum has continued to be the mainstay of the Iranian economy. The regime's energy and oil policy has steadily diverged from its revolutionary slogans.[13] The opposition had castigated the Shah's oil policy of producing close to 6 mb/d of crude oil as inimical to Iran's long-term national interest. During the first months after the revolution, virtually all political factions were in favor of reducing oil output and exports by 30–40 per cent. Yet the need for foreign exchange forced the authorities to push for maximum use of existing capacity and to persistently demand higher quotas within OPEC. The early policy stance on oil was finally reversed *in toto* with the launching of the current five-year plan, where a substantial portion of total fixed capital formation has again been earmarked for the expansion of the oil and gas sector. The National Iranian Oil Company has once again declared its intention to become 'one of the four major oil exporters' in the next century. The objective of creating an 'oil-free' economy has evidently been downgraded. Indeed, the dependence of the economy on oil revenues for financing national expenditure, essential imports, and domestic public investment has intensified. To be sure, the share of the oil sector in GDP has measurably declined, but its contribution to national income and standard of living has not been replaced by other economic activities: GDP itself has been hurt by reduced oil production and exports.

With the new focus on oil and gas expansion as a major engine of economic growth, the regime has once again been exposed to the same type of criticisms lodged against the Shah's strategy. The reliance on oil revenues to finance current consumption has resulted in the depletion of an exhaustible resource in order to feed present inhabitants at the expense of unborn generations. Every dollar of petroleum receipts not productively invested, and thus incapable of producing a future stream of income, has meant reduced future consumption. Moreover, the treatment of oil as an annual *income*, rather than as the exchange of one asset (a mineral) for another (a cash deposit), has distorted not only the government's overall fiscal position (and the country's future productive capacity), but also the Iranian rial's equilibrium rate of exchange. Commonly referred to as the 'Dutch disease', large and unrequited incomes from petroleum exports have given the false appearance of a more favorable balance-of-payments position than would otherwise have been possible, and an 'equilibrium' rate of exchange valued at a much higher level than would otherwise have been the case. This unwarranted and spurious feeling of well-being has discouraged non-oil exports, encouraged imports and foreign-dependent domestic production, and stimulated capital exports, instead of promoting internal investment. As a consequence, the economy has become more volatile in the short run as oil prices have fluctuated beyond the country's control in the global market. In the longer run, as oil is gradually depleted, the country is unlikely to be able to finance its accustomed levels of consumption because of the paucity of income-generating investments and the dwindling supplies of foreign exchange.

Industry has been a clear laggard in post-revolution developments. Due to shortages of raw materials and machinery, and damages incurred during the war, the industrial sector registered negative or stagnant growth in 7 of the 14 years under review. The share of the labor force in this sector fell from 34 per cent in 1976/77 to about 24 per cent ten years later. The regime blamed the slack mainly on shortages of foreign exchange. However, inexperienced management, overstaffing, poor coordination, and ideological constraints must also have played their parts.

Interestingly, the initial industrial policy position also seems to have undergone a significant turnabout. The previous regime's emphasis on rapid industralization, which had been bitterly attacked by the victorious revolutionaries as short-sighted, harmful, and based on unsound principles, seems to have come back in full force. Despite an early commitment by the new regime to change the country's direction of development in favor of agriculture, and to establish a genuine, indigenous, industrial sector totally coordinated with domestic farming and internal resources, no major change from the pre-revolution era can yet be detected.[14] Not only has the much criticized dependence of industry on imports of raw materials, machinery, spare parts, and technology failed to decline since the revolution but also the pattern of planned industrial development is hardly distinguishable from the Shah's time. In the current five-year plan, industry is once again expected to serve as the main engine of growth, alongside oil and gas. One fifth of the total fixed capital investment during the plan period is to be absorbed by industry. The sector's share in GDP is to reach 19.5 per cent from 17 per cent. Average annual real growth, projected at 14.3 per cent for manufacturing, is two-and-a-half times that of agriculture, and much faster than that of any other sector in the economy.

The broad objectives of the industrial sector once again refer to reduced dependence on imported inputs, expansion of the technological base, encouragement of non-oil exports, and an improvement in industrial management. Two-thirds of the total investment in industry is still to be provided by the public sector. But while the new strategy favors intermediate and capital goods industries at the expense of consumer goods, its orientation is still toward large, import-substituting (rather than export-promoting) industries – a strategy for which the old regime was severely (and rather unfairly) censored by many domestic and foreign analysts. Protection of home industries is expected to increase, as was the case in the past. Within the industrial sector, a turnabout also seems to have emerged in the case of nuclear power development. The Shah's plans to supply a major portion of the country's electric power needs through nuclear energy were rejected by the revolutionaries as inappropriate, wasteful, and foreign-dependent. All this seems now to have changed.

On **government finance**, the regime has been singularly unsuccessful in reducing its dependence on oil income. The promised substitution of oil revenues by taxes on domestic products and incomes in order to reduce 'dependency on the outside world' has been unfulfilled. Although the share of the general government budget in GDP declined measurably during the 1980s, the budget deficit has not yet been effectively dealt with by raising income taxes. The total cumulative deficit for the decade was almost totally financed by borrowing from the central bank. In addition, the substantial fall in central government expenditure after the revolution was realized almost totally at the expense of public investment. Tax revenues, in fact, slipped from an already low 8.3 per cent of GDP in 1977/78 to 4.4 per cent in 1988/89, before turning back toward 5.8 per cent in 1991/92.

The drop in government expenditure on development projects, the declining share of taxes in GDP, and the rising public debt were, of course, partly caused by extraneous circumstances. Yet the government itself was also partly responsible; by keeping the tax administration weak and understaffed; by clinging to an archaic 19-bracket tax system (from 12 per cent to a marginal rate of 75 per cent); and by failing to prevent the proliferation of tax exemptions, deductions and tax holidays. The tax burden as a whole was gradually shifted from income taxes to excises. Collected individual income taxes were increasingly concentrated on factory workers and civil servants who could not escape withholdings. Professional cadres, service traders, and the 'super rich' easily evaded paying their share.[15] Also, the major portion of corporate income taxes was collected from *public* enterprises, especially Bank Markazi.

The budget deficit – large by any measure or definition – would still not seem extraordinary or intractable for a country at war and suffering from several other economic handicaps. What made the growing budget deficit a particularly troublesome phenomenon was its method of financing. The leadership's decision to reduce the economy's dependence on foreign resources and funds, and the authorities' resolve to pay back long-term (and low-cost) foreign public debt, left no alternative for the treasury but to rely on meager domestic resources. The perennial budget deficit had to be made up by three sources of finance: unspent appropriations from previous years; ongoing savings from current appropriations; and borrowing from the banking system. As the first two sources were frequently insignificant or non-existent, the third source was always the only choice. And, since all major financial institutions were already nationalized and dependent on the central bank for their own requirements, Bank Markazi became the only viable source of finance. Borrowing from the private sector was not a realistic option because private savings outside the banking system were tapped in several different ways to finance the war and to help other semi-public foundations.

It is important to note here that the government's inability to collect taxes from individuals and businesses was partly compensated for by a number of informal schemes (and even some extra-legal mechanisms) through which people voluntarily or obligingly contributed part of their earnings and wealth to the state. One such scheme was the so-called *khodyari* (or self-help), under which funds were obtained from the main beneficiaries of public and merit goods directly, instead of taxing their income via the treasury. Thus, instead of spending funds on social services through the national budgets of the regular public agencies, some government officials prodded citizens to finance their collective needs themselves. For example, parents of school children were asked to make voluntary contributions to improve public schools where their children were enrolled. Merchants were urged to donate money to their precinct authority in order to clean up the streets. Violators of zoning laws were routinely exonerated and allowed to finish their projects if they contributed certain sums for city beautification. Municipalities routinely financed part of their needs through 'voluntary donations' by developers and large construction companies. The widespread bureaucratic shenanigans and public sector corruption, frequently reported in the domestic and foreign press, were also a form of *taxation without fiscal intermediation*. Fixed-income government employees, often described by the leadership as the group most adversely affected by perennial inflation, were allowed to maintain, if not augment, their real income through *ad hoc* 'tax collection' from the beneficiaries of public services, or, from individuals needing government assistance, through open bribe-taking.[16]

A sizeable proportion of the budget deficit was also financed by the so-called 'inflation tax', or forced private savings. As might be expected, price increases entailed a pro-government bias. In addition to its effect on the real incomes of various economic groups, domestic inflation caused a substantial transfer of resources from the private to the public sector as the government's own resources declined. High inflation, resulting from a rapid expansion of liquidity and aggregate demand, led to low rates of returns on bank deposits and lower real values of principal assets. In both instances, the net result was tantamount to a tax (an 'inflation tax') that transferred resources from currency holders and owners of low-yielding assets (for example, bank depositors) to the government. As the bulk of the public sector deficit was thus underwritten by positive net private savings, an internal net transfer took place from the private to the public sector. As a result of these hidden or informal transfers, therefore, the real tax burden on the population was much larger than official figures would indicate.

Housing was yet another activity where accomplishments fell short of expectations. As shown in a previous section (Table 12.2), public and private investment in housing fell steadily during the 1980s for a variety of reasons. Consequently, the number of housing units completed each year progressively declined, while the country's population steadily grew. Residential units completed or built in 1989/90, for example, amounted to slightly more than one-fifth of the number in 1976/77, and less than half of the new five-year-plan target of 294,000 a year.[17] Thus, while there were 16 dwellings built per 1,000 inhabitants each year before the revolution, the corresponding number 10 years later fell to less than 3 units. According to a housing official, the housing shortage, estimated at 3.1 million units in 1985/86, reached 3.7 million units in 1989/90. Apart from the war damage, the country was in need of 600,000 new houses annually for the next 20 years, but, at best, only 200,000 could be constructed.[18] Thanks largely to the efforts of the Construction Crusade in the rural areas, the number of houses with electricity and piped water increased by more than 50 per cent during the 1980s, but occupancy per housing unit, as well as congestion per room in each unit, measurably increased. Some 130,000 units totally destroyed by the war, and 110,000 units demolished by the 1990 earthquakes, added to the problem.

Among the factors responsible for the housing shortfalls were: declining per capita income; shortage of foreign exchange for financing foreign input needs of the construction industry; rising costs of land and building materials (lowering affordability of housing); declining private sector investment in multi-unit complexes; a precipitous fall in public sector investment in low-cost dwellings; ambiguities in landlord/tenant laws discouraging rental units construction; and the war.

In the area of **foreign trade** and exchange, the regime was partly successful in bringing foreign purchases and exchange transactions under state control. Although nationalization of external commerce was twice blocked by the Council of Guardians, the government exercised a near total control through its virtual monopoly of exchange earnings and its foreign currency allocation. Some discretion was also exercised over the initial price and distribution of imported goods. Customary tariffs and special profit taxes also served as supplementary devices to manage trade. Bilateral and other special arrangements were successfully used to change the direction of trade.

However, some of the other goals were harder to attain. The economy's dependence on the outside world, which was meant to decline, actually increased, both in absolute magnitude and as a percentage of GDP, between 1977/78 and 1991/92. The share of consumer goods in total imports, which was to be brought down substantially in favor of capital goods, actually increased slightly to an annual average of 19.6 per cent (compared with 18.4 per cent before the revolution – see Table 10.3). Non-oil exports, which were to rise, and eventually to replace oil export revenues, also displayed a rather disappointing performance up to 1991/92. Despite increasing incentives offered by the government (for example, reduced surrender requirements, 'rights to import' privileges, and favorable exchange rates), the average annual export of non-oil products at $718 million was only 15 per cent larger than the 1977/78 figure of $625 million, far less than the rate of inflation. In addition to this rather frustrating record, non-oil exports registered two additional disappointments: a renewed concentration on agricultural and traditional items, and a worsening in the terms of trade.

In the field of **banking** and **credit**, the transformation to Islamic banking was carried out without interruption in the internal financial market, largely because the change was essentially limited to the nomenclature. The regime's initial hopes to use the nationalized and Islamicized banking system as a means of restructuring the economy remained unfulfilled. The Islamic modes, that were supposed to shift investment funds away from consumerism and 'non-productive' services towards socially-justified productive projects, fell short of expectations. While short-term deposits were easily attracted under various incentives other than interest, banks were less successful in raising long-term deposits, or providing long-term loans. Hamstrung by a wide variety of regulations, direction and supervision, the state financial institutions were not able to compete for deposits or loans, and their efficiency steadily declined. As indicated before, the banking system was one of the poorest performing sectors of the economy during the 1980s. Nor was the system successful in raising national savings. The ratio of national savings to the gross national income (at adjusted market prices) remained virtually the same at the beginning and at the end of the decade – around 20 per cent. Also, credit was not diverted to the productive sectors, but was routinely attracted towards services and sales activities. National consumption was reduced, but only as a result of lower national income, and not by way of increased parsimony or voluntary frugality.

Due to the weaknesses in banking operations, the regime's new post-1989/90 liberalization strategy has had to improvise a novel scheme whereby 'non-bank' investment funds and institutions could be established in the private sector and could compete with regular banks in wide-ranging activities. Commercial banks are now reportedly allowed to participate in money market operations abroad. Joint ventures with foreign banks in industrial projects are also again sanctioned.

The **environment** seems to have been another casualty of the revolution. Article 50 of the 1979 Constitution calls for the prevention of damage to the environment from pollution and other eco-system imbalances. The Environment Protection Organization has been in charge of enforcing this mandate. Yet, according to a private report, destructive effects on the environment in the form of deforestation, systematic misuse of pasture, excessive soil erosion, a reduction in flora and fauna species, and pollution, have been considerable during the 1980s. Less than 2 million hectares of forest are said to remain in the Caspian region. The wild animal population has been reduced to between 50 and 80 per cent of what it was before the revolution. Air pollution in Tehran and other big cities has been rising rapidly. Only 10 per cent of the country's sewage is treated. Only 35 cities have hygienic systems for garbage disposal.[19]

Factors responsible for the deterioration of the environment are said to include: lack of attention to ecological issues in development planning and policies; excessive population and disorganized urban growth; uneven distribution of inhabitants, industries, and services around the cities; misuse of land; and lax enforcement of environmental regulations. No serious efforts have been made to protect coastal and inland waters from pollution, or to educate farmers in the use of fertilizers and pesticides.

EQUITY CONSIDERATIONS

The Islamic Republic's early national welfare policy in general, and its immediate social welfare engineering in particular, exhibited a clear populist slant and a strong lower-class bias. The revolution was portrayed by Ayatollah Khomeini and his supporters as the uprising of the poor and the deprived against the rich and powerful; and the 1979 Constitution, both in its preamble and in Chapter IV (on economic matters), placed the interests and needs of the poor at the top of the national agenda. The old and new five-year plans, as well as the annual budgets documents, have always officially been committed to this goal.

In the first two years after the revolution, the regime seemed actively to pursue and concretize its goal of redistribution. The takeover by 'the poor' of residential properties vacated by their owner/occupants, of factories abandoned by their owner/managers, of farms unattended by their landlords, and of other valuables left by emigrating followers of the Shah's regime, was ostensibly tolerated (if not surreptitiously sanctioned) by the government. Despite repeated declarations by many religious divines that such actions were not allowed under Islam, wholesale confiscation of the assets of several thousand individuals and families continued. More directly, the government launched a series of welfare measures – ranging from wage increases, price controls, and food subsidies, to land distribution, tax exemptions, and cash payments to special families – ostensibly designed to reduce poverty and income inequality.

Yet the consensus of informed opinion points to no notable success in this regard. In the absence of reliable data, the impact of the regime's public welfare measures on the condition of various social classes is hard to measure. Data published by the United Nations and the World Bank, based on information received from Iranian authorities, show that life expectancy at birth, adult literacy, daily per capita calorific intake, access to health services, availability of safe water, per capita energy consumption, and the number of students enrolled in all levels of education, have increased under the revolution. At the same time, infant mortality, population per physician and per nurse, and the primary pupil-teacher ratio have decreased. Countering progress in these socio-economic indicators has been the rate of growth of population, rising from 2.7 per cent a year before the revolution to an average of 3.5 per cent a year after 1979.[20]

To obtain a truer picture of the real improvements in public welfare, however, the raw quantitative data – even if totally accurate and reliable – need to be adjusted and refined for the *content* of education, the *skills* of added teachers and doctors, the *quality* of public health care, and the *nutritional value* of the calorie intake. Without such adjustments, the numerical comparisons of formal data between any two periods must be treated with extreme caution.

The lack of specific information on internal income distribution necessitates the resort of other indices in order to gain certain indications of change in the income status of various social groups. Available figures on the gross domestic product, the demographic development, and annual price movements during the 1979–1991 period, clearly indicate a downward trend in the national standard of living, and a worsening of the income gap between fixed and flexible income groups. As shown in Table 14.1, per capita income in 1991/92 (at constant 1982/83 prices) was about 62 per cent of the figure in 1977/78, reflecting changes in the national output and fluctuations in oil revenues.

As a general observation, it might be safe to conclude that, in an economy where real per capita income over a given period is down by nearly 40 per cent, not many people could be better off. Furthermore, since the two main sources of national income (namely, wages and earnings on liquid financial assets) have both demonstrably lagged behind rising prices during the 1980s, the majority of wage earners and liquid asset holders could not have been among the beneficiaries. Still further, most of the winners in a stagflated economy (like Iran's in the 1980s) could hardly be found in the relatively depressed sectors, such as oil or industry. Agriculture and services are, therefore, the only activities which could have produced some of the gainers. Consensual observations do indeed single out the revolution's major beneficiaries to be some mid-size, near-city, mechanized, farm owners; a number of strategically placed bazaar merchants; certain privileged importers/distributors; and well-connected deal-makers and speculators.[21] Those operating in the underground economy and in illicit traffics must also be placed among the top earners.[22] A special one-time luxury wealth tax, introduced in 1989/90 (The National Cooperation Tax for Reconstruction), and earmarked for reconstruction of war-damaged areas, was indicative of the government's concern about the new-rich.[23]

Worst off among white-collar workers were the fixed-income civil servants, retirees, and purged officials of the old regime. Despite several salary increases during the 1980s, widespread moonlighting by many state employees, and other means of supplementing monthly incomes, a majority of public employees and middle-class professional cadres were certainly hurt by rising prices and shortages of goods. Among blue-collar workers, the worst off consisted of unemployed job seekers, farm laborers, construction workers, and the poor urban proletariat. To this group should also be added the refugees from the war zones, those dislocated by war damage to their homes and businesses, and industrial workers laid off as a result of reduced capacity utilization.

Beyond these general observations, certain specific indications may also offer additional clues. For example, the surveys of urban and rural expenditures and incomes published by the Iranian Statistical Center show noteworthy changes in both the pattern and the level of living among the two groups. According to these surveys, between 1977/78 and 1987/88 annual incomes of urban families rose from nearly Rls 450,000 to Rls 1,150,000, while incomes of rural families increased from Rls 166,000 to Rls 723,000 – indicating a 155 per cent increase in the urban sector compared with a 340 per cent rise in the rural areas. In the same period, family expenditures in the urban centers rose from Rls 438,000 to Rls 1,490,000 while the figures for the rural sector were Rls 207,000 and Rls 908,000 respectively – indicating changes of 240 per cent vs. 338 per cent (Table 14.2). Thus, the ratio of urban expenditure to urban income deteriorated from 98 per cent to nearly 130 per cent, while the ratio for the rural families was almost unchanged at about 125 per cent. As a result, the income of rural families as a percentage of income of urban families, in the period under discussion, increased from 37 per cent to 63 per cent; while their expenditure rose from 47 per cent to 61 per cent.[24]

However, despite this apparent improvement in the rural/urban welfare position, the data fail to show that the lot of the rural poor was enhanced. Some analysts argue that the revolution has been equally harsh on low-income people from both urban and rural areas. The favourable shift of income share enjoyed by the rural populace has been due to the higher incomes of well-to-do farmers and rural middlemen rather than to improved incomes for farm workers. The rural poor, however, may have benefited from lower inflation in rural areas.

Although much of the discussion in the Iranian press and media regarding the plight of the poor is based on personal observation, individual inferences, and anecdotal evidence not always backed by scientific investigations, the issue frequently commands high priority in the leadership's agenda. Researchers in and out of the government hierarchy speak openly about the growing number of families (including nearly 9 million urban dwellers), comprising about 60 per cent of the population, who fall below the 'poverty line' – defined as a monthly income of Rls 250,000 ($158) in 1993. An estimated 2 million families reportedly earned less than Rls 120,000 a month ($76). The top 20 per cent of the population is said to receive 50 per cent of the national income, and control half of the national wealth, while the bottom 10 per cent get no more than 1.3 per cent. Iranian society is seen as being polarized into two classes, the very rich and the very poor.[25] Other studies also claim that income distribution has changed in favor of the top 20 per cent of families and against the average urban wage and salary earner.[26] On the other hand, there is a claim, based on an unreferenced Iranian Statistical Center calculation, that the Genie coefficient of income was slightly improved between 1977/78 and 1987/88, but was later reversed.[27]

In sum, analysts sympathetic to the Islamic Republic, as well as its opponents, seem to agree that public welfare measures adopted under the revolution have not yet resulted in a palpably fairer distribution of income, either within the urban and rural sectors, or between them. There also seems to be a consensus that, despite the government's price controls, rationing, subsidization, and other welfare measures, the steep rise in population and unemployment has offset any growth gains in GDP. A recent study devoted to this issue concludes that the Islamic Republic's early measures – a redistribution of assets through nationalization and confiscation, an increase in the official minimum wage rate, and a lowering of income tax rates – disfavored high-income households, had a favorable impact on middle-income families, and left very poor urban and rural people unaffected. After 1981, however, the possibilities of profiteering through both government-sanctioned activities and through illicit trade tended to widen income differences once again, so that the gap between the top and bottom deciles is now as wide as it was before the revolution for urban households, and even wider for the rural population.[28]

Finally, the leadership's repeated post-ceasefire promises to narrow the gap between the rich and poor are seen as an indication that the regime has failed in its pledge to redistribute wealth. Addressing the *Majles* in the spring of 1992, President Rafsanjani told deputies that Iran's oil revenues were 'devoured' by the rich, and that he intended to reverse the trend in income distribution.[29]

PERFORMANCE IN PROPER PERSPECTIVE

As the foregoing discussions indicate, the Iranian economy's overall performance since the revolution has largely failed the test of both equity and efficiency. Continued heavy reliance on oil export incomes as the mainstay of the economy, the main foreign exchange earner and a major source of state income also reveals that there has been no real progress toward economic diversification. As already shown earlier in this chapter, in terms of such basic common indicators as rapid growth, full employment, labor productivity, price stability fiscal sobriety, and external balance, the results have been on the whole disappointing.

Yet, it is from three other specific standpoints, that the Islamic Republic's economic record has been fatally flawed. First, despite extremely harsh political measures against its domestic opposition and strict control of private economic activity, the regime has been unable to deliver on its own promises. The economy's dependence on oil has not been diminished; agriculture has not become the pivot of development; self-sufficiency in food grains has not been accomplished; income distribution has not been turned in favor of the poor; and a consumption model has not yet been formulated. Instead, per capita income has declined; the infrastructure has deteriorated; labor productivity has fallen; shortages have been intensified; and unsavory practices have spread far and wide.

Second, and by far the more obvious failure, has been the regime's inability to establish a truly Islamic economy with its own distinct economic model, as long promised and advocated. Third, and most embarrassing of all, has been the theocracy's unabashed adoption of some of the Shah's policies mercilessly denounced during and shortly after the revolution. Thus, maximum oil production and exports have again taken center stage in the five-year development planning; industry rather than agriculture has once again become the axis of economic development; population control is now a top priority in government planning; foreign private investment is encouraged more than ever before; and, irony of ironies, military dominance in the Persian Gulf region is once more an overriding national goal. Some of the major points in the initial socioeconomic agenda (for example, foreign trade nationalization and land reform) have been quietly abandoned. Some others (such as encouraging population growth, and cutting down oil production and military expenditures) have undergone a complete reversal.[30] Certain strategies of the Shah's regime (for example, foreign borrowing and encouraging foreign investment), which were harshly criticized by the revolutionaries, are now gaining respectability and even Islamic legitimacy.

While the Islamic Republic's critics tend to blame all these shortfalls on systemic flaws and innate incompetence, the influence of some adverse factors and unforeseen events should by no means be ignored or underestimated. In any assessment of the Islamic Republic's record, allowance should be made for the unfavorable circumstances which were somewhat beyond the regime's control. Among the major impediments, the costly and destructive war with Iraq was by far the most outstanding, and is accordingly discussed in a special appendix to this chapter. In addition to the war, the Islamic regime also faced a number of other serious challenges that put its resolve to gruelling tests at every turn. The threats to the regime's success and survival included: a devastating revolt by Marxist contingents among the anti-Shah forces (particularly the *Mojahedin-e Khalq*) in the form of violent attacks, terrorist action, and political assassinations; the Kurdish and Baluchi uprisings in the west and southeast in demand of local autonomy; the wholesale exodus of managerial, entrepreneurial and technical talent from the country; a 14-month confrontation with the United States over the hostage crisis, and continued quarrels with Washington over a number of political issues; a Western arms and trade embargo and (later) economic sanctions; diplomatic isolation for most of the period from most of the industrial world; and an influx of 3 million or more Afghanis, Iraqi Shi'ites, and Kurdish refugees into the country.

Ayatollah Khomeini and his Islamic fundamentalist supporters fought their revolutionary cohorts for nearly two years in order to establish their special brand of Islamic governance. The new economic order which the secular groups hoped to build on democratic principles and socialist tenets after the revolution never came to pass. Its main architects lost their position and influence soon after, in successive stages. First to go were the National Front followers of former prime minister Mosaddeq, who had spearheaded a secular, democratic revolt against the Pahlavi regime back in 1977, and initially participated in Mehdi Bazargan's provisional government. Next came the Liberation Movement, headed by Bazargan himself, who was forced out, after a brief period of ineffective rule, by the uncompromising, fundamentalist, anti-Western groups. Third, were the vaguely Western-oriented, semi-pragmatist followers of Abol Hassan Bani-Sadr (the Islamic Republic's first president in 1980/81) whose economics of 'divine unity' was supposed to fuse certain unconventional economic principles with 20th-century economic and financial realities. The radical left (The *Mojahedin* and *Fadai'yan Khalq*), as well as the Communist elements (the Tudeh Party), never had a chance to participate in the government at high levels despite having played a pivotal role in the Shah's ousting. Ethnic rebellions in Kurdestan and Baluchistan were also decisively crushed, with almost no concessions given to separatist demands for local autonomy. During these skirmishes, the Islamic-fundamentalist faction lost almost two-thirds of its top leadership to domestic bombings, assassinations, and terrorist acts – and yet still kept a tight grip on the government. This faction gradually silenced *Bazaari* dissidents; purged the universities of troublesome instructors and students; defrocked and banned some clerical opponents (e.g., Shariatmadari, and Tehrani); and methodically placed the managements of industries, workers' councils, and major daily newspapers under clerical direction.

External challenges were also successfully fought off. As already touched upon, eight months into the revolution the Islamic Republic suddenly faced almost total international isolation when 52 American diplomats in Tehran were taken hostage by a shadowy group calling themselves the 'Students Following the Imam's Line'. Repeated refusals by the government to free these hostages unless certain onerous (to the US) conditions were met cost Tehran much creditability in world diplomatic circles.[31] Condemned by the United Nations Security Council and the International Court of Justice for its behavior in the hostage crisis, Iran was unable to mobilize international political support for its condemnation of aggression by Iraq. Nor was Tehran in a position to obtain foreign financial help to cope with a costly and damaging war with its western neighbor. Essential war supplies and badly needed spare parts (except for a limited range of light weapons and ammunition from North Korea, China, Libya, Syria and, ironically, Israel and the United States) were denied the Iranian government by Western countries to whom Tehran appealed. No one was anxious to jeopardize relations with Washington. The UN-imposed trade sanctions against Iran were largely observed, and national defense and survival needs had to be obtained from abroad at exorbitantly high prices.

The economic exploit, albeit modest, that was accomplished despite internal political turmoil, financial hardships, and military burdens can hardly be ignored. For example, despite the protracted and costly war – estimated to have absorbed an estimated 7–8 per cent of GDP each year – budgetary expenditure on defense rose by about 4 per cent a year, thanks largely to voluntary private financial contributions and popular sacrifice. Despite intense financial pressures on the public sector, the annual budget deficit was kept below 9 per cent of GDP on average through reductions on 'non-priority' outlays. Thanks to sizeable oil revenues, no recourse had to be made to long-term foreign borrowing. By sharply cutting down bank credit to the private sector, and by reducing capital expenditures, inflationary pressures were kept relatively in check. Furthermore, adverse effects of price rises on low- and fixed-income groups were mitigated in part through a system of subsidies, price ceilings, rationing, and direct distribution of essential goods and services through official channels. Finally, by strict control of imports and foreign exchange allocations, as well as incentives given to non-oil exporters, the overall balance-of-payments deficits were held down. In short, by avoiding universal catastrophes common to war, such as hyperinflation, life-threatening shortages, intolerable social disamenities, and mounting external debt, the economy showed remarkable resilience in the face of formidable odds.

The regime's leadership blames all its avowed failures and setbacks on these internal and external forces, and portrays all the aggravating circumstances as *force majeure* – whether or not they have been truly beyond its control. The list of obstacles routinely cited by public officials includes: the legacy of an unbalanced and dependent economy; damage caused by the so-called 'imposed' war with Iraq; Western hostility toward the Islamic Republic; the volatile oil market; internal sabotage; natural disasters; and a blanket category called 'Zionist/imperialist' machinations against Iran within the United Nations, OPEC, and other international agencies.[32]

As already indicated, there is no doubt that without certain handicaps and constraints, the Iranian economy would have been in different shape today. Yet the lion's share of the responsibility for the regime's misfortunes in the economic arena must be attributed to three specific factors: the Islamic Republic's highly unrealistic populist stance at home, and its visionary mission to export the Islamic revolution abroad; the choice of an anachronistic and discredited economic model throughout much of the 1980s; and a dogged determination to reverse the irreversible in traditional Persian culture.

IMPOSSIBLE MISSIONS AT HOME AND ABROAD

The populist mandates of the 1979 Constitution went beyond even the most generous provisions for a modern welfare state and required a very rapid rate of economic growth to finance them. At the same time, the regime's economic culture could hardly provide the necessary underpinning for such high expansion rates. Under the new constitution, the state was called upon to provide Iranian citizens with a cradle-to-grave welfare system which resembled something more like make-believe than a plausible platform. A cursory look at the people's rights under Articles 28–31 of the 1979 Constitution – the rights to free education, a suitable dwelling, all basic necessities such as food, clothing, and health care, the opportunity to work, social security with respect to retirement, unemployment, old age, disability and destitution benefits – suffices to show the lack of realism of this socio-economic manifesto. Ideal and distant goals, these provisions were akin to wishful dreams rather than a credible agenda. Even with the fullest realization of Iran's agricultural, industrial, and hydrocarbons potentials, no Iranian government could ever afford the unbearable costs of this constitutionally-mandated welfare nirvana.

Ironically, even a modest rate of growth that could finance part of this welfare state was undermined by the leadership's puritanical stance. Relentless exhortations from the pulpit for a simple, frugal life under an Islamic consumption model – while not essentially hostile to increased output – served as a strong disincentive to entrepreneurial endeavors. Although the regime's national economic planning called for substantial growth of output, and its brand of state capitalism was geared to optimum production, uncertainty about property rights, government ownership of large enterprises, and a distrust of the private sector and foreign investment, cut into the economy's potential for producing sufficient consumer goods. Elaborate patterns of restrictive rules and regulations also served as a fertile ground for widespread corruption. And, rather than running parallel with rapid economic growth, as it does in some countries, Iran's institutionalized corruption became pernicious, debilitating, and inimical to progress.

Another visionary mission – and a further heavy burden on the country's relatively meager resources – was the regime's self-adopted 'manifest destiny' in championing the cause of Islam, and the salvation of the world's down-trodden against the rich and the powerful. To Ayatollah Khomeini, Islam was not only a religion and a contemporary socio-political idiom for Iran, it was a way of life for mankind.[33] The Iranian government's overriding duty was not only to defend and practice Islam at home, but also to propagate and export it abroad. The nation's territorial integrity and economic prosperity had to go hand in hand with spreading the gospel beyond Iran's borders.[34] Thus, the preamble of the

Islamic Republic's 1979 Constitution calls for the continuation of the revolution at home and abroad towards the formation of a single world community and the liberation of all deprived and oppressed people in the world.[35] In pursuit of this manifest destiny, the regime vowed to: support Islamic extremist groups in the Middle East; stand against Soviet expansion in Afghanistan; conquer Baghdad from Saddam Hussein; liberate Jerusalem from Israeli hands; and assist fundamentalist Islamic revolution everywhere. This strategy sapped a good deal of the regime's energy, and resulted in the country's diplomatic isolation. Tehran's widely alleged involvement in Islamic fundamentalist movements in the Middle East, North Africa, and elsewhere caused a significant drain on the country's economic and manpower resources. The regime's determination to become a dominant power in the Persian Gulf, to champion singlehandedly the cause of the radical Palestinian groups, and to 'stand up' to the United States and Israel, pushed the government into a furious military build-up (including the purchase of advanced combat aircraft, missile launchers and submarines).

THE WRONG ECONOMIC MODEL

The second factor responsible for the economy's poor performance was the unfortunate choice of the wrong economic model during most of the 1980s. Under the influence of its powerful radical faction in the early 1980s, the Islamic Republic chose to adopt the old and repudiated Soviet-inspired Indian model for its economic management. At roughly the time when both Russia and India were ready to admit the failure of their inward-looking economic regimes, Iran stepped forward to embrace the flawed system. Economic self-sufficiency, a disdain for consumerism, a stress on national planning, the tightening of the state's clutches on industries, restrictions on foreign trade, maintenance of an overvalued currency, and hostility to foreign investment became the regime's pre-eminent agenda. The whole set of policies that had proved ruinous for both India and the former Soviet Union were written anew in the 1979 Constitution under the banner of the Islamic economics, anti-imperialism, and economic independence. The Pahlavis' notion of the state playing a guiding role in Iran's economic development was pushed forward to the untenable conclusion that the government's role must be primary, pivotal, and supreme. The result was a near-isolationist, insecure, and patrimonial economic strategy. Instead of limiting its guiding role to providing a legal and regulatory framework for the economy, and focusing its interventionist responsibility on activities such as high quality education, effective environmental protection, strict population control, and meaningful aid to the neediest, the Islamic Republic went far beyond the Pahlavi regime in wishing to micro-manage the economy.

Ironically, not only was the model itself a discredited one but also the new regime was ill-prepared to undertake its complex implementation. A crucial deficiency in this attempt at micro-management was the absence of a unified direction, and the inadequacy of policy coordination. Different ministries, agencies, and even semi-private organizations and revolutionary units often had joint responsibility over the same facets of the economy. Although economic issues were routinely discussed at various ministerial levels, in the council of ministers, and in numerous committees of the *Majles*, there was no disciplined management. Nor was there a mechanism for developing coherent policies among different economic sectors, or for coordinating essential economic variables. Policies involving output, prices, incentives, investment, trade, foreign exchange, ownership, and finance were often made without regard to their interaction and complementarity. In some sectors (for example, industry), decision-making on policies and procedures was haphazardly shared by a dozen different agencies. President Rafsanjani himself complained that, despite the government's desperate need to encourage non-oil exports, an exporter had to go to 80 places in order to finalize the foreign sale.[36]

Continued heavy dependence on oil exports as the main source of both foreign exchange and government revenues, and the resort to 'import compression' in the face of falling oil revenues in the mid-1980s, intensified this uncoordinated micro-management. Strict control of foreign currency expenditures through import quotas and licenses, and foreign exchange allocation, led to a gradual over-valuation of the official exchange rate – that is, a rising premium on the US dollar and other major currencies in the 'free market'. The maintenance of the highly over-valued official exchange rate throughout the post-revolution period in turn resulted in a number of harmful consequences for the economy.

The first unfavorable outcome of the overvalued rate was a severe misallocation of resources from the commodity-producing sectors, such as manufacturing, to trade and distribution. The shift of resources was particularly pronounced from export and import-competing industries to services and non-tradeable sectors – mainly for domestic consumption. Government sales of foreign exchange to favored importers at the artificially low price of Rls 70 for a US dollar encouraged imports, hit hard at competing domestic products, camouflaged subsidies to home consumers, and served as a hidden bonanza for foreign producers. Production for local use became increasingly more import-intensive as domestic prices rose faster than import prices. Ever increasing foreign exchange was demanded per unit of domestic output.

Secondly, there was a substantial increase in so called 'rent-seeking' activities at the expense of real production. As the difference between free-market and official rates widened over the years – from twice in early 1980 to more than 20 times in late 1992 – access to official foreign exchange became an end in itself. The staggering free-market premium – reportedly rare even among the economies of Latin American and African countries – turned foreign exchange transactions into a growing and highly lucrative economic activity. In addition to encouraging over-invoicing of imports and under-invoicing of exports, the rising premium created ample opportunity for corrupt practices in the allocation and use of foreign currencies at the official rate.

Thirdly, exchange control in the form of specific allocation in the annual foreign exchange budget to various ministries, agencies, activities, and semi-private foundations created a number of entrenched vested interests. Recipients of foreign exchange at the highly over-valued official rate formed a strong constituency against the rial's devaluation. All attempts at exchange rate unification within the development plan – recommended by the World Bank and the International Monetary Fund to correct internal and external imbalances – were successfully rebuffed by the strong interest groups that were steadfastly organized during the 1980s.[37]

Fourthly, the unrealistic fixed exchange rate further distorted, and often nullified, the government's agricultural support policies. Despite support prices offered for domestic farm products which were considered highly generous by government officials and a burden on the national budget, farmers had difficulty competing with imports priced artificially low. The low profit in agricultural pursuits relative to gains from trade and services accelerated farm migration, and added to the masses of under-employed urban proletariat.[38]

Finally, the highly overvalued currency wreaked havoc with the desired distribution of rationed goods. Due to the large and hidden subsidies involved in the import of 'essential' products (or their import components in domestic products) at the official exchange rate, their cost-based prices fixed by the government were considerably lower than those for similar items in neighboring countries. As a result, many items ranging from oil products and pharmaceuticals to trucks and tractors, purchased at subsidized prices with the help of legitimate or bogus coupons, were smuggled out of the country to be sold across the borders at reportedly 10 to 80 times profit.[39]

Central regulation of prices was another unfortunate aspect of this micro-management. Price controls, as always, entailed several unintended and undesirable side effects. Price ceilings were flagrantly violated by sellers through such means as reducing quality, cheating on weight, or selling the goods under the table. Furthermore, despite the authorities' desire to control domestic prices through rationing, these prices steadily increased in the free market in tandem with the free exchange rate. The gap between tradeable (import) and non-tradeable (domestic) prices also widened, with the result that the demand for foreign goods (and foreign exchange) relentlessly increased while their supply was limited. Still further, the shift in relative prices induced both producers and consumers to increase their use of tradeable items due to their lower costs. Finally, private investment tended to shift towards the production of non-controlled items: for example, services, brokering, middlemen activities, and others.[40]

All in all, price controls, rationing, and an overvalued fixed exchange rate produced a price system that did not reflect relative scarcity values. State intervention in favor of some priority sectors and certain social groups thus failed to achieve its intended objectives. Instead of optimizing output, and distributing it equitably among various socio-economic strata, the regime's extensive public controls and regulations led to misallocation of resources, intersectoral inefficiencies, and less-than-optimal income. Even the goal of keeping down import costs through an overvalued fixed exchange rate was effectively thwarted by large monopoly rents added to import prices in the market.[41]

In the final analysis, except for a very small minority of well placed individuals, everyone lost out as inward-looking economic policies disallowed export diversification as well as international competition to improve domestic output efficiency.

CULTURAL RESISTANCE

The third factor working against the regime's economic success has been its revolutionary promise to reverse not only the course of social modernization and political secularization launched by the Pahlavi regime, but also the rise of consumerism and the quest for a fuller life. However, in a society where material well-being – even conspicuous consumption – has had strong cultural roots not only among the well-to-do but also within the underclasses, this austere and puritanical policy could attract precious few. Ayatollah Khomeini's own ascetic lifestyle has had a scant following even among his closest associates. Local newspapers are filled with stories of high government officials enjoying lives of luxury and even extravagance.

Similar attempts to fit Iranian society into an Islamic mold have also proved impossible. After more than half a century of Westernization, liberation from old taboos, global contacts, and acceptance of new values and institutions, the state has been unable to reverse the irreversible. During more than 50 years of the Pahlavis' reign and rule, nearly all major elements in Iranian urban society, economy, and politics became too thoroughly immersed in 'modern' culture, and too profoundly dependent on the outside world to welcome any isolationist, puritanical, or absolutist tendencies. The Pahlavis' alliance with the West and the United States, and the transformation of Iran into a vibrant center of international trade, regional politics, and Third World leadership went too far to be quickly or drastically reversed – or to be reverted to seventh-century Islam as the new leaders have seemed to wish. The 'White Revolution' had moved too far for any permanent return to the days not only of Prophet Mohammad, but even the Qajar kings. No longer a backward, rural, weak, and illiterate society, Iran had become increasingly modern, urban, strong, and educated – dissatisfied with old-time religion and, at best, yearning for a 'new Islam'. The revolutionary leadership and their supporters have gradually discovered this, albeit grudgingly and with virtual astonishment.

STEPS TOWARD REALITY

By the end of the war with Iraq, a good number of new technocrats, and many 'moderate' clergymen within the establishment seemed to have finally come to the conclusion that early revolutionary objectives would not be easily achieved, and that the regime's very survival could not be guaranteed without rethinking the revolutionary agenda, relaxing central command and control, and realizing that time could not be turned back. It was also widely recognized that unless these perceptions became a firmly established national posture, the slogan 'Islam is the solution' would continue to have little effect. Ayatollah Khomeini's death saw the beginning of a serious movement toward structural adjustment, and away from revolutionary slogans. The final outcome is yet to unfold.

APPENDIX: THE IRAN–IRAQ WAR

Iran's war with Iraq began in September 1980 and ended in August 1988, under the UN Resolution 598 (1987), and has been the Islamic Republic's most devastating economic disaster by far. Iraq's responsibility for starting the war has now been formally declared by the UN Secretary General under Resolution 598.[42] The responsibility for prolonging the hostilities beyond UN Resolution 513 (1982) has been debated for years between the regime and its opponents; it is bound to be the subject of ceaseless discussion for years to come. The opposition at home and abroad has accused the Iranian government of intransigence in not accepting several mediation efforts throughout the 1980–1988 period by the United Nations, the Islamic Conference Organization, the Non-Aligned Movement, the Gulf Cooperation Council, and the Arab League.[43] The Islamic Republic's leadership has steadfastly defended its previous uncompromising stand as a legitimate moral, strategic and political position against 'naked aggression' and an 'imposed' war.

Many aspects of the war – historical, geographic, political, and religious – are beyond the purview of this work.[44] The extent of the Islamic Republic's interference in internal Iraqi affairs prior to Iraq's invasion, Baghdad's miscalculations in challenging Ayatollah Khomeini's pan-Islamic ambitions, the opportunities missed by Tehran on different occasions to settle the war peacefully and profitably, and the costly delay in accepting even the 1987 UN Resolution are issues that cannot be treated here. Of direct relevance to the focus of this study are the impact of the war on the Iranian economy; the material damage inflicted upon the country's productive base; and, to a much lesser extent, the regime's convenient resort to the 'imposed' war as the main cause of all its economic failures.

The war's impact on the Iranian economy has been virtually incalculable. By all accounts, the prolonged hostilities were, perhaps, the costliest calamity for Iran in this century. Apart from the human toll of dead and maimed, for which there can never be cost accounting, the war's economic impact has also been enormous. It has significantly affected the development of the Iranian economy during eight of the fourteen years of the Islamic rule. One of the most significant changes immediately brought about by the war was an increase in military spending and arms imports, which the Islamic Republic had initially vowed to cut from previous levels under the Shah, and which it succeeded in doing in 1978/79 and 1979/80. By affecting oil production and revenues, the war not only reduced the size of GDP in real terms, but also contributed to drastic reductions in public investment, and caused the virtual demise of the first five-year plan (1983/84–1987/88). Having suffered devastating blows to its production and transfer facilities, the oil sector lost a good part of its share in GDP (although the economy's dependence on oil for defense and development was not diminished). Furthermore, Iran was transformed from a net exporter of oil products before the war to a net importer afterwards. The reduced share of oil in the national output was picked up in part by the services sector, consisting mostly of non-productive activities, which resulted in lower government revenues, mounting budget deficits, and virulent inflation. Finally, Iran lost its previous foreign oil market share and position for many years.

The one positive impact of the war, however, was the boost it gave to the small local arms industry, and the reduced dependence on imports of small arms. The regime's claims, largely substantiated by foreign observers, point to Iran's growing capacity to manufacture small arms, machine guns, recoilless rifles and half the country's ammunition needs.[45] What is almost certain is that war, and the Western embargo on Iran's arms purchased abroad, greatly enhanced local ingenuity and the Iranian penchant for innovation.[46]

The second factor to be looked at here is war damage. In addition to the negative impact of the war on domestic output and oil revenues, the hostilities inflicted heavy losses to the country's infrastructure, industrial facilities, and farmland and population centers.[47] The nature and extent of the damage sustained by Iran has been detailed by a UN team of experts despatched to the country in mid-1991 by the Secretary General in pursuance of Resolution 598.[48] The team's preliminary report points out that 5 of the 24 Iranian provinces had been operational theaters of war, and 11 others were targets of repeated attacks by Iraqi aircraft and missiles. These 16 provinces housed two-thirds of the country's population. The land war was fought mainly on Iranian territory, 1,200 kilometers from Khuzestan to West Azerbaijan along the western border, and some 80 kilometers deep into Iran. Quoting Iranian authorities, the UN team further reports that over 50 cities and towns, and close to 4,000 villages, suffered varying degrees of damage, including total destruction. Over 130,000 houses were destroyed, with an additional 190,000 severely damaged. Some 1.25 million persons were displaced by the war. The oil industry suffered massive destruction. The Abadan refinery was virtually put out of operation, and three other refineries were damaged. Oil and gas fields, loading facilities at Kharg Island, and offshore drilling platforms were either destroyed or severely damaged. Transport, power and telecommunication installations, and facilities were heavily affected. The total destruction of Khorramshahr, a city of half a million people, deprived the country of its principal cargo and passenger port. The wreckage of ships in the Shat-al Arab has made navigation in the river impossible even once Khorramshahr is rebuilt. Damage to power stations and transmission lines has caused frequent power blackouts. Almost 800 light and heavy industrial enterprises were damaged or destroyed. Agricultural land, the structure of the plains, the soil's fertility, and river flows all suffered heavily as a result of embankments, tank traffic, mine fields, salinization and water-logging. Almost half of the date trees under production have been destroyed. Damage to the social sectors (health, education, and cultural facilities) remains to be appraised.

The estimated monetary value of the total damage varies considerably. Variations result from such factors as the inclusion of 'indirect' damages and their nature, different methods of cost accounting, and relevant exchange rate, notional oil prices in the absence of the war, and others. Differences in appraisals also reflect the exclusion of certain indirect cost items such as: military losses in hard and software gear; environmental damage; additional shipping and insurance charges for oil export through the Persian Gulf; lost earnings in war casualties; and a host of other imponderables.

Alnasrawi's calculations up to the end of 1985 give a figure of $240 billion for war costs plus estimated lost oil revenues. Amirahmadi's estimate for the entire war period puts the total at about $592 billion. A more inclusive estimate raises the total to $644 billion. The Islamic Republic's own estimate (given to the UN team) of *direct* damage to the economic sector is (an ambitiously precise) Rls 30,811,414 million. *Indirect* damage to the same sector is put at Rls 34,535,360 million. This total, at the official exchange rate at the time, would amount to about $900 billion. President Rafsanjani has, on many occasions, mentioned a round figure of $1 trillion. In the government's calculations *direct* damage consists of output capacities destroyed as a result of the war; *indirect* damage covers services and production capacities that would have been put to use in the absence of war. The latter still excludes psychological and physical pain and suffering endured by the population, and the value of human lives lost in battle. The aggregate number also masks the life-earning potentials of the war dead, not yet officially revealed.[49]

The final tally of the war's *direct* damage, computed at 1988 replacement costs, has been estimated by a special UN team to be a total of $97.2 billion.[50] This figure of directly calculable damage to the production and services facilities is clearly less than the Iranian government's own estimates of direct cost. However, the enormous extent of the destruction, and its long-term unfavorable impact on the economy, can hardly be ignored or belittled.

The third impact of the war has been to mask the regime's economic shortfalls. While the damage inflicted on Iran's infrastructure and production facilities should by no means be minimized, and while the reconstruction of the war-torn economy may require several years of rebuilding and repair, the war seems to have had some redeeming political value for the regime. The undeniable hardship, shortages, and physical destruction caused by the prolonged hostilities provided an unparalleled opportunity for the Islamic Republic to unite the people behind its 'war-until-victory' agenda. The conflict has also routinely been utilized as an excuse for explaining away some serious social and economic problems caused by the revolution itself, as well as the regime's own early mistakes and miscalculations.

In one of his Friday sermons, President Hashemi Rafsanjani concluded that the war, despite its destructive effects, had strengthened the nation spiritually. In his view, the people's revolutionary spirit, willingness for self-sacrifice, and attachment to Islamic values and culture had become second nature to the majority of Iranian citizens. The government's task, he said, is to preserve and nurture this spirit. Having said that, he singled out the war as the root cause of a dozen or so grave economic problems facing the nation.[51] Taking their cue from the leadership, village supervisors, mayors, agency heads, cabinet ministers, and others in the government hierarchy repeatedly blame their shortcomings on the 'imposed war'. There are also unconcealed hints by the Rafsanjani government that the Islamic Republic's performance record should begin in September 1988 and not in February 1979.

NOTES

1. One plausible explanation may be that, in Bank Markazi's accounting, 'changes in stock' are roughly estimated, and not calculated independently due to lack of sufficient information. Statistical discrepancies are derived from the difference between the total value of *sources* and *uses* of GDP. For this reason, the figures indicate a 'presumed' rather than an actual magnitude.
2. Shortly after the revolution, reports circulated in Iran and abroad that

the Ministry of Finance paid back a large part of the country's long-term debt carrying single-digit interest rates shortly before other public agencies had to borrow at double-digit rates in the short-term capital markets. Similarly, there were reports that Bank Markazi diverted part of its dollar holdings into gold at the highest record price for the metal, and later lost a great deal in that transaction.

3. See, for example, President A. A. H. Rafsanjani, Friday prayer sermon of 18 Mordad 1370, *Kayhan Havai*, August 14, 1991, pp. 9 ff; and Kamran Mofid, *The Economic Consequences of the Gulf War* (London: Routledge, 1990).

4. See, for example, *Negahi be Karname-ye Jomhuri-ye Eslami 1358–1367* (A Look at the Islamic Republic's Performance 1979–1988), p. 490. See also Hossein Azimi, 'Negahi be Naqsh-e Dowlat dar Towseh-e Eqtesadi', (A Look at the Role of the State in Economic Development) *Ettela'at Siasi-Eqtesadi*, 4, No. 1, Mehr 1368 and Masoud Kavoosi, 'The Postrevolutionary Iranian Economy', *Business Economics* (April 1988).

5. For a more elaborate and detailed list of these objectives, see the first post-revolution development plan outlined in Chapter 9.

6. For a litany of Iran's alleged economic ills under the Shah, see *Writings and Declarations of Imam Khomeini*, translated by Hamid Algar (Berkeley: Mizan Press, 1981); for details of specific objectives see Barrasi-e Tahavolat (1984). Cf. S. T. Hunter, *Iran After Khomeini* (New York: Praeger, 1992).

7. *Kayhan Havai*, August 14, 1991, pp. 9 ff.

8. See Sohrab Behdad, 'The Political Economy of Islamic Planning in Iran', in Amirahmadi and Parvin (1988), pp. 118–9.

9. Patrick Clawson, 'Dossier Iran', *Les Cahiers de L'Orient* (Third Quarter, 1990), p. 66.

10. For further discussion, see K. S. McLachlan and F. Ershad (eds.), *Internal Migration in Iran* (London: School of Oriental and African Studies, 1989).

11. McLachlan (1988), p. 221.

12. See *World Development Report, 1980* (Washington: The World Bank, 1980), p. 113.

13. See M. G. Renner, 'Determinants of the Islamic Republic's Oil Policies', in Amirahmadi and Parvin (1988), pp. 183 ff.

14. For a brief analysis of this dependence, see Sohrab Behdad, 'Foreign Exchange Gap, Structural Constraints and the Political Economy of Exchange Rate Determination in Iran', *International Journal of Middle East Studies*, No. 20 (1988), pp. 10–13.

15. See *Kayhan Havai*, 23 Day 1367 [1989].

16. See Dilip Hiro, 'War Unsettles Iran's Economy', *The Washington Post*, January 9, 1986.

17. Plan and Budget Organization, *Gozaresh-e Eqtesadi, 1368* (Tehran: PBO, 1990), p. 343.

18. See *Iran Focus*, June, 1989, p. 14. For a comparison of housing

shortage before and after the revolution see Mossalanejad (1986), p. 220.

19. See *Iran Focus*, April 1991, pp. 15–16.
20. See *World Development Report, 1979*, and *1992* (Washington: The World Bank, 1979 and 1992); and *Human Development Report 1992* (New York: *UNDP*, 1992).
21. It is also argued that, with nearly 42 per cent of Iran's population living in rural areas, agriculture supplying an average of 19 per cent of GDP, and the urban sector monopolizing the ownership of production factors, the city people appropriated a much larger share of income. Tehran, with only one-sixth of the population, reportedly received 40 per cent of national income in 1981 See *Ettela'at*, 9 Farvardin 1360.
22. See 'Drug Trafficking is Thriving in Iran', *The New York Times*, November 15, 1991.
23. The tax was levied on wealth exceeding Rls 100 million at progressive rates from 15 to 40 per cent. But collection proved low due to generous exemptions granted to private dwellings (which are normally a large part of an individual's wealth).
24. For the source of data, see annual statistical yearbook of the Iranian Statistical Center. For further details see *An Analysis of the Urban Family Budget Survey 1990/91* (Tehran: Bank of Markazi, n.d.).
25. For a sampling of these claims see, Hosain Azimi, 'Budgeh va Towse'h-e Eqtesadi dar Iran', *Ettela'at Siasi-Eqtesadi*, 5 Bahman, 1366; *Echo of Iran*, 'Political Bulletin' (3, 10 and 17 March, 1987, and 16 January, 1987); *Echo of Iran*, 'Economic Bulletin' (6, 13, and 27 October, 1987); *Ettela'at*, 8 Ordibehesht 1366; *Gozaresh-e Eqtesadi* (Tehran: Plan and Budget Organization, 1363); Amirahmadi (1990), pp. 194–203; and *Iran Times*, 7 Aban, 1367.
26. See *Negahi be Karnameh Jomhuri-e Islami* (1990), pp. 444–8.
27. For details, see *Kayhan Havai*, March 18, 1992, p. 15.
28. Sohrab Behdad, 'Winners and Losers of the Iranian Revolution', *International Journal of Middle East Studies*, No. 21 (1989), pp. 327–358.
29. *The Wall Street Journal*, May 29, 1992; see also 'Call is Out to Iran's Rich', *The New York Times*, April 12, 1992.
30. After the 1986/87 census, Prime Minister Musavi showed unabashed jubilation on television over the fact that Iran's population had grown by nearly 12 million since the revolution, which, he agreed, ensured the country's future power, wealth, and prosperity. By 1990, however, the Rafsanjani government had adopted a strict population control policy and program, offering free consultations and contraceptives to women through its health care centers – activities for which private doctors were reportedly enjoined 18 months earlier.
31. These conditions included return by the US of the ailing Shah and his wealth; recognition of the Iranian revolution; a promise not to interfere in Iran's internal affairs; withdrawal of all US claims against Iran; unfreezing of some $8 billion of Iranian assets in US banks, and

$420 million worth of military equipment paid for by Iran and not yet delivered; and an American apology for past 'misdeeds'.

32. For a typical litany of grievances see President Rafsanjani's Friday prayer sermon in *Kayhan Havai*, August 14, 1991.

33. In a letter to Mikhail Gorbachev shortly before his death, the Ayatollah advised the Soviet president to study the Qor'an in order to find solutions to some of Russia's enduring problems.

34. For a critical discussion of this mission, see Robin Wright, *In the Name of God: The Khomeini Decade* (New York: Simon and Schuster, 1989) particularly Ch. 4, and p. 196.

35. *The Constitution of the Islamic Republic of Iran* (Berkeley: Mizan Press, 1980), p. 19.

36. *Kayhan Havai*, August 14, 1991, p. 15.

37. For a full treatment of this subject see M. Hashem Pesaran, 'The Iranian Foreign Exchange Policy and the Black Market for Dollars', *International Journal of Middle East Studies*, (February 1992), pp. 102–125. See also Wolfgang Lautenschlager, 'The Effects of an Overvalued Exchange Rate on the Iranian Economy, 1979–84', *International Journal of Middle East Studies*, No. 18 (1986). For a rebuttal, close to the views of the radical faction within the hierarchy, see Sohrab Behdad (1988).

38. During much of the 1980s, the State Grain Organization, for example, imported wheat at $150 a ton on average (or Rls 10.5 per kilogram) at the official rate. The agency was thus reluctant to buy domestic wheat at the government support price of Rls 50 per kilo – arguing that it was nearly four times the cost of imports. Yet if the organization were denied access to the cheap petrodollars and had to procure its wheat imports at free-market rates of Rls 1000–1450 per US dollar, its imported cost would have been Rls 150–217.5 per kilo (or three to four times the domestic support price).

39. See *Kayhan Havai*, July 22, 1992, p. 26, for President Rafsanjani's complaint about the state of subsidized items.

40. The only benefit in maintaining parallel 'free' markets for goods and foreign currencies was the creation of an effective political safety valve for the regime. Large groups of well-to-do families were kept satisfied and out of political mischief. As long as fancy food, luxury items and foreign travel were readily available at free-market prices, there was little reason for the rich to agitate against the system on the grounds of austerity.

41. Import prices in Iran during the 1980s reportedly rose on average by 14.7 per cent a year while the annual rate of inflation in the countries supplying the bulk of Iran's imports was no more than 3.8 per cent. This huge difference is directly attributable to the high premiums enjoyed by traders in the free market. See Pesaran (1992).

42. *The Washington Post*, December 11, 1991.

43. See Dilip Hiro, *Iran Under the Ayatollahs* (London: Routledge & Kegan Paul, 1985), Ch. 6; and his *The Longest War* (London: Routledge, 1990).

44. For discussions of these issues, see (among major works on the subject) Tareq Y. Ismael, *Iran and Iraq: Roots of Conflict* (Syracuse: Syracuse University Press, 1982); J. M. Abdulghani, *Iraq and Iran: The Years of Crisis*, (Baltimore: Johns Hopkins University Press, 1985); Shahram Chubin and Charles Tripp, *Iran and Iraq at War* (Boulder: Westview Press, 1988); Majid Khadduri, *The Gulf War* (New York: Oxford University Press, 1988); Gary Sick, 'Trial by Error: Reflections on the Iran-Iraq War', *Middle East Journal* (spring 1989); and Efraim Karsh, *The Iran-Iraq War* (New York: St Martin's Press, 1989).

45. Government officials further claim the ability to make medium-range radar, pilotless aircraft, helicopters, speed boats, and even fighter planes. These are at best experimental prototypes, and not sufficient for Iran's defense against modern warfare.

46. See Karsh (1989), pp. 242–246.

47. On these issues, see Abbas Alnasrawi, 'Economic Consequences of the Iran-Iraq War', *Third World Quarterly* (July, 1986); Hooshang Amirahmadi, 'War Damage and Reconstruction in the Islamic Republic of Iran', in Amirahmadi and Parvin (1988); and Mansour Farhang 'The Iran-Iraq War', in *World Policy Journal* (fall 1985).

48. See UN Security Council, 5/22863, 31 July 1991.

49. An official of the National Iranian Oil Company said recently, 'We lost 1 million of the best young men in Iran – and for what?' *The Washington Post*, June 7, 1991.

50. See UN Security Council, Document S/23322, December 24, 1991. The figure does not include *indirect* losses due to 'the difficulty in defining their nature and extent'. The total damage in Iranian rials is converted into the US dollar at the rate of Rls 237=$1.

51. *Kayhan Havai*, August 14, 1991, pp. 9 ff.

15

From revolutionary slogans to economic reality

The post-revolution Iranian economy lacked a distinctive, home-grown, innovative, Islamic model. The anti-Shah opposition had an economic ideology that was neither totally Islamic, nor a matter of general consensus. The only common theme supported by all revolutionary factions was the allegation that the economy under the Pahlavis was unhealthy and non-viable. It was unhealthy because of: addiction to oil export revenues; highly inequitable income distribution among social strata and geographic regions; and subservience to superpower interests. It was non-viable because of: perilous dependence on the external world for raw materials, semi-processed goods, management, and capital equipment; excessive military expenditure; and neglect of agriculture in favor of rapid industrialization. There was no consensus of opinion on an appropriate new economic model. In fact, there were profound differences in analysis and outlook between traditional bourgeois elements in and out of the *bazaar* on the one hand, and radical reformers in and out of religious circles on the other.

A DECADE OF TRIALS AND TRIBULATIONS

Caught in the midst of these political cross-currents, the economy initially toyed with various versions of 'divine harmony' – while each group tried to promote its own socio-economic blueprint for the future. With the Iran–Iraq war disrupting normal business activities after 1980, and the radical/interventionist faction rising to power, a statist, command-type economic system emerged after

1982, with government control and wartime regulations gradually replacing the mechanism of the market.

The regime's statist strategy, designed to deal with internal and external challenges, was bent on 'economic stabilization'. To this end, controls and ceilings were imposed on domestic prices and wages; rationing was established on the consumption of basic necessities; the official exchange rate was kept deliberately overvalued; foreign currencies and imports were subjected to strict allocation; capital charges and profits (i.e., interest and dividends) were tightly regulated and kept low; bank credits were restricted; and the establishment of any new industrial enterprise required prior permits. In short, regulation and control encompassed all economic activities from production and foreign trade to distribution and final consumption. Parallel with this highly restrictive strategy, a series of new public agencies sprang up, charged with price control, procurement and distribution, and foreign trade. Also, new laws and rules concerning economic activity were enacted.

As already detailed in Chapter 14, the leadership's experience with this statist/Islamic model was anything but encouraging. The devastating and disruptive war with Iraq bore a large share of the responsibility for the country's misfortunes. But the regime's ambitious politico-economic stance and objectives also had a great bearing on the outcome. The idealistic dream of Ayatollah Khomeini and some of his followers to turn the clock back to Prophet Mohammad's 7th-century rule proved highly impractical. Putting the stamp of early Islam on 20th-century Iran, which had undergone at least half a century of near-total immersion in Western ways, was beyond the ingenuity, charisma, and administrative ability of the Ayatollah and his top aides. As a leading clergyman reluctantly acknowledged, even after a decade of earnest struggle to give the economy an Islamic face, no concrete and practical ways had been found 'to apply Islamic precepts to everyday decisions from banking to the law'. The same point was publicly acknowledged by the republic's President Ali Khamenei on the occasion of the revolution's tenth anniversary on February 11, 1989.[1]

A juxtaposition of the regime's intentions and its final results is highly illuminating. As already indicated, the victorious revolutionaries had promised to reduce Iran's dependence on the outside (especially the Western) world; to diversify the economy so as to cut the government's heavy reliance on oil revenues; to make agriculture the 'pivot of development' and to achieve self-sufficiency in food; to increase non-oil exports and slash imports (especially consumer-goods imports); to put an end to rural migration; to bring down military expenditure and foreign arms purchases; to divert defense outlays towards improving the living conditions of the poor (with better nutrition, housing, health care, and cultural refinement); and, finally, to create a society blessed by spiritual values, which had rejected crass materialism and consumerism.

The outcome, after a decade of endeavor, was great disappointment on almost all fronts. By the end of the 1980s – and the tenth anniversary of the revolution – the Iranian economy was plagued with high unemployment, double-digit inflation, a large budget deficit, a wide balance-of-payments gap, material shortages, power blackouts, air pollution, and over-population. Worse still, *none* of the economic goals enunciated at the outset had been reached, or even approached. The country's dependence on the external world (even the West) was, if anything, greater than ever. Economic diversification, and the reduction of oil's contribution to the economy and the government budget, still remained a distant goal. Agriculture's role in Iran's economic development was anything but crucial, and its self-sufficiency was further than ever from being realized. Rural migration had stubbornly continued. Military expenditure showed no signs of decreasing. A serene, puritanical, and just society was still a dream. In the meantime, corruption, bribery, smuggling, black-marketing, drug addiction, violent crime, and moral degradation were on the rise. The future had arrived, and it did not live up to promises and expectations.

In many respects, the regime's successes and failures were predetermined. Spurred on by revolutionary zeal, and supported by an extensive infrastructure, sizeable capital stock, and a large cadre of trained personnel left from the Shah's time, the Islamic Republic managed to withstand several threats to its rule, sustain a modest level of living for its growing population, and survive a bloody and debilitating war with Iraq. But, hampered by a host of domestic and foreign constraints, it also met many setbacks and reversals. The regime's ability to survive politically, against all the odds, without experiencing internal revolt, vital shortages, widespread starvation, runaway inflation, backbreaking foreign debt, massive unemployment, or even large negative growth ought to be chalked up to its undeniable credit. On the other hand, the inability to satisfactorily achieve any of its professed economic objectives must be considered a definite debit.

Top government officials have been fairly candid in acknowledging the country's economic plight at the end of the 1980s. As already mentioned, President Rafsanjani summed up Iran's economic problems at the time of his election in July 1989 as: the government's uncomfortable internal and external debt; falling real income of wage-earners; a large number of unfinished projects; extensive war damage and inadequate investment during the war years; lagging infrastructure facilities; plant obsolescence; excessive bureaucratic centralization; dependence by consumers and producers on state subsidies; continued deprivation of depressed geographic areas; rising popular expectations (particularly demands from veterans and their families); flight of capital; bank losses; a widening gap between the rich and poor; flourishing smuggling and contraband transactions; and inadequate tax collection.[2]

Another frank dissertation by a senior government official has been even more to the point. Writing in a local periodical, the observer attributes the economy's stagflation in the 1980s (e.g., unemployment, internal and external imbalances, flight of capital, and unhealthy short-term borrowings) mainly to the government's 'hasty and unscientific' economic policies. The overall outcome of these policies, he writes, has been 'increased poverty, economic insecurity, social tension, and rising dependence on oil exports'. The root causes of these problems are seen to lie in wrong pricing mechanisms, wrong monetary and credit policies, wrong production incentives, a poor tax system, and too many public subsidies. Price controls, designed to hold down inflation, are considered responsible for 'stagnation, hoarding, corruption, and a two-tier price system' where a ten-times difference between official and free-market prices favors not the producers, but brokers and intermediaries. Lack of initiative on the part of the nationalized banks is said to have confined their activities to accounting and cashing, ceding the credit field to usurers at home, and short-term 'usance' lenders abroad. Exchange controls and the artificial exchange rates are said to have succeeded in diverting demand towards imports and foreign contracts, and away from domestic production. The result has been recession in exports; unfruitful transactions in foreign currencies; extensive unemployment at home; wastage of domestic capital; and invisible subsidies. The tax system is faulted for disallowing legitimate capital depreciation, discouraging capital accumulation, and encouraging illegal transactions. Restrictions on the size of productive units, and the imposition of output ceilings on these units, are said to have depressed export-oriented production, and reduced capital goods imports. Unwise restrictions and regimentation have created a flourishing unhealthy market for influence peddling, and led to administrative corruption, decline in productivity, and inflationary pressures. Finally, keeping factory-gate prices artificially low in order to subsidize the low-income

classes resulted not only in growing losses for productive enterprises, but also unhealthy rural migration, plus the creation of an
intermediary group which reaped most of the profit.[3] In sum, the
country ended up with inadequate human resources, technical
skills, organization, and management.[4]

THE SHIFT IN ECONOMIC STRATEGY

The ceasefire with Iraq expectedly unleashed repressed demands by
a war-weary and impoverished nation for suitable rewards and
appropriate redemption. The end of hostilities also coincided with
the speedy breakdown of the bipolar world political system and
the gradual break-up of the Soviet empire. Subsequent trends in
the Iranian economy were profoundly influenced by these new
developments.

With the end of the Iran–Iraq war, greater transparency was
allowed in the Islamic regime's economic record. As a result, some
of the early criticisms of the Pahlavis' economic strategy began to
seem rather hasty and premature. Some of the initial populist
proclamations and revolutionary promises started to appear empty
and unrealistic. The overwhelming support the *bazaar* gave to
Ayatollah Khomeini in his revolt against the Shah began to wane.
Merchants and small businessmen who were now dominated by a
statist regime were unhappy about their fate. The lessons of Bani-
Sadr's economic dilettantism and Musavi's stark mismanagement
were not lost on the leadership that came to power after the
ceasefire. In the absence of Ayatollah Khomeini as mediator
between the warring factions, a fresh coalition between President
Rafsanjani and the new Supreme Leader, Ali Khamenei, began to
spearhead a calculated drive towards greater political sobriety and
economic realism.

The emergence of *perestroika* under Mikhail Gorbachev in
Moscow, and the imminent collapse of the centrally controlled
Soviet economy, also played into the new leadership's hands. From
all indications, it was manifestly clear that the unstoppable global
forces marching towards political democracy and economic free
enterprise did not augur well for the viability of Iran's politico-
economic *status quo*. To cope with the inevitable, however, the
leadership confronted a wrenching new dilemma: how to *secularize*
Iran without losing Islamic face. Fundamentalist/hardliners were
adamant that the country's opening to the West, and further
integration in the world economy, was likely to call into question
Ayatollah Khomeini's cardinal precepts, and his spiritual authority,

through gradual erosion of moral and ideological convictions. Whenever they were confronted with the obvious deterioration of the economy during the 'radical' rule of the 1980s, the fundamentalists usually invoked Ayatollah Khomeini's reported dictum that the people should make their choice: either welfare and consumerism, or hardship and independence.[5]

Moderate/pragmatists, however, were convinced that Iran's continued technological and diplomatic isolation threatened the very survival of the revolution and the Islamic Republic through deteriorating economic conditions, middle-class impoverishment, popular discontent, and rising social tension. Challenged by sweeping external pressures for change, stung by criticisms of their post-revolution stabilization strategy, and emboldened by popular sentiments against restriction and regimentation, the heirs to Ayatollah Khomeini's political leadership finally decided to embark on a new course. The new three-pronged strategy was based on reconstruction of war-torn areas and facilities; renewal and expansion of infrastructure badly neglected during the war; and structural adjustment (*ta'dil-e eqtesadi*) aimed at marketization of the economy.

This decisive policy shift applied to both politics and economics. In politics, the early objective of turning the economy back to the Islamic period, and exporting Islamic fundamentalist ideology to neighboring countries, took a new face. The Constitution was amended in favor of a strong presidential government that could interpret Islamic tenets in the public interest. A more conciliatory stance was also adopted in foreign relations. While remaining ostensibly faithful to the Islamic foundations of the revolution, and abiding by the spirit of the 1979 Constitution (as revised), the new public posture changed. Trying to save the slogan by adapting its ideological zeal to pragmatic politics, Hojatol-Islam Rafsanjani urged Iranians to export the Islamic revolution by taking part in every international arena from the United Nations to the Olympics.[6] Exporting the revolution through 'rhetorical fire power', in the opinion of a foreign academic supporter of the Islamic Republic, was to be replaced by more peaceful, practical and persuasive means. Islamic ideas and institutions such as social justice, welfare imperatives, and interest-free banking had to supersede political means or armed struggle.[7]

The launching of the five-year development plan for the first reconstruction period (1989/90–1993/94) set the stage for the new direction toward deregulation, privatization, free enterprise, and a return to the mechanisms of the market. In contrast to the early policy of avoiding foreign financial assistance – considered a threat to economic independence – the Rafsanjani government began to seek long-term external credit from the World Bank and elsewhere.[8]

The post-ceasefire economic recovery, and the need to sustain growth after several years of slump, prompted the leadership to take an even bolder step: reconciliation with the outside (and now largely capitalist) world. The first public declaration of this foreign policy stance was aired at an international petroleum conference held in Isfahan in May 1991. The Islamic Republic's foreign minister opened the meeting by declaring that: 'From a global perspective, a new order is gradually superseding in which economic considerations overshadow political priorities'. The startling significance of this trite statement was its stark contrast with Ayatollah Khomeini's oft-repeated admonition that the Iranian revolution was not meant to raise the *material* standard of living, but to disseminate Islam's *spiritual* values, and to free the world's oppressed billions from the yoke of imperialism and superpower hegemony. At the same conference, Iran's oil minister acknowledged that too high a price for crude oil was inimical to the interests of both producers and consumers. The novelty of this declaration, again, was not in its conventional wisdom, but in its unprecedented support of Saudi Arabia's long-standing position to which the Islamic Republic had always been adamantly opposed within OPEC.

Reflecting the same sentiments in a message read on his behalf at the conference, President Rafsanjani said that, in the new order which replaced the previous bipolar system, 'cooperation should replace confrontation'. In a related gesture of coming to terms with the past, the Islamic Republic called on expatriate Iranian professionals, industrialists, technicians, and managers to return to Iran and participate in the country's reconstruction. Finally, in a major policy address to representatives from the Group of 77 (gathered in Tehran in November 1991 to forge a common position in advance of UNCTAD 8), President Rafsanjani declared his government's intention to expand private ownership and to open up the economy to the outside world. He urged all developing countries to take similar steps in order to catch up with the rich nations, and to redress 'grave inequities' in North–South standards of living. The essential message in all these pronouncements was a pragmatic one: as far as the economy was concerned, the revolution was over.[9]

RAFSANJANI'S PERESTROIKA

While the new team still publicly blames the country's economic ills on the Shah's legacy, the 'imposed' war, natural catastrophes, and external forces hostile to the Islamic revolution, the political leadership and the technocrats in charge of the economy seem to realize that the inexorable economic laws which radical ideologues had stubbornly tried to repeal remain as valid as ever. They seem to feel that the borderline between divine law and economic management has to be carefully redrawn. As a Western diplomat put it, the regime has reached 'the limits of its contradictions'. A senior Iranian official has acknowledged the obvious outcome by admitting that: 'We must get rid of all we borrowed from Stalinistic economics, free ourselves of the bureaucratic tangle'.[10]

With the fate of its political survival in the balance after the ceasefire, the new leadership has also appeared ready to abandon all growth-impeding vestiges of a radical Islamic economy. Often referred to as Rafsanjani's *perestroika*, the objective has been to transform a vastly regulated, badly distorted, and mismanaged economy into an investment-driven, market-oriented, and more efficient system. As part of this economic liberalization policy, concerted efforts have been made towards the marketization and privatization of the economy. The exchange and trading system has been revamped and simplified. Price controls on many goods have been removed or relaxed. Rationing for most consumer items has been eliminated. Fiscal subsidies to producers and consumers have been reduced or terminated. The Iranian rial has been effectively devalued for many imports and for all non-oil exports. Credit policy has been rationalized through higher interest rates and keener competition among commercial banks. Several hundred state enterprises have been offered for sale to the private sector through the Tehran Stock Exchange and other means. And, not least, the rules governing labor relations have been tightened.

The reconversion to a market economy has been reflected in several other decisions which contrast with previous revolutionary slogans and early vows. For example, under a scheme established during the Shah's reign, and now actively followed by the new regime, the Financial Organization for the Expansion of Proprietorship of Production Units is engaged in purchasing shares of state enterprises and offering them to their workers and other state employees.

Another manifestation of the regime's economic liberalization has been its fairly relaxed position toward private foreign investment, joint-ventures, and association with multinational companies. At the time of the revolution, it was difficult to find an anti-Shah tract, writing, or commentary which did not denounce multinationals as the source of all evil. It was in pursuit of this economic xenophobia that all but a handful of foreign firms operating in Iran were ousted in the first year of the revolution.[11] With the launching of the new five-year development plan, however, joint-ventures with foreign enterprises have once again come into vogue. While the feeling in some quarters is still against such ventures, the leadership has boldly thrown its support behind foreign participation in the reconstruction efforts.

A showcase of the new pragmatic approach has also been the designation of several 'free trade zones'. The free trade areas were created by a *Majles* act in February 1990 with a number of special incentives: no taxes, guarantees against nationalization, unrestricted transfer of principal and profit of investment, minimum applications of Islamic law, a relative lack of social constraints, and even the waiver of majority ownership by Iranians. The law was bitterly opposed by radical hardliners as contrary to Iran's national interests; but the government finally prevailed.[12]

Still another sign of the times has been the acceptance by the *Majles* in May 1991 of Iran's increased quota in the International Monetary Fund, under the 9th quota exercise, from SDR 660 million to SDR 1078 million – after having twice refused to accept the country's assigned quota increases in the 7th and 8th quota adjustments during the 1980s. Throughout the first decade of the revolution, the regime shunned any contract with the IMF on the grounds that the latter was an imperialist-dominated institution. Tehran refused to pick up its approved quota which had been painstakingly pursued and obtained by the Shah's government. Had the Islamic Republic agreed to subscribe to its raised quota of SDR 1,076 million in the 7th review (1978/79), its subsequent share would now have reached at least SDR 1.66 billion, or more than 50 per cent, guaranteeing a safe seat on the IMF's board of executive directors. The regime's attempts to revive part of its previously lost shares have so far been unsuccessful.

REFORMS AND REACTIONS

The new liberalization and restructuring measures by the Rafsanjani administration have not gone unchallenged. Islamic fundamentalists and the radical clergy have opposed the government's reforms every step of the way. Followers of the Imam's line have insisted on keeping alive Ayatollah Khomeini's anti-materialism, the need to return to an early Islamic way of life, the export of Islamic revolution, and the establishment of a classless society of Islamic justice, piety and brotherhood. Hardliners in and out of the *Majles* have been protesting against billboards, posters, and advertisements for consumer goods which replaced religious and revolutionary slogans all over town.[13]

Faced with persistent attacks from the hardline fundamentalists, and sensitive to the poignancy of their charges, the 'moderate' clergy and their technocratic collaborators have attempted to present a kinder and gentler Islamic order where: wealth is no longer evil; austerity is not necessarily a virtue; social welfare is not the government's stepchild subservient to ideology; the state is not a big brother; and even consumerism is no longer taboo. In order not to appear as rejecting the policies of earlier Islamic administrations, government officials have embarked on a careful and calculated campaign to provide justification for the new reforms. Thus, the statist and interventionist policies of the Musavi administration are attributed to wartime exigencies and the imperatives of economic stabilization (*tasbit-e eqtesadi*). With the cessation of hostilities, it is painstakingly argued, there is need for structural adjustment (*ta'dil-e eqtesadi*). State officials have gone out of their way to show that the new reforms are within Islamic norms, and were all sanctioned by Ayatollah Khomeini before his death; that privatization does not subvert the Constitution; that links with the outside world would not lead to a loss of economic independence; and that foreign private investment could not erode the Islamic culture and values. The free-market system, in a cabinet minister's words, would result in the uprooting of economic corruption.[14]

Nevertheless, the tug-of-war between the two clerical factions, their newspapers and lay spokesmen continues. The radical group – largely represented by several dailies and some defeated 3rd *Majles* deputies – routinely accuse the government of deviating from the Imam's line and subverting the Constitution. The administration, in turn, is quick to invoke Ayatollah Khomeini's previous consent, and the current spiritual leadership's blessings to justify its policies. Backtracking and mid-course corrections needed to cope with reform-created hardships are explained away as part of the basic strategy. For example, when the consumer price index in 1991/92 rose to more than double the rate of the previous year, and a nationwide clamor arose for restraint in mid-August 1992, the government announced a new program of 'price-labeling' whereby consumers' rights were to be protected against price-gougers and speculators.[15] Acutely aware of the fact that the opposition was quick to portray this price policy reversal as evidence of his failed price de-control and liberalization strategy, President Rafsanjani took great pains in one of his Friday prayer sermons to present the new program as an integral part of that strategy, and a necessary adjustment.[16]

CHANGE AND CONTINUITY

Of all the expected consequences of Iran's 1979 revolution, the fundamentally unchanged status of the economy remains the most puzzling. An epocal event that rightfully ranks with the Russian and Cuban revolutions as one of the great national upheavals of the century has, astonishingly and unlike the other two, left the essential features of the inherited economy undisturbed. While profound and far-reaching changes have occurred in the structure of political power, the economy's institutional bases have remained fundamentally the same. This continuity amidst change stands out as one of the most curious aspects of the Islamic Republic.

Since the fall of the monarchy in February 1979, Iran has undergone considerable change in many respects. *Politically*, a multi-polar system of public decision-making has emerged whereby government policy has become subject to effective checks and balances. The Supreme Leader, the President, the *Majles*, the Council of Guardians, the Assembly of Experts, the Council for the Determination of Expediency and Discernment, and other *loci* of power (e.g., individual grand ayatollahs, the press, and Friday prayer leaders) all exert an influence on national destiny. Although not totally independent of one another in their source of power, nor necessarily receiving their legitimacy from the popular voice, each of these centers can often obstruct a particular decision or help to move others. While the Pahlavi regime was never effectively a one-man rule as commonly believed, its successor has been much more politically decentralized.

Institutionally, several revolutionary organs (*nahad-e engelabi*) have been established to parallel the functions of regular government agencies inherited from the previous regime. Thus *Sepah-e Pasdaran* (the Revolutionary Guards Corps) and *Basij* (a popular army made up mostly of very young or over-aged volunteers from less-favored social classes) have been formed alongside regular armed forces. Neighborhood *komitehs* (committees) took the enforcement of law and order into their own hands side by side with the regular police and gendarmerie units before they were all merged in 1990. The Construction Crusade was placed next to the Plan and Budget Organization as a development agency, and a competitor to the Ministry of Agriculture. A number of semi-private foundations have been given the task of performing parallel public functions, and providing certain public services. Through these duplicate organs, the regime has managed to ensure the fulfilment of its own mandates via its trusted institutions while not risking hazardous political instability or economic chaos by a wholesale replacement of inherited agencies.

Administratively, the Islamic Republic has adopted a basically totalitarian approach (in contrast with the authoritarian character of the Shah's regime). This totalitarianism has been evident in the pervasiveness of Islamic contingents in almost all centers of economic decision-making. Every public or parastatal economic organization is obligated to have a representative of the clergy on its board; every ministry, agency or bureau has an Islamic committee in its midst; all major trade unions are run by an Islamic workers' council. The presence of these Islamic 'commissars' in the midst of the major economic organizations has turned the state bureaucracy into fragmented, semi-independent, and uncoordinated centers of power. With religious representatives or managers beholden to no single source of religious authority or emulation (*marja'-e taqlid*), decisions made by a given bureau (even a court of law) are often ignored, delayed, or countermanded by other bureaus. Due to this pulverization of authority, the outcome of any economic effort is never certain until the result is actually in hand. The uncertainty inherent in such a system continues to be one of the regime's major handicaps.[17]

Notwithstanding these political, administrative, and institutional changes, and despite the Islamic Republic's efforts to present its management of the Iranian economy as truly 'Islamic' – and diametrically opposed to the Shah's – a good measure of continuity seems to have been the rule rather than the exception. During the 14 years since the revolution, the Iranian economy has been managed not so much according to Islamic ideals and ideas, but largely in an *ad hoc*, improvised, pragmatic, and not infrequently contradictory manner. While the slogans of street demonstrators have continued to display a pro-Islamic and anti-Western tone, the essential guiding light of the economy has been a mixture of capitalism, socialism, populism, and pragmatism with a dose of Islamic topping – an economic system not essentially different from the Shah's time except for outward appearances. And, apart from some cosmetic and superficial changes in the nomenclature, economic reality has triumphed over revolutionary slogans.[18]

Without trying to over-emphasize the prevalence of continuity, reference can be made to some striking similarities between the two regimes. The Shah often spoke of five imperative tenents of social justice under his 'White Revolution': the right of every citizen to a decent minimum of food, clothing, housing, medical care, and education.[19] Not coincidentally, Article 43 of the 1979 Constitution also singles out exactly the same 'basic' rights in similar order. In another context, the Shah defined one of the main principles of his 'economic democracy' as the absence of exploitation of the fruits of a man's labor by other men.[20] The Islamic opposition subscribed to the same slogan. The so-called *Ashura* Manifesto of Islamic demonstrators in December 7, 1978 – which Ayatollah Khomeini called a 'referendum' on the monarchy – had, as one of its main demands (and in astonishingly similar language), the eradication of 'exploitation of man by man'.[21] The Shah's economy democracy emphasized 'growth first, distribution later'. The Islamic Republic initially repudiated this strategy; it advocated 'social justice first, prosperity later'. However, faced with declining output, growing unemployment, persistent inflation, reduced private investment, material shortages, and rising popular discontent, the Rafsanjani government finally had to make an about-face. Social justice, once an overriding priority in Iran's Islamic economics, has now in effect taken a back seat to rapid economic growth.

Under close scrutiny, interesting parallels can also be found in the conduct of domestic economic policy. In fighting a new surge of inflation, the Islamic Republic early in 1989 passed a law requiring shopkeepers to affix government-controlled price labels on their goods, or face being hauled before the courts as 'hoarders and profiteers'. Remarkably akin to the Shah's 14th principle of the White Revolution – price stabilization and campaign against profiteering – the new law targeted the symptom rather than the cause of the price rise. Instead of stemming excess demand, or increasing needed supplies, the government edict in both instances induced shopkeepers to hide their wares, thus contributing to yet higher prices.

Privatization through the sale of nationalized industries is another example. The Shah's program to denationalize state factories (the 3rd and 13th principles of the White Revolution), was designed to tap private funds, and to increase industrial productivity. The Rafsanjani government's post-ceasefire decision to return public enterprises to the private sector contains similar goals. It has also faced similar hurdles. Since the most eligible candidates for sale, at both times, have been overstaffed, unprofitable, debt-ridden, under-capitalized, and politicized state companies tied up in legal complications, there have been few customers except at fire-sale prices. Furthermore, since the private sector has been invited to invest in new enterprises when the general public climate has been regarded as insufficiently stable, secure, or pro-business, the necessary confidence for such undertakings has been lacking. In both cases, private businessmen have hesitated to risk their fortunes without solid assurances of a safe environment for making profit.

Even in the delicate area of foreign economic relations, the regime has been unable to separate itself totally from the past. The conditions stipulated by a top government official in mid-1992 for welcoming foreign private investment to Iran during the current five-year plan (that is, 'meeting domestic needs, generating exports, and bringing in high technology') are identical to those prevailing during the Shah's time.[22] Some of the obstacles to such investment (such as liberal labor laws, shortage of trained workers, and systemic inefficiency) may also be the same, although the Islamic Republic's brand of bureaucracy, its anti-Western stance, its moral codes, and other restrictions, may present additional obstacles to such prospective ventures.[23]

Still further, the continuity of economic strategy and policy has been plainly evident in the current structure and on-going orientation of the Iranian economy. After more than 14 years of Islamic rule, and despite the Islamic Republic's declared intention to alter the economy's development course, few radical changes in the shape and outlook of the economy can yet be detected. Iran is still an oil-based economy, dependent on foreign supplies and technology for almost all of its basic development and modern defense needs, as well as for a considerable portion of its food consumption. Industry continues to enjoy top priority in national planning. Services still constitute the largest sector of the economy and largest provider of employment. Consumerism, and people's craving for a good life, remain as popular as ever. The list of economic bottlenecks has hardly changed.[24]

Nor has the state bureaucracy been prevented from sinking deeper and deeper into inefficiency and corruption. In fact, in Iran's traumatized society, where maintenance of law and order has fallen into the hands of innumerable political claimants, the old and endemic Third World corruption, rooted in poverty and discrimination, has become widely institutionalized. A government officeholder – be it the local prosecutor, ecclesiastic judge, *komiteh* chieftain, revolutionary guardsman, or strategically-placed functionary – has been able to exact a tithe for performing his duty, or ignoring an offence. Frequent reports in the local press regarding state employees' malfeasance are dwarfed by myriad stories recounted by individuals who have come face to face with the 'lawless', inefficient, uncoordinated, and flagrantly abusive bureaucracy. With average government salaries continually lagging behind inflation, many public servants have become independent tax collectors for themselves. As recounted not only by ordinary citizens, but also by the regime's official newspapers, every transaction with the government has now acquired its open private price. This practice – direct taxation without state intermediation – seems to have been readily accepted by all, even if officially or privately denounced and deplored.[25]

One finds also a curious similarity of perception regarding Iran's international position on the part of successive leaders. In the midst of the oil boom and Iran's rising economic star in 1975, Mohammad Reza Shah ordered the government not to refer to his country as a 'Third World nation' any longer, since Iran was thought ready to join the ranks of industrial economies. On November 25, 1991, President Rafsanjani, inaugurating a gas distribution project near Tehran, told his audience: 'Iran is not a poor country and should not be classified as a Third World nation. We can turn Iran into a prosperous and a model country, capable of helping Islamic and poor countries'.[26]

Finally, even the Shah's quest for the much derided 'Great Civilization' seems to have come curiously close to becoming one of the regime's new goals. President Rafsanjani's 'ideal' (i.e. ultimate) goal, according to a top aide and confidant, is 'to bring Iran to the highest level of its economic, industrial, and cultural potential'. This objective is, in turn, defined as creating a new image and reputation for the country, giving it a position of power in the region, with the ability to meet the people's economic needs.[27]

In short, few fundamental changes can be readily identified in the structure or orientation of the Iranian economy. Slogans have changed from the Shah's time, but economic realities remain as inexorable as ever. Economic warlords have new faces; but basic economic relationships among productive factors are not materially altered. The new rich are now a different group; so are the new poor. But income gaps have, if anything, probably grown farther apart. Power is now exercised by a new ruling class; but the rule of law seems as distant as ever. The bureaucracy has grown out of all proportion and become far less efficient.[28] An Islamic government has been firmly established, but the promised Islamic social justice remains a dream. A sombre dress code, and a drastic ban on drinking, gambling, and display of affection in public, have been brutally enforced in order to fight Westernization; but the public's yearning for most things Western has hardly been dented.

In sum, the principal economic challenges that faced the Shah's regime have, if anything, become more serious and more problematic under the Islamic Republic. Leading the list of these critical problems are: controlling the recent demographic explosion; reversing the troubling rural migration; creating enough productive work for new entrants into the job market; reducing the acute shortage of urban housing and curbing real estate speculation; winning the race between the rising number of students and the number of new classrooms and teachers at all levels of education; and, finally, redressing the steady decline in the standard of living.

Assuming that rapid economic growth and rising standards of living will enjoy high priority in the forthcoming second development plan (as they did in the first), these problems can neither be ignored nor explained away by ideological slogans. And the regime's success in coping with them ultimately depends upon substitution of truth over dogma; respect for personal freedom, where individual liberties lead to the betterment of the human condition; emphasis on private enterprise over state operation where no overriding public interest is evident; and further integration into the global economy.

NOTES

1. See *The New York Times*, July 17, 1988, and February 12, 1989.
2. *Kayhan Havai*, August 28, 1991, p. 11.
3. Passenger cars, for example, were reportedly sold by a state factory at Rls 710,000 each, absorbing Rls 700,000 loss on each unit. The same unit was then resold in the free market at Rls 7 to 8 million – providing quick profit to favored middlemen.
4. See 'Senior Officials Outline Policies', *Iran Focus*, May 1990, pp. 14–15.
5. 'Khomeini Predicts Hardships for Iran', *Reuters*, January 10, 1989.
6. *The New York Times*, January 2, 1989.
7. *The New York Times*, January 24, 1989.
8. Liesl Graz, 'Iran Under Rafsanjani', *Middle East International*, January 5, 1990.
9. *The New York Times*, May 28, 1991.
10. See *The New York Times*, July 2, 1991, and May 28, 1991.
11. *US News and World Report*, December 3, 1979, p. 31. For the list of foreign firms whose operation was terminated, see *Mossallanejad* (1986), pp. 147–153.
12. See 'Island of Laissez-Faire', *The New York Times*, July 2, 1991; and The Economist Intelligence Unit, 'Iran: Country Report No. 3', 1991.
13. See *Kayhan Havai*, March 11, and June 17, 1992; and *MEED*, November 15, 1991.
14. *Iran Focus*, January 1991, p. 15.

15. *Kayhan Havai*, August 9, 1992, p. 10.
16. *Kayhan Havai*, September 2, 1992, p. 9.
17. See *The New York Times*, March 23, 1992.
18. In one of the latest moves to finesse the issue of interest-free banking, three ranking members of the Council of Guardians have suggested that interest payments by banks – called 'realized profit' since 1983 – should now be termed 'expected' or 'interim' profit, and that loans granted by financial institutions should be labelled commercial 'facilities'. See *Iran Times*, September 18, 1992.
19. See R. K. Karanjia, *The Mind of a Monarch* (London: Allen & Unwin, 1977), pp. 146, 150.
20. *Iran's Domestic and Foreign Policy* (Washington: Embassy of Iran, 1976), pp. 12, 33.
21. Akbar Khalili, *Gam be Gam ba Engelab* (Step by Step with the Revolution) (Tehran: Soroush, 1360 [1981]), pp. 114–116.
22. See *The New York Times*, June 29, 1992, and Jahangir Amuzegar, *Iran: An Economic Profile* (Washington: The Middle East Institute, 1977), p. 216.
23. For a discussion of similarities in the Pahlavi monarchy and the Islamic Republic on foreign policy issues, see S. T. Hunter, *Iran and the World: Continuity in a Revolutionary Decade* (Bloomington: Indiana University Press, 1990).
24. Compare the list presented by the head of the Plan and Budget Organization in March 1983 and another cited by President Rafsanjani in August of 1990. *Ettela'at*, 28 Esfand 1362, and *Kayhan Havai*, August 14, 1990.
25. See *US News and World Report*, April 15, 1991, pp. 34–36, and, particularly, *Kayhan Havai*, July 9, 1992.
26. *Kayhan Havai*, December 4, 1991, p. 4.
27. See Elaine Sciolino, 'Rafsanjani Drives for Goals', *The New York Times*, April 19, 1992.
28. In 1980, one ministry, with an annual budget of Rls 850 million, was in charge of the whole industrial sector. In 1991, there were three ministries, with a budget of Rls 11 billion, overseeing the same sector.

Conclusion

An examination of the Iranian economy under the Islamic Republic would not be complete without brief reference to the country's current politico-economic problems, and a glance at its prospects.

As detailed in the foregoing fifteen chapters, Iran's economy during 1979–92 has been plagued with severe internal and external disequilibria. Reflecting these serious imbalances have been widespread wage/price distortions, a decline in the standard of living, the proliferation of parasitic activities, and a host of other socioeconomic ills.

While some of these disequilibria may have been caused by forces largely beyond the regime's control, there is no doubt that the government's monetary, fiscal, and foreign exchange policies were mainly responsible for exacerbating the impact of those forces. And there can be no question that without an investment-friendly environment and without supporting politico-economic policies, the prospects could hardly be brighter.

The outcome of the nationwide elections of the 4th *Majles* held in April and May 1992 was widely interpreted as confirmation of President Rafsanjani's pragmatic/nationalist policies, and a good omen for sustained economic growth and political stability. The first year of the current legislature, however, have belied all those expectations. Whether the new *Majles* can still surprise its legion of skeptics remains to be seen in the light of past experience and forthcoming events.

LESSONS IN RETROSPECT

Between 1978/79 and 1991/92, the economy's political framework went through three distinct phases. First there was a two-year period of ideological turmoil when the nation's political arena witnessed a power struggle between various revolutionary factions. The second phase, roughly corresponding to the duration of the Iran–Iraq war, was dominated by religious hardliners and theocratic socialists. The third phase following the ceasefire with Iraq has been characterized as one of reconstruction and structural adjustment.

Each of these political phases has had its own distinct economic model. The first phase, 1979–81, saw the state poised to make a total break with the past. Prevailing in intellectual circles was a novel brand of economic theory called 'divine harmony' whose basic premise was not *scarcity* and the need for resource allocation, but *plenty* and the task of income redistribution. This amorphous model was short-lived as was the political fortune of its author, Abol Hassan Bani-Sadr. The second period was that of wartime restrictions and big-brother protection. The economic model adopted by the government was an Indian–Soviet variety characterized by economic insularity and a tendency toward self-sufficiency, domination of the state over the economy, denunciation of consumerism, and emphasis on import substitution rather than export promotion. The third period, 1989 to the present, has followed a nationalist/pragmatist stance under what may be called a Chinese–Saudi Arabian model where a capitalist, free-enterprise, marketized economy is to coexist with non-capitalist ideology as its ultimate point of reference and political beacon.

The overall economic development over these three periods point to three broad conclusions. First, despite the new regime's earnest desire to break with the past, the economy's basic character has not been changed into a distinctly Islamic mold. Except for some cosmetic and superficial changes in the nomenclature and the façade, no Islamic economic model has been devised. Abstracting from the slogans and metaphors, the economy's structure and direction bear scant relation to the regime's early intentions and designs. In fact, the Islamic Republic which won the revolution by effectively turning the Pahlavis' economic strategy into symbols of weakness and failure appears now to be moving in the direction of similar policies as part of its own economic platform. The irony in the government's current reconstruction and restructuring programs is inescapable. What was considered a bankrupt and decadent politico-economic landscape is now being passed off as a legitimate blueprint for action. This policy reversal reflects the impossibility of managing an oil-based and petro-dollar-led economy self-sufficiently and independent of the rest of the world – as the Islamic revolutionaries intended and promised.

Second, the attempt to reconcile even a watered-down 'Islamic' economic ideology with the underlying characteristics of a modern, semi-industrial economy has proved more difficult than initially expected. Thus, some of the thorny socio-economic problems for which the Shah's regime was called to task – and which an Islamic economy was supposed to remedy – have actually been intensified. In addition to inflation, power blackouts, water shortage, traffic congestion, and air pollution, which have all exceeded the levels prevailing before the revolution, other problems have been created or aggravated. According to reports published in the local press and recited by travellers, serious crime has increased, white-collar offences have been on a steep rise, and drug addiction has reached 2 million inhabitants despite relentless executions of drug dealers throughout the country. Submission to the moral and spiritual teachings of Islam has been conspicuous by its absence in many vital areas. Nepotism, cronyism, corruption, and blatant extortion of the assets of the old ruling class are rampant.[1]

Third, while the official policy has consistently aimed at imposing an ascetic and puritanical 'Islamic' value system onto traditional Persian culture, objective reality has triumphed over ideological dogma. The 'cultural engineering' seems to have produced contradictions, deception, and escape instead of spiritual unity (*vahdat-e kalameh*) or social harmony (*ommat-e vahed*). The regime's experimentation with the economy under an 'Islamic' banner has triggered a profound and far-reaching backlash which the leadership may not wish to acknowledge, but can neither easily ignore nor escape.

The Islamic Republic's critics at home and abroad tend to interpret the recent policy reversals towards privatization, deregulation, and market discipline as the beginning of a return to the old way of life, or what is known in Iran as 'Westoxication'. The regime's sympathizers, on the other hand, argue that the new 'structural adjustment strategy' is not meant to abandon, or even de-emphasize, revolutionary principles. The pragmatic economic policies adopted by the Rafsanjani government, they contend, are not to be regarded as a deviation from Islamic idealism. Nor should ideological moderation be taken to signal any fissure in the theocratic state. The turnaround, it is insisted, is only a new *tactic* chosen to achieve the same revolutionary and religious objectives.

Perhaps. But a more plausible view is to regard the change as *de facto* recognition of the inevitable.

THE PRESENT QUANDARY

From all indications the regime is now determined to make up for the 'lost decade'. The Rafsanjani administration seems resolved to increase the economy's efficiency through speedy marketization and deregulation; to improve social equity through expansion of social services (particularly health and education); and to ensure balanced economic growth through increased investment in non-oil industries using the proceeds from exports of hydrocarbons, as well as foreign joint-ventures. With eventual restoration of political stability and the return of business confidence, it is now hoped that a large part of domestic liquidity finds its way into productive endeavors, and part of the previously exported capital repatriated. In short, the regime's structural adjustment policies are said to be moving in the right direction. The challenges, however, are formidable.

To begin with, the enormity of the regime's economic task can hardly be exaggerated. The damage inflicted on the economy by revolutionary dislocations, the war, and economic mismanagement can only be repaired with time and concerted effort. With per capita real income in 1991/92 down to 62 per cent of the pre-revolution level (Table 14.1), it might take some 20–25 years – even under a highly optimistic scenario[2] – for the people again to be able to enjoy a standard of living equal to that of 1977/78, unless a new economic miracle takes place. The revolution's 'costs' in economic terms have been staggering.[3] To cut the restoration and recuperation period to, say, ten or fifteen years, would require a much faster growth – something in the order of 9–10 per cent a year without interruption.

Judged by the regime's own published data, while the economy's upward trend since the ceasefire has reversed the downward course of the three previous years, serious structural and political problems still remain to be solved, and the new challenges that have emerged must be dealt with. Output growth and lower inflation in the first two years after the ceasefire have been due in part to such fortuitous circumstances as good rainfall, benefits derived from the Gulf War, availability of additional resources (particularly foreign exchange released from the Iran–Iraq war), the presence of excess industrial capacity, and increased short-term foreign credit. These favorable circumstances may not, however, be long-lived. Inflation has already reappeared as a problem due to a *de facto* devaluation of the rial, an increased money supply, the lifting of controls, and higher wages and salaries granted to industrial workers and public employees. At the same time, a substantial increase in the 1992/93 and 1993/94 budgetary outlay seems to reaffirm the government's inability to reduce its size, or raise its productivity. The freedom given to non-oil exporters to sell their foreign exchange proceeds in the free market has helped increase foreign sales. However, these proceeds, no longer in government hands, have been used to import 'luxury' consumer items rather than capital and investment goods.

The new liberalization and reform measures have further aggravated the plight of the poor and fixed-income groups, and renewed a frantic call in the *Majles* and elsewhere to continue (and even increase) fiscal subsidies. The continuation of food and other subsidies, however, is likely to impede or postpone the needed structural adjustment. In one of his Friday prayer sermons, President Rafsanjani highlighted the plight of his government by referring to this fiscal burden.[4] The government battle for harnessing the 'supra-governmental' *bonyads* also remains a nearly heroic task. These clergy-dominated giant foundations – operating as semi-independent manufacturers, farmers, traders, importers, and real estate developers – cannot be prised free without shaking the regime's very foundations and threatening its power base. The government's technocratic elite is still subservient to the clergy's established authority and status. It may take years before the regime can rid itself of its major power brokers.

Finally, and by far the most stubborn obstacle facing the economy, is the difficulty of reconciling free-market principles with the 'Islamic' precepts incorporated in Iran's 1979 Constitution. Such concepts as the primacy of consumer sovereignty, sanctity of private property, legitimacy of the profit motive, propriety of capital accumulation and individual enrichment, acceptability of material comfort, and separation of faith from science, seem to present irreconcilable differences with the 'Islamic' values propagated by Iranian clerical authorities. The Moslems' duty of 'enjoining good and forbidding evil' is widely interpreted by large groups in the Iranian religious establishment to mean: shunning capital and capitalists as the root of evil; renouncing materialism; cherishing frugality, self-sacrifice, and wealth-sharing; rejecting competition for bigger profits; fighting the satanic lure of greed; disdaining concentration of wealth; acknowledging the superiority of the faithful over experts; forbidding interest on loans; and accepting the supremacy of social justice and equitable distribution of income over social welfare.[5] The clearest reaffirmation of this conflict can be seen in the guidelines given to the president and the council of ministers by Iran's head of state, Ali Khamenei, in August 1992 when he said: 'Free-market economics is a Western concept, and we are not followers of the West. Ours is a proper Islamic approach to the needs of our own society, and the exigencies of our own order'.[6] Among the regime's familiar demons, Western capitalism is high on the list.

While the regime vehemently denies foreign press reports concerning a rift within the top leadership, pre-agenda speeches in the *Majles* and lengthy editorials in local newspapers testify to a bitter and endless debate on the choice of an appropriate economic model. Left-of-center Islamic fundamentalists still rail against the so-called new world order based on 'super-capitalism', and consider the Islamic government's comprehensive and direct intervention in the economy as the sole safeguard against sectoral imbalances and social injustice. They are against limitless foreign direct investment, wholesale privatization of industry and agriculture, price decontrol, and exchange devaluation. Technocratic moderates and pragmatists, by contrast, root for an outward-looking, integrated, and free economy.

Given the depth and complexity of this ideological conflict, the prospects for real economic progress in the short run remain contingent upon the adoption of a consensual national agenda, backed by appropriate structural adjustment measures and forward-looking policy reforms on both the domestic and foreign fronts. In the economic arena, the exchange and trade system needs to be further overhauled toward liberalization. Significant reforms must be made in the fiscal policy field through widening of the tax base, improvement of tax elasticity, and greater diligence in tax collection. Hidden subsidies should be gradually replaced by direct assistance such as negative-income compensation to the poorer strata in society. Harmful controls over prices and wages should be discontinued, and greater flexibility allowed in market price formulation. More competition must be introduced among commercial banks, and there should be progressive increases in the share of the private sector in total credit allocation. Government administration should be streamlined through the consolidation of duplicate ministries and agencies. The state's regular expenditures should be reduced in favor of infrastructural investments, coupled with reduced budget deficits. Speedier steps should be taken toward privatizing non-strategic public enterprises, improving the accountability of parastatal organizations, and cutting down budgetary losses of fat and lazy government corporations.

Other distortions, rigidities, and imbalances must also be eliminated. Serious measures should be taken to reduce the attractiveness of unproductive activities (for example, multi-layered distribution networks, petty trades, and duplicate services) in favor of investment of money and labor in agriculture and industry. Indeterminate boundaries in the public, cooperative and private sectors under the current Constitution ought to be more precisely delineated, and their interrelations clarified. Uncertainty should be removed regarding legitimate private ownership, foreign trade engagements, land tenure, and the status of confiscated properties belonging to individuals rightly or wrongly associated with the previous regime. It is also necessary to provide adequate incentives for private investors, and to take full advantage of the human resource potential (particularly women) at home and abroad.[7]

On the external front, efforts should be made to transcend the current diplomatic isolation and to improve relations with the outside world, in order to be able to attract foreign capital, management, and technology badly needed for the country's internationally competitive development. Needless to say, any new defense build-up beyond the level necessary to deter foreign aggression — that is, any attempt to gain politico-military prominence in the region, to dominate regional security arrangements, or to foster ideological and religious ambitions in neighboring countries — is likely to further complicate the task of domestic economic reconstruction and growth.

Beyond the immediate and short term, Iran's long-term economic problems call for a series of additional reforms in domestic and foreign strategies. Internally, there is need for effective population control, proper resource mobilization, improved labor productivity, enhanced international competitiveness, reduced income disparity, and a clean bureaucracy. On the external front, the need is for a credible foreign policy stance devoid of xenophobia, religious intolerance, political subversion, and hegemonic intention — a policy within accepted international norms of diplomacy, observance of human rights, and a search for peace and stability in the region and elsewhere.

What seems certain is that without a substantial restructuring of the economy and foreign policy along these lines, sustained economic recovery and continued real growth will be stifled. But making reasonable headway toward these objectives requires the rethinking of a number of political, ideological, and even constitutional preferences, priorities and perceptions over which there seems as yet to be no national consensus.

POLITICAL DILEMMAS

The Pandora's box that such basic constitutional, political, and economic restructuring is bound to open will be a formidable one. In the first place, the needed reforms are not without cost. If the experience of Eastern Europe and the former Soviet Union can serve as a guide, Rafsanjani's *perestroika* (that is, the raising of taxes, rationalizing of interest rates, cutting off subsidies, liberalizing trade, and linking wage hikes to productivity) will have similar widely unpopular repercussions. These restructuring measures, although ultimately rewarding, are bound, in the short run, to produce further inflation, unemployment, bankruptcies, and deprivation – developments that are unwelcome not only to the domestic opposition, but to an overwhelming majority of the rank-and-file. It thus remains to be seen how this 'surgery without anaesthetic' can be performed on and tolerated by the patients.

Secondly, after fourteen years of war, austerity, deprivation, unemployment, inflation, shortages, and sacrifices, the people now expect the leadership to provide them with a new and credible socio-economic agenda for the future. The past objectives of saving the revolution, winning the war with Iraq, and preserving the Islamic Republic have all been achieved, or have outlived their appeal. The much-heralded political and economic independence from East and West must now be supplemented by a fuller and freer economic life. Living conditions must be palpably improved if popular support is to continue. In short, demonizing the Pahlavi regime and sanctifying the revolution will no longer suffice. As a Western reporter put it, for the first time since the revolution, no outside force can be blamed for the absence of prosperity – not the Shah's policies, not the revolutionary turmoil, not the 'imposed war', not a hostile *Majles*.[8]

However, any economic initiatives for carrying out needed policy reforms are fraught with high political risks, and confront the regime with another political dilemma. The leadership may wish to proceed with the new reforms only within the confines of an 'Islamic' fundamentalist order. However, the momentum of liberalization may be hard to stop. In the same way that *style* pushed to the limit may become *essence*, tactical maneuvers also have a way of becoming an accepted strategy, if not an implicit objective. Revolutionary purity may not be easily immunized against non-revolutionary practices.

Interestingly enough, this point has not been lost on the domestic opposition. The radical faction that is now challenging the government from within the clerical establishment have already intensified their criticism of the Rafsanjani administration in a new way. Referring to the government's liberalization measures obliquely as part of the 'enemy's cultural onslaught', a relentless campaign has been launched against the 'experts and specialists' who, backed by high government officials, tend to ignore Islamic values and follow the West's 'debauched culture'. A theologian on the Council of Guardians warns: 'If efficiency is the criterion, let the liberals in; and then read the last rites of the revolution'.[9]

The ultimate dilemma for the regime is how to contain the momentum that will be generated by economic restructuring without negating its beneficial results. Most analysts believe that the new and needed *economic* reforms, if successful, would be more than likely to lead to a demanding *political* climate. The abandonment of economic insularity, adoption of free market and private enterprise, attraction of foreign investment and technology, and further integration into the world community are bound to unleash fresh popular demands for truly democratic elections, greater personal freedoms, respect for human rights, and the emancipation of women and minorities. Any attempts to meet these demands are certain to undercut the very status and power of the ruling clergy, and challenge the incumbents' monopoly on statecraft. And therein lies the gravest challenge yet to the theocracy's survival. To ward off this threat (or to cope with it), the leadership needs every bit of ingenuity, courage, cunning, charisma – and luck – that it can summon.

POSTSCRIPT

The basic data and analysis of this book extend through March 1992. Certain subsequent developments, however, have made it necessary to update the discussion through March 1993.

After the hopeful elections of the 4 *Majles* in April–May 1992, most analysts predicted the dawning of a kinder and gentler Islamic regime, with increased political freedom, reduced social restrictions, and promised economic reform. By the end of the year, however, those predictions still remain to be realized. In fact, the revolutionary fervor that appeared to be subsiding only a few months before, seemed to be on the rise again under the banner of fighting the Western 'cultural onslaught'. The socio-cultural backlash was accompanied by new doubts about full-speed economic restructuring. President Rafsanjani's successful mobilization of 'moderate' elements in the spring elections was unexpectedly followed by a process of demobilization in favor of the *status quo*.

The government's structural adjustment program hit serious snags on both domestic and foreign fronts. Internally, effective depreciations of the Iranian rial and the elimination of certain subsidies caused the consumer price index to more than double in 1991/92 and to remain at that level in 1992/93. Since the record trade gap and the unprecedented current account deficit in 1991/92 could no longer be financed, imports had to be cut. Falling oil prices and the declining value of the US dollar vis-à-vis the currencies of Iran's major trading partners during much of 1992 placed Bank Markazi's hard currency reserves under considerable strain, causing continued delays in letter-of-credit payments. The country's short-term debt in the form of 'usance' reportedly reached $13 billion, and export credit agencies in the West refused to grant further credit to Iranian importers without Bank Markazi guarantees.

Externally the government's efforts to obtain badly needed long-term foreign financing and technology were thwarted by the growing perception of the Islamic Republic as a new international menace. Iran's rapid military build-up and foreign press reports about the country's nuclear ambitions raised new fears and suspicion regarding Tehran's expansionist designs. Accusing Iran of the unlawful takeover of Abu Musa island in the Persian Gulf, and the supply of arms and funds to Islamic militants in Lebanon, Sudan, Algeria, Egypt and elsewhere, a US–Arab campaign was launched to isolate and contain it. The US Congress passed a bill in October 1992 banning exports of advanced weapons and technology to Iran, and urging other industrialized countries to follow suit.[10]

Faced with the rather bleak prospect of obtaining needed foreign exchange, renewed inflationary pressures, and considerable opposition from the newly elected *Majles* deputies, President Rafsanjani announced on December 1, 1992, the decision to abandon his original plan to unify the multi-tiered exchange rates by March 1993. Not willing to give the economy 'a sudden shock', the government chose to 'separate the path of exchange-rate unification from reforms aimed at balancing the economy'.

Challenged by these new developments, Rafsanjani's reform program has reached a fateful crossroad. Further delays in rectifying current cost/price distortions, and allowing continued uncertainty about the trade and exchange system are likely to make subsequent adjustment and normalization much costlier and more painful. But classic shock therapy, given the current fragile state of the economy, would be fraught with incalculable risks of social unrest and political instability. If it is to find its way through the impasse, now more than ever before the regime needs the full support of a national consensus at home, and a much friendlier image abroad.

NOTES

1. See 'Clergy Capitalism', *The Wall Street Journal*, May 5, 1992; and 'A frank talk with the President', *Kayhan Havai*, July 9, 1992.
2. This assumes an average annual real economic growth rate of 5 per cent – the average for the World Bank's group of middle-income countries during 1965–1990 – and an annual population growth of no more than 2.7 per cent (Iran's own current five-year plan's target).
3. Had the country's annual growth rate of over 9 per cent on average during 1965–1978 continued, with population growth limited to no more than 2.7 per cent a year, real GDP in 1990/91 would have been 2.5 times larger, rather than 3 per cent smaller, than the 1977/78 level. Real per capita income would have been at least twice as much, rather than only about 60 per cent.
4. According to the president, the government bought wheat, sugar, and cooking oil from producers and sold them to consumers at subsidized prices that recouped only 7–8 per cent of their costs. Some 1.2 mb/d of oil products were delivered to households and businesses virtually free, as not even actual costs of their delivery were covered. Domestic airlines did not cover more than a fraction of even their variable costs. See *Kayhan Havai*, March 11, 1992, and April 22, 1992.
5. For a partial list of these tenets, see the statement by the 'Supreme leader' in *Kayhan Havai*, July 22, 1992, pp. 3, 14, and other articles in the same issue.
6. *Kayhan Havai*, September 2, 1992, p. 3.
7. Although women constitute nearly 49 per cent of the population, they provide only 18 per cent of the active labor force. See *Kayhan Havai*, June 17, 1992, p. 4.
8. *The New York Times*, April 14, 1992.
9. *Foreign Broadcast Information Service*, 11 August, 1992, p. 62.
10. For the major provisions of the bill in brief see *MEED*, December 4, 1992.

Table 1.1
Gross Domestic and National Product
The Fifth Development Plan, 1352–1356 (1973/74–1977/78)
(In billions of Iranian rials at 1974/75 prices)

	1352 1973/74	1353 1974/75	1354 1975/76	1355 1976/77	1356[1] 1977/78
Agriculture[2]	280	290	304	326	327
Oil	1448	1434	1259	1384	1363
Industry[3]	331	385	475	601	592
Service[4]	743	1026	1205	1518	1642
Imputed service charges[5]	−64	−109	−138	−170	−182
GDP at factor cost	2738	3026	3105	3659	3923
Net indirect taxes	100	64	71	99	121
GDP at market prices	2838	3090	3176	3758	3864
Consumption	1362	1819	2055	2409	2521
Gross investment	463	529	875	1181	1083
Net foreign trade	1010	802	321	340	95
Errors & omissions	−121	−95	−88	37	382
Changes in stock	124	35	13	−209	−217
GDE at market price	2838	3090	3176	3758	3864
Net factor income	−36	−11	−14	1	−38
GNP at market prices	2802	3079	3162	3759	3826
Terms-of-trade adjustment	−411	–	−34	69	108
GNP (adjusted)	2391	3079	3128	3690	3934

Source: Bank Markazi, *Hesabhay-e Melli-e Iran, 1338–1356* (Iran's National Accounts 1959/60–1977/78)

[1] Original figures.
[2] Including livestock, fisheries, and forestry.
[3] Including manufacturing, construction, water, power, and gas.
[4] Including transport and communications, banking and insurance, trade, and social services.
[5] Imputed service charges are explained in the source.

Table 1.2
Sectoral Trends during the Fifth Plan, 1973/74–1977/78
(Annual percentage change at constant 1974/75 prices)

	1352 1973/74	1353 1974/75	1354 1975/76	1355 1976/77	1356 1977/78	1352–56
Agriculture[1]	6.0	3.5	4.8	7.3	0.3	4.4
Oil	9.2	−1.0	−12.2	9.9	−1.6	0.9
Industry[2]	22.1	16.3	23.4	26.5	−1.6	17.5
Services[3]	4.5	37.9	17.5	25.8	8.2	18.3
GDP (factor cost)	9.2	10.5	2.6	17.8	2.3	8.5

Source: Bank Markazi, *Iran's National Accounts, 1959/60–1977/78*.

[1] Including livestock, fisheries and forestry.
[2] Including manufacturing, construction, water, power, and gas.
[3] Including transport and communications, banking and insurance, trade, and social services.

Table 1.3
Selected Data on the Iranian Economy
1963/64–1977/78
(Percentage share in total)

	1342 (1963/64)	1347 (1968/69)	1352 (1973/74)	1356 (1977/78)
Gross domestic product[1]	100.0	100.0	100.0	100.0
Agriculture	30.3	21.8	13.1	8.5
Oil	14.3	17.3	34.9	32.5
Industry	13.4	17.1	16.9	18.7
Services	42.0	43.8	35.1	40.3
Employment	100.0	100.0	100.0	100.0
Agriculture	47.5	44.3	43.2	32.1
Oil	0.6	0.6	0.7	0.6
Industry	23.5	25.6	26.9	33.4
services	24.7	25.5	25.8	31.0
(Unemployed)	3.7	4.0	3.4	2.9
Gross domestic expenditures[1]	100.0	100.0	100.0	100.0
Consumption	78.0	72.2	68.2	64.1
Investment	15.7	23.1	23.1	27.5
Other[2]	6.3	4.7	8.7	8.4

Memorandum Items

	1342–1346	1347–1351	1352–1356
GDP growth[3]	9.8	13.0	8.5

	1342	1347	1352	1356
Real per capita income[4]	25.3	32.8	69.5	105.7

Source: Bank Markazi, *Iran's National Accounts 1959/60–1977/78.*
1. At current prices.
2. Includes changes in stock, net foreign trade, and statistical discrepancies.
3. Annual percentage in real terms.
4. Rls 1,000 at constant prices.

Table 4.1
Gross Domestic and National Product
(In billions of Iranian rials at current prices)

	1356[1] 1977/78	1357 1978/79	1358 1979/80	1359 1980/81	1360 1981/82	1361 1982/83	1362 1983/84	1363 1984/85	1364 1985/86	1365 1986/87	1366 1987/88	1367 1988/89	1368 1989/90	1369 1990/91	1370 1991/92
Agriculture	518.6	669.0	882.1	1164.4	1693.1	2091.4	2334.7	2826.9	3109.8	3752.9	4891.3	5208.7	6669.9	8419.1	11340.5
Oil[2]	1619.7	1171.9	1606.6	838.6	995.5	1947.7	1983.3	1662.5	1490.2	644.0	893.7	990.6	1714.5	3793.8	3839.7
Industry	1037.7	1026.5	1002.5	1264.5	1479.8	1884.0	2533.4	2788.8	2714.8	2772.3	3317.0	3769.0	4629.4	6419.8	9884.1
Mining & manufacturing	515.2	480.5	472.5	651.9	829.6	1061.9	1228.5	1402.9	1400.8	1456.8	1948.2	2397.6	3037.0	4587.1	7484.3
Construction	470.7	494.9	448.1	540.4	554.2	695.5	1166.8	1262.1	1174.3	1152.9	1167.8	1110.7	1287.6	1437.5	1798.5
Water, power & gas	51.8	51.1	81.9	72.2	96.0	126.6	138.1	123.8	139.7	162.6	201.0	260.7	304.8	395.2	601.3
Services	2156.5	2424.4	2823.6	3396.2	3871.9	4543.4	6161.1	7068.1	7939.4	8525.8	10188.1	11922.2	14162.8	17398.9	22093.0
Trade	397.8	452.6	492.9	561.2	636.8	751.1	1510.3	1949.3	2280.7	2753.4	3568.8	4468.8	5528.8	6541.6	8636.2
Transport & communication	331.5	355.8	441.6	560.1	628.9	769.7	1030.9	1169.4	1182.1	1132.7	1315.9	1491.4	1790.9	2652.4	3331.7
Banking & insurance	234.9	245.5	165.9	307.4	281.0	265.2	251.4	192.3	189.6	188.4	166.9	204.5	218.0	358.2	488.5
Ownership & dwellings	453.4	473.8	496.0	646.9	840.6	1039.4	1362.7	1702.5	1905.3	2028.9	2352.5	2796.9	3395.5	3937.9	4923.0
Public services	650.8	798.4	1098.6	1172.4	1324.0	1498.7	1682.2	1736.6	1979.3	2043.9	2330.0	2400.9	2606.8	3091.6	3626.7
Private services	88.1	98.3	128.6	148.2	183.5	219.3	323.6	318.0	402.4	378.5	454.0	559.7	622.8	817.2	1086.9
Less: Imputed service charges	-155.5	-196.3	-156.6	-192.6	-156.0	-131.1	-82.5	-103.9	-86.4	-81.0	-6.1	-136.9	-147.8	-276.6	-380.5
GDP (factor cost)	5177.0	5095.5	6158.2	6471.1	7884.3	10335.4	12930.0	14242.4	15167.8	15614.0	19284.0	21753.6	27028.8	35755.0	46776.8
Net indirect taxes	186.9	176.5	4.8	161.3	125.0	204.4	446.2	561.3	607.6	612.9	665.0	550.5	758.3	889.6	1105.5
GDP (market prices)	5363.9	5272.0	6163.0	6632.0	8009.3	10539.8	13376.2	14803.7	15775.4	16226.9	19949.0	22304.4	27787.1	36644.6	47882.3
Net factor income	-52.4	-185.8	54.8	25.6	32.9		-6.6	-11.1	-33.8	-18.7	-39.3	-116.4	-211.7	-263.4	-186.6
GNP (market prices)	5311.5	5086.2	6217.8	6658.0	8042.2	10539.8	13369.6	14792.6	15741.6	16208.2	19909.7	22187.7	27575.4	36381.2	47695.7

Source: Bank Markazi: *Iran's National Accounts 1353–1366* (1974/75–1987/88); *Iran's National Accounts 1367–1369* (1988/89–1990/91); and *Annual Review, 1991/92*.

[1] Revised figures.
[2] Includes oil extraction and refining.

Table 4.2
Gross Domestic and National Produce
(In billions of Iranian rials at constant 1982/83 prices)

	1356 1977/78	1357 1978/79	1358 1979/80	1359 1980/81	1360 1981/82	1361 1982/83	1362 1983/84	1363 1984/85	1364 1985/86	1365 1986/87	1366 1987/88	1367 1988/89	1368 1989/90	1369 1990/91	1370 1991/92
Agriculture	1640.4	1747.2	1851.2	1914.9	1952.7	2091.4	2193.0	2353.7	2537.6	2650.5	2715.8	2648.0	2746.0	2967.5	3118.8
Oil[1]	4408.3	3144.0	2535.2	866.1	882.6	1947.7	2006.3	1625.6	1644.4	1403.0	1598.7	1754.0	1889.5	2264.7	2488.8
Industry	2330.0	2104.3	1773.7	1874.4	1875.1	1884.0	2254.6	2364.3	2232.2	2032.7	2084.1	1978.1	2109.1	2391.8	2834.3
Mining & manufacturing	1161.4	1041.8	910.9	1018.7	1097.9	1061.9	1186.3	1326.4	1297.5	1210.3	1341.1	1358.1	1476.5	1706.9	2044.0
Construction	1070.0	963.7	757.9	763.2	671.1	695.5	936.6	889.9	772.9	648.9	549.8	433.4	425.9	438.2	476.8
Water, power & gas	98.6	98.8	105.0	92.5	106.1	126.6	131.7	148.0	161.8	173.5	193.2	186.3	206.7	246.7	313.5
Services	4817.3	4841.1	4964.4	4855.0	4507.2	4543.4	5135.6	5260.5	5373.2	4654.7	4340.5	4030.2	4100.9	4499.6	4738.9
Trade	999.5	1024.1	905.6	785.8	732.0	751.1	1071.6	1230.7	1171.5	1045.1	1042.2	1008.4	1068.9	1136.4	1246.1
Transport & communication	874.4	813.4	890.9	903.4	735.9	769.7	889.6	906.3	906.9	785.5	642.9	599.7	654.9	796.2	839.9
Banking & insurance	520.8	495.0	300.0	450.0	307.6	265.2	219.2	152.1	140.6	113.0	78.0	74.1	67.3	101.5	115.8
Ownership & dwellings	788.1	721.2	681.8	809.4	949.0	1039.4	1204.2	1354.5	1400.5	1249.4	1222.4	1195.1	1237.3	1290.3	1345.1
Public services	1443.0	1609.7	1986.6	1716.5	1578.1	1498.7	1466.6	1372.8	1468.3	1226.1	1093.4	870.8	805.1	876.3	859.6
Private services	191.6	177.7	199.5	189.9	204.6	219.3	284.4	244.1	285.4	235.6	261.6	282.1	267.4	298.9	332.4
Less: Imputed service charges	-344.7	-395.7	-283.2	-282.0	-185.9	-131.1	-71.9	-82.0	-63.8	-48.4	-2.9	-49.7	-45.6	-78.4	-90.2
GDP (factor cost)	12851.3	11440.9	10841.3	9228.4	9031.7	10335.4	11517.6	11522.1	11723.6	10692.5	10736.2	10360.6	10799.9	12045.2	13090.6
Net indirect taxes	403.7	348.8	8.2	232.4	145.5	204.4	398.0	456.7	464.9	387.2	348.3	233.7	266.6	265.3	276.9
GDP (market prices)	13255.0	11789.7	10849.5	9460.8	9177.2	10539.8	11915.6	11978.8	12188.5	11079.7	11084.5	10594.3	11066.8	12310.5	13367.5
Net factor income	-258.8	-494.1	22.8	4.1	25.0	0	4.3	4.0	-14.7	1.8	-8.9	-16.9	15.5	67.3	220.4
GNP (market prices)	12996.2	11295.6	10872.3	9464.9	9202.2	10539.8	11919.9	11982.8	12173.8	11081.5	11075.6	10577.4	11082.3	12377.8	13587.9
Terms-of-trade adjustment	-1667.5	-1370.1	-298.2	94.7	143.5	0	19.1	65.0	-116.2	-830.8	-716.4	-1126.3	-1285.3	-1380.3	-1374.6
Gross national income	11328.7	9925.5	10574.1	9559.6	9345.7	10539.8	11939.0	12047.8	12057.6	10250.7	10359.2	9451.1	9797.0	10997.5	12213.3
Depreciation	781.8	923.2	1027.6	1095.1	1165.2	1228.1	1321.0	1436.5	1039.7	935.3	754.0	1273.7	1303.6	1331.9	1368.0
Net national income (factor cost)	10143.2	8653.5	9538.3	8232.1	8035.0	9107.3	10220.0	10154.6	11017.9	9315.4	9605.2	7943.7	8226.5	9400.4	10568.4

Source: Bank Markazi: *Iran's National Accounts 1974/75–1987/88*; *Iran's National Accounts 1988/89–1990/91*; and *Annual Review 1991/92*.

[1] Includes oil extraction and refining.

Table 4.3
Gross Domestic and National Expenditure
(In billions of Iranian rials at current prices)

	1356 1977/78	1357 1978/79	1358 1979/80	1359 1980/81	1360 1981/82	1361 1982/83	1362 1983/84	1363 1984/85	1364 1985/86	1365 1986/87	1366 1987/88	1367 1988/89	1368 1989/90	1369 1990/91	1370 1991/92
Consumption	3297.2	3748.3	4250.1	4911.2	6329.0	7853.4	9922.6	11116.4	12069.7	12809.3	14932.8	18104.2	21741.8	28124.9	36931.9
Private sector	2172.8	2502.9	3027.1	3531.4	4652.9	5943.3	7771.2	8926.8	9627.1	10438.7	12225.5	14905.5	18448.1	24070.7	32011.8
Public sector	1124.4	1245.4	1223.0	1379.8	1676.1	1910.1	2151.4	2189.6	2442.6	2370.6	2707.3	3198.7	3293.7	4054.2	4920.1
Gross domestic fixed capital formation	1784.0	1564.6	1176.5	1442.1	1527.9	1841.5	2869.7	3095.9	2759.0	2494.3	2662.4	2956.8	3709.2	5662.6	8054.7
Private sector	780.1	502.2	565.2	754.8	745.3	784.3	1607.9	1834.1	1672.3	1400.5	1562.1	1755.6	2285.2	3046.4	4359.8
Public sector	1003.9	1062.4	611.3	687.3	782.6	1057.2	1261.8	1261.8	1086.7	1093.8	1100.3	1201.2	1424.0	2616.2	3694.9
Changes in stock	-53.9	-205.9	-20.1	519.7	294.6	-165.3	226.2	507.8	562.0	1098.5	2416.6	1296.3	2891.1	4827.2	4959.9[1]
Net foreign trade	253.1	188.7	784.4	-205.9	-314.8	475.4	27.6	-35.1	-15.0	-381.8	-113.3	-242.0	-820.0	-1396.9	-2064.2
Statistical discrepancy	83.5	-23.7	-27.9	-34.7	172.6	534.8	330.1	118.7	399.7	206.6	50.5	188.8	265.5	-573.0	–
Capital GDE=(market prices)	5363.9	5272.0	6163.0	6632.4	8009.3	10539.8	13376.2	14803.7	15775.4	16226.9	19949.0	22304.1	27787.1	36644.6	47882.3
Net factor income	-52.4	-185.8	54.8	25.6	32.9	0	-6.6	-11.1	-33.8	-18.7	-39.3	-116.4	-211.7	-263.4	-186.6
Gross national product/expenditure	5311.5	5086.2	6217.8	6658.0	8042.2	10539.8	13369.6	14792.6	15741.6	16208.2	19909.7	22187.7	27575.4	36381.2	47695.7
Depreciation	429.6	549.4	674.7	864.5	1034.2	1288.1	1473.9	1724.3	1866.6	2298.6	2886.1	3290.3	3956.7	5442.6	7159.8
Net indirect taxes	186.9	176.5	4.8	161.3	125.0	204.4	446.2	561.3	607.6	612.9	665.0	550.5	758.3	889.6	1105.5
Net national income (factor cost)	4695.0	4360.3	5538.3	5632.2	6883.0	9107.3	11449.5	12507.0	13267.4	13296.7	16358.6	18346.9	22860.4	30049.0	39430.4

Source: Bank Markazi: *Iran's National Accounts 1974/75–1987/88*; *Iran's National Accounts 1988/89–1990/91*; *and Annual Review 1991/92*

1 Including statistical discrepancy.

Table 4.4
Gross Domestic and National Expenditure
(In billions of Iranian rials at constant 1982/83 prices)

	1356 1977/78	1357 1978/79	1358 1979/80	1359 1980/81	1360 1981/82	1361 1982/83	1362 1983/84	1363 1984/85	1364 1985/86	1365 1986/87	1366 1987/88	1367 1988/89	1368 1989/90	1369 1990/91	1370 1991/92
Consumption	7629.7	7777.4	7782.4	7328.5	7481.2	7853.4	8733.8	8981.1	9188.7	8051.3	7544.1	7567.9	7516.5	8900.1	9510.9
Private	5322.6	5430.5	5615.1	5360.1	5533.3	5943.3	6803.7	7170.3	7290.6	6543.7	6141.3	6171.8	6327.1	7563.5	8108.8
Public	2307.1	2346.9	2177.3	1968.4	1947.9	1910.1	1930.1	1810.8	1898.1	1507.6	1402.8	1396.1	1189.4	1336.6	1402.1
Gross domestic fixed capital formation	3231.0	2623.0	1815.8	1848.4	1724.2	1841.5	2551.1	2562.2	2229.5	1733.9	1358.2	1143.6	1216.8	1378.8	1545.6
Private	1450.1	873.1	898.7	987.1	851.2	784.3	1406.8	1484.8	1338.8	1004.1	819.1	679.3	748.0	765.8	856.7
Public	1780.9	1749.9	917.1	861.3	873.0	1057.2	1144.3	1077.8	890.7	729.8	539.1	464.3	468.8	613.0	688.9
Changes in stocks	-135.8	-468.0	-37.2	726.9	337.5	-165.3	159.1	318.0	286.0	411.3	697.8	288.3	549.2	821.8	1455.9
Net foreign trade	2222.2	1778.4	1455.0	-306.1	-447.3	475.4	16.2	-92.2	94.4	274.2	551.5	938.1	920.1	958.4	855.1
Statistical discrepancy	307.9	78.9	-176.5	-136.9	81.6	534.8	455.4	209.7	466.1	697.0	930.5	656.4	864.2	231.4	–
Gross domestic product/expenditure	13255.0	11789.7	10839.5	9460.8	9177.2	10539.8	11915.6	11978.8	12188.5	11079.7	11084.5	10594.3	11066.8	12310.5	13367.5
Net factor income	-258.8	-494.1	22.8	4.1	25.0	0	4.3	4.0	-14.7	1.8	-8.9	-16.9	15.5	67.3	220.4
Gross national product (market prices)	12996.2	11295.6	10862.3	9464.9	9202.2	10539.8	11919.9	11982.8	12173.8	11081.5	11075.6	10577.4	11082.3	12377.8	13587.9
Terms-of-trade adjustment	-1667.5	-1370.1	-298.2	94.7	143.5	0	19.1	65.0	-116.2	-830.8	-716.4	-1126.3	-1285.3	-1380.3	-1374.6
Gross national income	11328.7	9925.5	10574.1	9559.6	9345.7	10539.8	11939.0	12047.8	12057.6	10250.7	10359.2	9451.1	9797.0	10997.5	12213.3
Depreciation	781.8	932.2	1027.6	1095.1	1165.2	1228.1	1321.0	1436.5	1475.8	1578.5	1550.4	1273.7	1303.6	1331.8	1368.0
Net indirect taxes	403.7	348.8	8.2	232.4	145.5	204.4	398.0	456.7	464.9	387.2	348.3	233.7	266.9	265.3	276.9
Net national income (factor cost)	10143.2	8653.5	9538.3	8232.1	8035.0	9107.3	10220.0	10154.6	10116.9	8285.0	8460.5	7943.7	8226.5	9400.4	10568.4

Source: Bank Markazi: *Iran's National Accounts 1353–1366*; (1974/75–1987/88); *Iran's National Accounts 1367–1369* (1988/89–1991/92); and unofficial estimates.

344 Tables

Table 4.5
Composition of Domestic Expenditure
(In percentage of GDE at current prices)

	1356 1977/78	1357 1978/79	1358 1979/80	1359 1980/81	1360 1981/82	1361 1982/83	1362 1983/84	1363 1984/85	1364 1985/86	1365 1986/87	1366 1987/88	1367 1988/89	1368 1989/90	1369 1990/91	1370 1991/92
Consumption	61.5	71.1	69.0	74.1	79.0	74.5	74.2	75.1	76.5	78.9	74.8	81.1	78.2	76.7	77.1
Private	40.5	47.5	49.2	53.2	58.0	56.3	58.0	60.3	61.0	64.3	61.3	66.8	66.4	65.6	66.8
Public	21.0	23.6	19.8	20.8	21.0	18.2	16.1	14.7	15.5	14.6	13.5	14.3	11.8	11.1	10.3
Gross domestic fixed capital formation	33.2	29.7	19.1	21.7	19.1	17.5	21.4	20.9	17.5	15.3	13.3	13.2	13.3	15.4	16.8
Private	14.5	9.5	9.2	11.4	9.3	7.4	12.0	12.4	10.6	8.6	7.8	7.8	8.2	8.3	9.1
Public	18.7	20.2	9.9	10.3	9.8	10.1	9.4	8.5	6.9	6.7	5.5	5.4	5.1	7.1	7.7
Changes in stocks and statistical discrepancy	0.6	-4.4	-0.8	7.3	5.8	3.5	4.2	4.2	6.0	8.0	12.3	6.6	11.3	11.6	10.3
Net foreign trade	4.7	3.6	12.7	-3.1	-3.9	4.5	0.2	-0.2	0	-2.2	-0.4	-0.9	-2.8	-3.7	-4.2
GDE (market prices)	100	100	100	100	100	100	100	100	100	100	100	100	100	100	100

Source: Table 4.3.

Table 4.6
Macroeconomic development and Sectional Change

	1356 1977/78	1357 1978/79	1358 1979/80	1359 1980/81	1360 1981/82	1361 1082/83	1362 1983/84	1363 1984/85	1364 1985/86	1365 1986/87	1366 1987/88	1367 1988/89	1368 1989/90	1369 1990/91	1370 1991/92
Agriculture															
Growth rate[1]	0.3	6.5	5.9	3.4	1.9	7.1	4.8	7.3	7.8	4.4	2.4	-2.5	3.7	8.0	5.1
Share in GDP[2]	9.7	12.6	14.0	17.4	21.1	20.0	17.9	19.7	20.4	23.9	25.4	23.8	24.5	23.4	24.0
Oil															
Growth rate[1]	-1.6	-28.7	-19.4	-65.8	1.9	120.7	3.0	-18.9	1.1	-14.7	13.9	9.7	7.7	19.8	9.9
Share in GDP[2]	30.4	22.2	25.4	12.6	12.3	18.6	15.2	11.6	9.8	4.1	4.6	4.5	6.3	10.5	8.1
Industry															
Growth rate[1]	-1.8	-9.7	-15.7	5.6	0.04	0.5	19.6	4.8	-5.5	-8.9	2.5	-5.0	6.6	13.4	18.5
Share in GDP[2]	19.4	19.4	15.9	19.0	18.4	18.0	19.6	19.4	17.8	17.6	17.2	17.2	17.0	17.8	21.0
Services															
Growth rate[1]	8.2	0.4	2.5	-2.2	-7.2	0.8	13.0	2.4	2.1	-13.3	-6.7	-7.1	1.7	9.7	5.3
Share in GDP[2]	40.5	45.8	44.7	51.0	48.2	43.4	47.3	49.2	52.0	54.4	52.8	54.5	52.1	48.3	46.9
Gross domestic product (factor cost)															
Growth rate[1]	1.3	-10.9	-5.2	-14.9	-2.1	14.4	11.4	0.04	1.7	-8.8	0.4	-3.6	4.2	11.5	8.6

Source: Tables 4.1 and 4.2.
1. Percentage of real growth over the year at constant 1982/83 prices
2. At current prices; factor cost.

Table 5.1
Employment and Unemployment
(In millions of persons; age range: 10–64 years.)

	1355 1976/11	1356 1977/78	1357 1978/79	1358 1979/80	1359 1980/81	1360 1981/82	1361 1982/83	1362 1983/84	1363 1984/85	1364 1985/86	1365 1986/87	1366 1987/88	1367 1988/89	1368 1989/90	1369 1990/91	1370 1991/92
Agriculture	2.99	3.01	3.03	3.05	3.07	3.09	3.11	3.13	3.15	3.17	3.19	3.21	3.25	3.31	3.37	3.58
Oil	0.09	0.09	0.09	0.09	0.09	0.10	0.10	0.10	0.10	0.10	0.11	0.11	0.11	0.11	0.11	0.11
Industry[1]	2.93	2.89	2.86	2.83	2.81	2.78	2.75	2.74	2.71	2.68	2.66	2.63	2.70	2.84	3.04	3.24
Services[2]	2.79	3.00	3.21	3.43	3.64	4.03	4.34	4.60	4.88	4.97	5.04	5.33	5.40	5.52	5.67	6.02
Total employment[2]	8.80	8.99	9.19	9.40	9.61	10.00	10.30	10.57	10.84	10.92	11.00	11.28	11.46	11.78	12.19	12.95
Unemployed	0.90	1.06[3]	1.13	1.21	1.28	1.36	1.45	1.53	1.62	1.72	1.82	1.95	2.16	2.21	2.18	1.67
(percentage)	(9.2)	(10.5)	(10.9)	(11.4)	(11.7)	(12.0)	(12.3)	(12.6)	(13.1)	(13.6)	(14.0)	(14.8)	(15.9)	(15.8)	(15.1)	(11.4)
Labor force[4]	9.79	10.06	10.32	10.61	10.89	11.36	11.75	12.10	12.46	12.64	12.82	13.24	13.62	13.99	14.37	14.62
Population	33.7	34.7	36.0	37.9	39.6	41.2	42.8	44.4	46.2	47.8	49.4	51.0	52.8	54.4	56.1	58.1
Urban	15.8	16.6	17.4	18.4	19.4	20.6	21.8	23.1	24.5	25.8	26.8	28.1	29.5	30.9	32.4	33.3
Rural	17.9	18.1	18.6	19.5	20.2	20.6	21.0	21.3	21.7	22.0	22.6	22.9	23.3	23.5	23.7	24.8

Source: Bank Markazi; and Plan and Budget Organization. For 1355 and 1365, official census; for other years, best estimates.

[1] Including water, power, and gas, and construction
[2] Including unclassified categories
[3] Figure considerably higher than previously reported.
[4] Adjusted for discrepancies in the source data.

Table 5.2
Employment Characteristics: 1986/87
(In thousands of persons)

	Total	Percentage	Overall		Urban			Rural		
			Male	Female	Total	Male	Female	Total	Male	Female
Managers	341	3.1	328	14	206	200	5	134	126	8
Self-employed	4,398	39.9	4,217	181	1,742	1,693	48	2,613	2,482	131
Public sector employees	3,454	31.3	3,047	408	2,594	2,225	369	858	819	39
Private sector employees	1,882	17.1	1,782	100	1,074	1,023	41	803	745	58
Family businesses	497	4.5	283	214	47	34	13	440	240	199
Other	464	4.2	393	71	297	247	51	165	145	20
Total	11,036[1]	100.0	10,049	987	5,960	5,433	527	5,013	4,558	455

Source: *Iran Statistical Yearbook, 1990/91.*

[1] The overall figure includes migrant workers and non-residents.

Table 6.1
Price Developments[1]
(Percentage change, Mid-year)

	1356 1977/78	1357 1978/79	1358 1979/80	1359 1980/81	1360 1981/82	1361 1982/83	1362[2] 1983/84	1363 1984/85	1364 1985/86	1365 1986/87	1366 1987/88	1367 1988/89	1368 1989/90	1369 1990/91	1370 1991/92
Wholesale prices	14.6	9.4	19.8	30.5	19.4	13.7	7.8	7.6	7.3	25.1	29.7	22.0	18.4	23.9	28.1
Domestic products	15.6	9.2	21.2	33.4	22.2	14.5	8.4	8.4	6.9	22.5	27.0	22.0	20.0	22.2	28.1
Imported goods	12.1	10.4	15.0	21.6	10.5	10.7	4.6	3.8	7.9	29.4	32.9	24.7	13.2	34.4	22.5
Exported goods	12.2	3.7	24.6	28.8	18.9	16.6	−0.8	15.5	21.5	198.8	107.9	6.4	4.5	13.2	67.8
Cost of living	25.1	9.9	11.4	23.5	22.8	19.2	14.8	10.4	6.9	23.7	27.7	28.9	17.4	9.0	19.6
Food	20.5	18.0	22.2	29.0	28.9	16.6	11.4	9.3	10.0	28.5	19.2	18.8	15.3	4.3	27.8
Housing	37.8	0	−0.5	7.3	9.5	12.2	14.6	10.4	8.0	19.6	23.3	28.1	17.7	7.6	20.2
Implicit price deflator															
GDP (factor costs)	14.7	16.4	20.6	26.6	16.9	16.8	14.0	4.6	4.8	20.8	20.0	18.6	15.5	15.9	20.8
Non-oil GDP (factor cost)	15.7	17.8	20.5	25.6	17.8	21.1	17.1	3.9	6.7	27.2	21.9	22.3	15.8	16.8	…

Memorandum Items:

	1977/78–1981/82	1982/83–1990/91
Wholesale Price Index, Weights	100.00	100.00
Domestic products	69.02	83.33
Imported goods	27.89	15.97
Exported goods	3.09	0.70
Consumer Price Index, Weights	100.00	100.00
Food	35.48	40.06
Housing	21.14	25.37
Other	43.38	34.57
Inflation base	1974/75 = 100	1982/83 = 100

Source: Bank Markazi; International Monetary Fund; and other data.

[1] Urban areas.
[2] New series.

Table 7.1
General Government Fiscal Position[1,7]
(In billions of Iranian rials)

	1356 1977/78	1357 1978/79	1358 1979/80	1359 1980/81	1360 1981/82	1361 1982/83	1362 1983/84	1363 1984/85	1364 1985/86	1365 1986/87	1366 1987/88	1367 1988/89	1368 1989/90	1369 1990/91	1370 1991/92	1371 1992/93	1372 1993/94
Total Revenue	2035	1599	1700	1431	1925	2701	2996	2993	2969	2016	2681	2655	3831	6618	7920	11656	25251
Oil and gas revenues	1498	1013	1220	889	1056	1690	1779	1373	1189	435	853	809	1515	3376	3549	5174	15815
of which SFE[2]	-	-	-	-	-	-	-	-	-	18	87	141	744	2257	2511	4073	-
Non-oil revenues	537	586	480	437	714	812	994	1342	1478	1273	1318	1276	1660	2257	3454	5497	7723
Tax revenues	444	466	368	340	554	614	797	899	1034	1025	1030	986	1188	1695	2765	3608	5420
Non-tax revenues	93	120	112	97	160	199	198	443	444	248	288	290	472	562	689	1889	2303
Special revenues	-	-	-	105	154	199	223	278	302	309	342	415	450	627	917	985	1713
OPCP[3] revenues (net)	-	-	-	-	-	-	-	-	-	-	167	155	206	358	-	-	-
Total expenditure	2492	2208	2228	2403	2861	3367	3896	3632	3616	3437	4066	4702	4932	7338	9008	12452	25426
Current expenditures	1430	1515	1588	1728	2032	2253	2524	2476	2560	2389	2900	3387	3381	4475	5564	7504	13903
Capital expenditures	1062	693	640	570	675	915	1149	878	765	746	729	816	931	1832	2527	3962	9810
Special expenditures	-	-	-	105	154	199	223	278	302	309	342	415	450	627	917	985	1713
Net lending	-	-	-	-	-	-	-	-	-11	-6	-4	-8	-2	-	-	-	-
OPCP expenditure	-	-	-	-	-	-	-	-	-	-	98	91	171	403	-	-	-
Deficit (excl. SFE)	-	-	-	-	-	-	-	-	-	-1439	-1472	-2188	-1845	-2977	-3599	-	-
Overall deficit	-458	-609	-528	-972	-937	-666	-899	-639	-647	-1421	-1385	-2047	-1101	-720	-1088	-796	-175
Financing	379	351	444	975	1000	778	955	659	685	1432	1444	2082	1217	710	1118	-	-
Domestic[4]	350	250	350	952	949	762	934	647	659	1386	1419	2083	1216	714	1118	796	175
Foreign[5]	29	101	94	23	51	16	21	12	28	46	25	-1	1	-4	-	-	-
Discrepancies[6]	79	258	85	48	64	113	56	20	37	11	58	35	116	-9	30	-	-

Source: Bank Markazi; Plan and Budget Organization; and estimates.

[1] For 1356 to 1370, actual; for 1371, approved budget; for 1372, proposed budget.
[2] Sale of foreign exchange in the open market.
[3] Organization for the Protection of Consumers and Producers.
[4] Includes borrowing from the banking system as well as carryover from previous year.
[5] Primarily repayments of principal and interest on previous loans.
[6] Mainly reflecting the delay in settling the accounts of provinces.
[7] Details may not add up due to rounding.

Table 7.2
Structure of Government Revenues
(In billions of Iranian rials)

	1356	1357	1358	1359	1360	1361	1362	1363	1364	1365	1366[6]	1367[7]	1368[6]	1369[6]	1370[6]	1371[7]
	1977/78	1878/79	1979/80	1980/81	1981/82	1982/83	1983/84	1984/85	1985/86	1986/87	1987/88	1988/89	1989/90	1990/91	1991/92	1992/93
Total Revenue[1]	2035	1599	1700	1431	1925	2701	2996	2993	2969	2016	2514	2500	3625	6259	7548	10473
Oil and gas revenues[2]	1498	1013	1220	889	1056	1690	1779	1373	1189	435	853	809	1515	3375	3549	5042
Of which SFE[3]	-	-	-	-	-	-	-	-	-	18	87	141	744	2257	2511	4073
Non-oil general revenues	537	586	480	437	714	812	994	1342	1478	1273	1318	1276	1660	2256	3384	4445
Tax Revenues	444	466	368	340	554	614	797	899	1034	1025	1030	986	1188	1694	2765	3414
Income taxes	[230]	[269]	[228]	[129]	[322]	[269]	[332]	[405]	[530]	[580]	[612]	[646]	[660]	[923]	[1396]	[1737]
Public corporations	(107)	(145)	(101)	(11)	(185)	(114)	(123)	(125)	(190)	(373)	(374)	(392)	(340)	(496)	(775)	(961)
Private corporations[4]	(53)	(53)	(42)	(35)	(43)	(60)	(85)	(132)	(167)	(205)	(190)	(198)	(127)	(162)	(245)	(391)
Wages and salaries	(40)	(44)	(60)	(52)	(56)	(65)	(59)	(73)	(87)	(168)	(184)	(194)	(213)	(333)	(530)	(570)
Professions	(11)	(9)	(8)	(9)	(17)	(21)	(22)	(24)	(36)	(93)	(71)	(70)	(89)	(127)	(229)	(204)
Real estate	(6)	(5)	(4)	(20)	(18)	(29)	(36)	(42)	(38)	(70)	(96)	(102)	(134)	(182)	(253)	(366)
Other	(13)	(11)	(13)	(3)	(4)	(6)	(7)	(11)	(11)	(43)	(71)	(82)	(96)	(119)	(138)	(206)
Wealth surtax	-	-	-	-	-	-	-	-	-	-	-	-	(19)	(12)	(14)	(30)
Taxes on production and consumption	[44]	[53]	[39]	[50]	[63]	[101]	[118]	[148]	[230]	[220]	[217]	[195]	[178]	[269]	[417]	[545]
Cigarettes	(32)	(43)	(33)	(8)	(16)	(42)	(44)	(53)	(119)	(136)	(109)	(93)	(71)	(120)	(122)	(165)
Petroleum products	(4)	(3)	(1)	(29)	(25)	(27)	(25)	(10)	(56)	(39)	(48)	(35)	(39)	(54)	(44)	(52)
Beverages	(7)	(6)	(1)	(1)	(1)	(7)	(10)	(10)	(11)	(9)	(20)	(29)	(29)	(36)	(41)	(48)
Automobiles	(1)	(1)	(4)	(4)	(3)	(5)	(7)	(8)	(15)	(30)	(33)	(27)	(23)	(47)	(141)	(202)
Other	-	-	-	(9)	(17)	(20)	(32)	(34)	(30)	(7)	(7)	(11)	(15)	(12)	(68)	(78)
Taxes on foreign trade	[169]	[144]	[101]	[161]	[170]	[218]	[346]	[346]	[274]	[225]	[201]	[146]	[350]	[502]	[952]	[1131]
Custom duties	(95)	(67)	(62)	(100)	(101)	(74)	(126)	(139)	(109)	(76)	(66)	(50)	(70)	(115)	(180)	(190)
Commercial profit tax	(51)	(36)	(33)	(52)	(54)	(81)	(142)	(136)	(115)	(119)	(87)	(57)	(91)	(161)	(389)	(427)
Registration fee	-	-	-	(7)	(6)	(27)	(50)	(30)	(27)	(20)	(45)	(35)	(179)	(215)	(306)	(429)
Other	(23)	(41)	(6)	(2)	(8)	(35)	(27)	(40)	(22)	(9)	(4)	(3)	(9)	(11)	(76)	(85)

Non-tax revenues	93	120	112	97	160	199	198	443	444	248	288	290	472	562	619	1031
Public monopolies	(35)	(52)	(36)	–	(56)	(61)	(35)	(34)	(34)	(22)	(16)	(21)	(26)	(30)	(35)	(97)
Sales of goods and services	(20)	(21)	(22)	(29)	(37)	(72)	(81)	(312)	(220)	(166)	(203)	(227)	(361)	(387)	(399)	(717)
Foreign investment	(20)	(21)	(26)	(25)	(12)	(9)	(9)	(6)	(5)	(5)	(5)	(4)	(4)	(4)	(4)	1
Other	(18)	(31)	(28)	(42)	(55)	(56)	(72)	(91)	(185)	(55)	(64)	(38)	(81)	(141)	(181)	(216)
Special Revenue[5]	–	–	–	105	154	199	223	278	302	309	342	415	450	627	615	986

Source: Ministry of Economy and Finance; and Plan and Budget Organization.

[1] Excludes OPCP revenues.

[2] Includes revenue from forward sales of crude oil on consignment basis.

[3] Sale of foreign exchange in the open market.

[4] Includes enterprises and agencies under government supervision.

[5] Revenue earmarked for special expenditure.

[6] Preliminary actual. Figures differ from actual summary in Table 7.1

[7] Proposed budget. Figures differ from approved summary in Table 7.1

Table 7.3
Structure of Government Expenditures
(In billions of Iranian rials)

	1356 1977/78	1357 1978/79	1358 1979/80	1359 1980/81	1360 1981/82	1361 1982/83	1362 1983/84	1363 1984/85	1364 1985/86	1365 1986/87	1366[5] 1987/88	1367[5] 1988/89	1368[5] 1989/90	1369[5] 1990/91	1370[5] 1991/92	1371[6] 1992/93
Total expenditure[1,3]	2492	2208	2228	2403	2861	3367	3896	3632	3616	3466	3983	4625	4767	6677	9279	11269
Regular expenditure:	2492[3]	2208[3]	2228[3]	2298	2707	3167	3672	3354	3313	3157	3640	4211	4317	6050	8664	10283
General services	202	161	185	277	290	381	377	413	311	313	321	368	398	558	816	954
National defence	561	590	314	375	326	334	330	360	480	470	461	526	634	729	892	968
Social services	545	604	644	771	800	848	1037	1060	1092	1141	1299	1554	1835	2663	3302	4049
Education	–	–	–	(446)	(444)	(451)	(430)	(447)	(468)	(536)	(582)	(705)	(817)	(1138)	(1449)	(1725)
Health	–	–	–	(148)	(152)	(164)	(194)	(205)	(206)	(191)	(203)	(285)	(365)	(459)	(582)	(713)
Housing	–	–	–	(54)	(54)	(65)	(70)	(47)	(32)	(21)	(39)	(30)	(17)	(108)	(25)	(32)
Other	–	–	–	(123)	(150)	(166)	(344)	(360)	(385)	(393)	(469)	(534)	(636)	(960)	(1247)	(1578)
Economic services	894	632	563	560	626	791	870	891	722	597	698	717	789	1382	1727	1912
Agriculture	–	–	–	(72)	(74)	(89)	(120)	(118)	(100)	(109)	(111)	(125)	(162)	(236)	(335)	(369)
Water resources	–	–	–	(50)	(55)	(65)	(77)	(81)	(61)	(56)	(70)	(78)	(93)	(197)	(254)	(381)
Energy	–	–	–	(165)	(125)	(189)	(211)	(289)	(162)	(115)	(188)	(183)	(101)	(183)	(197)	(167)
Manufacturing	–	–	–	(87)	(97)	(148)	(168)	(113)	(97)	(105)	(131)	(108)	(142)	(226)	(207)	(152)
Transport and communication	–	–	–	(126)	(142)	(158)	(172)	(156)	(165)	(150)	(164)	(177)	(241)	(413)	(556)	(649)
Other	–	–	–	(60)	(132)	(142)	(122)	(134)	(136)	(62)	(35)	(46)	(50)	(126)	(178)	(193)
Other expenditure	290	221	–	316	664	813	1058	629	708	635	861	1045	660	715	1927	2399
Special expenditure[4]	–	–	522	105	154	199	223	278	302	309	342	415	450	627	615	986

Source: Ministry of Economy and Finance; and Plan and Budget Organization

1 Details may not add up to totals due to rounding.
2 May differ from data in Tables 7.1 because of exclusion of repayments of foreign loans.
3 Includes special expenditures.
4 Expenditure financed by special revenue.
5 Preliminary actual. Figures differ from Table 7.1
6 Proposed budget. Figures differ from Table 7.1

Table 7.4
Subsidies by Commodities[1]
(In billions of Iranian rials)

	1359 1980/81	1360 1981/82	1361 1982/83	1362 1983/84	1363 1984/85	1364 1985/86	1365 1986/87	1366 1987/88	1367 1988/89	1368 1989/90	1369 1990/91	1370 1991/92
Consumer items:												
Wheat	3.7	24.0	37.0	24.3	27.0	51.0	68.3	40.0	38.5	45.2	155.0	250.2
Sugar	12.0	18.7	6.0	15.0	14.7	15.0	13.0	13.5	11.0	36.3	98.0	100.3
Vegetable oil[2]	3.0	8.6	10.4	10.0	31.1	8.0	–	0.9	–	–	–	–
Milk	3.2	2.4	3.6	5.9	8.2	8.1	9.1	9.0	10.3	21.3	20.0	30.0
Meat	–	–	6.3	8.3	–	–	–	0.2	–	–	–	–
Producer items:												
Fertilizer	14.6	20.0	27.0	25.3	27.8	22.0	20.5	19.0	13.8	23.7	39.0	78.6
Pesticides	–	–	–	–	–	–	–	–	5.9	12.7	–	–
Others[3]	0.8	7.6	19.4	17.3	11.4	12.3	16.4	15.2	12.0	32.3	91.0	55.8
Total	37.3	81.3	109.7	106.1	120.2	116.4	127.3	97.8	91.5	171.5	403.0	514.9

Source: The Organization for the Protection of Consumers and Producers; and Bank Markazi.

[1] Financed through budgetary allocations as well as contributions from OPCP.
[2] Transfers for vegetable oil have become self-liquidating.
[3] Includes transfers to agribusiness complexes.

Table 8.1
New Facilities under the Islamic Banking[1]
(In billions of Iranian rials)

	1363 1984/85	1364 1985/86	1365 1986/87	1366 1987/88	1367 1988/89	1368 1989/90	1369 1990/91	1370 1991/92
Instalment sale	247	604	990	1657	2454	3489	5470	7668
Trade partnership (*Mozarabeh*)	135	294	429	491	570	802	1142	1582
Civil partnership	109	244	384	539	609	959	1261	2901
Hire purchase	28	37	52	83	99	107	125	232
Forward purchase (*Salaf*)	27	59	109	151	255	497	589	809
Legal partnership	26	136	182	277	372	435	510	785
Direct investment	4	66	74	64	67	98	143	212
Service contract	3	26	38	71	144	384	740	1142
Debt purchase	85	186	176	120	53	42	32	17
Interest-free loan (*Qarz ol-Hassaneh*)	78	199	321	412	507	564	640	682
Other	2	22	46	70	135	169	230	395
Total[2]	744	1872	2804	3937	5266	7546	10882	16425

Source: Bank Markazi; and Plan and budget Organization.

[1] For the characteristics of these various modes, see the text.
[2] Totals may differ from actual due to rounding.

Table 8.2
Monetary Accounts of the Bank Markazi
(In billions of Iranian rials)

	1356 1977/78	1357 1978/79	1358 1979/80	1359 1980/81	1360 1981/82	1361 1982/83	1362 1983/84	1363 1984/85	1364 1985/86	1365 1986/87	1366 1987/88	1367 1988/89	1368 1989/90	1369 1990/91	1370 1991/92
Foreign assets	843	830	1088	729	1061	936	833	590	688	736	727	681	774	1350	1374
Gold¹	(14)	(14)	(39)	(86)	(39)	(29)	(66)	(24)	(28)	(23)	(121)	(96)	(116)	(302)	(393)
Foreign exchange	(818)	(786)	(1011)	(602)	(964)	(789)	(658)	(374)	(408)	(537)	(434)	(437)	(518)	(921)	(844)
Bilateral foreign exchange	0	0	(1)	0	(16)	(75)	(65)	(147)	(206)	(130)	(125)	(114)	(96)	(83)	(101)
Subscription to international organization	(15)	(15)	(15)	(15)	(15)	(15)	(15)	(15)	(15)	(16)	(16)	(16)	(16)	(16)	(16)
SDR allocation	(6)	(15)	(21)	(27)	(27)	(28)	(29)	(30)	(31)	(31)	(32)	(18)	(29)	(29)	(20)
Notes and coins in till	8	12	8	23	20	9	7	9	33	11	27	45	43	19	45
Claims on the public sector	599	1042	1551	2420	3207	4007	4850	5696	6418	8087	9541	11652	12865	13928	15388
Government²	(239)	(661)	(939)	(1858)	(2608)	(3480)	(4191)	(5038)	(5725)	(7456)	(8904)	(10976)	(12180)	(12707)	(13730)
Public agencies and corporations	(360)	(481)	(612)	(562)	(599)	(528)	(659)	(658)	(693)	(631)	(637)	(676)	(685)	(1221)	(1658)
Claims on banks	175	194	266	394	422	465	468	506	356	295	315	320	322	384	1317
Guarantees and acceptances	309	319	288	354	378	503	445	352	333	347	355	351	491	604	562
Other	25	50	9	18	72	64	25	45	196	46	58	129	76	50	122
Total assets = total liabilities	1959	2547	3210	3938	5160	5984	6628	7198	8024	9522	11023	13178	14571	16336	18807
Notes and coins in circulation	407	919	1033	1368	1503	1818	2032	2176	2328	2771	3112	3725	3965	4484	5009
Deposits in banks	340	303	519	644	1172	1597	1729	2073	2615	3302	4457	5840	6388	6247	7354
Public sector deposits³	463	522	837	697	872	1083	1220	1283	1171	1280	1534	1672	1879	2617	3126
Capital account	64	94	96	156	174	196	210	222	228	239	243	248	253	253	258
Foreign exchange liabilities	14	23	39	58	33	51	109	43	44	61	47	62	74	125	237
Import registrations deposits	34	30	29	26	19	24	32	22	20	12	11	10	22	30	27
Advanced payments on letters of credit	169	173	167	204	209	240	361	300	231	297	313	317	439	565	460
Guarantees and acceptances	309	319	288	354	378	503	445	352	333	347	355	351	491	604	562
Other	159	164	202	431	800	472	490	728	1054	1213	951	953	1060	1412	1774

Source: Bank Markazi

¹ Including Rls 3.1 billion in IMF
² Including government securities
³ Including deposits of municipalities and non-financial public enterprises

Table 8.3
Consolidated Accounts of Commercial and Specialized Banks
(In billions of Iranian rials)

	1356 1977/78	1357 1978/79	1358 1979/80	1359 1980/81	1360 1981/82	1361 1982/83	1362 1983/84	1363 1984/85	1364 1985/86	1365 1986/87	1366 1987/88	1367 1988/89	1368 1989/90	1369 1990/91	1370 1991/92
Reserves	413	407	616	758	1212	1708	1840	2191	2733	3419	4559	6074	6666	6592	7738
Notes & coins	73	104	97	114	76	111	111	118	117		102	234	278	345	384
Deposits with Bank Markazi	340	303	519	644	1136	1597	1729	2073	2615	3302	4457	5840	6388	6247	7354
Foreign assets	56	52	125	176	150	167	204	145	163	138	104	120	159	262	252
Gold	1	2	5	5	5	5	3	1	1	1	1	1	1	1	1
Foreign exchange[1]	55	50	120	171	145	162	201	144	162	137	103	119	158	261	251
Claims on government[2]	414	267	492	500	694	1179	1269	1317	1194	1235	1252	1248	1348	1346	1322
Claims on public enterprises	26	26	27	25	34	16	22	43	34	124	167	352	471	822	953
Claims on private sector[3]	1869	2199	2577	3060	3219	3485	4257	4501	5082	5578	6416	7479	9697	13157	18247
Unclassified assets[4]	513	698	747	979	818	1016	1150	815	1112	1367	1513	2037	2856	4492	6808
Total assets = Total liabilities	3291	3651	4584	5498	6127	7572	8741	9012	10317	11862	14011	17310	21197	26671	35321
Demand deposits (Private sector)[5]	465	434	738	1156	1434	1786	1956	2509	2747	3169	3794	4312	5342	7076	9061
Time & savings deposits (Private sector)[5]	1306	1342	1884	2134	2404	2947	3645	3409	4078	4912	5891	7929	9766	11774	14988
Government deposits[6]	238	260	245	198	232	214	195	210	223	214	250	279	252	207	291
Foreign liabilities	253	269	186	161	171	167	163	57	62	68	76	78	103	171	205
Credit from bank Markazi[7]	175	194	266	394	422	465	468	506	356	295	315	320	323	384	1317
Capital accounts	267	298	-	-	-	349	363	353	315	296	281	233	238	197	432
Unclassified liabilities[8]	587	854	1265[8]	1455[8]	1464[8]	1644	1952	1967	2535	2910	3404	4158	5174	6862	9028

Source: bank Markazi; and other data.

1 Includes foreign exchange deposits with Bank Markazi.
2 Includes government securities and bank losses before 1364.
3 Includes equity participation in companies, some of which public enterprises.
4 Includes interbank claims.
5 Includes deposits of some non-financial public enterprises.
6 Includes Government Lending Funds.
7 Includes repayment of government debt caused by bank losses due to nationalization.
8 Includes capital accounts.

Table 8.4
Monetary Survey[1]
(In billions of Iranian rials)

	1356 1977/78	1357 1978/79	1358 1979/80	1359 1980/81	1360 1981/82	1361 1982/83	1362 1983/84	1363 1984/85	1364 1985/86	1365 1986/87	1366 1987/88	1367 1988/89	1368 1989/90	1369 1990/91	1370 1991/92
Foreign assets (net)	631	590	989	706	1021	898	777	646	756	744	707	660	756	1316	1184
Domestic assets (net)															
Domestic credit	1467	1988	2561	3491	4396	5751	7015	7602	8507	9979	11961	15028	17997	21653	27444
Claims on government (net)[2]	2038	2680	3564	5232	6217	7600	9248	10331	11583	13530	11593	18779	22251	25667	31317
Claims on public enterprises	169	481	-987	1584	2365	3571	4311	5129	5774	7428	8748	10542	11679	11712	12238
(net)	–	–	–	587	633	544	680	701	726	524	497	758	875	1624	2009
Claims on private sector	1869	2199	2577	3060	3220	3485	4257	4501	5082	5578	6348	7479	9697	12331	17070
Other items[3]	-571	-692	-1003	-1290	-1821	-1849	-2233	-2729	-3076	-3551	-3632	-3751	-4254	-4014	-3872
Broad money (M2)	2098	2578	3550	4648	5417	6648	7792	8248	9263	10723	12668	15688	18753	22969	28628
Money (M1)	791	1236	1666	2511	3009	3680	4127	4835	5180	5811	6777	7758	8987	11195	13641
Currency	(205)	(802)	(928)	(1231)	(1407)	(1698)	(1914)	(2049)	(2176)	(2642)	(2983)	(3446)	(3645)	(4119)	(4580)
Demand deposits	(585)	(434)	(738)	(1280)	(1602)	(1983)	(2213)	(2787)	(3004)	(3169)	(3794)	(4312)	(5342)	(7076)	(9061)
Quasi money	1307	1342	1884	2136	2408	2968	3665	3413	4083	4912	5891	7930	9766	11774	14988

Source: Bank Markazi.

1 Figures may differ from those published by the International Monetary Fund due to differences in definition. Details may not add up due to rounding.
2 Includes government bonds.
3 Includes capital accounts of the banking system, private sector import registration deposits, and public sector's LC advanced payments.

Table 9.1
First Five-Year Plan
Projection of Gross Fixed Capital Formation by Sectors
1989/90–1993/94
(In billions of Iranian rials)

	Development Budget	Public Enterprise	Private Savings	Banking System	Total
General affairs	519.6	–	152.0	51.0	722.6
Social affairs	2466.4	468.4	6244.6	4849.5	14028.9
Education	(1635.5)	(24.7)	(201.2)	(322.2)	(2183.6)
Health	(456.0)	–	(158.5)	(28.0)	(624.5)
Welfare	(23.1)	–	(700.5)	–	(723.6)
Housing	(115.6)	(443.7)	(4212.9)	(4494.1)	(9336.3)
Other	(236.2)	–	(901.5)	(5.2)	(1142.9)
Economic affairs	4002.8	5198.4	1670.7	2492.5	13364.4
Agriculture	(787.2)	(128.8)	(726.3)	(1225.7)	(2868.0)
Water & power	(958.4)	(1418.2)	(132.0)	(183.4)	(2692.0)
Industry & mines	(963.2)	(613.6)	(370.1)	(522.3)	(2469.2)
Oil & gas	–	(1792.9)	–	–	(1792.9)
Transport & communications	(1248.8)	(1081.8)	(4.0)	(270.4)	(2605.5)
Trade & tourism	(45.2)	(14.6)	(438.3)	(290.2)	(788.3)
Other	1200.2	–	–	–	1200.2
Total	8189.0	5666.8	8067.3	7393.0	29316.1

Source: Plan and Budget Organization

Table 9.2
First Five-Year Plan, 1989/90–1993/94
Sectoral Origins of Domestic Product
(In billions of Iranian rials at constant 1367 prices)[1]

	1368 1989/90	1369 1990/91	1370 1991/92	1371 1992/93	1372 1993/94	5-Year Avg. Growth (percentage)
Agriculture	5430	5678	6026	6454	7001	6.1
	(22.0)	(21.3)	(21.0)	(20.8)	(20.8)	
Oil	2500	2741	2834	3155	3250	9.5
	(10.1)	(10.3)	(9.9)	(10.2)	(9.7)	
Manufacturing	1623	1835	2090	2415	2750	14.2
	(6.6)	(6.9)	(7.3)	(7.7)	(8.1)	
Mining	241	314	372	451	512	19.2
	(1.0)	(1.2)	(1.3)	(1.4)	(1.5)	
Water & power	490	525	587	618	914	9.1
	(2.0)	(2.0)	(2.0)	(1.9)	(2.7)	
Construction	1593	1844	2073	2282	2429	14.5
	(6.5)	(6.9)	(7.2)	(7.3)	(7.2)	
Services	12758	13663	14650	15681	16794	6.7
	(51.8)	(51.4)	(51.3)	(50.7)	(50.0)	
Imputed service charges[2]	346	67	286	309	335	
GDP (factor cost)	24289	26533	28346	30747	33315	8.1
	(100)	(100)	(100)	(100)	(100)	
Population[3] (millions)	54.4	55.7	57.4	59.3	61.3	
Per capita GDP[3]	450	476	493	518	543	4.9

Source: *The Law of the First Economic, Social and Cultural Development Plan of the Islamic Republic of Iran, 1989/90–1993/94.* (In Persian).

[1] Figures in parentheses denote percentage share of sector in GDP.
[2] See *Iran's National Accounts, 1959/60–1977/78* for explanation of these charges.
[3] Figures are adjusted for inconsistencies in the original source.

Table 9.3
Planned Consumption and Investment 1989/90–1993/94
(In billions of Iranian rials at 1367 prices)[1]

	1368 1989/90	1369 1990/91	1370 1991/92	1371 1992/93	1372 1993/94	1368–72 1989/90–1993/94
Consumption:	16332	17212	18244	19514	20973	
	(1.4)	(5.3)	(6.0)	(6.9)	(7.4)	(5.4)
Public	2772	3021	3107	3269	3488	
	(−4.1)	(9.0)	(2.8)	(5.2)	(6.7)	(3.8)
Private	13560	14191	15137	16245	17485	
	(2.6)	(4.7)	(6.7)	(7.3)	(7.6)	(5.7)
Investment:	4132	5451	5610	5596	5663	
	(26.4)	(31.9)	(2.9)	(−0.2)	(1.2)	(11.6)
Public[2]	1789	2709	2741	2679	2574	
	(17.0)	(51.4)	(1.2)	(−2.3)	(−3.9)	(10.8)
Private[3]	2343	2742	2869	2917	3089	
	(34.7)	(17.0)	(4.6)	(1.7)	(5.9)	(12.2)

Memorandum Items
(as percentage of real GDP)

Aggregate consumption	67.2	64.8	64.3	63.4	62.9	
(private)	(55.8)	(53.4)	(53.4)	(52.8)	(52.4)	
Gross domestic investment	17.0	20.5	19.8	18.2	16.9	
(public)	(7.3)	(10.2)	(9.6)	(8.7)	(7.7)	

Source: *The Law of the First Economic, Social and Cultural Development Plan*, and Table 9.2.

[1] Figures in parentheses denote the rate of annual growth in real terms.
[2] Including investments by public enterprises.
[3] Including investments by the banking system.

Table 9.4
Projected Sources and Uses of Foreign Exchange in 1989/90–1993/94
(In billions of U.S. dollars)

Sources		Uses	
Export of oil, gas, and products	83.1	Import of goods	114.3
Crude oil	72.6	Current	52.2
Natural gas	1.6	(Industry)	(19.6)
Hydrocarbon products	8.9	(Oil)	(6.4)
		(Commerce)	(18.4)
		(Defense)	(1.4)
Export of non-oil products	17.8	Development	62.1
Traditional	8.8	(Industry)	(14.1)
(Carpet)	(4.4)	(Oil)	(8.3)
Industrial	9.0	(Commerce)	(1.1)
		(Defense)	(8.8)
Export of services	2.8	Import of services	4.5
Income from foreign investment	2.6	Debt servicing	0.9
Foreign credit	12.4	President's discretion	1.0
Other	2.0		
Total	120.7	Total	120.7

Source: *The Law of the First Economic, Social, and Cultural Development Plan.*

Table 9.5
First Five-Year Plan Performance 1368–1369 average
(1989/90–1990/91)

	Planned	Actual
Output growth of GDP (percentage)	8.5	7.0
Agriculture	4.4	4.2
Oil	15.3	11.0
Manufacturing	13.9	12.5
Mining	22.4	13.3
Water, power, and gas	6.8	11.9
Construction	22.1	1.7
Transport	5.4	14.6
Other services	6.1	4.4
GFCF growth (percentage)	24.2	15.4[1]
Private consumption (rate of annual growth)	3.6	10.3
Public consumption (rate of annual growth)	17.0	20.3
Private consumption/GDP	53.0	61.0
Government's fiscal position		
Revenue/GDP ratio	13.0	13.7
Deficit/GDP ratio	5.3	3.0
Development outlays/total expenditure	26.3	25.3
Private liquidity (percentage growth)	10.8	21.0
Inflation (CPI)	18.6	13.2

Source: Plan and Budget Organization, *Annual Report, 1990/91.*
[1] Estimates of the Plan and Budget Organization differ from those of Bank Markazi.

Table 10.1
Composition and Value of Imports
(In millions of U.S. dollars)

	1356 1977/78	1357 1978/79	1358 1979/80	1359 1980/81	1360 1981/82	1361 1982/83	1362 1983/84	1363 1984/85	1364 1985/86	1365 1986/87	1366 1987/88	1367 1988/89	1368 1989/90
Food and live animals	1534	1031	1518	1541	2161	2164	2368	2070	1538	1039	1466	1374	2779
Dairy and eggs	179	113	259	357	482	351	530	364	255	151	206	190	265
Grains & derivatives	565	391	450	562	943	673	1018	956	723	455	611	568	1856
Sugar, its derivatives, and honey	168	61	293	157	32	395	86	70	112	99	101	75	221
Coffee, tea, cocoa, spices, etc.	65	60	95	39	61	37	54	147	84	84	50	175	43
Fruits and vegetables	99	37	24	7	12	8	17	15	3	5	2	4	8
Others	458	369	397	419	631	700	663	518	361	245	496	362	386
Beverages and tobacco	131	117	52	46	88	7	90	82	99	109	107	47	77
Raw non-edible products (excluding petroleum fuels)	453	318	312	661	667	461	802	522	314	282	257	243	392
Raw caoutchouc	49	39	17	35	49	54	75	58	35	43	52	56	72
Textile fibers unlisted elsewhere	164	117	140	182	301	199	410	199	94	80	59	72	137
Various raw fertilizers and minerals	55	35	24	54	50	45	68	48	31	20	26	17	63
Others	185	127	131	390	267	163	249	217	154	139	120	98	120
Mineral products, fuel, oily products and their derivatives	43	28	16	88	214	207	205	299	247	401	411	347	319
Vegetable and animal shortening	186	152	267	113	294	192	338	361	310	184	373	130	359
Vegetable shortening	156	139	231	51	207	171	304	344	292	163	339	109	316
Others	30	13	36	62	87	21	34	17	18	21	34	21	43
Chemical products	1040	792	1085	1521	2180	1679	2084	1768	1163	1369	1428	1304	2048
Chemicals and their compounds	170	130	141	161	291	267	351	252	268	274	288	259	429
Raw materials for paints, dyes and tanning	93	74	82	90	124	71	132	213	71	50	62	46	74
Medical & pharmaceutical products	277	247	354	468	525	398	356	206	156	258	258	226	254
Plastic, cellulose and artificial resins	263	170	239	425	450	304	514	393	218	275	212	204	368
Other unlisted chemicals	121	90	134	124	297	253	306	348	157	211	317	208	479
Others	116	81	135	253	493	386	425	356	293	301	291	351	444

Goods classified according to their composition	4251	2974	2908	3335	3986	3507	5326	3561	3356	2258	1952	1623	2553
Paper, cardboard and derivatives	230	123	166	276	333	216	285	207	193	138	224	190	326
Various textile yarns and related products	664	335	422	655	921	739	1476	998	595	450	218	210	423
Non-metal mineral goods	403	331	249	310	150	84	174	131	87	97	87	81	104
Iron and steel	1405	1313	1223	1033	1415	1557	1902	1105	1768	1031	820	794	1059
Others	1549	872	848	1061	1167	911	1489	1120	713	542	603	348	641
Transportation vehicles, machinery & tools	6310	4534	2989	3055	3527	3331	6317	5452	3896	3315	3066	2804	3842
Non-electric machinery	3592	2693	1599	1403	1854	1732	3042	2828	1873	1798	1717	1706	2051
Elec. machinery, tools and appliances	1247	876	779	987	893	693	1346	1089	834	792	787	540	715
Transportation vehicles	1471	965	611	665	780	906	1929	1535	1189	725	562	558	1076
Miscellaneous finished products	520	358	489	484	393	284	530	358	293	392	307	271	381
Scientific and professional tools	269	237	294	321	236	202	365	251	206	250	221	214	267
Artificial goods unlisted elsewhere	130	68	115	135	118	58	119	71	69	106	68	50	95
Others	121	53	80	28	39	24	46	36	18	36	18	7	19
Goods not classified according to their type	158	68	59	6	5	13	43	21	192	6	2	34	57
Total	14626	10372	9695	10850	13515	11845	18103	14494	11408	9355	9369	8177	12807

Source: Bank Markazi; and Customs Administration, *Foreign Trade Statistics.*

Table 10.2
Composition of Non-Oil Exports
(Volume in 1000 tons)
(Value in millions of U.S. dollars)

	1356 1977/78	1357 1978/79	1358 1979/80	1359 1980/81	1360 1981/82	1361 1982/83	1362 1983/84	1363 1984/85	1364 1985/86	1365 1986/87	1366 1987/88	1367 1988/89	1368 1989/90	1369 1990/91	1370[1] 1991/92
Agricultural and traditional goods	443	369	725	602	321	255	318	295	371	781	991	770	894	1112	1884
Carpets	83	84	409	425	149	67	89	90	115	356	482	309	345	475	1115
Fruits	119	75	115	62	58	79	125	80	113	272	272	253	319	374	431
Skins and leather	40	39	49	49	53	41	35	49	60	61	103	78	94	53	55
Others	201	171	152	66	61	68	69	76	83	92	134	130	136	210	283
Metal ores	47	11	21	19	5	7	12	39	30	25	38	33	27	46	41
Industrial goods	136	163	66	24	13	21	26	27	64	110	132	233	123	189	456
Inorganic chemicals	18	44	4	–	–	–	–	1	4	11	17	33	34	28	43
Copper ingots, sheets	–	–	–	–	–	–	–	–	29	61	42	143	17	79	27
Ready-made clothes, etc	24	20	12	10	9	10	10	14	9	15	10	7	5	33	62
Construction materials	2	1	–	–	–	3	1	1	1	3	10	7	6	12	6
Transport vehicles	13	9	2	7	3	5	8	7	–	2	2	4	2	8	4
Others	79	89	48	4	1	3	7	4	21	18	51	44	59	29	314
Total value[2]	625	543	812	645	339	284	357	361	465	915	1161	1036	1044	1373	2533
Total volume	1138	1336	579	129	154	162	231	269	458	654	1133	1224	1445	2168	2490

Source: Customs Administration; and Bank Markazi.

[1] Estimates based on first nine months.

[2] Total value reported by the Customs Administration often differs from figures in balance-of-payments reported by Bank Markazi due to barter arrangements, sale of proceeds in the free market, and other statistical shortfalls.

Table 10.3
Composition of Imports and Exports by Use
(In millions of U.S. dollars)

	1356 1977/78	1357 1978/79	1358 1979/80	1359 1980/81	1360 1981/82	1361 1982/83	1362 1983/84	1363 1984/85	1364 1985/86	1365 1986/87	1366 1987/88	1367 1988/89	1368 1989/90	1369 1990/91
Imports														
Raw materials and processed goods	7910	5350	5301	6207	8225	6861	10840	8310	7411	5461	5498	4829	7548	11854
Capital goods	4019	9208	1835	1738	2149	2308	4352	3867	2421	2199	2209	1869	2915	4363
Consumer goods	2697	2114	2559	2905	3141	2676	2911	2318	1576	1695	1662	1479	2344	2505
Total[1]	14626	10372	9695	10850	13515	11845	18103	14494	11408	9355	9369	8177	12807	18722
Exports														
Raw materials and processed goods[2]	273	297	217	122	111	100	84	145	195	240	325	389	308	307
Capital goods	49	28	23	2	–	–	4	2	1	2	3	6	4	6
Consumer goods	303	218	572	521	228	183	269	213	269	673	833	641	733	1060
Total[3]	625	543	812	645	339	283	357	361	465	915	1161	1036	1044	1373

Source: Customs Administration and Bank Markazi.

[1] Total excludes imported items not under classification.
[2] Excluding oil and gas.
[3] Total may differ from figures in the balance-of-payments table 10.6.

Table 10.4
Distribution of Imports by Countries
(In millions of U.S. dollars)

	1356 1977/78	1357 1978/79	1358 1979/80	1359 1980/81	1360 1981/82	1361 1982/83	1362 1983/84	1363 1984/85	1364 1985/86	1365 1986/87	1366 1987/88	1367 1988/89	1368 1989/90	1369 1990/91
Germany	2804	2142	1750	1639	2252	1936	3443	2775	1900	1708	1795	1472	2024	3430
Japan	2319	1757	1343	1061	1619	1250	3022	2064	1609	1267	1053	836	973	1933
Italy	809	596	547	601	715	552	839	643	553	609	569	417	803	1499
Brazil	–	–	–	43	84	222	425	481	239	246	552	343	362	645
United Kingdom	1031	843	666	791	852	709	1087	1211	677	634	550	556	567	1015
Turkey	41	23	23	111	292	774	853	523	898	587	474	425	699	726
United Arab Emirates	60	42	132	461	404	121	335	302	350	537	390	276	949	971
Argentina	–	–	–	15	62	152	421	382	472	254	381	169	457	545
Australia	228	151	184	139	193	295	292	388	315	243	327	216	451	684
Belgium	347	257	256	275	318	338	417	560	347	341	316	393	493	797
South Korea	139	77	160	424	614	400	503	428	292	234	242	127	477	635
Netherlands	488	215	299	334	444	312	404	358	289	293	232	286	410	576
Switzerland	444	275	273	450	530	296	356	265	389	229	212	216	306	546
Soviet Union	273	195	182	819	194	270	221	88	116	93	198	217	200	305
New Zealand	95	38	40	80	206	290	304	287	238	161	166	76	182	23
Austria	143	78	140	355	336	194	329	265	250	163	146	161	226	450
Thailand	68	25	29	100	248	124	118	116	72	52	136	70	186	199
Bulgaria	70	46	84	154	180	229	200	135	164	89	106	94	104	57
Spain	147	172	110	234	412	359	384	301	210	133	106	110	219	287
Denmark	–	–	–	118	117	100	176	138	100	95	105	102	139	147
Yugoslavia	26	20	39	69	172	208	285	186	119	86	102	124	169	210
Canada	–	–	–	47	83	173	227	200	70	66	101	79	384	414
Romania	199	142	164	207	301	463	313	168	398	85	95	95	109	49
France	661	508	556	526	456	382	291	138	69	48	91	243	266	489
Others[3]	4242[2]	770[2]	6736[2]	1791	2431	1690	2858	2092	1272	1102	917	1084	1652	2090
Total[3]	14626	10372	9695	10844	13515	11839	18103	14494	11408	9355	9369	8177	12807	18722

Source: Customs Administration; and Bank Markazi.

[1] Figure refers to countries not consistently among the top 25 partners.

[2] Column does not add up because of different composition of countries on the list before and after the revolution.

[3] Total may differ from Table 10.6 due to differences in coverage and statistical discrepancy.

Table 10.5
Distribution of Non-Oil Exports by Countries
(In millions of U.S. dollars)

	1356 1977/78	1357 1978/79	1358 1979/80	1359 1980/81	1360 1981/82	1361 1982/83	1362 1983/84	1363 1984/85	1364 1985/86	1365 1986/87	1366 1987/88	1367 1988/89	1368 1989/90	1369 1990/91
Germany	81.5	75.4	281.7	291.9	108.2	53.3	73.4	64.2	113.6	283.1	355.9	321.7[1]	363.7[1]	399.8[1]
United Arab Emirates	15.9	7.5	19.3	4.3	4.1	18.1	50.2	33.0	65.2	163.3	155.1	145.8	143.6	152.5
Italy	26.3	24.7	56.4	52.5	46.3	35.6	33.0	38.6	54.1	68.8	116.0	106.9	134.3	159.0
Switzerland	6.5	8.1	45.1	55.6	26.3	9.8	13.2	24.1	34.1	55.4	94.1	77.8	80.3	100.1
Soviet Union	132.7	72.2	72.5	80.2	39.8	55.5	40.0	43.2	30.3	22.0	90.9	63.7	22.8	26.9
Japan	12.7	49.9	14.2	4.2	1.2	7.0	8.4	5.2	3.9	12.9	31.9	36.9	52.9	52.1
France	16.4	17.6	28.1	20.1	8.0	9.9	7.9	3.5	4.3	16.9	29.2	19.2	25.7	36.1
Netherlands	7.2	5.1	8.5	6.0	2.6	4.3	3.8	3.5	4.0	20.2	26.2	1.5	7.5	7.4
United Kingdom	17.2	13.7	23.6	22.6	9.2	8.6	16.3	17.7	15.3	20.3	25.1	99.3	18.8	50.1
Austria	3.1	1.7	7.3	10.4	4.4	2.0	3.7	4.3	8.0	15.1	18.2	12.1	17.1	17.7
China	–	–	–	–	–	–	–	–	2.5	0.4	15.7	3.8	3.6	3.8
Belgium	3.9	3.4	14.0	8.4	3.3	4.1	2.3	2.8	2.4	9.4	11.6	7.2	8.4	10.4
Czechoslovakia	9.2	9.4	10.2	7.6	8.1	7.9	5.1	24.4	0.3	6.2	10.8	17.9	4.7	1.9
Turkey	–	0.5	0.3	0.1	1.0	0.3	2.0	5.8	11.0	6.2	10.3	3.4	5.5	106.1
East Germany	4.2	2.4	3.8	3.5	8.9	4.4	5.8	9.9	13.6	18.1	10.1	–	–	–
Canada	1.9	1.4	5.7	3.2	2.2	1.2	0.9	1.3	1.6	4.5	8.1	8.0	11.3	18.2
India	4.1	3.7	3.0	2.2	1.0	1.4	1.2	0.8	4.2	12.1	7.0	5.3	9.3	24.4
Hungary	21.8	20.7	11.8	3.5	1.2	1.4	10.7	16.5	16.6	6.3	5.8	3.0	1.4	1.7
Denmark	1.5	1.0	4.7	3.1	1.0	0.7	1.0	0.8	1.0	4.7	5.7	3.9	4.5	5.0
Others	276.3[2]	224.4[2]	204.5[2]	65.8	62.7	58.2	77.7	61.5	79.0	169.6	133.1	98.4	128.5	199.2
Total	652.2	542.8	811.8	645.2	339.5	283.7	356.6	361.1	465.0	915.5	1160.8	1035.8	1043.9	1372.2

Source: Customs Administration; and Bank Markazi.

[1] Includes former East Germany's share.

[2] Includes Saudi Arabia, Kuwait, Lebanon, Syria, Pakistan, Australia and Bahrain who were among Iran's top 25 trading countries before the revolution.

Table 10.6
Balance of Payments
(In millions of US dollars)

	1356 1977/78	1357 1978/79	1358 1979/80	1359 1980/81	1360 1981/82	1361 1982/83	1362 1983/84	1363 1984/85	1364 1985/86	1365 1986/87	1366 1987/88	1367 1988/89	1368 1989/90	1369 1990/91	1370⁴ 1991/92
Trade balance	4876	4982	8284	1450	-1307	7900	3480	2358	2169	-3414	-89	101	-367	975	-6560
Exports	21429	18533	19829	12338	11831	20452	21507	17087	14175	7171	11916	11709	13081	19035	18415
Oil and gas	20905	18116	19386	11693	11491	20168	21150	16726	13710	6255	10755	9673	12037	17993	15802
Non-oil exports	524¹	417¹	443¹	645	340	284	357	361	465	916	1161	1036	1044	1312	2613
Imports²	-16553	-13551	-11545	-10888	-13138	-12552	-18027	-14729	-12005	-10585	-12005	-10608	-13448	-18330	-24975
Services	-3781	-5483	-2175	-3885	-2139	-2167	-3122	-2772	-2645	-1741	-2001	-1970	-2324	-3148	-3849
Receipts	4162	4204	2829	1735	1451	1121	1335	1069	763	607	437	467	798	892	1684
Passenger services				33	27	49	76	56	43	32	52	55	68	36	61
Travel				29	18	10	12	19	28	19	11	11	15	28	57
Investment income				1004	895	612	795	594	393	365	206	223	352	456	472
Other				(669)	(511)	(450)	(452)	(400)	(299)	(191)	168	178	363	372	1094
Payments	-7943	-9687	-5004	-5621	-3590	-3288	-4457	-3841	-3408	-2348	-2437	-2437	-3122	-4040	-5533
Freight & insurance				-2553	-1877	-1793	-2576	-2103	-1715	-1242	-1231	-1088	-1346	-1992	-2470
Passenger services				-60	-44	-38	-100	-139	-115	-63	-31	-103	-43	-64	-127
Travel				-1700	-681	-400	-464	-488	-508	-247	-246	-69	-129	-340	-734
Investment income				-398	-275	-227	-184	-143	-100	-66	-66	-82	-104	-78	-85
Other				-910	-713	-830	-1133	-968	-970	-720	-864	-1095	-1500	-1566	-1117
Current balance	1095	-501	6109	-2435	-3446	5733	358	-414	-476	-5155	-2090	-1869	-191⁵	327⁵	-7909⁵
Capital account	1505	316	-110	-8238	1441	-1847	-2474	-2818	544	3127	1711	441	3207	354	5530
Long-term capital				-5261	289	-1866	-271	-421	-160	802	719	-37	1036	49	1137
Government sector (net)³				-5246	424	-1791	-151	-306	-115	840	-757	-16	-1038	-49	1137
Others				-15	-135	-75	-120	-115	-45	-38	-38	-53	-2		–
Short-term capital				-2977	1152	19	-2203	2397	704	2325	992	478	2171	305	4393
Government sector				287	-504	-544	752	-1605	-1000	1076	-192	117	501	387	-492
Banks				-1027	446	-255	-483	-504	-351	291	546	-159	-216	-551	611
Other sectors (net)				-2162	1210	818	-2472	-288	2055	958	638	520	1886	469	4274

Errors and omissions	-586	-394	-348	945	1745	1052	864	-906	549	856	193	472	-682	-981	282
Overall balance	2014	-579	5651	-9728	-260	4938	-1252	-4138	617	-1172	-186	-956	2334	-300	-2097
MEMORANDUM ITEMS															
Official Exchange Rate (Rials/$)	70.62	70.48	70.48	70.62	78.33	83.60	86.36	90.03	91.05	78.76	71.46	68.68	72.02	68.10	67.51

Source: Bank Markazi; International Monetary Fund; and Organization of Petroleum Exporting Countries.

1 Foreign exchange bought by Bank Markazi from non-oil exporters. Figures may differ from those in Table 10.2.
2 Includes payments for imports not subject to bilateral arrangements. Figures differ from those in Table 10.1.
3 Assets have a minus sign.
4 Estimates.
5 Includes an estimated $2.5 billion of unregistered private capital inflow, financing private imports.

Table 10.7
Estimates of External Debt: Stock and Flows
(In millions of U.S. dollars)

	1359 1980/81	1360 1981/82	1361 1982/83	1362 1983/84	1363 1984/85	1364 1985/86	1365 1986/87	1366 1987/88	1367 1988/89	1368 1989/90	1369 1990/91	1370 1991/92
Total debt stock	4508	3793	8237	7107	5160	6057	5827	6144	5831	6518	9021	11511
Long-term	4508	3793	3468	2968	2457	2390	2413	2280	2055	1862	1797	2736
Short-term[1]	–	–	4769	4139	2703	3667	3414	3864	3776	4657	7224	8775
Total debt flows												
Disbursements (Long-term)	264	95	209	94	5	87	42	11	157	–	139	1086
Repayments (Long-term)	531	523	481	545	370	354	321	214	334	124	225	174
Interest payments												
Long-term	432	221	693	508	374	259	246	228	291	333	430	603
Short-term	432	221	181	115	79	58	61	38	62	44	28	25
Short-term	–	–	512	393	295	201	185	190	229	289	402	578
Total debt service	963	744	1174	1059	744	613	567	442	625	457	655	777
Long-term	963	744	662	659	449	412	382	252	396	168	253	199
Short-term	–	–	512	393	295	201	185	190	229	289	402	578

Source: The World Bank; and the Organization for Economic Cooperation and Development.

[1] Largely export credits.

Table 11.1
Output, Area, and Yield of major Crops[1]
(Production in thousands of tons; area in thousands of hectares; and yield in kilograms per hectare)

	1356 1977/78	1357 1978/79	1358 1979/80	1359 1980/81	1360 1981/82	1361 1982/83	1362 1983/84	1363 1984/85	1364 1985/86	1365 1986/87	1366 1987/88	1367 1988/89	1368 1989/90	1369 1990/91	1370 1991/92
Cotton															
Production	557	427	321	219	275	358	300	351	324	359	341	380	395	437	358
Area	316	280	215	145	194	206	184	212	188	188	192	192	228	221	–
Yield	1761	1524	1493	1510	1418	1738	1630	1656	1723	1910	1776	1979	1732	1977	–
Wheat															
Production	5517	5660	6025	5744	6610	6660	5956	6207	6631	7740	7600	7265	6010	8547	8758
Area	5451	5442	5352	5954	6124	7192	6042	5959	6195	6497	6591	6553	6257	6360	–
Yield	1012	1040	1128	965	1079	926	986	1042	1070	1191	1163	1109	961	1343	–
Barley															
Production	1230	1217	1353	1265	1700	1903	2034	2293	2297	2528	2731	3394	2847	3748	3196
Area	1277	1177	1255	1577	1565	1841	2006	2163	2084	1956	2220	2576	2651	2638	–
Yield	963	1034	1078	802	1086	1034	1014	1060	1102	1292	1230	1318	1074	1420	–
Rice															
Production	1399	1527	1348	1181	1624	1605	1215	1474	1772	1784	1929	1419	1854	2273	2430
area	404	386	381	402	459	483	429	442	475	471	586	467	519	605	–
Yield	3465	3955	3273	2938	3538	3323	2832	3335	3731	3788	3292	3039	3572	3757	–
Sugar Beets															
Production	4187	3660	3807	3917	3231	4321	3648	3392	3924	4965	4500	3454	3535	3641	4960
Area	166	150	160	160	142	193	168	134	145	177	178	147	149	149	–
Yield	25262	24385	23855	24481	22754	22389	21714	25313	27062	28051	25281	23497	23725	24436	–
Oil Seeds															
Production	105	126	99	69	81	123	188	118	138	129	229	298	236	145	155
Area	107	–	–	63	78	87	108	89	94	98	148	142	179	142	–
Yield	981	–	–	1095	1038	1414	1741	1326	1468	1316	1547	2098	1318	1021	–
Pistachio															
Production	27	69	9	23	122	95	84	94	100	110	114	126	131	163	–
Area	–	–	97	112	114	115	102	127	130	146	153	168	130	154	–
Yield	–	–	92	205	1070	826	824	740	769	753	745	750	1007	1058	–

Table 11.1 (cont.)
Output, Area, and Yield of major Crops[1]
(Production in thousands of tons; area in thousands of hectares; and yield in kilograms per hectare)

	1356 1977/78	1357 1978/79	1358 1979/80	1359 1980/81	1360 1981/82	1361 1982/83	1362 1983/84	1363 1984/85	1364 1985/86	1365 1986/87	1366 1987/88	1367 1988/89	1368 1989/90	1369 1990/91	1370 1991/92
Green tea															
Production	116	120	136	143	147	157	162	194	148	181	192	193	124	166	–
Area	27	–	–	31	31	30	35	31	32	35	32	32	32	32	–
Yield	4295	–	–	4613	4594	5233	4629	6258	4625	5171	6000	6031	3875	5187	–
Tobacco															
Production	15	13	18	24	27	25	21	22	28	28	25	9	15	19	–
Area	13	14	17	23	24	22	20	20	23	22	22	5	15	17	–
Yield	1120	925	1065	1043	1125	1136	1050	1100	1217	1273	1136	1800	1000	1117	–
Onions															
Production	392	393	596	631	675	965	736	844	719	809	923	612	692	1213	1200
Area	34	31	36	41	40	54	41	43	39	42	44	25	25	60	–
Yield	11538	12677	13596	15390	16875	17870	17951	19628	18436	19262	20977	24480	27680	20216	–
Potatoes															
Production	697	735	973	1270	1540	1814	1740	1784	1725	2349	2348	1443	2033	2809	3025
Area	63	57	75	93	99	110	115	116	111	145	150	105	121	162	–
Yield	11400	12695	12906	13656	15556	16491	15130	15379	15541	16200	15653	13743	16802	17339	–

Source: Ministry of Agriculture; and Food and Agriculture Organization.
[1] Some figures differ from data published by Bank Markazi.

Table 11.2
Imports of Selected Foodstuffs
(In 1,000 metric tons)

	1356 1977/78	1360 1981/82	1362 1983/84	1364 1985/86	1366 1987/88	1368 1988/90	1370[3] 1991/92
Cereals[1]	2660	3982	4739	4178	5066	8221	–
Of which wheat	1197	1945	3031	2137	3770	4780	2500
Sugar and candy	387	668	660	573	555	468	200
Edible oil	259	356	603	555	463	858	–
Red meat	199	161	229	184	195	182	100
Memorandum Items							
Cereal imports Per capita (kg)	77	97	107	87	99	152	
As percentage of domestic output[2]	33	40	51	39	41	77	
As percentage of aggregate supply	25	27	34	28	29	43	

Source: Bank Markazi; Iranian Statistical Center; and Tables 5.1 and 11.1

[1] Includes wheat, barley, rice and corn.
[2] Includes wheat, barley and rice.
[3] Estimates.

Table 12.1
Production, Employment and Compensation[1]
in
Large Manufacturing Establishments
1361 = 100
(Annual averages)

	1359 1980/81			1360 1981/82			1361 1982/83			1362 1983/84			1363 1984/85		
	P	E	C	P	E	C	P	E	C	P	E	C	P	E	C
Food, beverage & tobacco	95.1	97.4	93.1	95.4	97.1	90.7	100.0	100.0	100.0	109.4	101.4	114.3	114.0	102.3	121.4
Textiles, clothing and leather	76.3	92.1	79.1	93.3	95.6	88.0	100.0	100.0	100.0	115.6	105.5	114.4	120.2	110.6	128.7
Wood and wooden products	63.9	97.0	87.8	75.8	95.7	87.9	100.0	100.0	100.0	107.0	110.6	112.5	116.2	117.9	128.6
Paper, cardboard & derivatives	64.3	70.3	67.3	74.3	73.5	74.2	100.0	100.0	100.0	116.4	105.7	111.6	131.7	107.7	124.4
Chemical materials and products	80.0	93.4	92.8	84.9	97.4	95.8	100.0	100.0	100.0	122.8	108.2	113.9	134.0	115.6	131.1
Non-metallic minerals[2]	77.3	91.9	76.0	86.6	95.4	86.8	100.0	100.0	100.0	108.5	105.2	112.6	114.7	108.0	122.4
Basic Metals	69.5	90.4	85.2	61.5	92.0	88.6	100.0	100.0	100.0	148.5	116.8	128.7	171.4	135.3	160.6
Machinery and equipment	70.2	93.4	79.2	88.9	97.0	90.5	100.0	100.0	100.0	136.8	115.1	123.2	151.0	124.5	140.8
General index	77.3	92.5	82.2	87.5	95.4	89.4	100.0	100.0	100.0	121.9	108.6	117.4	131.3	115.3	133.1

Source: Bank Markazi.

[1] Excludes sugar industry and slaughterhouses

[2] Excludes oil and coal

Table 12.1 (cont.)
Production, Employment and Compensation[1]
in
Large Manufacturing Establishments
1361 = 100
(Annual averages)

	1364 1985/86			1365 1986/87			1366 1987/88			1367 1988/89			1368 1989/90			1369 1990/91	
P	E	C	P	E	C	P	E	C	P	E	C	P	E	C	P	E	C
120.7	104.2	136.6	104.1	102.5	137.3	95.2	100.4	152.8	92.5	101.9	176.8	93.6	101.8	199.5	108.5	105.6	200.6
121.8	112.9	144.8	102.3	111.4	144.3	95.3	110.3	157.6	84.8	109.9	177.9	82.4	107.6	190.6	90.8	108.0	190.8
102.4	122.8	148.2	96.4	128.3	150.5	99.6	128.8	166.1	97.2	128.3	190.3	111.9	138.7	217.4	112.2	148.1	216.4
117.8	108.5	137.1	81.2	103.8	128.2	77.7	98.0	143.6	88.2	95.4	159.8	90.3	93.5	179.6	134.5	98.6	186.2
127.9	119.4	144.1	108.7	117.3	144.8	113.6	114.6	159.1	95.6	115.8	192.6	117.6	117.3	215.4	161.5	122.9	240.8
116.6	112.0	139.0	108.5	109.5	138.3	115.3	109.3	152.8	108.4	104.4	167.7	120.2	106.5	179.8	134.5	108.7	192.4
166.1	141.8	183.2	133.6	134.8	177.6	105.0	131.1	191.0	108.1	136.2	225.2	123.2	143.8	263.4	201.0	152.2	302.1
133.4	128.0	155.5	83.6	116.6	138.9	71.6	108.4	144.2	65.2	107.8	164.9	66.6	108.4	185.8	104.6	113.0	196.6
126.9	118.5	149.0	100.6	114.0	144.0	94.3	110.8	155.9	86.7	111.1	178.7	91.8	111.2	199.7	118.4	114.7	244.8

Table 12.2
Housing and Construction

	1356 1977/78	1357 1978/79	1358 1979/80	1359 1980/81	1360 1981/82	1361 1982/83	1362 1983/84	1363 1984/85	1364 1985/86	1365 1986/87	1366 1987/88	1367 1988/89	1368 1989/90
Housing units completed[1]	576	495	496	504	504	371	371	329	328	215	–	–	–
Urban areas	322	306	306	294	294	207	207	189	189	134	–	128	116
Rural areas	254	189	190	210	210	164	164	140	139	81	–	–	–
Investment in construction[2]	655	578	425	434	378	403	510	474	423	384	351	318	316
Private	246	218	227	237	192	186	293	286	274	233	218	193	207
Public	409	360	198	197	186	217	216	188	149	151	133	125	109
Total cumulative units[1]											8217		
Urban											4670		
Rural											3547		

Source: Bank Markazi; and Iranian Statistical Center.

[1] In thousands of units. Figures for 1357–58, 1359–60, 1361–62, and 1363–64 are combined in the source, and divided here.
[2] In billions of Iranian rials at 1974/75 prices.

Table 12.3
Electricity Generation and Sales

	1356 1977/78	1365 1986/87	1369 1990/91	1372[1] 1993/94
Nominal installed capacity (MW)	7105	15540	17950	20305
Power generation (MKWH)	17400	42550	59100	73200
Peak demand (MKWH)	3490	7464	9480	14600
Load factor (%)	56.9	62.7	60.1	59.1
Total sales (MKWH)[2]	13950	32620	45100	63300
Domestic	3800	12420	17345	21300
Commercial	3420	7810	11930	14900
Industrial	5820	8700	10220	21300
Agricultural	440	2160	3715	3900
Others	670	1530	1890	1900
Losses	3240	6425	10200	13100

Source: Ministry of Energy; and Iranian Statistical Center.

[1] Projected.
[2] Ministry of Energy only.

Table 13.1
Production, Export and Domestic Consumption of Oil
(In millions of barrels per year)

	1356 1977/78	1357 1978/79	1358 1979/80	1359 1980/81	1360 1981/82	1361 1982/83	1362 1983/84	1363 1984/85	1364 1985/86	1365 1986/87	1366 1987/88	1367 1988/89	1368 1989/90	1369 1990/91	1370 1991/92
Output of crude oil	2038.8	1551.9	1253.0	540.9	538.0	979.7	988.8	865.4	914.0	794.2	897.9	933.3	1075.6	1179.0	1285.9
(per day)	(5.58)	(4.25)	(3.43)	(1.48)	(1.47)	(2.68)	(2.71)	(2.37)	(2.50)	(2.17)	(2.46)	(2.55)	(2.94)	(3.23)	(3.36)
Export of crude oil[1]	1757.8[2]	1261.0[2]	960.6[2]	278.1[2]	289.4	615.4	746.4	586.5	532.9	456.2	564.3	601.6	684.4	811.8	897.9
(per day)	(4.81)	(3.45)	(2.63)	(0.76)	(0.83)	(1.98)	(2.06)	(1.64)	(1.71)	(1.25)	(1.55)	(1.65)	(1.87)	(2.22)	(2.46)
Net exports of refined products	77.3	74.0	85.7	51.4	30.1	35.4	-32.6	-26.9	-45.6	-60.5	-71.5	-69.2	-31.1	-23.4	-24.2
Export on consignment	–	–	–	–	12.2	106.5	7.5	13.4	91.3	98.7	75.9	85.0	62.0	50.0	–
Domestic consumption	186.2	190.7	200.3	192.0	199.0	213.0	263.0	284.4	309.6	287.9	294.2	304.8	327.7	335.2	412.2
Discrepancy[3]	17.5	26.2	6.4	19.4	7.3	9.4	4.5	8.0	25.8	11.9	35.0	11.1	35.6	5.4	–

Source: Ministry of Petroleum; and Bank Markazi.

[1] Including exports for refining.
[2] Including exports on consignment.
[3] Discrepancies include change in inventories, crude oil in pipelines, and refining wastage.

Table 13.2
Natural Gas Production and Uses
(In billions of standard cubic meters)[1]

	1356 1977/78	1357 1978/79	1358 1979/80	1359 1980/81	1360 1981/82	1361 1982/83	1362 1983/84	1363 1984/85	1364 1985/86	1365 1986/87	1366 1987/88	1367 1988/89	1368 1989/90	1369 1990/91	1370 1991/92
Gross output	59.5	44.4	41.7	16.6	15.7	30.0	27.8	29.2	35.0	25.9	31.4	34.6	45.9	56.3	61.8
Exports	9.2	5.3	3.5	-	-	-	-	-	-	-	-	-	-	2.1	2.9
Domestic consumption	23.9[2]	16.6[2]	21.4[2]	9.4[2]	5.1	7.0	8.0	9.1	9.1	8.8	11.0	11.0	13.1	16.1	22.6
Sector use and losses	-	-	-	-	2.2	3.6	3.6	3.6	5.8	3.6	3.6	4.0	8.4	11.7	8.0
Gas reinjection	-	-	-	-	2.6	7.3	4.0	7.3	9.9	4.0	6.2	9.1	13.5	15.0	17.2
Flare	26.4	22.5	16.8	7.2	5.8	12.1	12.2	9.2	10.2	9.5	10.6	10.5	10.9	11.4	11.1

Source: National Iranian Oil Co.; OPEC Secretariat; and unofficial estimates.

[1] One billion cubic meters = 34.642 billion cubic feet.
[2] Includes gas reinjections, sector use and losses.

Table 14.1
Gross National Product and Per Capita Income

	1356 1977/78	1357 1978/79	1358 1979/80	1359 1980/81	1360 1981/82	1361 1982/83	1362 1983/84	1363 1984/85	1364 1985/86	1365 1986/87	1366 1987/88	1367 1988/89	1368 1989/90	1369 1990/91	1370 1991/92
Population[1]	34.7	36.0	37.9	39.6	41.2	42.8	44.4	46.2	47.8	49.4	51.0	52.7	54.5	56.4	58.2
Net national income:															
Nominal[2]:	4695	4360	5538	5632	6883	9107	11449	12507	14048	15195	17680	18347	22860	30049	39430
(Per capita)[3]	(135)	(121)	(126)	(142)	(167)	(213)	(258)	(271)	(294)	(307)	(347)	(348)	(419)	(533)	(677)
Real[4]:	10143	8653	9538	8232	8035	9107	10220	10155	11593	9829	9891	7944	8226	9400	10568
(Per capita)[5]	(292)	(240)	(251)	(208)	(195)	(213)	(230)	(220)	(242)	(199)	(194)	(151)	(151)	(167)	(181)
Private consumption[6]	5323	5430	5615	5360	5533	5943	6804	7170	7306	6634	6307	6172	6327	7563	8108
(Per capita)[7]	(153)	(151)	(148)	(135)	(134)	(139)	(153)	(155)	(153)	(134)	(124)	(117)	(116)	(134)	(139)

Source: Tables 4.3, 4.4, and 5.1.

[1] In millions of inhabitants.
[2] In billions of Iranian rials at current market prices.
[3] In thousands of Iranian rials at current prices.
[4] In billions of Iranian rials at constant 1361 prices.
[5] In thousands of Iranian rials at constant 1361 prices.
[6] In billions of Iranian rials at constant 1361 prices.
[7] In thousands of Iranian rials at constant 1361 prices.

Table 14.2
Average Annual Budget of Households
(In thousands of Iranian rials)[1]

	1356 1977/78	1358 1979/80	1361 1982/83	1362 1983/84	1363 1984/85	1364 1985/86	1365 1986/87	1366 1987/88	1367 1988/89	1368 1989/90
Urban households										
Total income	448.7	514.4	709.6	918.4	1034.1	1037.0	1126.6	1149.2	1339.9	1467.4
Wages & salaries										
Public sector			207.1	266.1	284.3	303.2	312.3	298.7	320.3	346.1
Private sector			98.7	116.5	130.8	133.7	137.7	154.8	180.9	194.9
Self-employment										
Agriculture			20.4	26.7	20.7	21.5	35.3	29.2	56.2	55.5
Other			169.2	224.5	260.3	232.4	269.5	293.3	352.3	361.2
Misc. income			213.9	284.2	337.8	346.2	370.6	373.1	430.1	509.5
Total expenditure[2]	438.2	528.2	883.5	1113.1	1240.1	1280.0	1314.6	1488.8	1800.3	2086.1
Food			355.0	436.0	480.1	500.0	546.6	634.5	802.9	916.1
Non-food			528.5	677.1	760.4	780.0	768.0	854.3	997.3	1170.0
Rural households										
Total income	166.3	227.3	391.8	471.8	524.6	531.1	568.6	723.2	908.6	1012.2
Wages & salaries										
Public sector				60.3	66.0	65.7	69.8	101.7	100.8	89.2
Private sector			110.0	90.8	90.0	92.8	91.0	109.7	135.8	156.2
Self-employment										
Agriculture			162.3	170.1	196.6	198.6	238.8	283.0	390.4	444.9
Others			54.2	67.7	70.8	71.7	64.7	90.0	114.6	131.6
Misc. income			65.1	91.0	101.0	102.0	104.0	138.7	166.8	191.0
Total expenditure[2]	207.2	288.4	505.4	611.7	670.7	677.6	761.6	908.4	1058.4	1307.2
Food			271.8	309.9	346.8	347.0	426.5	504.0	553.1	676.9
Non-food			233.6	301.8	323.9	330.6	335.1	404.4	505.2	630.2
Ratio of urban/rural Incomes	2.7	2.3	1.8	1.9	2.0	2.0	1.98	1.59	1.47	1.45
Ratio of urban/rural Expenditures	2.1	1.8	1.7	1.8	1.9	1.9	1.73	1.64	1.70	1.59

Source: Iranian Statistical Center.

[1] Decimals may not add up due to rounding.

[2] Expenditure refers to actual or imputed value of goods and services consumed by households or given away as gifts, (including purchased, service-related, home-made, and bartered items), and gifts received.

Select Bibliography*

Abdulghani, J. M., *Iraq and Iran: The Years of Crisis* (Baltimore: The Johns Hopkins University Press, 1984).

Ahmad, Kurshid, *Studies in Islamic Economics* (Leicester: Islamic Foundation, 1981)

Afshar, Haleh, *Iran: A Revolution in Turmoil* (Albany: SUNY Press, 1985).

Ajami, Fouad, 'The Impossible Revolution', in *Foreign Affairs*, January 1989.

Akhavi, Shahrough, 'Elite Factionalism in the Islamic Republic of Iran', in *The Middle East Journal*, Spring 1987.

Algar, Hamed, *Constitution of the Islamic Republic of Iran* (Berkeley: Mizan Press, 1980).

Alizadeh, Mohammad, *Vizhegiha-ye Rahbordi-ye Bazaar-e Kar-e Iran 1355–1365* (Tehran: Plan and Budget Organization, 1367 [1988].

Alnasrawi, Abbas, 'Economic Consequences of Iran–Iraq War', in *Third World Quarterly*, July 1986.

Amirahmadi, H., and Parvin, M., (eds.), *Post-Revolutionary Iran* (Boulder: Westview Press, 1988).

Amirahmadi, Hooshang, *Revolution and Economic Transition: The Iranian Experience* (Albany: SUNY Press, 1990).

---

* The bibliography includes only the major works cited in this book or specifically consulted for writing it. Internal agency reports, memoranda, position papers and unpublished materials which have also been examined are left out due to the lack of space. Excluded are also numerous references in footnotes to domestic and foreign newspapers.

Amuzegar, Jahangir, *Iran: An Economic Profile* (Washington: The Middle East Institute, 1977).

Amuzegar, Jahangir, 'Growth Without Pain: The New Iranian Development Strategy', Middle East Problem Paper No. 18 (Washington: The Middle East institute, September 1978).

Amuzegar, Jahangir, *The Dynamics of the Iranian Revolution* (Albany: SUNY Press, 1991).

Amuzegar, Jahangir, and Fekrat, M. A., *Iran: Economic Development under Dualistic Conditions* (Chicago: The University of Chicago Press, 1971).

Ashraf, Ahmad, *Masa'el-e Arzi va Dehqani* (Tehran: Agah Press, 1361 [1882]).

Bakhash, Shaul, *The Politics of Oil and Revolution in Iran* (Washington: The Brookings Institution, 1982)

Bakhash, Shaul, 'The Politics of Land, Law, and Social Justice in Iran', in *The Middle East Journal*, Spring 1989.

Bakhash, Shaul, *The Reign of the Ayatollahs* (London: I.B.Tauris, 1985)

Bani-Sadr, A. H., *Eqtesad-e Towhidi* (n.p., 1357 [1978]).

Bank Markazi Jomhuri-ye Eslami-ye Iran, Hesabha-ye Melli-ye Iran 1338–1356 [1959/60–1977/78] (Tehran: 1360).

Bank Markazi Jomhuri-ye Eslami-ye Iran, Hesabha-ye Melli-ye Iran 1353–1366 [1974/75–1987/88] (Tehran: 1370).

Bank Markazi Jomhuri-ye Eslami-ye Iran, *Gozaresh-e Eqtesadi va Taraznameh* (Tehran: 1357 to 1369 [1978/79–1990/91]).

Bank Markazi Jomhuri-ye Eslami-ye Iran, *Barrasi-e Tahavolat-e Eqtesadi-ye Keshvar baad az Enqelab* (Tehran: n.d. [1984?]).

Bashiriyeh, Hossein, *The State and Revolution in Iran 1962–1982* (London: Croom Helm, 1984).

Bayat, Assef, *Workers and Revolution in Iran* (London: Zed Books, 1987).

Behdad, Sohrab, 'Foreign Exchange Gap, Structural Constraints and the Political Economy of Exchange-Rate Determination in Iran', in *International Journal of Middle East Studies*, February 1988.

Beheshti, M. H., *Eqtesad-e Eslami* (Tehran: n.p., 1370 [1990]).

Benard, C., and Khalilzad, Z., *The Government of God* (New York: Columbia University Press, 1984).

Bina, C., and Zanganeh, H., *Modern Capitalism and Islamic Ideology in Iran* (New York: St Martin's Press, 1992).

Carswell, Robert, 'Economic Sanctions and the Iran Experience', in *Foreign Affairs*, Winter 1981–82.

Choudhuri, M. A., and Malik, U. A., *The Foundations of Islamic Political Economy* (London: Macmillan, 1992).

Christopher, Warren, *American Hostages in Iran* (New Haven: Yale University Press, 1985).

Chubin, S., and Tripp, C., *Iran and Iraq at War* (London: I.B.Tauris, 1988).

Clawson, Patrick, 'Islamic Iran's Economic Politics and Prospects', in *The Middle East Journal*, Summer 1988.

Clawson, Patrick, 'Dossier Iran: la situation economique: prospective et politique', in *Les Cahiers de L'orient*, 3ème trimestre 1990.

Embassy of Iran, *Iran's Domestic and Foreign Policy* (Washington: 1976)

Farazmand, Ali, *The State, Bureaucracy and Revolution in Modern Iran* (New York: Praeger, 1989).

Farhang, Mansour, 'The Iran–Iraq War', in *World Policy Journal*, Fall 1985.

Fesharaki, Fereidun, *Revolution and Energy Policy in Iran* (London: The Economist Intelligence Unit, 1980).

Food and Agriculture Organization, *Production Yearbook*, 1979 to 1991.

Food and Agriculture Organization, *Trade Yearbook*, 1980 to 1991.

Ghasimi, M. R., 'The Iranian Economy After the Revolution', in *International Journal of Middle East Studies*, November 1992.

Graham, Robert, *Iran: The Illusion of Power* (New York: St Martin's Press, 1979).

Graz, Liesl, 'Iran Under Rafsanjani', in *Middle East International*, January 5, 1990.

Halliday, Fred, 'The Iranian Revolution: Uneven Development and Religious Populism', in *Journal of International Affairs*, Winter 1983.

Hashemi-Rafsanjani, A. A. *Siasat-e Eqtesadi* (Tehran:Hezb-e Jomhuri-ye Eslami, 1362 [1983]).

Hiro, Dilip, *Iran Under the Ayatollahs* (London: Routledge, 1985).

Hiro, Dilip, *The Longest War* (London: Routledge, 1990).

Hooglund, Eric, *Land and Revolution in Iran 1960–1980* (Austin: University of Texas Press, 1982).

Hunter, S. T., *Iran and the World: Continuity in a Revolutionary Decade* (Bloomington: Indiana University Press, 1990).

Hunter, S. T., *Iran After Khomeini* (New York: Praeger, 1992).

Hussain, Asaf, *Islamic Iran* (New York: St Martin's Press, 1985).

International Monetary Fund, *Direction of Trade Statistics* (Washington: 1979 to 1992).

International Monetary Fund, *International Financial Statistics Yearbook* (Washington: 1979 to 1992).

International Monetary Fund, *Government Finance Statistics Year-book* (Washington: 1988 to 1992).

International Monetary Fund, *Exchange Arrangements and Exchange Restrictions* Annual Report, 1992 (Washington: 1992).

Iqbal, Z., and Mirakhor, A., *Islamic Banking*, Occasional Paper No. 49 (Washington: International Monetary Fund, 1986).

Iranian Statistical Center, *Iran in the Mirror of Statistics* (Tehran, 1990).

Ismael, T. Y., *Iran and Iraq: Roots of Conflict* (Syracuse: Syracuse University Press, 1982).

Jacqz, J. W. (ed.), *Iran: Past, Present, and Future* (New York: Aspen Institute, 1975).

Karanjia, R. K., *The Mind of a Monarch* (London: Allen & Unwin, 1977).

Karimi, Setareh, 'Economic Policies and Structural Changes Since the Revolution', in N. R. Keddie and E. Hooglund (eds.), *The Iranian Revolution and the Islamic Republic* (Syracuse: Syracuse University Press, 1986).

Karsh, Efraim, *The Iran–Iraq War* (New York: St Martin's Press, 1989).

Karshenas, Massoud, *Oil, State, and Industrialization in Iran* (Cambridge: Cambridge University Press, 1990).

Kavoosi, Masoud, 'The Post-Revolutionary Iranian Economy', in *Business Economics*, April 1988.

Khadduri, Majid, *The Gulf War* (New York: Oxford University Press, 1988).

Khalili, Akbar, *Gam be Gam ba Enqelab* (Tehran: Soroush, 1360 [1981]).

Khomeini, Rouhollah, *Islam and Revolution: Writings and Declarations* (London: Routledge, 1981).

Lautenschlager, Wolfgang, 'The Effects of an Overvalued Exchange Rate on the Iranian Economy, 1979–1984', in *International Journal of Middle East Studies*, February 1986.

Lenczowski, George, *Iran Under the Pahlavis* (Stanford: The Hoover Institution Press, 1978).

Malek, M. M. H., *The Political Economy of Iran under the Shah* (London: Croom Helm, 1986).

Mannan, M. A., *Islamic Economics* (Cambridge: The Islamic Academy, 1986).

Markaz-e Amar-e Iran, *Salnameh-e Amari-ye Keshvar* (Tehran: 1366 to 1370 [1987 to 1990]).

McLachlan, K. S., *The Neglected Garden: The Politics and Ecology of Agriculture in Iran* (London: I.B.Tauris, 1988).

McLachlan, K. S., and Ershad F., (eds.), *Internal Migration in Iran* (London: SOAS, 1989)

Milani, M. M., *The Making of Iran's Islamic Revolution* (Boulder: Westview Press, 1988).

Ministry of Economics and Finance, Jomhuri-ye Eslami-ye Iran, *Law and Regulations Concerning the Attraction and Protection of Foreign Investments in Iran* (Tehran: details unavailable).

Mofid, Kamran, *Development Planning in Iran: From Monarchy to Islamic Republic* (Cambridgeshire: MENAS Press, 1987).

Mofid, Kamran, *The Economic Consequences of the Gulf War* (London: Routledge, 1990).

Moghadam, V. M., 'Workers' and Peasants' Councils in Iran', in *Monthly Review*, October 1980.

Moghadam, V. M. (S. Azad), 'Women, Work, and Ideology in the Islamic Republic', in *International Journal of Middle East Studies*, May 1988.

Mojtahed, A., and Esfahani, H., 'Agricultural Policy and Performance in Iran: The Post-Revolutionary Experience', in *World Development*, June 1989.

Mossallanejad, Ezat, *The Political Economy of Oil* (New Delhi: Criterion Press, 1986).

Mossavar-Rahmani, Bijan, *Energy Policy in Iran: Domestic Choices and International Implications* (New York: Pergamon Press, 1981).

Nehzat-e Moqavemat-e Melli-ye Iran, *Negahi be Karnameh-e Jomhuri-ye Eslami 1358–1367* (Paris: 1369 [1990]).

Najmabadi, Afsaneh, *Land Reform and Social Change in Iran* (Salt Lake City: University of Utah Press, 1987).

Pesaran, M. H., 'The Iranian Foreign Exchange Policy and the Black Market for Dollars', in *International Journal of Middle East Studies*, February 1992.

Plan and Budget Organization, *Iran's Fifth Development Plan, Revised 1973–1978: A Summary* (Tehran: January 1975).

Plan and Budget Organization, *A Summarized Version of the First Five-Year Economic, Social, and Cultural Development Plan of the Islamic Republic of Iran* (Tehran: May 1990).

Rahnema, A., and Nomani, F., *Iran: The Secular Miracle* (London: Zed Books, 1990).

Rajaee, Farhang, *Islamic Values and Worldview: Khomeini on Man, the State, and International Politics* (Lanham: University Press of America, 1983).

Ramazani, R. K., *Revolutionary Iran: Challenge and Response* (Baltimore: The Johns Hopkins University Press, 1986).

Razavi, H., and Vakil, F., *The Political Environment of Economic Planning in Iran, 1971–1983* (Boulder: Westview Press, 1984).

Razzaqi, Ebrahim, *Eqtesad-e Iran* (Tehran: Nashr-e Ney, 1367 [1988]).

Rodinson, Maxime, *Islam and Capitalism* (Austin: University of Texas Press, 1978).

Rosen, B. M. (ed.), *Iran since the Revolution* (New York: Columbia University Press, 1985).

Sadr, Imam Musa, *Eqtesad dar Maktab-e Eslam* (Tehran: Entesharat, 1350 [1971]).

Sadr, M. B., *Eqtesad-e Ma* (transl.) (Tehran: Entesharat Borhan, 1350, 1357 [1971, 1978]).

Sadr, M. B., *Islam and Schools of Economica* (transl.) (Accra: Islamic Seminary Publications, 1982).

Salmanzadeh, Cyrus, *Agricultural Change and Rural Society in Southern Iran* (Canterbury: MENAS Press, 1981).

Sazman-e Barnameh va Budjeh, Jomhuri-ye Eslami-ye Iran, *Nezam-e Barnameh Rizi-ye Keshvar* (Tehran: 1360 [1981]).

Sazman-e Barnameh va Budjeh, Jomhuri-ye Eslami-ye Iran, *Ahdaf-e Kami-ye Towseh-e Eqtesadi-Ejtema'i-ye Jomhuri-ye Eslami-ye Iran dar Dowreh-e 1361–1381* (Tehran: 1360 [1987]).

Sazman-e Barnameh va Budjeh, Jomhuri-ye Eslami-ye Iran, *Barnameh-e Avval-e Eqtesadi, Ejtema'i, Farhangi-ye Jomhuri-ye Eslami-ye Iran 1362–1366* (Tehran: 1362 [1984]).

Sazman-e Barnameh va Budjeh, Jomhuri-ye Eslami-ye Iran, *Gozaresh-e Eqtesadi* (Tehran: 1368, 1369 [1989/90, 1990/91]).

Schneider, S. A., *The Oil Price Revolution* (Baltimore: The Johns Hopkins University Press, 1982).

Siddiqi, M. N., *Muslim Economic Thinking* (Leicester: Islamic Foundation, 1981).

Simpson, John, *Inside Iran: Life under Khomeini's Regime* (New York: St Martin's Press, 1988).

Stowasser, B. F. (ed.), *The Islamic Impulse* (London: Croom Helm, 1987).

Taleqani, S. M., *Society and Economics in Islam* (Berkeley: Mizan Press, 1982).

Taleqani, S. M., *Islam and Ownership* (Lexington: Mazda Press, 1983).

Tehrani, Ali, *Eqtesad-e Eslami* (Mashad: Khorasan Press, 1353 [1974]).

Tehrani, Bahram, *Pajouheshi dar Eqtesad-e Iran 1354–1364* (Paris: Khavaran, 1986).

United Nations Development Program, *Human Development Report 1992* (New York: UNDP, 1992).

Vezarat-e Bazargani, Jomhuri-ye Eslami-ye Iran, *Gozaresh-e Towzihi-ye Layeh-e Dowlati Kardan-e Bazargani-ye Khareji* (Tehran: 1360 [1981]).

Westberg, J. A., *Case Law of the Iran–US Claims Tribunal* (Washington: ILI, 1991).

World Bank, *World Debt Tables* (Washington: 1992).

World Bank, *World Development Report* (Washington: 1979 to 1992).

Wright, Robin, *In the Name of God: The Khomeini Decade* (New York: Simon and Schuster, 1989).

Yeganeh, Cyrus, 'The Agrarian Structure of Iran', in *State, Culture and Society*, Spring 1985.

Zabih, Sepehr, *Iran Since the Revolution* (Baltimore: The Johns Hopkins University Press, 1982).

Index